"*Holy War, Inc.* is one of those books that makes the reader want to read passages aloud to other people because it so clearly reflects the opinion of someone who knows what he is talking about."
—Deirdre Donahue, *USA Today*

"An interesting journey with a trustworthy guide. . . . Bergen has a fine eye for detail. . . . Given the hysteria and half-truths surrounding bin Laden, Bergen steers a sensible course, sorting through competing stories."
—Ethan Bronner, *The New York Times*

"Peter Bergen . . . has done the world a favor by writing something that is at once lively, literate, and authoritative—equal parts journalism, history, and even whimsical travelogue."
—Jeff Stein, *The Washington Post*

"Bergen has a wonderful ear for the absurd and a great sense of humor, is a marvelous storyteller and a companionable escort on this journey into bin Laden's world."
—Adrienne Miller, *Esquire*

"A confident, easily digestible explanation of the evolution of radical Islamic movements and their global Jihad. The final product is impressive in scope and spookiness, underscoring both the grim determination of bin Laden and his comrades and the threat they pose to international stability."
—Daniel Fierman, *Entertainment Weekly*

"Fascinating."
—John Micklethwait and Adrian Woolridge, *The Wall Street Journal*

"Readable, reliable, and thoughtful, *Holy War, Inc.* goes beyond the news accounts without straying far into conjecture or pushing pet hypotheses. . . . Vivid storytelling . . . a lively read."
—Scott Shane, *The Baltimore Sun*

"A reader finishes *Holy War, Inc.* having more than satisfied basic course requirements for 'Introduction to the Enemy.'"
—Sheryl Connelly, *Daily News* (New York)

PETER L. BERGEN

Holy War, Inc.

Inside the Secret World of
Osama bin Laden

A Touchstone Book
Published by Simon & Schuster
NEW YORK LONDON TORONTO SYDNEY SINGAPORE

TOUCHSTONE
Rockefeller Center
1230 Avenue of the Americas
New York, NY 10020

First Touchstone Edition 2002

TOUCHSTONE and colophon are
trademarks of Simon & Schuster, Inc.

For information about special discounts for bulk purchases,
please contact Simon & Schuster Special Sales:
1-800-456-6798 or business@simonandschuster.com

Manufactured in the United States of America

1   3   5   7   9   10   8   6   4   2

Library of Congress Cataloging-in-Publication Data

Bergen, Peter L.
Holy War, Inc. : inside the secret world of Osama bin Laden / Peter L. Bergen.
p.   cm.
Includes bibliographical references and index.
1. Bin Laden, Osama, 1957–   2. Terrorism—Religious aspects—Islam.
3. Terrorism—Government policy—United States.   4. Jihad.   I. Title : Inside the
secret world of Osama bin Laden.   II. Title.

HV6430.B55 B47 2002
95.805'3'092—dc21

[B]   2001054732

ISBN 0-7432-0502-2
0-7432-3495-2 (Pbk)

Both author and publisher will donate a portion of their proceeds
from this book to the International Committee of the Red Cross.

For my parents with love

Sarah Lampert Bergen
D. Thomas Bergen

CONTENTS

NOTE FROM THE AUTHOR

In transliterating names and other items from Arabic, Pushtu, and Urdu, I have generally used conventional English spellings, for example, "Koran" rather than "Qu'ran." Sometimes, as in the case of the bin Laden family surname, I have of necessity used different spellings in different contexts, as appropriate.

Nothing in this book should be construed to represent the views of CNN or any other news organization for which I have done reporting. Any errors of fact and interpretation are my responsibility.

Holy War, Inc.

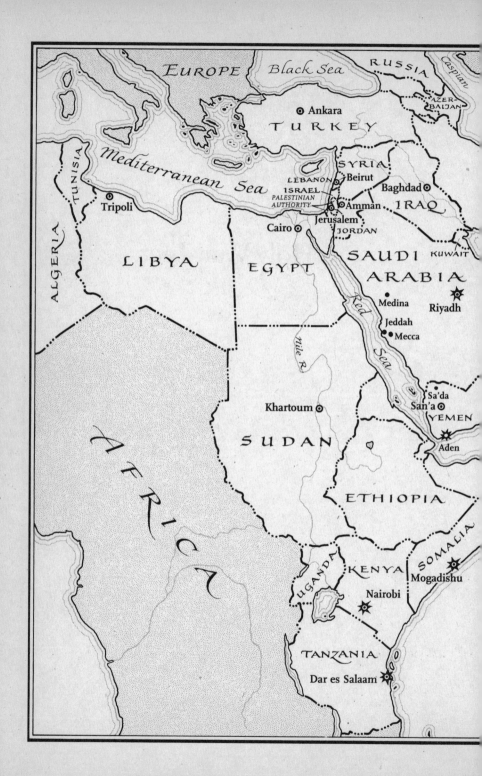

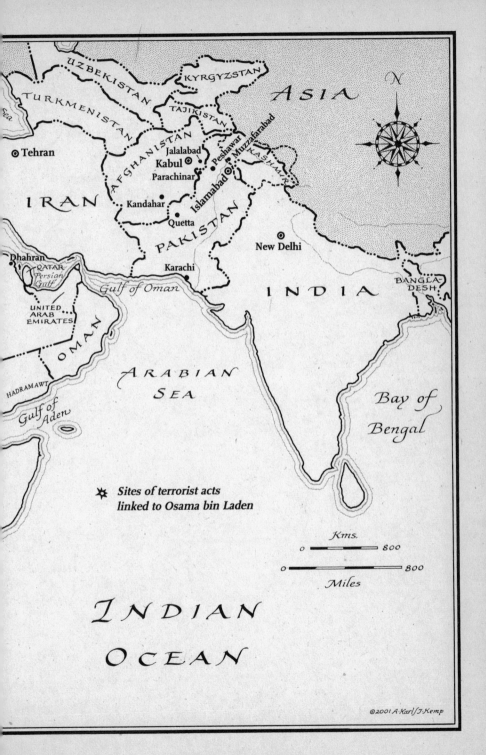

UZBEKISTAN

KYRGYZSTAN

TURKMENISTAN

ASIA

N

TAJIKISTAN

Sea

AFGHANISTAN

Jalalabad

Peshawar

Muzzafarabad

⊙ Tehran

Kabul ⊙

KASHMIR

Parachinar

Islamabad ⊙

I R A N

Kandahar ●

Quetta ●

PAKISTAN

New Delhi ⊙

Dhahran

QATAR
Persian
Gulf

Karachi ●

I N D I A

BANGLA-
DESH

Gulf of Oman

UNITED
ARAB
EMIRATES

O M A N

HADRAMAWT

A R A B I A N

Gulf of
Aden

S E A

Bay of
Bengal

✵ Sites of terrorist acts
   linked to Osama bin Laden

Kms.

0 ⸻⸻⸻ 800

0 ⸻⸻⸻ 800

Miles

I N D I A N

O C E A N

©2001 A·Karl/J·Kemp

How to Find the World's Most Wanted Man

When you go looking for Osama bin Laden, you don't find him: he finds you. It was March 1997 when the phone rang.

"Osama has agreed to meet with you in Afghanistan," said the voice at the other end of the line.

Bin Laden and his advisers had concluded that CNN, my then employer, was the best forum to broadcast his first television interview to the English-speaking world.

My interest in Afghanistan had been sparked in 1983, when I made a documentary about the millions of Afghan refugees pouring into Pakistan following the Soviet invasion of their country. A decade later, I traveled to Afghanistan to explore the links between the CIA-funded rebels who fought the Soviets and the 1993 bombing of New York's World Trade Center.

To me there was always an unresolved quality to the U.S. government's investigation of the first attempt to destroy the World Trade Center, which was also the first time international terrorists had successfully carried out a bombing operation on American soil. The government had convicted the actual bombers, but who was the mastermind of the operation? Who had bankrolled two of the bombers to fly from Pakistan to New York to carry out the attack? The more I read about bin Laden, the more plausible a candidate he seemed. By 1996 the U.S. State Department was calling him "the most significant financial sponsor of Islamic extremist activities in the world today" and accusing him of running terrorist training camps in Afghanistan and Sudan. In August of that year, bin Laden issued his first public call to Muslims to attack U.S. military targets, a summons that was well publicized in the Middle East.

My quest to find the mysterious Saudi multimillionaire began in North London. The quiet suburb of Dollis Hill is favored by Arab immigrants, who have set up mosques and Islamic schools on its leafy avenues. On an unassuming street of 1930s Tudor-style houses lived Khaled al-Fawwaz, the spokesman for a Saudi opposition group founded by bin Laden, the Advice and Reformation Committee. I had called from the United States a few weeks earlier, but Khaled had cut the conversation short.

"There are matters I do not want to discuss on the telephone," he said. It was a sensible precaution, since anyone remotely connected to bin Laden is likely to have a tapped phone.

When I arrived at Khaled's house, all the curtains were drawn. He answered the door dressed in a floor-length white robe and a red-and-white-checked headdress, wearing his full, bushy beard in the same manner that the Prophet Muhammad had worn his nearly a millennium and a half ago. Entering the house, I took my shoes off, as if I were already in the Middle East. Khaled conducted me into the tidy sitting room that also served as his office. On one side of the room were computers, printers, and faxes, and on another wall, shelves filled with books in Arabic. Khaled was thirty-four, but he seemed older—worn down, perhaps, by the cares of a man who was once an entrepreneur in Saudi Arabia but was now a full-time opposition figure. Although England's liberal tradition of hospitality to dissidents allowed Khaled to function, he found London a worrisome place to bring up his children, given the constant assault of its hypersexualized, commercialized culture.

With an elaborate courtesy I came to recognize as one of his defining traits, Khaled offered me some flavored coffee and a plate of dates from an oasis town in Arabia. Then we got down to business, of a sort. Khaled seemed more interested in discussing the Koran and Saudi politics than in addressing the logistics of how exactly we would secure the interview with bin Laden.

Khaled repeatedly referred to himself as a "reformer" of the Saudi regime, not a revolutionary. He was not referring to reform in the nineteenth-century liberal sense, but to a literal reformation that sought to take Islam in Arabia back to the way it was practiced at the time of the Prophet Muhammad in the seventh century. I was struck by how this desire to *reform* Islam echoed the Protestant Reformation's attempt to correct the abuses of the medieval Catholic Church and to return Christianity to its founding principles. Islam had seen countless such attempts to restore the perfect society of Muhammad and his immediate successors, the four "Rightly Guided" caliphs.[1]

During the first week of meetings, Khaled gave me a preliminary picture of his friend Osama, describing him, in an accent tinged with the recently acquired cadences of North London, as "humble, charming, intelligent, a really significant wealthy chap for Islamic causes who gave up everything to go and fight in Afghanistan." Bin Laden's role in the war against the Soviet occupation of Afghanistan in the 1980s had made him a hero throughout the Middle East.

Khaled said that bin Laden, now back in Afghanistan, was "violently opposed to the presence of U.S. troops in Saudi Arabia," troops who had arrived there in response to Saddam Hussein's 1990 invasion of Kuwait.

Bin Laden also believed the House of al-Saud, the family that has ruled Arabia for generations, were "apostates" from Islam. Apostasy is a grave charge to level against the Saudi royal family, who style themselves the protectors of the two holiest places in Islam, Mecca and Medina, and practice the most traditional form of Sunni Islam. Bin Laden's antipathy to the Saudi regime was peculiar because his family had grown extraordinarily rich as a result of their close relations with the royal family.

Khaled endorsed bin Laden's critique of the Saudi monarchy and the American presence on the holy land of the Arabian Peninsula. In his view, the Prophet Muhammad had banned the permanent presence of infidels in Arabia; hence bin Laden's opposition to the thousands of American troops based there. But Khaled added that while he would not condemn bin Laden's calls for violence against those soldiers, he could not condone them either.

When I pressed Khaled on the matter of the interview, he said that there were a number of potential problems. Bin Laden's personal safety was the paramount concern: several assassination attempts had been mounted against him by Saudi intelligence services.

"Are you sure none of your team are agents of the CIA?" he asked abruptly.

I assured him we were not—but it is hard for some Middle Easterners to believe that journalists are not on the government payroll, as is sometimes the case in their own countries.

Nevertheless, Khaled said he would relay our interview request.

The telephone infrastructure in Afghanistan had been destroyed by years of war, so the only means of communication was by satellite phone. Bin Laden himself communicated only by radio, Khaled said, because he was well aware that intelligence agencies could easily monitor satellite phone calls. He told me that bin Laden hadn't wanted to do a television interview until recently. Of course, we were not the only ones interested in talking to the exiled Saudi; Khaled showed me a stack of interview requests from news organizations around the world. Still, Khaled said we had a chance. In the interim he suggested I go and speak to Dr. Saad al-Fagih, another Saudi dissident, for more background on bin Laden.

Dr. al-Fagih's office was not far from Khaled's house. A wiry, intense intellectual whose thin face is framed by heavy glasses, Dr. al-Fagih was a professor of surgery at the prestigious King Saud University and had studied at the Royal College of Surgeons in Scotland. Al-Fagih told me that he had performed surgery on the day he left Saudi Arabia for exile in England in 1994. In short, he was an unlikely revolutionary.

Al-Fagih's critique of the Saudi regime is as much political as religious, a fact reflected in his dress, which is invariably a suit. Certainly al-Fagih favors a conservative Islamic state, but his criticisms of the regime also focus on its corruption and mishandling of the economy. Al-Fagih calls his opposition group the Movement for Islamic Reform in Arabia (MIRA). His approach to undermining the regime is determinedly modern. When I visited his office there were usually several earnest, bearded young men hunched over computer screens updating the group's web site, *www.miraserve.com*, in Arabic and English. The site analyzes news and trends in Saudi Arabia in a reasonably accurate and fair-minded manner. Dr. al-Fagih also proudly showed me his newly built radio studio, from which he planned to broadcast his message via satellite directly to the Saudi kingdom.

During the eighties, Dr. al-Fagih had traveled to Peshawar, Pakistan to lend his services as a surgeon during the Afghan jihad against the Soviets.[2] "I estimate that between twelve and fifteen thousand men served with bin Laden in the war in Afghanistan against the Soviets," al-Fagih told me. "Of those there are four thousand now committed to bin Laden's cause around the world." He said that some of these men were linked to bin Laden by a chain of command, but that the majority operated as part of a loose network "whose common link is respect for bin Laden as a great leader."

In London I was also introduced to an Arab I will call Ali, who had served with bin Laden's guerrillas as a medic for three years during the Afghan war against the communists. He would be the person guiding us to bin Laden if we got the green light to meet him. Our conversations were somewhat stilted since he spoke no English and I no Arabic, forcing us to communicate in rudimentary French.

Ali had spent more than a decade in Europe and had written extensively on Islamist struggles in the Middle East and Asia. A compact, muscular man not given to smiling from behind his bushy red beard, Ali projected an intense seriousness of purpose. One had the sense that he would be very calm under fire.

Despite the years he had spent in Europe, Ali could be somewhat reductive in his views. During one of our chats he said, "You realize that the U.S. foreign policy is run by three Jews? Albright, Berger, and Cohen." I resisted the impulse to tell Ali that it was the two most powerful men in Washington—Bill Clinton and Al Gore—who drove Washington's undoubtedly pro-Israel policy. And they were both Southern Baptists.

Our philosophical differences and his somewhat gruff manner notwithstanding, Ali seemed to warm to me. He explained the logistics of securing the interview, saying the trip to meet bin Laden could take as little as ten days, but might take more than two weeks. Like all estimates about time in Afghanistan, the more pessimistic one proved accurate. As one wag puts it: "When you are in Afghanistan, the clock slows down and your bowels speed up."

Ali's parting comment, delivered matter-of-factly, was that we should speak in code on the phone. On no account were we to use bin

Laden's name, and our trip to Jalalabad, Afghanistan, where he was living, should be referred to as a trip to "meet the man in Kuwait."

Then Khaled summoned me back to see him, saying he had received a call from bin Laden's media adviser. The adviser was favorably disposed to either the BBC, CBS' *60 Minutes*, or CNN doing bin Laden's first television interview. Khaled said he supported either CBS or CNN. I pointed out that CNN's programs were shown in over a hundred countries, while CBS was broadcast only in the United States. He seemed to take that point on board. I returned to the United States to wait for Khaled's call.

It came a month later. We were on.

The correspondent would be Peter Arnett, who had won a Pulitzer Prize during his ten years of reporting in Vietnam and whose courageous decision to remain in Baghdad during the Gulf War had helped put CNN on the map. The cameraman was a former British army officer, Peter Jouvenal, who has probably spent more time inside Afghanistan than any journalist in the world. (He even rented a house in Afghanistan's war-torn capital, Kabul, where he would go *on vacation*.) Four years before our trip to meet bin Laden, I had traveled to Afghanistan with Arnett and Jouvenal at a time when the prime minister, Gulbuddin Hekmatyar, was staking out his claim to be perhaps the only prime minister in history to shell his own capital on a daily basis.

We began our journey in Britain flying from London to Pakistan. The stewardesses on our Pakistan International Airlines (PIA) flight were dressed in pantsuits and headscarves, serving curries that were a foretaste of our destination. Just before takeoff, a recorded prayer was offered up to Allah for a safe journey. Given the age of PIA's fleet, this seemed a sensible precaution.

We landed in Pakistan's capital, Islamabad, early in the morning. Leaving the plane, I breathed in the first intoxicating smell of the sweet, pungent, rotting vegetation that characterizes the Indian subcontinent. Once our van was loaded, we drove through the quiet streets of the city, which is nestled in the verdant hills of northern Pakistan. While most Pakistani cities are hymns to chaos, overpopulation, and manic energy, Islamabad is divided into orderly zones with names like G6 and F1. We passed the pleasant white-walled villas of government bureaucrats and foreign diplomats. The scent of wild marijuana drifted through my window. The weed grows in profusion in Islamabad, even outside the headquarters of Pakistan's drug police.

Recovered from jet lag, I visited the U.S. embassy to get an update on the security situation in Afghanistan. Like many embassies in countries where the United States is admired and hated in equal measure, the building looked like a medium-security jail. A long brick wall surmounted by razor wire surrounded the compound. On the way in to the embassy I passed through two bulletproof checkpoints. The embassy seemed to be under siege, which in some ways it was. In 1979 a mob had burned down the old embassy. In 1988 the U.S. ambassador was killed in a mysterious plane crash while on a trip with the country's military dictator. And in 1999 unidentified militants attacked the embassy with rockets.

A couple of days later we loaded up our van to make our way to Peshawar, the jumping-off point for Afghanistan. That would mean a drive along the Grand Trunk Road, where you were more likely to be killed than you were in the middle of the civil war then smouldering inside neighboring Afghanistan. The Grand Trunk Road is one of the world's most formidable automotive experiences, its drivers all engaged in a protracted and high-speed game of chicken. Testaments to this distinctive style of driving can be seen in the numerous burned-out vehicles that lie by the side of the road. The mangled hulks of buses predominate—a consequence, perhaps, of the copious quantities of hashish the drivers ingest while making the trip.

About halfway into the journey we crossed the Indus River, which rises in a torrent in Tibet but by this point has slowed to a meandering, muddy flow irrigating the plains around it. Nearing Peshawar, we passed perhaps the largest religious school in Pakistan, the Darul Uloom Haqqania, which has provided hundreds of recruits to bin Laden's cause and is sometimes described as the Harvard of the Taliban movement, at the time the de facto government of Afghanistan.[3]

And suddenly we were in Peshawar, a dusty, Wild West kind of town. Peshawar is the capital of Pakistan's North-West Frontier province, the gateway to the Khyber Pass, which runs through the Hindu Kush mountains into Afghanistan. During the Afghan war, Peshawar became an Asian Casablanca, awash in spies, journalists, aid workers, and refugees. Among the visitors was a rich young Saudi by the name of Osama bin Laden.

Our first stop was the Pearl Continental Hotel. Displayed prominently in the lobby was a sign stating: "Hotel Guests are asked that their bodyguards kindly deposit all firearms at the Front Desk." In my bedroom a green arrow on a table pointed toward Mecca, the direction for prayer.

I soon repaired to the hotel bar, one of a handful of public places in Pakistan where you can drink legally, provided you are a non-Muslim. Hidden away on the top floor of the hotel, the Gul Bar is a large room devoid of both customers and decoration, except for a set of white cabinets displaying a selection of locally brewed spirits. The bartender, a sad, cadaverous-looking chap, passed me a sheaf of typewritten pages, starting with the somewhat off-putting FORM PR-IV, (See Rule-13-(I); APPLICATION FOR GRANT OF PERMIT FOR THE POSSESSION AND CONSUMPTION OF FOREIGN LIQUOR BY NON-MUSLIM FOREIGNERS. The permit included this splendidly mystifying sentence: "This permit is hereby granted to the above named, authorizing him to possess, Purchase, transport For consume liquor is detailed above under the provision of prohibition (Enforcement Hadd)." After filling the form out in triplicate, I really did need a drink.

We whiled away a few days in Peshawar while Ali and a friend, now dressed in their *shalwar kameez,* the loose-fitting shirt and pants that are Pakistan's national dress, went off to make "contact."

Seeking some relief from the noise and pollution of the city, I paid a visit to the leafy graveyard where dozens of British officers and soldiers were buried. Peshawar had been critical to the "Great Game" played by Britain and Russia as they wrestled for control of Central Asia during the nineteenth century. The graveyard was testament to the difficulties of life on the frontier. One headstone read, "Lt. Colonel Edward Henry LeMarch, shot to death by a fanatic, 25th March 1898, aged 40." Another read, "George Mitchell Richmond Levit, 20th Punjab Infantry, died aged 23, on the 27th October, 1863 of a wound received the previous day in the defense of the Eagle's Nest Picket, Umbeyla Pass. A good soldier and a true Christian." Another inscription recalled the way of life the British imported wholesale to remind them of their green and pleasant land: "Lt. Colonel

Walter Irvine, who lost his life in the Nagoroman River when leading the Peshawar Vale Hunt, of which he was the Master." The trip to the British graveyard was a refreshing interlude, but was going to do little to solve more immediate conundrums.

The week before our trip the Taliban had decreed it was against Islam to film or photograph any living being, which would pose a bit of a problem for our project. This was the latest in a long list of what might be called "Tali-bans." Soccer, kite-flying, music, television, and the presence of females in schools and offices were all banned.[4] Some of the decrees had a Monty Python–esque quality, like the rule banning the use of paper bags on the remote chance the paper might include recycled pages of the Koran.[5] Behavior the Taliban deemed deviant was met with inventive punishments. Taliban religious scholars labored over the vital question of how to deal with homosexuals: "Some say we should take these sinners to a high roof and throw them down, while others say we should dig a big hole beside a wall, bury them, then push the wall on top of them."[6]

To straighten out such matters as videotaping and visas, I decided to pay a visit to the Taliban consulate in Peshawar. There I was greeted by a group of ragged teenagers who seemed to have stepped out of a Hogarth print. I felt sorry for them. Afghanistan had been at war continuously since 1978. War was all they knew. When I said that I was looking for the consul, they mimed that he was out. One of them grabbed my shirt as the others started pressing around me, leering and grimacing. I wasn't quite sure what was happening, but I wasn't going to stay to find out. We'd take our chances in Afghanistan.

A couple of days later Ali returned, saying we had the okay to proceed.

The next morning our van set off from the hotel at the crack of dawn, as we had to reach the base of the Khyber Rifles regiment no later than nine A.M. The regiment would provide us with an armed escort through the no-man's-land surrounding the Khyber Pass between Pakistan and Afghanistan. This buffer zone, known as the Khyber Agency, is a holdover from the days when Britain ruled the North-West Frontier. The British had difficulty subduing the unruly tribesmen on the frontier, so a deal was struck: the tribes could manage their own affairs, but British law would apply to the road that runs through the Khyber Pass. A similar arrangement applies in Pakistan today. Once you step off the road that runs through the pass you are in tribal territory, where tribal, not Pakistani, law prevails. As the tribes surrounding the Khyber pass enjoy a rich tradition of kidnapping, internecine feuds, and heroin smuggling, the prospect of escort by the Pakistani government was a welcome one. We were less comforted, however, when we met the man who was to be our protector, an elderly soldier with a slight stoop, whose Lee Enfield rifle had probably last seen action in World War I.

We arrived at the offices of the Khyber Agency, a courtyard of low-slung, whitewashed nineteenth-century offices presided over by well-fed Pakistani civil servants surrounded by piles of rarely disturbed papers tied up with ribbons. Tribesmen milled about seeking redress for their various grievances. In the middle of the courtyard sat a little jail where prisoners were kept in conditions that would probably not have pleased Amnesty International.

After an epic display of paper shuffling and stamping, we obtained our pass. The ancient rifleman jumped into the front of our van, where he promptly fell asleep. Then we drove through the outskirts of Peshawar, arriving at a checkpoint where a sign announced: ATTENTION: ENTRY OF FOREIGNERS IS PROHIBITED BEYOND THIS POINT. We roused our escort from his slumbers and he showed the soldiers manning the barrier that we had the requisite authorization to continue. We were allowed to pass on. Now we were in tribal territory. Along the road were rows of shops selling guns, and later shops with sheep tails in the window to signify hashish for sale.

Twenty-five miles to the south was the town of Darra, which might be the world's largest outlet store for weaponry. There you can buy guns that are disguised as pens and shoot only one bullet—a bargain at seven bucks. Or, for the more sportive customer, there are flamethrowers, machine guns and rocket-propelled grenades (RPGs). Prefer to start with a test drive? For fifty dollars they'll let you fire a bazooka. The gunsmiths in Darra do a brisk business. No self-respecting male in tribal territory would leave home without his firearm.

We continued east into the Khyber Pass, where the Indian subcontinent meets Central Asia. Alexander the Great's soldiers came this way during his campaign to conquer India.[7] On one wall of the pass were reminders of another empire—the insignia of the British regiments that served on this blood-soaked frontier of the Raj during the nineteenth century. (The Khyber had, less gloriously, also given the English language the Cockney rhyming slang "Khyber Pass" for "arse.")

The hills soon grew into mountains. Scattered on the peaks were the houses of tribal families, miniature fortresses whose gun ports were not merely decorative. Close to the road was the massive fortified compound of Haji Ayub Afridi, allegedly one of Pakistan's most important drug lords. His reputation did not prevent him from serving for a period as a legislator in the National Assembly.[8] I had once met with a Pakistani who worked as a valued informant for the U.S. Drug Enforcement Administration. Like most informants, he looked as though he hadn't had a good night's sleep in years. He told me that Afridi's house had taken four years to build. "There are hidden tunnels within the walls," he added. "It has its own power station. There are orchards in the grounds. It's defended by cannons and anti-aircraft guns. It could hold off a brigade-strength attack."

About midway through the pass we reached the small town of Landi Khotal, a seemingly innocuous place that has long been one of the world's largest heroin-smuggling posts.[9] Armed men, some wearing little purple caps, others in turbans, sauntered up and down the street, their rifles casually slung across their backs. We did not pause for refreshments. The pass climbed higher and higher until we reached a fortress of Pakistan's army.

And then, suddenly, stretched out before us was Afghanistan.

The very word is an incantation. I never get over the thrill of seeing the country. In my imagination it has always seemed like something out of Tolkien's *Lord of the Rings*. It promises mystery, a movement back into a time of medieval chivalry and medieval cruelty, an absence of the modern world that is both thrilling and disturbing, a place of extraordinary natural beauty that opens the mind to contemplation. The Spanish conquistador Hernán Cortés was once asked to describe what Mexico looked like. He answered by taking a piece of parchment and crumpling it up to illustrate the endless mountain ranges of the country. Cortés could have been describing much of Afghanistan.

And then there is the light: pure and crystalline, foreshortening distances and bathing everything in a pristine glow. One simply cannot take a bad picture in Afghanistan. Although a country deeply scarred by war, it is a place where one can find a species of personal tranquillity rarely experienced in the West.

The scene at the border itself was bedlam. Our hope was that the Taliban guards would assume we were workers for an aid agency and would wave us through without demanding to see our visas, which is exactly what they did. As we made our way over the border crossing I noticed that it was festooned with long black strings of audiotape—the remains of music cassettes that the guards had confiscated from heedless travelers. Thank God, I thought, that they hadn't searched our van and done the same with all our videotapes.

Shortly after we cleared the border post we passed a graveyard dotted with fluttering green flags marking the graves of Arabs who had died fighting the Soviets. "Here is where I took part in fighting the Russians," Ali said, as the mountainous terrain gave way to a lunar landscape. These men must have been extraordinarily committed to take on the Soviets here. Other than an occasional rocky outcrop, there was no cover on these plains. The bravery of the Arabs who had fought under bin Laden's command was lunatic, but impressive.

According to the Pakistani journalist Rahimullah Yusufzai, the Arabs would pitch white tents out in the open in the hopes of attracting Soviet fire, hoping for martyrdom. "I saw one person who was crying because he survived an air attack," Yusufzai said.[10] A Muslim killed in the course of jihad is *shaheed*, a martyr who is guaranteed entry to Paradise. According to some traditions, the martyrs are attended by seventy virgins who will cater to their every desire.

We drove past what had once been a large village but now looked like an archeological dig of a Sumerian city. The only evidence that this had once been a bustling town were the jagged fragments of walls. The Soviets had destroyed thousands of such villages, creating five million refugees and killing at least a million Afghans, out of a prewar population of fifteen million or so.[11]

The plains soon turned into cultivated fields and orchards. Before long, we arrived in Jalalabad, the compact town where we would be staying while we waited to see bin Laden. Ali told us that bin Laden's wives and children lived in a little tented complex on the city outskirts, in a place called Hadda.

As we drove into Jalalabad's bazaar area I was puzzled by the many carpets in the middle of the streets. Someone explained to me that this was a trick of local merchants, who laid out the carpets so that passing cars and trucks would roll over them and give them the authentic "aged" look prized by gullible Western buyers.

Our lodgings would be the Spinghar Hotel, named after the snow-capped mountains that dominated the view to the south. I had stayed at the Spinghar four years earlier. Then it had been one of the grimmest hotels imaginable, having once served as housing for Soviet officers. But since my last visit a remarkable transformation had taken place. An Afghan entrepreneur who had moved to California during the war had returned to take over the place, sprucing it up with amenities like hot water, fresh paint, and landscaped gardens. Unfortunately, his business acumen did not extend to an understanding of how the Taliban operated. Just before we arrived, Taliban officials had convened a clerical kangaroo court in the Spinghar's dining room and ruled that the hotel should be commandeered. Occasionally the owner could be seen walking through the hotel, a dazed expression on his face.

Our location gave us an interesting window on the Taliban. The word is the plural of *talib,* meaning "religious student," and refers to a group of students from religious schools in Pakistan and Afghanistan who took control of much of the country during the mid-1990s.[12] The Taliban protected bin Laden because they admired him for the role he had played in helping to dislodge the Soviets. The admiration was mutual. When I asked Khaled al-Fawwaz, bin Laden's London contact, what present regime in the world most resembled his vision of how an Islamic state should be run, he said the Taliban were "getting there."

In Jalalabad the Taliban roared through town in Japanese pickup trucks with white flags fluttering from their antennae. The pickups were filled with fierce fighters recognizable by their black or white turbans—bringing back the Middle Ages on a fleet of Toyotas. The women in town, following Taliban edicts, were covered from head to foot in the *burqa,* an all-enveloping garment out of which one can barely see.

Once, driving through town, we encountered the first traffic jam I'd seen in tiny Jalalabad. After a couple of minutes I realized the source: the Taliban had stopped all traffic during prayer time. Out of the window of our car I could see a Talib fighter beating one hapless man with a stick because he hadn't stopped riding his bicycle.

Despite the ferocious reputation of the Taliban, we were able to stay in Jalalabad for several days without any official asking us why we were there. Either the Taliban were incompetent, I thought, or they knew of our mission and had sanctioned the interview at the highest level. Like so many things in Afghanistan, this was never really clear.

The Taliban were pariahs on the world stage. Because of their antediluvian treatment of women in particular and their dismal human rights record generally, only three countries recognized their government. But even the Taliban's harshest critics could not deny their one remarkable achievement: they had restored order to much of the country.

During the early 1990s, Afghanistan had become a patchwork of fiefdoms held by competing warlords. On a visit in 1993 I witnessed the anarchy in the country at first hand. Kabul, the capital, a once lovely city nestling in a vast valley, was then being destroyed by religious and ethnic militias. At a post manned by a Shia militia unit, the soldiers laughingly urged me to get in the seat of an anti-aircraft gun and let off some shots. They did not seem to appreciate, or perhaps care, that the rounds would eventually have to land somewhere in the crowded city.

A good number of the foot soldiers in these militias were boys. I have a photograph I took of a group of three child soldiers. One boy holds a grenade; another self-consciously holds up a rocket launcher. The third boy holds his rifle nonchalantly to his side as he looks unblinkingly into the camera, ready to meet his obligations. He appears to be ten.

The fighting had left whole neighborhoods in ruins. Ancient palaces were pockmarked by shells. The Kabul Museum, which once housed masterpieces of Buddhist art, was now open to the sky, its ceiling blown off by mortar shells. A 1930s Rolls-Royce that had once belonged to the king of Afghanistan lay in a heap of twisted metal on the grounds of the museum. The runway at Kabul airport was littered with burnt-out aircraft.

It was as if the Afghans were applying the demented logic of their national passion, *buzkashi*, a distant and violent cousin of polo, to their capital. *Buzkashi* is played by horsemen who compete to grab hold of the headless carcass of a calf. That's pretty much it for the rules. As a book on the sport observes: "The calf is trampled, dragged, tugged, lifted and lost again as one competitor after another tries to gain sole control."[13] Now the carcass was Kabul.

It was out of the sort of anarchy I witnessed in 1993 that the Taliban emerged in the southeastern Afghan city of Kandahar. Local residents had been angered for years by the payoffs demanded by the various militias at checkpoints on the roads around town. The final straw was a perhaps apocryphal story—the kind journalists say is "too good to check": in 1994 two local warlords, competing for the favors of a young boy, had waged a full-scale tank battle in Kandahar's bazaar.[14] To much local applause, a small group of religious students under the leadership of a shadowy, one-eyed cleric named Mullah Mohammed Omar took over the city.[15] Within two years Mullah Omar and his men had taken control of most of the country, partly by paying off local commanders and partly because of their dynamic tactics, based on fast-moving fleets of pickup trucks, each carrying eight or so heavily armed fighters.[16]

And certainly the Taliban had made the country safer. The road between Kandahar and Quetta, Pakistan, had once been a gauntlet of militia checkpoints whose occupants would "tax" and rob you at will.[17] But when I traveled it in January 2000, the only untoward obstacle was a pair of camels copulating in the middle of the road. It was an operation that seemed to give little satisfaction to either party.

Indeed, all types of crime and socially unacceptable behavior fell precipitously under the Taliban. This could be partially explained by the brutal punishments meted out by the religious warriors: convicted robbers had their hands amputated, adulterers were stoned to death, and murderers could be personally executed by male members of the victim's family.[18] The amputations and executions were the only public entertainment in a country starved of diversions. So when knife-wielding surgeons and executioners performed their grisly duties in Kabul's soccer stadium on Fridays, thousands filled the stands to cheer on the proceedings.[19] However, when I visited the stadium on a random Friday afternoon in December 1999 a soccer game was in progress. According to locals, the number of executions had declined over the years.

Despite the improvements in public security, many Afghans found the Taliban's social policies anathema. In my hotel in Jalalabad I met two men who wanted to talk. They worked for Afghanistan's national airline, ARIANA, as pilots. They were working on growing their Taliban-mandated beards, but the beards looked suspiciously well-trimmed to be truly Taliban-certified. Smoking furtively (cigarettes being another vice discouraged by the Taliban), they explained in hushed voices that the religious warriors' policies might suit the almost medieval villages of the countryside, but that for more urbanized Afghans they were utterly foreign.

When I pointed out that the Taliban had brought safety to most of the country, one replied, "Yes, but you can be secure in a prison."

One morning I was walking toward the center of Jalalabad with Arnett when we were approached by a woman completely covered in a black *burqa*. As she drew nearer I saw a pair of bright red shoes poking out below the hem of her garments. As she reached us she nodded and, in a clear, amused voice said in English, "Hello. How are you? Good morning." We took it to be her way of saying: "The Taliban may make me wear this getup, but they can't control my thoughts."

After several days of waiting in the Jalalabad hotel, we were visited by a bin Laden emissary. The man, who introduced himself as bin Laden's "media adviser," was young and wore shoulder-length hair, a headdress, and sunglasses that concealed much of his face. He was not unfriendly, but businesslike, asking if he could take a look at our camera and sound equipment. Following a perfunctory survey of our gear he announced: "You can't bring any of this for the interview." To have gotten so far, and to have spent this much time and money, only to learn that the interview would be sabotaged—this was rather bad news.

Things looked up again when the media adviser said that we could shoot the interview on his hand-held digital camera. I knew that our professional gear would do a better job, but there was clearly little point in arguing. Bin Laden feared that strangers with electronic equipment might be concealing some type of tracking device that would give away his location. (Ali had mentioned the example of Terry Waite, an Anglican church envoy negotiating for the release of Western hostages in Beirut in the 1980s, who was himself taken captive because he was suspected of carrying such a device.)

Bin Laden's men left nothing to chance: we were not even to bring our watches. The media adviser's parting words were: "Bring only the clothes you are wearing." He told us we would be picked up the next day.

The following afternoon a beaten-up blue Volkswagen van drew up at our hotel. Ali motioned hurriedly for us to get in and then drew curtains over the windows of the van. As the sun dipped, we drove west on the road to Kabul. Inside the van were three well-armed men.

The trip passed mostly in a heavy silence.

After driving through a long tunnel, Ali finally broke the silence, saying almost apologetically: "This is the point in the journey when guests are told if they are hiding a tracking device, tell us now and it will not be a problem." We took it that any potential "problem" would likely result in a swift execution. I glanced nervously at my two colleagues. Could I be absolutely sure neither of them had such a device? I assured him we were clean.

It was now nightfall and under an almost full moon we turned onto a little track heading into mountainous terrain. After a few minutes we arrived at a small plateau and were told to get out. Each of us was given a pair of glasses with little cardboard inserts stuffed in the lenses, making it impossible to see. We were then transferred into another vehicle, in which we were later allowed to take off our glasses. We found ourselves inside a jeep with heavily tinted windows. The path wound upward, becoming steeper. In places, the road seemed to be just the rock bed of a mountain stream; elsewhere, improvements had been made to the track. My colleagues and I exchanged almost no words during this surreal trip. None of us had any idea how it would end.

Suddenly a man leaped out of the darkness, pointing an RPG, or rocket propelled grenade, at our vehicle. He shouted at us to halt and then exchanged some quick words with the driver before letting us pass on. This happened again a few minutes later. Finally, a group of about half a dozen men appeared and signaled us to get out of the vehicle. They were armed with Russian PK submachine guns and RPGs.

"Don't be afraid," said their leader, a burly Saudi, who politely asked us to get out of the car. "We are going to search you now," he said in barely accented English. They patted us down in a professional manner and ran a beeping instrument with a red flashing light over us. I assumed it was a scan for any tracking device we might have secreted.

We drove into a small rock-strewn valley at about five thousand feet. March in the Afghan mountains is cold and I was glad I had brought a down jacket for the trip. We were led to a rough mud hut lined with blankets; here we were to meet bin Laden. Nearby were other huts, grouped around a stream. The settlement was probably used from time to time by Kuchis, nomads who roam Afghanistan's mountains and deserts with their flocks. We could hear the low rumble of a generator that bin Laden's men had set up for us so that we could run the lights and camera.

Inside the hut, a flickering kerosene lamp illuminated the faces of bin Laden's followers. Some were Arabs; others had darker, African complexions. They served us a dinner of heaping platters of rice, nan bread, and some unidentifiable meat. Was it goat? Chicken? Hard to tell in the dim light. I have generally made it a rule of the road never to eat anything I am not too sure of, ever since an eventful encounter with some curried sheep brains in Peshawar. But by now I was ravenous, so I tucked in with gusto.

I calculated that it was sometime before midnight when bin Laden appeared with his entourage—a translator and several bodyguards. He is a tall man, well over six feet, his face dominated by an aquiline nose. Dressed in a turban, white robes, and a green camouflage jacket, he walked with a cane and seemed tired, less like a swaggering revolutionary than a Muslim ascetic. Those around him treated him with the utmost deference, referring to him with the honorific "sheikh," an homage he seemed to take as his due. We were told we had about an hour with him before he would have to go. As he sat down, he propped up next to him the Kalashnikov rifle that is never far from his side. His followers said he had taken it from a Russian he had killed.

Jouvenal fiddled with the lights and camera and then said the welcome words "We have speed," which is cameramanese for "We're ready."

Peter Arnett and I had worked up a long list of questions, many more than could be answered in the hour allotted to us. We had been asked to submit them in advance, and bin Laden's people had excised any questions about his personal life, his family, or his finances. We were not going to find out, Barbara Walters–style, what kind of tree bin Laden thought he was. But he was going to answer our questions about his political views and why he advocated violence against Americans.

Without raising his voice, bin Laden began to rail in Arabic against the injustices visited upon Muslims by the United States and his native Saudi Arabia: "Our main problem is the U.S. government. . . . By being loyal to the U.S. regime, the Saudi regime has committed an act against Islam," he said. Bin Laden made no secret of the fact that he was interested in fomenting a revolution in Saudi Arabia, and that his new regime would rule in accordance with the seventh-century precepts of the Prophet Muhammad. "We are confident . . . that Muslims will be victorious in the Arabian peninsula and that God's religion, praise and glory be to Him, will prevail in this peninsula. It is a great . . . hope that the revelation unto Muhammad will be used for ruling."

Bin Laden coughed softly throughout the interview and nursed a cup of tea. No doubt he was suffering from a cold brought on by the drafty Afghan mountains. He continued on in his soft-spoken but focused manner, an ambiguous, thin smile sometimes playing on his lips: "We declared jihad against the U.S. government because the U.S. government . . . has committed acts that are extremely unjust, hideous, and criminal whether directly or through its support of the Israeli occupation of [Palestine]. And we believe the U.S. is directly responsible for those who were killed in Palestine, Lebanon, and Iraq. This U.S. government abandoned humanitarian feelings by these hideous crimes. It transgressed all bounds and behaved in a way not witnessed before by any power or any imperialist power in the world. Due to its subordination to the Jews, the arrogance and haughtiness of the U.S. regime has reached to the extent that they occupied [Arabia]. For this and other acts of aggression and injustice, we have declared jihad against the U.S., because in our religion it is our duty to make jihad so that God's word is the one exalted to the heights and so that we drive the Americans away from all Muslim countries."

Throughout bin Laden's diatribe perhaps a dozen of his followers listened in rapt attention as he went on to clarify that the call for jihad was directed against U.S. armed forces stationed in the Saudi Kingdom.

"We have focused our declaration on striking at the soldiers in the country of the Two Holy Places [Mecca and Medina]." This was Bin Laden's name for Saudi Arabia, a term he avoids using, as he loathes the Saudi royal family.[20]

He continued: "The country of the Two Holy Places has in our religion a peculiarity of its own over the other Muslim countries. In our religion, it is not permissible for any non-Muslim to stay in our country. Therefore, even though American civilians are not targeted in our plan, they must leave. We do not guarantee their safety."

This was the first time that bin Laden had told members of the Western press that American civilians might be casualties in his holy war. A year later he would tell ABC News that he made no distinction between American military and civilian targets, despite the fact that the Koran itself is explicit about the protections offered to civilians.

Bin Laden went on to say that the end of the Cold War had made the United States overreach: "The collapse of the Soviet Union made the U.S. more haughty and arrogant and it has started to look at itself as a master of this world and established what it calls the New World Order."

It was ironic that bin Laden was critical of the post–Cold War environment. It was precisely the end of the Cold War, which brought more open borders, that allowed his organization to flourish. According to the U.S. indictment against him, his network had established cells in twenty countries during the 1990s. Some of those countries, such as Croatia, Bosnia, Tajikistan, and Azerbaijan, owed their very existence to the end of the Cold War. And bin Laden represented a shift in the way terrorists operated, a shift made possible by the changing rules of the New World Order. While bin Laden transferred his millions from Saudi Arabia to Sudan to Afghanistan, his followers enthusiastically embraced the artifacts of globalization. They communicated by American satellite phones and kept their plans on Japanese-made computers. Bin Laden's *fatwas*, or religious rulings, were faxed to other countries, particularly England, where Arabic-language newspapers reprinted them and transmitted them throughout the Middle East. Thus was bin Laden able to create a truly global network.

Bin Laden envisaged his own counterpoint to the march of globalization—the restoration of the *Khalifa*, or caliphate, which would begin from Afghanistan.[21] Not since the final demise of the Ottoman Empire after the end of World War I had there been a Muslim entity that more or less united the *umma,* the community of Muslim believers, under the green flag of Islam. In this view, the treaties that followed World War I had carved up the Ottoman Empire, "the Sick Man of Europe," into ersatz entities like Iraq and Syria. Bin Laden aimed to create the conditions for the rebirth of the *Khalifa,* where the *umma* would live under the rule of the Prophet Muhammad in a continuous swath of green from Tunisia to Indonesia, much as the red of the British empire colored maps from Egypt to Burma before World War II. As a practical matter, the restoration of the *Khalifa* had about as much chance as the Holy Roman Empire suddenly reappearing in Europe, but as a rhetorical device the call for its return exercised a powerful grip on bin Laden and his followers.

During the interview bin Laden's translator, who spoke precise English, gave us rough translations of what bin Laden was saying. Occasionally, though, bin Laden would answer questions before they had been translated. So he clearly understood some English. "The U.S. today has set a double standard, calling whoever goes against its injustice a terrorist," he said at one point. "It wants to occupy our countries, steal our resources, impose on us agents to rule us . . . and wants us to agree to all these. If we refuse to do so, it will say, 'You are terrorists.' With a simple look at the U.S. behaviors, we find that it judges the behavior of the poor Palestinian children whose country was occupied: if they throw stones against the Israeli occupation, it says they are terrorists, whereas when the Israeli pilots bombed the United Nations building in Qana, Lebanon, while it was full of children and women, the U.S. stopped any plan to condemn Israel." (This was a reference to April 18, 1996, when Israeli forces seeking to attack Hezbollah guerrillas shelled a U.N. building in Qana, Lebanon, killing 102 Lebanese civilians. Israel characterized the attack on the U.N. building as an accident, a claim the U.N. later dismissed.)[22]

Bin Laden angrily continued. "At the same time that they condemn any Muslim who calls for his rights, they receive the top official of the Irish Republican Army [Gerry Adams] at the White House as a political leader. Wherever we look, we find the U.S. as the leader of terrorism and crime in the world. The U.S. does not consider it a terrorist act to throw atomic bombs at nations thousands of miles away, when those bombs would hit more than just military targets. Those bombs rather were thrown at entire nations, including women, children, and elderly people, and up to this day the traces of those bombs remain in Japan."

Bin Laden then surprised us by claiming that Arabs affiliated with his group were involved in killing American troops in Somalia in 1993, a claim he had earlier made to an Arabic newspaper.[23] We all remembered the grisly television images of the mutilated body of a U.S. serviceman being dragged through the streets of Mogadishu. What was not known at the time was the possible involvement of bin Laden's organization in training the Somalis who carried out the operation.

Bin Laden told us: "Resistance started against the American invasion, because Muslims did not believe the U.S. allegations that they came to save the Somalis. With Allah's grace, Muslims in Somalia cooperated with some Arab holy warriors who were in Afghanistan. Together they killed large numbers of American occupation troops." For bin Laden, Somalia was clearly an intoxicating victory. He exulted in the fact that the United States withdrew its troops from the country, pointing to the withdrawal as an example of the "weakness, frailty and cowardice of the U.S. troops."[24]

Asked what message he would send President Clinton, bin Laden answered: "Mentioning the name of Clinton or that of the American government provokes disgust and revulsion. This is because the name of the American government and the name of Clinton and Bush directly reflect in our minds . . . the picture of the children who died in Iraq." (He was referring to the fact that, by May 1996, an estimated 500,000 Iraqi children had died as a result of U.N. sanctions imposed on Iraq in 1990, for its continued violations of U.N. resolutions.[25])

He continued: "The hearts of Muslims are filled with hatred towards the United States of America and the American president. The president has a heart that knows no words. A heart that kills hundreds of children definitely knows no words. Our people in the Arabian Peninsula will send him messages with no words because he does not know any words. If there is a message that I may send through you, then it is a message I address to the mothers of the American troops who came here with their military uniforms walking proudly up and down our land. . . . I say that this represents a blatant provocation to over a billion Muslims. To these mothers I say if they are concerned for their sons, then let them object to the American government's policy."[26]

The interview came to an end, but bin Laden lingered for a few minutes, courteously serving us cups of tea. The talk turned to Iraq and Saddam Hussein, whom Arnett had interviewed during the Gulf War. Bin Laden said that the Iraqi dictator wanted the oil of Kuwait for his own aggrandizement and was not a true Muslim leader.

After posing for a couple of photos, bin Laden left as quickly as he had arrived. He had spent a little over an hour with us. But the "media adviser" was reluctant to give up the interview tapes. First, he wanted to erase some shots of bin Laden he considered unflattering. With several of bin Laden's guards still present, there was no way to stop him. I watched as he proceeded to erase the offending images by taping over the interview tape inside the camera. Not content with this little display, he then started an argument with Ali about giving us the tapes at all. A tugging match ensued. Finally, Ali prevailed, giving me both interview tapes, which were hardly larger than a pair of matchbooks. I put them in the most secure place I could think of: inside my money belt, which I wore under my trousers.

"Will you use the bit of the interview where bin Laden attacks Clinton?" Ali asked. We were standing outside the mud hut, where the interview had taken place, underneath a vast sky. There is no light pollution or smog in Afghanistan, so the heavens can be seen in their natural state. It was a beautiful night, clear and cold and utterly, utterly silent. "Of course," I told him. Ali seemed surprised. He was used to firm government control of the media.

During the next weeks we wrote and edited the script for our profile, which was broadcast on May 12, 1997, in the United States and over a hundred other countries. In Saudi Arabia, authorities confiscated copies of newspapers that ran items about our story, while in the U.S. the Associated Press wire service ran a piece that was picked up by a number of American papers. Otherwise, the story had little impact.

But a line kept resonating in my mind, the final words in our broadcast. When asked about his future plans bin Laden had replied:

"You'll see them and hear about them in the media, God willing."

CHAPTER 1

While America Slept

"I have always dreamed," he mouthed, fiercely, "of a band of men absolute in their resolve to discard all scruples in the choice of means, strong enough to give themselves frankly the name of destroyers, and free from the taint of resigned pessimism which rots the world. No pity for anything on earth, including themselves, and death enlisted for good and all in the service of humanity . . ."

—Joseph Conrad, *The Secret Agent*

You will soon be, with God's permission, with your heavenly brides in Heaven. Smile in the face of death young man. You are headed to the Paradise of Eternity . . .

—From a document found by the FBI in one of the hijacker's cars after 9/11

Seperember 11, 2001, was the kind of morning when everything seemed right with the world. On the East Coast of the United States, the air was cool and clear, the sky a limitless, cloudless, azure blue. It was a very *American* morning, somehow. It was the perfect morning to take a dog for a walk, to stop for a coffee and bagel on the way to work. And it was the perfect morning for flying.

That was a matter of vital importance to the nineteen Middle Eastern men who boarded flights leaving Boston, Newark, and Washington for the West Coast. Any weather-related delay, however slight, could sabotage their carefully synchronized plans to wreak unimaginable havoc against their enemy, the United States of America.

At 7:45 A.M., American Airlines flight 11 left Boston for Los Angeles, followed thirteen minutes later by United Airlines flight 175, also heading to L.A. Within three minutes, United Airlines flight 93 left Newark for San Francisco. At 8:10 A.M., American flight 77 left Washington's Dulles Airport for Los Angeles.[1]

Armed with boxcutters and knives, the men quickly seized control of the four planes and steered them to their targets in Manhattan and Washington. At 8:45 A.M., American flight 11—laden, like the other planes, with fuel for its long haul—slammed into the North Tower of the World Trade Center, setting off a giant fireball inside the building. Twenty minutes later, United flight 175, now in effect a massive flying bomb, crashed into the South Tower. Within an hour and a half, both skyscrapers had collapsed. At 9:39 A.M., American flight 77 plowed into the side of the Pentagon.[2] Only the heroism of passengers who fought the hijackers on United flight 93 prevented its use in another kamikaze attack. After a struggle, the exact details of which will never be known, the jet went down southeast of Pittsburgh, Pennsylvania at 10:10 A.M., killing all on board.

In little more than an hour, some three thousand Americans perished: the most catastrophic act of terrorism in the history of the United States. And Americans were not the only victims of this unimaginable crime. Also killed were men and women from more than fifty other countries, among them Great Britain, which, having lost seventy-eight citizens, had experienced the single most deadly act of terrorism in its history too. Until that grim morning, the average American was statistically more likely to be killed by a bolt of lightning than an act of terrorism. But everything had now changed.[3]

The dual attacks in New York and Washington were the deadliest salvo in Osama bin Laden's holy war against the United States—a war that had begun almost a decade earlier with the little-noticed bombing of two hotels in Yemen housing American soldiers. An Australian tourist was the sole casualty of that assault, but with every passing year the attacks became more sophisticated and more deadly. The bombings in 1998 of two U.S. embassies in Africa killed more than two hundred people; the October 2000 bombing of an American warship, the U.S.S. *Cole*, in Yemen left seventeen American sailors dead.

A terrible irony is that among the World Trade Center victims was John O'Neill, who probably knew more about bin Laden than anyone in the U.S. government: he had led the FBI investigation of the embassy bombings and the attack on the *Cole*. A blustery, can-do man who did not endear himself to more bureaucratically minded officials in the U.S. government, O'Neill had retired from the Bureau only two weeks before and gone to work as the head of security at the Trade Center. He died trying to rescue people.

Although the September assaults came as an utter surprise, there were indications that bin Laden was planning to attack an American target sometime in the months before 9/11. The clearest signal of this was a two-hour al-Qaeda propaganda videotape circulating around the Middle East that summer. I acquired a complete copy of the tape three weeks before the Trade Center attacks and had it translated. It was an eye opener. The skillfully edited tape was the most wide-ranging distillation of bin Laden's views to date, and it predicted additional anti-American actions. I decided the best forum to explain in detail what was on the tape was a story in *The New York Times*. To that end I wrote a letter to John Burns, one of the best reporters at the paper, who shared my view that the threat from bin Laden had been underestimated. An abbreviated version of the letter follows:

August 17, 2001

John,

I think there is a major story to be told wrapping around the new bin Laden videotape and the various threats against U.S. facilities in past months which can paint both a compelling picture of the bin Laden organization today, and responsibly suggest that an al-Qaeda attack is in the works. . . . As you know there were very strong indications of attacks on U.S. targets in Yemen in June. Also in June two men were picked up in New Delhi, who said they were planning to blow up the busy visa section of the U.S. embassy. . . . On July 18, the State Department issued a statement that the USG [U.S. government] has "strong indications that indi-

viduals may be planning imminent terrorist actions against U.S. interests in the Arabian Peninsula."

Clearly, al-Qaeda was and is planning something.

Now comes the two-hour bin Laden recruitment-propaganda tape, brief snippets of which were shown on CNN and Reuters ran a story about it when it surfaced in Kuwait in late June. But no one has looked at the entire tape, or if they have, they did not bother to sit down and translate the whole thing . . .

Also no one has thought to put the videotape in the context of al-Qaeda's modus operandi which is to subtly indicate a plot is in the works before it takes place. We saw this in May 1998 when bin Laden held a press conference in Afghanistan where he talked of "good news in coming weeks" and a few days later told ABC News that he predicted a "black day for America." Nine weeks later the embassies in Africa were bombed. . . .

A few months before the Cole bombing, as you know, a tape appeared which is notable for two things: bin Laden is wearing the jambiya Yemeni dagger, which he had never previously worn in any of the dozens of photos that exist of him, and his deputy Ayman al-Zawahiri specifically called for attacks on American forces in Yemen. This tape is of more than passing interest to U.S. investigators, and again shows how al-Qaeda subtly signals its next move.

Now the videotape I have in hand is circulating around the Middle East, which has all sorts of juicy stuff on it detailed below, not least of which is that on the tape bin Laden makes a set of statements taking credit for a number of anti-American actions, his most explicit and wide-ranging to date . . .

On the tape, bin Laden and his advisers make impassioned speeches about Muslims being attacked in Chechnya, Kashmir, Iraq, Israel, Lebanon, Indonesia, and Egypt; speeches which are laid over graphic footage of Muslims being killed, beaten, and imprisoned. The videotape devotes ten to fifteen minutes to images of Palestinians under attack by Israeli soldiers. . . .

For bin Laden, however, the greatest insult to Muslims is the continued presence of Americans in the holy land of Arabia. Bin Laden says: "These Americans brought women and Jewish women who can go anywhere in our holy land" adding "the Arab rulers worship the God of the White House." These statements are made over images of Saudi royal family members meeting American leaders such as Colin Powell.

Bin Laden says that Muslims must seek revenge for these insults: "If you don't fight you will be punished by God." The Saudi exile says the solution to these problems is that Muslims should travel to Afghanistan, and receive training about how to do jihad. The tape then shows hundreds of bin Laden's masked followers training at his al-Farouq camp in eastern Afghanistan, holding up black flags and chanting in Arabic "fight evil." Bin Laden's fighters shoot off anti-aircraft guns and RPGs, hold up their Korans and their Kalashnikovs [AK-47s], run across obstacle courses, dive into pools of water, blow up buildings and shoot at images of President Clinton. Bin Laden himself looses off some rounds fromn an automatic rifle. Chillingly, the tape also shows dozens of young boys, most of whom appear to be around ten, dressed in military camouflage uniforms, chanting for jihad . . .

Towards the end of the tape, bin Laden implies more action against the United States: "The victory of Islam is coming. And the victory of Yemen will continue . . ." The entire video is now available in a DVD format and is also circulating in clandestine chat rooms on the Internet, according to those familiar with bin Laden's organization . . . [who also say] "these threats on the videotape are genuine, that bin Laden's followers are making real preparations against more than one American target . . ."

After Burns obtained a copy of the videotape, we spoke again, and he said that it provided the starkest evidence yet that some major new al-Qaeda attack was afoot. After reviewing the videotape with a distinguished scholar of Islamic history, Professor Tarif Khalidi of Cambridge University, Burns wrote a full account of the tape and the menace is contained which appeared on *The New York Times* Web site on September 9 under the headline: "On Videotape, Bin Laden Charts a Violent Future." But strangely that was the only version of the story that ever appeared, and it was later expunged by the newspaper from the Web site archive. A spokesperson for the *Times* explained to me that Burns's article was "inadvertently published on the Web site," adding that "I can't comment on why it didn't make it into the print version. Routinely many articles are held from print."[4] So the last, best warning to America of what might be ahead failed to see the light of day. (The *Times* would publish a story by Burns a day after 9/11 that referenced the bin Laden videotape; a piece that had few of the details of the original story and was, alas, too late to make a difference.)

The al-Qaeda videotape, which was widely distributed on the Internet, is a graphic demonstration of how bin Laden and his followers have exploited twenty-first-century communications and weapons technology in the service of the most extreme, retrograde reading of holy war. The result is a fusion I call Holy War, Inc.

No single event better illustrates this fusion than the attacks on the World Trade Center and the Pentagon. Bin Laden's men, several of whom had trained in the United States as pilots, flew passenger jets into two of the world's most famous buildings in a martyrdom operation that would, in their view, instantly take them to Paradise. They saw themselves as *shuhadaa*—martyrs in the name of Allah—and their attacks as acts of worship.

These were not, however, impoverished suicide bombers of the type usually seen in the Palestinian *intifada*. Instead, they were generally well-educated, technically savvy young men who blended all too well into their various American communities in California, Florida, and Virginia. They did not wear the full beards of the typical Islamist militant, but were clean-shaven. They worked out at gyms, ordered in pizza, and booked their flights on the Internet. Some even drank on occasion—a grave sin for a serious Muslim but an excellent cover for bin Laden's operatives. In short, the hijackers looked and acted like the increasingly diverse United States of the twenty-first century.

This grafting of entirely modern sensibilities and techniques to the most radical interpretation of holy war is the hallmark of bin Laden's network. One of his Afghan training camps during the late nineties was named al-Badr, after a key seventh-century battle fought by the Prophet Muhammad, yet al-Qaeda members training there were tutored in the use of high-tech explosives such as RDX and C4. Members of al-Qaeda perform *bayat,* a quasi-mediaeval oath of allegiance to bin Laden their *emir,* or leader. But while based in Sudan in the early nineties, they also drew monthly paychecks and supported themselves with a wide range of legitimate businesses. When bin Laden declared war on Americans in 1996, he described U.S. soldiers stationed in the Middle East as "the Crusaders," as if the crusades of the Middle Ages were still being fought, and signed his declaration "from the peaks of the Hindu Kush mountains of Afghanistan," a place barely touched by the modern world. That declaration of war was written on an Apple computer and then faxed or e-mailed to supporters in Pakistan and Britain, who in turn made it available to Arabic newspapers based in London, which subsequently beamed the text, via satellite, to printing centers all over the Middle East and in New York.[5] Thus, a premodern message was delivered by postmodern means.

In a 2001 interview the head of the secretive U.S. National Security Agency said that bin Laden had better technology for communications than the United States.[6] The Saudi militant's followers communicate by fax, satellite phone, and e-mail. They encrypt memos on their Macintosh and Toshiba computers.[7] And in the mid-1990s, members of al-Qaeda made a CD-ROM containing hundreds of pages of information about various kinds of weaponry, as well as instructions on how to build bombs and conduct terrorist and paramilitary operations. Bin Laden's methods of travel are equally modern: when he lived in Sudan, he generally kept a couple of pilots on call. And when he traveled from Pakistan to Sudan with his family and followers in 1991, they made the trip in his personal jet.[8]

When he first turned his attention to holy war, bin Laden also applied business techniques picked up from his years working for the family company. During the 1980s Afghan war, he set up offices in Pakistan and the United States; raised funds in Saudi Arabia; recruited fighters from every country in the Muslim world; and used the resources of his family company to build bases inside Afghanistan for his holy warriors.

The older generation of Islamist radicals, such as Palestinian Abdullah Azzam, Egypt's Sheikh Omar Abdel Rahman, and Yemen's Sheikh Abdul Majid Zindani studied at Cairo's al-Azhar University, the Oxford of Islamic learning.[9] By contrast, the men attracted to bin Laden's standard, like so many of the newer generation of Islamist militants, are more likely to have studied technical subjects such as medicine and engineering, or had careers in business, than to have studied the finer points of Islamic jurisprudence.

So it should not be surprising that bin Laden's top aide is a physician from an upper-class Egyptian family, or that his former media representative in London was a Saudi entrepreneur, born in Kuwait, who worked in the import-export business. His military adviser in the United States graduated from an Egyptian university with a degree in psychology and worked as a computer network specialist in California.[10] Egyptian militant Rifia Ahmed Taha, a cosignatory of bin Laden's 1998 declaration of war against Americans, is an accountant.[11] Another top al-Qaeda official, Mamdouh Mahmud Salim, studied electrical engineering in Iraq.[12] Bin Laden himself studied economics in college and worked for his family's construction business in Saudi Arabia when he was a young man.[13] During the early 1990s he set himself up as one of the most active businessmen in Sudan.

Indeed, al-Qaeda functions as an interesting analogue of the Saudi Binladin Group, the giant construction company founded by bin Laden's deeply religious father, which operates in countries across the Middle East and Asia. One of bin Laden's aliases is simply "the Director," which is probably as good a description as any other of his role in al-Qaeda.[14] Bin Laden organized al-Qaeda in a businesslike manner—he formulates the general policies of al-Qaeda in consultation with his *shura* council. The *shura* makes executive decisions for the group. Subordinate to that council are other committees responsible for military affairs and the business interests of the group, as well as a *fatwa* committee, which issues rulings on Islamic law, and a media group.[15] The contents of an al-Qaeda computer discovered in Kabul after the fall of the Taliban underscores that the group thought of itself as a corporation. In a document about an al-Qaeda cell in Yemen a report notes: "The general management shall be consulted on issues related to joining and firing from the company, the general strategy and the company name."[16]

Once decisions on overall policy are made by bin Laden and his closest advisers, they are relayed to the relevant committee and then—at the appropriate moment—to lower-level members of the group. Many of these foot soldiers have had little or no contact with bin Laden himself. In 1997, for instance, the media information officer for bin Laden's Kenyan cell, who would later play a key role in the bombing of the American embassy in Nairobi, noted in a document on his computer that the cell's mission was to attack Americans, but added: "We, the East Africa cell members, do not want to know about the operations plan since we are just implementers." [17] The suicide bombers in the Kenya embassy bombing were never directly given instructions by bin Laden, and some of his followers have not even met their hero.[18] A case in point is Khalfan Khamis Mohamed, a Tanzanian who helped blow up the American embassy in Tanzania in 1998. In an interview with ABC News after that attack, bin Laden aptly summarized his role in al-Qaeda: "It is our job to instigate. By the Grace of God we did that and certain people responded to this instigation." [19]

In short, it's fruitful to think of al-Qaeda as a sort of multinational holding company, which was headquartered in Afghanistan, under the chairmanship of bin Laden. The traditional structure of a holding company is a core management group controlling partial or complete interests in other companies.[20] Holding companies are also sometimes used by criminals to disguise their illegal activities and are often based in countries where they can operate with little or no regulatory scrutiny. True to form, al-Qaeda incorporates, to various degrees, subsidiary militant organizations in Egypt, Pakistan, Bangladesh, Algeria, Libya, Yemen, Syria, and Kashmir.[21]

Al-Qaeda's Afghan training camps have also attracted a rainbow coalition of Jordanians, Turks, Palestinians, Iraqis, Saudis, Sudanese, Moroccans, Omanis, Tunisians, Tanzanians, Malaysians, Bangladeshis, Indians, Filipinos, Chechens, Uzbeks, Tajiks, Chinese Uighurs, Burmese, Germans, Swedes, French, Britons, Arab-Americans, and African-Americans.[22] The graduates of those camps have gone on to export terrorism and holy war to pretty much every corner of the world. As bin Laden himself put it: "I would say that the number of the brothers is large, thank God, and I do not know everyone who is with us in this base or this organization." [23] Spoken like a true CEO.

Osama bin Laden inspires superlatives, for or against. Shades of gray are rarely applied to any portrait of the world's most famous Islamist militant. And that makes trying to understand him a complicated task. Testifying before the U.S. Senate in 1999, the CIA director,

George Tenet, observed that bin Laden "and his global network of lieutenants and associates remain the most immediate and serious threat" of terrorism directed against the United States. That observation would prove to be prescient. Addressing Congress nine days after the World Trade Center and Pentagon attacks, President George W. Bush painted bin Laden as a sort of terrorist godfather when he declared that "al-Qaeda is to terrorism what the Mafia is to crime."

The headmaster of one of the largest religious schools in Pakistan expressed a rather different view when he said that bin Laden is a "hero because he raised his voice against the outside powers that are trying to crush Muslims." A small boy carrying a Koran in the remote village in southern Yemen where the bin Laden family originates told me: "We love him. He fights for God's sake and he is in Afghanistan." Similar adulation could be heard at a conference I attended in London in the spring of 2000: before an audience of several hundred enthralled men and women, the keynote speaker lauded bin Laden as "this man who sacrificed his life for Islam."

And so we will encounter several different bin Ladens in the course of this book: bin Laden the hero; bin Laden the über-terrorist; bin Laden the banner carrier of Islamist militancy; perhaps even bin Laden the man.

Further clouding our understanding of bin Laden is the fact that a vast amount has been written about him, a good deal of it rubbish. A database search for news items about bin Laden turns up tens of thousands of stories. Take the respectable *Jane's Intelligence Review*, which reported that bin Laden may have obtained an engineering degree in the United States and was financed by the CIA during the 1980s war against the Soviets in Afghanistan. Bin Laden has never visited the United States, let alone studied here, and saying the CIA funded him during the Afghan war is a fundamental misunderstanding of the Agency's operations in Afghanistan.[24]

Or consider the report by NBC News from December 1998: "U.S. officials" have been told by a "friendly foreign intelligence service" that bin Laden has only "months to live."[25] The story went on to explain that the Saudi exile was suffering from heart problems and possibly cancer. Reports of bin Laden's imminent demise were plainly exaggerated, as he remains stubbornly alive years later.

These reporting lapses may be explicable by the pressures of daily journalism, but books that have tried to address the bin Laden phenomenon at greater length have often fared no better. One such, *Study of Revenge: Saddam Hussein's Unfinished War Against America,* argues that Iraq probably sponsored the 1993 bombing of the World Trade Center. This theory is supported by at least some of the facts. But the writer goes on to suggest that the bombing of two U.S. embassies in Africa in 1998 could have been a joint operation between Iraq and bin Laden.[26] In the tens of thousands of pages of court filings in the New York trial of four men who conspired to bomb those embassies there is simply no evidence of Iraqi involvement.

Another book, *Dollars for Terror: The United States and Islam,* by the Swiss journalist Richard Labevière, makes a number of bizarre claims about bin Laden: that he is a former CIA agent; that in 1997 he flew into London's Heathrow airport—unnoticed on his private jet!—to attend a meeting of terrorists planning attacks on tourists in Egypt; and that in Yemen he "controls the principal routes of qat, the hallucinogenic leaf which is consumed in the Horn of Africa and the southern part of the Arabian peninsula." Perhaps Labevière was chewing qat himself when he wrote this.

Other examples of misinformation about bin Laden can be found in a tome by Yossef Bodansky, who enjoys the title of director of the Congressional Task Force on Terrorism. In *Bin Laden: The Man Who Declared War on America,* Bodansky describes the teenage bin Laden visiting Beirut to drink, womanize, and get involved in bar brawls.[27] Those who know bin Laden, however, describe a deeply religious teenager who married at the age of seventeen. Perhaps Bodansky confused Osama with one of his twenty or so half-brothers. Bodansky also writes that in 1994 bin Laden traveled to London, where he "settled" in the London suburb of Wembley, a notion that Arab dissidents and journalists living in London find amusing.[28]

Bodansky makes another fantastic assertion: that the 1996 crash of TWA flight 800 off Long Island, which killed 230 people, was a joint operation between Iran and bin Laden.[29] However, an exhaustive two-year investigation by the National Transportation Safety Board and the FBI ruled out terrorism in the TWA 800 crash.

In the unintentionally hilarious *Bin Laden: Behind the Mask of a Ter-*

rorist, Adam Robinson describes bin Laden watching the events of 9/11 live on CNN in his Afghanistan hideout; landing his helicopter in Peshawar's bazaar (a place where maneuvering a motorcycle is tricky); scanning in pornographic photos on his computer; drinking himself into a stupor on Johnny Walker Black Label whisky; and consorting with prostitutes. Robinson seems to be endowed with a lively imagination.[30]

Why is there so much unreliable reporting about bin Laden? First, what is written about him is largely uncheckable because he is more or less incommunicado. Second, bin Laden has largely avoided questions about his personal life, and his family has remained determinedly silent, except to issue brief statements distancing themselves from the black sheep of the family. Finally, he is libel proof: one can say pretty much anything about him and know one isn't going to be sued.

Reporting on bin Laden is also made difficult by the fact that he plays multiple roles. The first is as the leader of a core cadre of hundreds of militants who have sworn an oath of allegiance to him. Another is as the ideologue for a larger group of thousands of holy warriors around the globe who may not be part of his organization, but who look to him for guidance and inspiration. As a result of the U.S. cruise missile attacks directed against bin Laden in August 1998, he also gained literally millions of admirers who viewed him as a symbol of resistance to the West. Finally, when announcing those American missile strikes, Clinton administration officials from the president down painted bin Laden as the mastermind of every conceivable terrorist attack in recent memory, a dastardly villain out of a James Bond movie—a portrait that in the light of the events of September 11 may be almost understated.

For his sympathizers, bin Laden became a turbaned Robin Hood, hiding out not in the forests of Nottingham during the Middle Ages, but in the mountains of almost medieval Afghanistan, gathering around him his band of unmerry men, armed not with crossbows but with rocket-propelled grenades and C4 explosives, tweaking the noses of the great powers of the West. But bin Laden is perhaps better understood as the Pied Piper of jihad; his invitation to holy war resonates among disaffected and underemployed Muslim youths from Algeria to Pakistan to California, leading them to sacrifice themselves in a conflict that cannot be won in any conventional sense.

What then is the attraction of bin Laden's call? He espouses a somewhat coherent ideology of anti-Americanism and opposition to Middle Eastern governments he deems "un-Islamic," and he supports guerrilla movements in countries as diverse as Chechnya and the Philippines. So it is bin Laden's political ideas as well as the terrorist operations he has mounted that makes understanding him a matter of vital importance.

In an interview a few months before the September 11 attacks, General Pervez Musharaf, the military ruler of Pakistan's 140 million Muslims, aptly summarized bin Laden's appeal at the time: "The Western demonization of OBL, as he is known in Pakistan, made him a cult figure among Muslims who resent everything from the decline in moral values as conveyed by Hollywood movies and TV serials to America's lack of support for Palestinians being killed by Israeli occupation forces, to what Russia is doing to Muslims in Chechnya, [to] what the West did to Muslims in Bosnia and Kosovo, [to] India's oppression of Muslims in Kashmir. . . . It is a very long list of complaints that has generated a strong persecution complex that the OBL cult figure has come to embody. He is a hero figure on the pedestal of Muslim extremism."[31]

The prototype of the technically savvy, worldly young men who are the shock troops of Holy War, Inc., is Ramzi Yousef, the operational leader of the 1993 World Trade Center bombing. Yousef, whose family are Baluch Pakistanis, was brought up in Kuwait.[32] He was educated as an electrical engineer in Wales, where he learned excellent English; his subsequent terrorism career took him to Afghanistan, New York, Thailand, the Philippines, and Pakistan. While in Pakistan, Yousef tried to assassinate the country's first woman prime minister, Benazir Bhutto.[33] Truly, a one-man global jihad.

Yousef was not the typical Islamist militant; he seemed to enjoy the good life. Yet he plugged into the al-Qaeda network many times during his career as globe-trotting terrorist: training at a bin Laden camp on the Afghan-Pakistan border; working closely with one of bin Laden's followers in the Philippines; and staying at a bin Laden guesthouse in Pakistan.[34]

Yousef's terrorist plots against the West culminated in plans for blowing up a dozen or so American passenger jets, assassinating Pope John Paul II, and crashing a plane into CIA headquarters in Virginia.[35] The plots were discovered when Filipino police found their outlines on his laptop computer in his Manila apartment in 1994 and subsequently interrogated one of Yousef's co-conspirators, who supplied details of the plan the terrorists code-named Bojinka.[36]

When Yousef was finally captured in 1995, in Pakistan, FBI agents flew him back to New York. The helicopter that would take Yousef to his American jail cell in Manhattan flew past the World Trade Center, and one of the agents commented that the towers were still standing. "They wouldn't be if I had enough money and explosives," came the reply.[37]

Al-Qaeda would have more money and more time, and the September 11 plotters, who began arriving in the United States in 2000, would execute a breathtakingly ambitious plan—one that combined, in effect, the most spectacular elements of the 1993 World Trade Center attack with the Bojinka plot.

Mohamed Atta, an Egyptian who was one of the cell leaders of the World Trade Center operation, embodies the marriage of religious zeal and technical accomplishment typical of al-Qaeda's elite recruits. Atta was born in 1968 to a religious, middle-class family in Cairo.[38] In 1992, he moved to Germany, where he studied urban planning and preservation at Hamburg's Harburg Technical Institute. Living the life of a semipermanent student, he took seven years to graduate. One of his professors, Dittmar Machule, remembers Atta as a precise thinker who was skeptical of the Western world; he never drank alcohol or had relationships with women. Atta's religiosity led him to found an Islamic student group at the university. Its fifty members included two of his roommates, who would join the Trade Center conspiracy.

On May 18, 2000, Atta applied for an American visa at the U.S. embassy in Berlin. He took a circuitous route to the United States, traveling via Prague, where he is thought to have met with an Iraqi intelligence agent—an encounter that might or might not be significant, since one meeting makes not an al-Qaeda-Iraqi conspiracy.[39] A senior U.S. counterterrorism official insisted to me that "no one has drawn any conclusion of any sort about that meeting."[40]

Atta left Prague for Newark on June 3. One of his first stops was a flight school in the university town of Norman, Oklahoma—the same place where one of al-Qaeda's American recruits, Ihab Ali, had learned to fly in the early nineties before going on to serve as one of bin Laden's pilots in Sudan.

After a few weeks, Atta moved to Venice, Florida, where he took up flying at Huffman Aviation between July and November. He paid $25,000 for his lessons and was subsequently certified to fly single-engine and multi-engine aircraft. In December, Atta spent several hours at another flight school, where he practiced on its Boeing 727 simulator.[41] The instructor was puzzled by the fact that, unlike other pupils, who were interested in the arts of taking off and landing, Atta wanted only to practice turns. While Atta was living in the United States, he was wired $110,000 from the United Arab Emirates—money that he distributed to other plotters and that probably paid for his flying lessons.

In February 2001 Atta visited the tiny airport at Belle Glade, Florida, where he made inquiries about how far the crop-dusting planes could fly and the volume of poisons they could carry.[42] One nightmare scenario of counterterrorism planners involves crop dusters modified to disperse chemical or biological agents over a major American city. Atta and his confederates clearly were interested in exploring that possibility. In a remarkable act of chutzpah, they even made inquiries about securing a loan from the U.S. Department of Agriculture to finance the purchase of a crop duster.[43]

On August 28, Atta bought a ticket for American Airlines flight 11 from Boston to Los Angeles. A week or so later he and one of his Hamburg friends went drinking at a bar in Hollywood, Florida—a puzzling aspect of the story, since Atta had shunned alcohol for years. Four days later, early on the morning of September 11, an airport security camera captured him entering the departure area for a flight from Portland, Maine, to Boston, where he connected with flight 11.

In Atta's bags, which never made it onto that flight, investigators found a five-page document in Arabic that contained instructions for Atta's final moments on earth. Under a section headed "When you enter the plane" the document exhorted its reader to pray: "Oh God. Open all doors to me. Oh God who answers prayers and answers those who ask you for your help, I am asking you for forgiveness. I am asking you to lighten the way. I am asking you to lift the burden I feel."[44]

Exactly one hour after takeoff, Mohamed Atta guided American flight 11 into the North Tower of the World Trade Center. The former student of urban preservation had now become the architect of the most spectacular act of urban demolition in history.

Of course, bin Laden is hardly the only Islamist militant who has espoused opposition to the United States and to Middle Eastern governments that are "un-Islamic," but he is now the focus of those ideas. Moreover, bin Laden is a quite different figure from the Arab terrorists of the seventies and eighties, none of whom enjoyed his worldwide celebrity, or espoused an overarching and coherent philosophy that went beyond opposition to Israel and calls for a Palestinian state. Bin Laden articulates an all-encompassing worldview with a much wider appeal than simple hatred of Israel. Of course, he is opposed to Israel, but he also calls for the end of U.S. military actions against Iraq; demands the creation of a "Muslim" nuclear weapon; claims it is a religious obligation to attack American military and civilian targets worldwide because of the continued presence of U.S. troops in the Gulf; criticizes the governments of countries like Egypt and Saudi Arabia for not instituting what he sees as true Islamic law; and supports a multitude of holy wars around the globe.

Most important, while the state-sponsored Arab terrorist groups of the 1980s are now largely out of business, bin Laden's al-Qaeda and its affiliates are constantly planning new operations. And the success of the September 11 attacks will only embolden bin Laden's followers, who will see that success as a sign of Allah's favor.

Then there is the ripple effect. In an increasingly globalized culture, bin Laden's ideas are influencing the beliefs and actions of militants from Yemen to Kenya to England. In part, this is simply a matter of timing: in the twenty-first century communication is ever easier and bin Laden's message can spread with a speed and reach unimaginable two decades ago. Bin Laden's interviews with CNN, *Time,* and *Newsweek* circulated internationally. Arab media outlets such as Qatar's al-Jazeera television and London's *Al-Quds Al-Arabi* newspaper relay news about bin Laden all over the Middle East. That coverage is in turn picked up by Western television networks and wire services.

The Internet has had as great an impact on Holy War, Inc. as it has on many other concerns. The recruitment videotape made by al-Qaeda in 2001 was converted to DVD format, which makes it easy to copy by computer, and was made available in several chatrooms.[45] There are also Web sites devoted to bin Laden and jihadist sites, such as the London-based *azzam.com*, which deliver a wide range of products and services.[46] *Azzam.com* details the lives of holy warriors martyred in conflicts around the world, sells videotapes of those wars, carries interviews with jihadist leaders, and sells books by the leading ideologues of jihad.[47] A measure of the site's global reach can be seen in the reaction to the death of a Saudi named Khallad al-Madani, who was killed in Chechnya in February 2000 while fighting under the command of a bin Laden protégé. In the course of one day, messages of support for al-Madani's family poured in from South Africa, the United States, Lebanon, Malaysia, Canada, New Zealand, Saudi Arabia, Turkey, Sri Lanka, and India.[48]

The rapidly globalizing world of the past decade has been the subject of many encomiums, but the triumphalist proponents of globalization made the understandable mistake of confusing "progress" with an improvement in the moral condition of man. The Catholic doctrine of Original Sin remains a useful concept, and while it is true that globalization brought many people the benefits of open borders, the speed-of-light communication of the Internet, freer markets, and cheap travel, it was precisely in this new environment that Holy War, Inc. flourished. A globalized world benefited all manner of non-state actors from AOL to Amnesty International to al-Qaeda. Indeed, al-Qaeda has been aptly described as "the ultimate NGO."[49]

The Middle Eastern terrorist groups of the 1970s and 1980s needed the patronage of states to supply the money and infrastructure that allowed them to do business. (The archetype of that model was the Abu Nidal Organization, whose serial assassinations and hijackings were sponsored first by Iraq in the 1970s, then by Syria and Libya during the 1980s.) Bin Laden, however, is an individual with deep enough pockets to operate largely without sponsorship, while a rapidly globalizing world, propelled by new technologies, allows his message to be taken up with a click of a mouse by holy warriors from Azerbaijan to Yemen. Holy War, Inc., thus represents a *privatization* of terrorism that parallels the movement by many countries in the past decade to convert their state-supported industries to privately held companies. Nothing better underlines this development than the contrast between the American bombing of Libyan targets in 1986, for that *government's* role in the killing of U.S. soldiers based in Germany, with the U.S. Navy's cruise missile attacks, in 1998, on bin Laden, an *individual,* for his role in the African embassy bombings.

Bin Laden's message also differs qualitatively from the slogans of earlier Arab militants, who were focused on the more strictly political goals of pan-Arabism or the creation of a Palestinian state. Bin Laden is truly conducting a religious war, his actions sanctified by *ulema,* or clergy, and he has wholeheartedly embraced the most extreme reading of jihad, not only against the infidel West, but also against every "apostate" regime in the Middle East, and countries like India or Russia that oppress Muslims.

The wider Islamist militant movements that look to bin Laden for inspiration also follow the Holy War, Inc., paradigm. The men who lead these movement are generally well-educated and utilize the latest in technology in their various jihads.

In 1999 I visited Abdullah Muntazir, the spokesman for Pakistan's Lashkar-e-Taiba, the largest Kashmiri militant organization, founded in 1985 as an Afghan jihad group. Dressed in *shalwar kameez* shirt and pants—and a jean jacket—Muntazir, who studied mathematics in college and guerrilla tactics in Afghanistan, was a walking embodiment of both the East and West. It was Ramadan and he was fasting, but he nonetheless offered me a drink of tea. The organization's small office in Islamabad, was packed with fax machines and computers. Muntazir had just been checking out a Web site maintained by Chechen rebels for whom Lashkar helps raise money for their war against the Russians. "This technology is a good thing," Muntazir explained with a wave of his hand, "but we reject the civilization of the West."

The Holy War, Inc., phenomenon is also exemplified by the Islamic Army of Aden, an affiliate of al-Qaeda that is based in southern Yemen and that kidnapped a group of Western tourists in December 1998.[50]

The kidnappers equipped themselves with a satellite phone.[51] Their media representative is Abu Hamza, an Egyptian engineer, now a British citizen, who maintains an extensive Web site where militants have swapped tips about how to get jihad training and post bank account numbers for terrorist groups.

Ahmed Omar Sheikh, a leader of Pakistan's terrorist Army of Mohammed, embodies many of the traits of Holy War, Inc. Sheikh is a British citizen from a prosperous Pakistani immigrant family who speaks four languages. As an undergraduate he attended the prestigious London School of Economics. Later, traveling the globe in search of holy wars from the Balkans to Afghanistan, he trained in an al-Qaeda camp, and eventually landed in Pakistan where he allegedly orchestrated—via email—the kidnapping-murder of American journalist Daniel Pearl in January 2002.

The Algerian Armed Islamic Group, known by its French initials, GIA, maintains close ties to al-Qaeda, and shows the global reach of Holy War, Inc. During the past decade GIA operated on four continents. Members of the group robbed banks in Belgium, organized cells in Canada and London, bombed a subway station in Paris, set up a passport-forging operation in Europe, tried to bomb Los Angeles International Airport, trained at bin Laden's camps in Afghanistan, fought in Bosnia, and murdered countless civilians in their own country.[52]

The transnational character of Holy War, Inc., and its embrace of Western technologies, can also be seen in the wars that have racked Chechnya, in southern Russia, since 1994. One of the key leaders of the Chechen resistance is a Saudi known as Khattab. Khattab fought in Afghanistan under bin Laden before moving to Chechnya, where he helped launch the second Chechen war in 1999. On the Internet, Chechen groups maintain Web sites in more than a dozen languages, from Albanian to Swedish.[53] The 2001 al-Qaeda recruitment videotape, accessible on the Web in Real Player format, lauds Khattab's exploits. Chechens honed their battle skills in Afghan training camps, and graduates of Pakistan's religious schools fight alongside the rebels in Chechnya.[54]

While the foot soldiers of Holy War, Inc. have now gone global, dispersed in dozens of countries around the world, the ideological roots and formative experiences of those holy warriors can generally be found in one place, Afghanistan, to which many of them were drawn during the Soviet-Afghan war. Like thousands of his followers, Osama bin Laden would leave the comforts of his home on the Arabian peninsula for the dangers of the Afghan holy war, and from the crucible of that conflict he would emerge steeled as a holy warrior. It is to the biography of the chief executive officer of Holy War, Inc., that we will turn now.

CHAPTER 2

The Afghan Jihad:
The Making of a Holy Warrior

"The acme of this religion is jihad."
> —Osama bin Laden, reflecting on his
> experience in the Afghan war [1]

Death of the martyr for the unification of all the people in
the cause of God and His word is the happiest, best, easiest
and most virtuous of deaths. [2]
> —The medieval Muslim scholar Taqi al-Din ibn
> Taymiyyah, who is often cited by bin Laden

As with so many stories, it is best to begin this one at the beginning, and the bin Laden family saga begins not in Riyadh, Saudi Arabia, where Osama was born in 1957, but several hundred miles to the south in Hadramawt, Yemen, where the bin Ladens originate. [3]

Hadramawt is a vast region of deserts and mountains, broiling under an unremitting sun, bounded to the north by Saudi Arabia's Empty Quarter and to the south by the Arabian Sea. Like Afghanistan, bin Laden's adopted home on and off over the past two decades, Hadramawt might as well be in the Middle Ages. There are few signs of the modern world intruding on its mud-brick houses and impoverished villages, where donkeys are the commonest form of transportation.

In the harsh Hadramawt climate, where agriculture is not much more than a subsistence activity, Hadrami have for centuries turned to two other occupations: trade and construction. The frankincense and myrrh that the Three Wise Men brought as gifts to the Christ child may have come from the trees of Hadramawt.[4] Later Hadramis plied the world's oceans seeking their fortunes in the Middle and Far East. A testament to their wanderlust—and their success—are the Hadrami roots of the Sultans of Oman and Brunei.[5]

And then there are the buildings of Hadramawt. As soon as I saw the centuries-old skyscrapers of the town of Shibam, rising sheer from the desert floor as high as fifteen stories, it hit me: Here was why Osama's father made his fortune in construction. Hadramis are builders of genius.

It is in the largest of the Hadramawt wadis, or valleys, Wadi Doan, that the bin Laden ancestral village of al-Rubat can be found. From this valley, which is about a hundred miles long, a remarkable genera-tion of men went north to Saudi Arabia in the early part of the twen-tieth century. Their names are a roll call of some of Saudi Arabia's richest families: the bin Mahfouz, who founded the country's largest bank, the National Commercial Bank; the al-Amoudis, who made a fortune in oil, mining, and real estate; the Baroum, who are traders; and the bin Ladens—perhaps the richest of the lot—who own the largest construction concern in the Saudi kingdom.[6]

These families did business with one another, intermarried, and brought with them from Hadramawt a distinctive culture that may ex-plain both their worldly success and their piety. As far as business goes, Hadramis are, by their own description, both frugal and scrupu-lously honest. A deal can be worth "millions and millions and not a riyal will be missing," according to Nabil al-Habshi, a tour operator in the area.[7] Hadramawt is also conservative in its observance of Islam. Hadrami women don't drive, and shops close at prayer time. Women from these valleys have so little contact with the outside world that they have developed their own distinctive dialect, and the imperative to keep them rigorously segregated has even influenced the architec-ture of Hadramawt's towerlike houses, which are mazes of corridors and dead ends.[8]

Osama's father, Mohammed bin Awad bin Laden, emigrated to what would soon become the Kingdom of Saudi Arabia from Hadramawt around 1930.[9] Freya Stark, the redoubtable English travel writer, visited Hadramawt and the bin Laden ancestral village of al-Rubat in the early 1930s. One of the few Europeans to have ventured there at that time, she paints a contemporaneous portrait of the kind of society Mohammed bin Laden lived in as a young man. In al-Rubat, Stark chatted with the locals about the affairs of the wadi, describing it as a place of "poverty and little commerce"; surely it was for this reason that Mohammed embarked on the difficult trip to Jeddah, hundreds of miles to the north. Stark notes that "most of the men of Hadramawt" left their native villages to find work in Malaysia to the south or Egypt to the north; they stayed away for up to twenty years.[10]

Mohammed bin Laden would follow this pattern, although he would not return to al-Rubat. Mohammed's brother Abdullah, with whom he set off for Saudi Arabia, must have felt some nostalgia for his hometown, because he later built a massive mud-brick house in al-Rubat that is now home to four extended families, including some bin Laden cousins, who evidently never shared in the family billions.[11] The house is so large that one part of it is now the village school. Despite its continued use, the house has fallen into disrepair. Graffiti marks some of its walls, and its window ledges are rotting away. The last time any of the rich bin Ladens visited al-Rubat was in 1997, when a number of women from the village who had married into the family came to pay what amounted to a state visit for three days. The bin Ladens also continue to support a vital irrigation project in the village that waters crops of dates and corn, and there are plans for the bin Laden family company to set up a small office in the town.[12]

Arriving in Jeddah, Mohammed found work first as a porter. Jeddah is a transit point for large numbers of pilgrims en route to perform the Hajj, the pilgrimage to the neighboring holy city of Mecca. In the days before the oil bonanza, servicing the Hajj pilgrims was one of the principal sources of income for the al-Saud family. Later in life, Mohammed proudly displayed his porter's bag in a reception room of his palace.

In 1931 Mohammed founded a contracting company, which prospered.[13] Other Hadramis traveled north to work for the new company. The tourism executive Nabil al-Habshi says his father went when he was fifteen, in 1945. "He worked for the bin Laden family building villas," al-Habshi said. "He spent ten years in Saudi Arabia, saving enough to buy a small clothing shop."[14]

During the 1950s, under the reign of King Saud, Mohammed underbid other contractors to work on the king's palaces. He impressed Saud, but also became close to other members of the royal family, especially Saud's brother, Faisal. Later, in 1964, when Saud and Faisal struggled for power, Mohammed played a role in getting Saud to step down in favor of Faisal.[15] King Faisal then appointed Mohammed minister of public works for a period, and the bin Laden construction company became known as "the King's private contractors."[16]

During this period Mohammed bin Laden would also jump-start the career of another Saudi billionaire, Adnan Khashoggi, known in the West for his flamboyant spending, his walk-on part in the Iran-contra scandal, and his nephew Dodi Fayed, who died along with Princess Diana in the Paris car crash. In the early 1950s Mohammed needed some trucks for his construction business in a hurry. Khashoggi was able to make a $500,000 purchase of trucks in the United States, for which Mohammed paid him a commission of $50,000. It was Khashoggi's first business deal.[17]

Osama, which means "young lion" in Arabic, was born on March 10, 1957, in Riyadh.[18] His family moved to Medina when he was six months old, later dividing its time between Jeddah and the holy cities of Mecca and Medina.[19] Osama was the seventeenth son of Mohammed, who sired fifty or so sons and daughters by several wives. Mohammed himself would get confused about which children were the offspring of which wife.[20] Osama's mother, a Syrian, also bore Mohammed a couple of daughters, but no other sons.[21] According to someone authorized by the family to speak to me, the bin Ladens do not consider Osama's mother to be part of their family, because she was divorced from Osama's father decades ago. A Yemeni cousin of bin Laden's, Khaled al-Omeri, says Osama's mother has since remarried. She remained close to her son, whom she visited in Sudan during the early 1990s, and later in Afghanistan in early 2001, to celebrate the wedding of one of her grandsons.[22]

The bin Laden family is generally devout, so it must have been a source of pride to be asked in the late 1960s to help rebuild the al-Aqsa mosque in Jerusalem—the site to which the Prophet was transported in his Night Journey from Mecca—after a mentally unbalanced Australian tourist had set the mosque on fire.[23] The family company also renovated the holy places of Mecca and Medina, so the bin Ladens can claim with justifiable pride that they have reconstructed Islam's three holiest sites. In a 1999 interview, Osama bin Laden said that "because of God's graciousness to him [my father] sometimes prayed in all three [of those cities'] mosques in one single day."[24]

It is not surprising then that Mohammed, a stern taskmaster, brought his children up in a strict way that combined piety and respect for the family business. From a young age Osama worked on roads the family was building.[25] Osama was also exposed to a good deal of Islamic teaching as a child: during the Hajj, Mohammed would host hundreds of pilgrims, some of whom were leaders of Muslim movements or senior *ulema*, clergy.

In 1967, when Osama was ten, his father died in a plane crash. Mohammed's estate passed to his children in the form of shares in the family company.[26] Salem, Osama's oldest brother and ten years his senior, eventually took over the business. Salem had attended a posh prep school in England and married Caroline Carey, an Englishwoman from an upper-class family, whose stepfather is the Marquess of Queensberry. Salem was fond of playing the guitar and maintained a fleet of jets that he piloted himself, sometimes performing stunts to the surprise of his passengers. Salem acted as a sort of court jester for King Fahd, who like many others found him amusing and original; Fahd sent many lucrative contracts his way.

Victor Henderson, a British diplomat posted to Saudi Arabia in 1969, says that by the beginning of the 1970s the bin Ladens were already very much part of the Saudi establishment, having constructed the major highway connecting Jeddah to Taif.[27] Salem was to turn the family company into an international conglomerate that went beyond the core construction business into industrial and power projects, oil exploration, mining, and telecommunications.[28]

Unlike his younger brother Osama, Salem was drawn to the United States. In 1976 Salem asked James Bath, a well-connected Houston businessman, to represent the bin Laden family's business interests there.[29] The following year, Bath purchased a small airport in Houston on behalf of Salem.[30] Bath was friendly, for example, with George W.

Bush, then an aspiring oilman whose father was director of the CIA and would serve as Ronald Reagan's vice-presidential running mate in 1980.[31] (Between 1979 and 1980, Bath would also help out his old pal George, with whom he had served in the Texas Air National Guard, by investing fifty thousand dollars in his first venture into the energy business, a company named Arbusto—Spanish for "bush" or, more precisely, "shrub"—taking a 5 percent share in the company.)[32]

Salem bought a house in Orlando, where he often vacationed when he traveled to the United States. Like his father before him, Salem died in a plane accident, when a microlite plane he was piloting crashed into some power lines in San Antonio, Texas in 1988.[33]

Despite Salem's untimely death, the bin Ladens have maintained numerous ties to the United States. Several have resided in the country (although they fled within days of the September 11 attack, fearing for their safety); the family owns property in New Jersey and Texas[34]; there is a fellowship in Islamic architecture at Harvard University named after the family; and one of Osama's brothers sat on the board of a subsidiary of the American communications giant Motorola. Furthermore, the family company maintained a satellite office in Maryland during the 1990s, employs a public relations agency in Manhattan, and receives legal advice from the white-shoe law firm Sullivan & Cromwell.[35]

The family company is now run by another of Osama's brothers, Bakr, who is chairman of the Saudi Binladin Group (SBG). The other top jobs in the company are also held by brothers: Yahia is vice chairman, Omar is president, and Hasan is vice president.[36] Another brother, Yeslam, based in Geneva, handles the family's financial transactions.

By the mid-1990s, the bin Laden group of companies had grown into a colossus whose worth was estimated at $5 billion.[37] The main family company, SBG, employed 37,000 people in 1999.[38] A sampling of the construction projects SBG has undertaken in recent years includes the renovation of the Cairo airport's runways; the reconstruction of the Aden airport, in Yemen; and the construction of a new suburb of Cairo, a Hyatt in Amman, Jordan, a seaside resort in Latakia, Syria, a mosque in Kuala Lumpur, a thirty-story office building in Riyadh, and a $150 million base for more than four thousand U.S. servicemen in Saudi Arabia.[39] (Ironically, that base was built in the middle of the Saudi desert as the result of two bombing attacks on facilities housing U.S. troops in Riyadh and Dhahran in the mid-1990s. At least one of those attacks was inspired by Osama bin Laden. And in a further irony, it was from this base that American military planners coordinated airstrikes against bin Laden's Afghan hideouts.)

The bin Laden family has also diversified into a vast array of businesses, from manufacturing spare parts for cars to managing resorts in Saudi Arabia.[40] According to a source close to the family, the bin Ladens own large tracts of property in Dubai, the tiny emirate city-state. And another source familiar with bin Laden businesses says much of the family wealth is tied up in landholdings in Saudi Arabia.

SBG is also the distributor for Snapple drinks and Porsche and Volkswagen cars in the Middle East and is licensed by Disney to produce a wide range of Arabic books based on its animated features. When you order a hamburger at a Hard Rock Café in the Middle East, the bin Laden family takes a bite of the profits.[41] And in the late 1990s, SBG was an investor in Motorola's ultimately ill-starred Iridium venture to launch a global network for mobile phones served by sixty-six low-orbit satellites. Finally, SBG continues to maintain and renovate the holy mosques of Mecca and Medina and has expanded their capacity to up to a million worshippers each.

While Salem was taking over the family business, Osama was showing increasing signs of the religiosity that has marked his life. At age seventeen, he married a Syrian relative, the first of his four wives.[42] Soon after, he attended Jeddah's prestigious King Abdul-Aziz University, from which he received a degree in economics and public administration in 1981.[43]

It was there that bin Laden first became associated with the Muslim Brotherhood, an Islamist group, and first came under the spell of two prominent teachers of Islamic studies, Abdullah Azzam and Muhammad Qutb. The influence of these men on bin Laden cannot be underestimated—it's as if Ronald Reagan and Milton Friedman's brother had taught him about capitalism. Azzam would go on to create the modern world's first truly international jihadist network, and Muhammad Qutb, himself a well-known Islamist scholar, was the brother of Sayyid Qutb, author of *Signposts*, the key text of the jihadist movement. After Sayyid's execution in Egypt in 1966, Muhammed would become the keeper of his brother's flame and the chief inter-preter of his written works.[44]

Those writings would have a profound effect on bin Laden and the Islamists allied with him. Qutb argues that modern societies, including most Muslim ones, are in *Jahiliyyah*, the state of ignorance that existed in pre-Islamic Arabia before the perfect revelations of the Koran.[45] True Muslims must free themselves from the "clutches of jahili society," and the only way to do that is by jihad. Qutb rails against the notion that jihad is simply a defensive war, as some verses of the Koran suggest. Qutb says those who make this argument "diminish the greatness of the Islamic way of life." [46] By implication, Qutb makes the case that the way to establish this Islamic order is through an offensive jihad against the enemies of Islam, whether they be non-Islamic societies or Muslim societies that are not following the precepts of the Koran. This is the ideological underpinning of bin Laden's followers, who target not only the West but also Muslim regimes such as Saudi Arabia, which they regard as apostates from Islam.

Bin Laden was soaking up these ideas in 1979, a year of tremendous ferment in the Muslim world. It was the dawn of a new century in the Muslim calendar, traditionally a time of change.[47] And what changes there were. In January the Shah of Iran was overthrown and the Ayatollah Khomeini subsequently returned to Tehran. Then, in March, to the consternation of many Muslims, Egypt and Israel signed a peace deal. In November came the shocking news that hundreds of armed Islamist militants had seized Islam's holy of holies, the Grand Mosque in Mecca, and engaged in a days-long bloody battle with security forces that left hundreds dead and dealt a severe blow to the prestige of the House of Saud.[48] Finally, in late December, the Soviets invaded Afghanistan. This was arguably the most earthshaking news of all: the godless communists had taken a sovereign Muslim nation by force.

The invasion was an event of signal importance for the West. President Carter, who had previously taken an accommodationist approach with the Soviets, now espoused a hard line. But its loudest echo was in the Muslim world. Just as in the 1930s an international cast of liberals and socialists—men like George Orwell, Ernest Hemingway, and John Dos Passos—were drawn to Spain to the war against Franco's Fascists, so Muslims from around the globe were drawn to fight the USSR in the Afghan war in the 1980s.

The Soviet war in Afghanistan was one of the most brutal wars of our brutal era. The Russians killed over a million people and forced about five million, a third of the country, into exile. It was also one of the most significant conflicts since World War II, giving the lie to the might of the Soviet military machine. Paradoxically it was also one of the most underreported wars of past decades. As the historian Robert D. Kaplan has pointed out, at least ten times more people died in Afghanistan than in the civil wars that started in Lebanon in 1975, yet "Afghanistan, which on the scale of suffering vastly overshadowed any other military conflict of the 1980s was, quite simply, almost unconsciously ignored."[49]

This was not surprising. Journalists who went into Afghanistan had to endure weeks of walking over some of the most difficult terrain in the world, in constant fear of being attacked by helicopter gunships, eating rice if they were lucky, and exposing themselves to a wide range of unpleasant diseases. During the Vietnam war, by contrast, a reporter could go to the front lines in a U.S. helicopter and be back at the hotel swimming pool later the same day, sipping a cold one. This is not to denigrate the many brave reporters in Vietnam, but simply to say that for those covering the Afghan war the risks were orders of magnitude higher, and the interest of news editors orders of magnitude lower, since no American soldiers' lives were at stake.

The journalist Rob Schultheis was one of the admirable few who repeatedly traveled inside Afghanistan. He described it as "the holiest of wars," and memorably wrote: "Those hopelessly brave warriors I walked with, and their families, who suffered so much for faith and freedom and who are still not free, they were truly the people of God."[50]

Indeed, if any conflict deserved to be called a just jihad, the war against the Soviets in Afghanistan surely was. Unprovoked, a superpower invaded a largely peasant nation and inflicted on it a total, totalitarian war. The population rose up under the banner of Islam to drive the infidels out. In a 1985 report, an independent human rights organization summed up the Russians' unforgiving approach: "The Soviet air force is bombing populated areas . . . killing uncounted numbers of villagers. Soviet ground forces, now reinforced by specialized commando units, have carried out even larger indiscriminate massacres. The Soviets continue to scatter anti-personnel mines in inhabited areas."[51] Afghanistan would become one of the most heavily mined countries in the world.

Despite these tactics, the Soviets obviously weren't paying much attention to Afghan history. From the mid-nineteenth century to the early twentieth, the British, the world's superpower of the time, had tried to subdue the unruly Afghans in three wars. Ultimately, the British came to realize that to occupy Afghanistan was to invite disaster. They subsequently preferred to exercise influence over the country by indirect means.

A nineteenth-century British account of a battle in the First Afghan War tells you all you need to know about the Afghan fighting spirit: "In the military history of this country there is no darker page than the destruction of a considerable British force in the terrible defiles between Cabul and Jellalabad in January 1842. . . . Dr. Brydon [a British medic] reached Jellalabad alive, the sole survivor of four thousand five hundred fighting men and twelve thousand camp followers."[52]

Until recently a copy of a famous Victorian oil painting of that Dr. Brydon hung in the American Club in Peshawar. Brydon, later known as the Messenger of Death, slumps wounded on his exhausted pony, the only witness to the destruction of an entire British army.[53] If only the gerontocracy in the Kremlin had seen this painting before they launched their ill-starred invasion, they might have saved Afghanistan and delayed their own rendezvous with the dustbin of history.

Within weeks of the Soviet invasion, bin Laden, then twenty-two, voted with his feet and wallet, heading to Pakistan to meet with the Afghan leaders Burhanuddin Rabbani and Abdul Rasool Sayyaf, whom he had previously encountered during Hajj gatherings. He then returned to Saudi Arabia and started lobbying his family and friends to provide money to support the Afghan guerrillas and continued making short trips to Pakistan for his fund-raising work.

In the early 1980s bin Laden, already an expert in demolition from time spent working in his family's construction business, made his first trips into Afghanistan, bringing with him hundreds of tons of construction machinery, bulldozers, loaders, dump trucks, and equipment for building trenches, which he put at the disposal of the *mujahideen*. The machinery would be used to build rough roads, dig tunnels into the mountains for shelter, and construct rudimentary hospitals.[54] Bin Laden's followers also set up mine-sweeping operations in the Afghan countryside.[55]

Despite the fact that the United States was also supporting the mujahideen, bin Laden was already voicing anti-American sentiments during the early eighties. Khaled al-Fawwaz, bin Laden's London contact, recalls his friend saying in 1982 that Muslims should boycott American products. In a 1999 interview, Bin Laden himself said that during the mid-1980s he gave lectures in Saudi Arabia urging attacks on U.S. forces and the boycott of American products.[56]

In 1984 bin Laden set up a guesthouse in Peshawar for Muslims drawn to the jihad. It was called *Beit al-Ansar,* or House of the Supporters, an allusion to the Prophet Muhammad's followers who helped him when he had to flee his native Mecca for Medina.[57] Initially the house was simply a way station for those who would be sent for training with one of the Afghan factions. Later, bin Laden would form his own military operation. At about the time bin Laden founded Beit al-Ansar, his former professor Abdullah Azzam established the *Mekhtab al-Khadamat,* or Services Office, in Peshawar.[58] The Services Office started publishing reports about the Afghan war and engaged in a global campaign to recruit Muslims for the jihad. Bin Laden was its principal funder. Eventually there would a dozen or so guesthouses in Peshawar under the aegis of the Services Office.[59]

Azzam was both the ideological godfather and the global recruiter par excellence of Muslims drawn to the Afghan jihad; he would exert a strong pull on bin Laden by virtue of his Islamic credentials and greater experience of the world. According to the Palestinian journalist Jamal Ismail, who was a student in Peshawar during the 1980s and met with bin Laden repeatedly after 1984: "It was Azzam who influenced Osama to finance the Arab fighters who came to Afghanistan." In an interview with an Arabic-language television station, bin Laden himself describes Azzam as "a man worth a nation."[60] Those who knew Azzam and bin Laden during this period recall that while Azzam was eloquent and charismatic, bin Laden, then in his mid-twenties, seemed sincere and honest but not a potential leader.[61]

Having lost his deeply religious father while he was still a child, bin Laden would, throughout his life, be influenced by religiously radical older men—first, Azzam and, to a lesser extent, the Afghan commander Abdul Rasool Sayyaf; later, the second-in-command in his jihadist organization, Ayman al-Zawahiri. All of these men had a very definite vision of how to conduct a life devoted to holy war. But bin Laden clearly sees his father as the ultimate inspiration for his jihad. He has told a Pakistani journalist: "My father was very keen that one of his sons should fight against the enemies of Islam. So I am the one son who is acting according to the wishes of his father." [62]

To understand the impact that Azzam had on bin Laden, and the whole of the subsequent jihadist movement, allow me a brief detour here to trace Azzam's life. Abdullah Azzam was born in a village in Palestine in 1941, near Jenin.[63] He graduated with a degree in theology from Damascus University in 1966. Already a firm believer in jihad, and a passionate hater of Israelis, whom he blamed for taking Palestinian land to create their own state in 1948, Azzam fought them in the 1967 war. Afterward, he studied at al-Azhar University in Cairo, the preeminent center of Islamic thought. There he received first a master's degree and later, in 1973, a doctorate in Islamic jurisprudence. While studying in Cairo, Azzam befriended the family of jihad ideologue Sayyid Qutb. Studying at al-Azhar at the same time as Azzam was the Egyptian Sheik Omar Abdel Rahman, later the spiritual leader of the jihadist movement in Egypt and a close colleague of Azzam's in the effort to create an international network of holy warriors during the 1980s.[64]

In the late 1970s, Azzam joined the faculty of the University of Jordan in Amman, where he taught Islamic law. Soon dismissed because he fought with university authorities over their secular attitudes, he moved to Saudi Arabia to teach. In 1980 he met with Afghan mujahideen leaders and decided to devote all his energies to the jihad in Afghanistan. He then moved to Pakistan, where he was appointed a lecturer at the Islamic University in Islamabad, later settling in Peshawar.

A barrel-chested man whose enormous gray beard and fiery rhetoric made him a commanding presence, Azzam believed that jihad was an absolute necessity to restore the *Khalifa*, the dream that Muslims around the world could be united under one ruler. His motto was "Jihad and the rifle alone: no negotiations, no conferences and no dialogues." And he put that belief in practice, often joining the *mujahideen*, "holy warriors," battling the Soviets in Afghanistan.[65]

For Azzam the jihad in Afghanistan was an *obligation* for every Muslim, as he explained in a widely distributed pamphlet entitled "Defending Muslim Territory Is the Most Important Duty." And it was not simply from Afghanistan that the infidels had to be expelled.[66] Azzam wrote: "This duty will not end with victory in Afghanistan; jihad will remain an individual obligation until all other lands that were Muslim are returned to us so that Islam will reign again: before us lie Palestine, Bokhara, Lebanon, Chad, Eritrea, Somalia, the Philippines, Burma, Southern Yemen, Tashkent and Andalusia [southern Spain]."[67]

Azzam traveled all over the world to recruit men and money for the Afghan jihad, preaching that "to stand one hour in the battle line in the cause of Allah is better than sixty years of night prayer."[68] Khaled al-Fawwaz recalls that Azzam was a one-man "wire service" for the jihad movement, traveling to Kuwait, Yemen, Bahrain, Saudi Arabia, and the United States to gather and spread news, recruit men, and raise millions of dollars for the cause.

The power of Azzam's message was so strong that even via the medium of videotape observant Muslims felt the pull of his call to holy war. Mohamed Odeh, a Jordanian citizen of Palestinian descent who would play a role in the 1998 bombing of the American embassy in Kenya, was a student of engineering in the Philippines in the late eighties, when he watched a video by Azzam extolling the Afghan jihad. Odeh soon traveled to Afghanistan, where he was trained in the use of a wide variety of weapons, including AK-47s, machine guns, and antitank and antiaircraft missiles, and of explosives such as C3, C4, and TNT. He also subsequently swore an oath of allegiance to bin Laden.[69]

Azzam was often seen in the company of the Egyptian militant Sheikh Rahman in Peshawar.[70] Rahman also founded a guesthouse in the city, traveling there at least twice during the 1980s.[71] In 1985, Rahman made his first trip into Afghanistan under the aegis of the ultra-Islamist Afghan leader Gulbuddin Hekmatyar. The sheikh, who had been blinded by diabetes when he was a baby, wept as he heard the crashing of artillery shells in the distance, bemoaning the fact that he could not see for himself his dream of jihad in action.[72]

Another influential figure in the Arab effort to support the war was Muhammad Abdurrahman Khalifa, a Jordanian, who would later go on to marry one of bin Laden's sisters. Khalifa headed the Jordanian branch of the Muslim Brotherhood, which supplied recruits for the Afghan jihad.[73] Khalifa also worked in Peshawar as head of the Saudi Muslim World League office during the Afghan jihad.[74]

Meanwhile, bin Laden traveled back and forth to Saudi Arabia, bringing donations for various Afghan parties, including that of the military commander Ahmad Shah Massoud, a moderate Islamist. But bin Laden would form his closest ties with the ultra-Islamist Hekmatyar and with Abdul Rasool Sayyaf, an Afghan leader who was fluent in Arabic and had studied in Saudi Arabia.[75] Sayyaf also subscribed to the purist Wahhabi Islam dear to bin Laden's heart.[76] Because of his close ties to Arabia, Sayyaf would receive hundreds of millions of dollars in Saudi aid.

Afghan commanders in the field understood the importance of Arab funding. Peter Jouvenal, the British cameraman who traveled into Afghanistan dozens of times during the war against the Soviets, described visiting a base in Pakistan built during the early 1980s by Jalaluddin Haqqani: "He decided to build [it] so he could show off to Arab donors," Jouvenal recalled. "When I visited there were underground bunkers. You could have been inside a house. There was wallpaper, carpets, toilets, and a generator for electricity. The bunker I was in slept four people. It was built into a cliff. The complex was spread out over a five-kilometer radius. In 1982 I saw a raid by the Russians on the base. It lasted about ten minutes. Four or so planes dropped high explosives, but no one was killed. The base had its own PR department. They shot videos of executions of Russians and sent them to Saudi Arabia for fund-raising purposes." (This base would later be used by al-Qaeda in the 1990s.)

With the establishment of the Services Office by Azzam and bin Laden in 1984, Arab support for the *mujahideen* became more overt. The recruits for the Afghan jihad came to be known as the Afghan Arabs. None of them was Afghan, and while most were Arabs, they also came from all over the Muslim world. Some of them were high school students who went on trips to the Afghan-Pakistan border that were not much more than the equivalent of jihad summer camp. Some were involved in support operations along the border, working for charities and hospitals. Others spent years in fierce battles against the communists.

According to the Palestinian journalist Jamal Ismail, three countries provided the lion's share of the Afghan Arabs: Saudi Arabia, Yemen, and Algeria. Saudi Arabia's national airline even gave a 75 percent discount to those going to the holy war.[77] By Ismail's account, fifty thousand Arabs came to Peshawar to fight. Bin Laden's friend Khaled al-Fawwaz told me the figure was 25,000. Milt Bearden, who ran the CIA's Afghan operation between 1986 and 1989, also puts the figure at 25,000.[78] No one really knows the exact figure, but it seems safe to say that the total number of Afghan Arabs who participated in the jihad over the course of the entire war was in the low tens of thousands.

It is worth noting here that the maximum combined strengths of the various Afghan *mujahideen* factions averaged somewhere between 175,000 and 250,000 in any given year.[79] These numbers demonstrate that the Afghan Arabs' contribution to the war against the Soviets was insignificant from a military point of view. The war was won primarily with the blood of Afghans and secondarily with the treasure of the United States and Saudi Arabia, who between them provided approximately $6 billion in support.

Of course, bin Laden and various other Afghan Arabs served as conduits for some of this money. Milt Bearden estimated that about $20 million a month was flowing into the Afghan jihad from Saudi sources after the summer of 1986. Prince Turki al-Faisal Saud, the head of the Saudi General Intelligence agency, managed the Saudi contribution, aided by Prince Salman, the governor of Riyadh.[80] Bin Laden worked closely with Prince Turki during this period, effectively working as an arm of Saudi intelligence.[81] In addition the Muslim World League, headed by the leading Saudi cleric Sheikh Abd al-Aziz bin Baz, provided funding.[82] (It is ironic that billions of dollars of Saudi government aid helped create a cadre of well-trained militants who would later turn against the Saudi royal family. This is part of a continuing larger pattern of Saudi funding of militant Islamist organizations, known as riyalpolitik, which is supposed to shore up Saudi legitimacy, but actually undermines it, because it funds the very groups most opposed to the Saudi regime.)[83]

Still, in the grand scheme of things the Afghan Arabs were no more than extras in the Afghan holy war. It was the lessons they learned from the jihad, rather than their contribution to it, that proved significant. They rubbed shoulders with militants from dozens of countries and were indoctrinated in the most extreme ideas concering jihad. They received at least some sort of military training, and in some cases battlefield experience. Those who had had their tickets punched in the Afghan conflict went back to their home countries with the ultimate credential for later holy wars. And they believed that their exertions had defeated a superpower. "The Afghan jihad plays a central role in the evolution of the Islamist movement around the world," writes Gilles Kepel, a scholar of militant Islam. "It replaces the Palestinian cause in the Arab imagination, and symbolizes the movement from [Arab] nationalism to Islamism."[84]

Jamal Ismail recalls that by about December 1984, bin Laden had become an important figure in the jihad effort. Around this time Azzam announced that bin Laden would pay the living expenses of the families of men who came to fight in the Afghan war. Since Pakistan was inexpensive, that sum was about $300 a month per family. Still, it added up. According to Essam Deraz, an Egyptian filmmaker who covered bin Laden in the late 1980s, the Saudi was subsidizing the Afghan Arabs at a rate of $25,000 a month during this period. Bin Laden's friend al-Fawwaz said bin Laden also started thinking about how he could create a mobile force. "He bought four-wheel-drive pickups and equipped every one with antitank missiles and mine detection so that each unit would be capable of dealing with any kind of situation," recounted al-Fawwaz in his London office.[85]

In 1986 bin Laden moved to Peshawar permanently, directing his operation from a two-story villa in the suburb of University Town where he both worked and lived.[86] It was at this time that bin Laden founded his first camp inside Afghanistan, named al-Ansar, near the village of Jaji in Paktia province, a few miles from a portion of Pakistan's North-West Frontier that juts into Afghanistan. At Jaji, bin Laden and his men would receive their baptism by fire: a week-long siege by the Soviets that has become a cornerstone of the popular legend surrounding bin Laden.[87]

According to Deraz, who said he witnessed the battle of Jaji from a distance of about two miles, the Soviet assault began on April 17, 1987.[88] The Arabs had based themselves at Jaji because it was close to the Soviet front lines, and had used bin Laden's construction equipment to dig themselves into caves in the heights around the village. For about a week they endured punishing bombardment by two-hundred-odd Russians, some of whom were wearing the uniform of Spetsnaz, Russia's special forces. Of about fifty Arabs, more than a dozen were killed before the group realized they could no longer hold their position and withdrew.[89]

Despite this retreat, Jaji was celebrated as a victory in the Arab world. It was the first time the Afghan Arabs had held their ground for any length of time against such superior forces. Arab journalists based in Peshawar wrote daily dispatches about bin Laden's battlefield exploits that were widely published in the Middle East and brought a flood of new recruits to the Afghan jihad.[90] Osama, "the lion," was lionized for leaving behind the typical Saudi multimillionaire's life of palaces in Jeddah and hotel suites in London and Monte Carlo for the dangers of the war in Afghanistan. This was in sharp contrast to the thousands of members of the al-Saud ruling family, none of whom seem to have fought in Afghanistan despite awarding themselves the title of "Custodians" of Islam's holiest sites in 1986.[91]

Another man who made his name at Jaji was Abu Ubaidah, an Egyptian, who later drowned in a ferry accident in Kenya. The U.S. government indictment of bin Laden names Abu Ubaidah as his "ranking military commander" until his death in 1996.

If the battle of Jaji was dangerous, the rigors of daily life were nearly as taxing for bin Laden. In a slim Arabic biography published in 1991, Deraz wrote that bin Laden's health problems during this period forced him to lie down intermittently for hours at a time. He suffered from low blood pressure, which was treated by an Egyptian doctor from Peshawar, and diabetes, for which he received insulin shots. One of the photographs in the book shows bin Laden getting a shot after being exposed to "poisonous gas." Another shows bin Laden tending a wound in his foot.[92]

I met Deraz in Cairo in December 2000 to talk about bin Laden. Deraz, now in his mid-fifties, went to the Afghan war zone at the age of forty as a journalist and documentary filmmaker. A slightly rotund, balding man dressed innocuously in a blue car coat, Deraz sipped a glass of orange juice in a hotel lobby a stone's throw from the Nile as he told me about his life and how it had intersected with bin Laden's. He wanted to make it clear from the start of our meeting that he "hated bin Laden's way," and that his past association with the Saudi exile had caused him to endure years of harassment by the Egyptian security forces.

Deraz said he met bin Laden, who until that point had avoided journalists, in 1987. From their first encounter, which took place in Peshawar, Deraz says he told bin Laden that "one day you [the Afghan Arabs] are all going to prison." But bin Laden was unmoved. "He thought we would be like heroes [back home]. He did not understand that our [Middle Eastern] governments hate any kind of popular movement."[93]

But bin Laden wasn't focusing on politics. For him, the Afghan war was an extraordinary spiritual experience. During his CNN interview he told us: "I have benefited so greatly from the jihad in Afghanistan that it would have been impossible for me to gain such a benefit from any other chance. . . . What we benefited from most was [that] the glory and myth of the superpower was destroyed not only in my mind, but also in [the minds] of all Muslims."[94] So convinced was bin Laden of the spiritual greatness of the struggle he was undertaking that he asked his eldest son, Abdullah, then aged twelve, to visit him during the war.[95]

Thousands of other Afghan Arabs were similarly moved. A case in point is Mansoor al-Barakati, a Saudi from Mecca, whose story is told on an Islamist Web site. Al-Barakati traveled to Afghanistan in 1987 to bring home a younger brother who had gone for jihad. When he crossed the border between Pakistan and Afghanistan he felt his "heart shake" with the feeling of entering a divine place. Giving up the search for his brother, al-Barakati traveled to Jalalabad, training at one of bin Laden's camps for two months. From there he moved to the deserts around Kandahar, which saw some of the worst fighting of the war. Al-Barakati distinguished himself by exceptional acts of heroism, rising to become the leader of the Arab *mujahideen* in the area. During the summer of 1990, a 120mm rocket hit the rooftop of a house on which al-Barakati was sitting. Bleeding heavily, he was driven to Pakistan for medical attention. On the way he pleaded for death, crying, "I am fed up with this worldly life. I really love Allah." Finally he died and, as in many accounts of the Arabs who are *shaheed,* "martyred," a witness recounted that a "beautiful scent the likes of which I have never experienced in my life" emanated from the body.[96]

The Afghan war did not only move men like bin Laden spiritually; it also enabled them to meet key figures in terrorist organizations in the Arab world. In 1987 bin Laden was introduced to members of Egypt's Jihad group, the organization behind the 1981 assassination of Egyptian President Anwar Sadat. A leader of the group, Ayman al-Zawahiri, had settled in Peshawar and was putting his skills as a physician to work at a hospital for Afghan refugees.[97] In 1989, bin Laden founded al-Qaeda, "the base" in Arabic, an organization that would eventually merge with al-Zawahiri's Jihad group.

Jamal Ismail says al-Qaeda's initial goals were prosaic. Most Arabs continued to arrive under the umbrella of the Services Office and bin Laden's guesthouse, Beit al-Ansar, remained open to all comers. But there were concerns that Middle Eastern governments, worried about Islamist movements in their own countries, had penetrated these organizations, so al-Qaeda was formed as a more secure unit. "They had a separate guesthouse," Ismail recalled. "Unless you were part of the inner circle you could not enter this house."

The Saudi dissident Saad al-Fagih suggests yet another reason for the founding of al-Qaeda. In 1988, bin Laden realized that there was little documentation to give to the families of those missing in Afghanistan; to solve this problem, he set up al-Qaeda to track those who were full-fledged *mujahideen,* those who were involved only in charity work in Peshawar, and those who were simply visitors. Movements between the guesthouses and military training camps were also recorded. Al-Fawwaz says these documents were subsequently used by Middle Eastern governments to identify potential Islamist militants.

The fullest accounting of the founding of al-Qaeda comes from Jamal al-Fadl, the U.S. government's first witness at the New York trial of four bin Laden associates in 2001. Al-Fadl, a Sudanese then in his early twenties, fought with bin Laden's group on the Afghan front lines in 1989. He was also trained to shoot down helicopters and attended courses on the use of explosives. In 1989 he was approached to become part of al-Qaeda, which planned to continue holy wars beyond the Afghan conflict. He performed *bayat*, an oath of fealty, to the group's jihad agenda and signed papers indicating his allegiance to the *emir*, bin Laden.[98] Al-Fadl was al-Qaeda's third member.

Al-Fadl defected after it was discovered that he had embezzled $110,000 from the organization, and he later became a U.S. government informant. At the Manhattan trial, al-Fadl outlined the operational structure of al-Qaeda and the responsibilties of various committees, among them the media operation, run by a man with the alias Abu Reuter.[99]

In February 1989 the Soviets withdrew from Afghanistan and bin Laden turned his attention to other struggles. He returned to Jaji, a place that had assumed tremendous symbolic importance, and made it a base. Peter Jouvenal was in the area around that time. "I witnessed them digging huge caves, using explosives and Caterpillar digging equipment. I was told that I wasn't safe and should move on."

One of bin Laden's initial targets was the first woman to lead a modern Muslim nation: Pakistan's prime minister, Benazir Bhutto, regarded as a liberal because of her education at Oxford and Harvard.[100] Bhutto's predecessor, the military dictator General Zia ul-Haq, had died in a mysterious plane crash the year before her election.[101] Zia had been a strong supporter of Islamist groups in Pakistan, and these groups saw Bhutto as a threat.

I met with the former prime minister at a well-kept suburban New Jersey home just across the George Washington Bridge from Manhattan, on a dank, freezing day in March 2000. She is a handsome, charismatic woman in her late forties, with the strong opinions of someone who is rarely contradicted. In his novel *Shame*, Salman Rushdie gave her the moniker Virgin Ironpants. Bhutto was born into what the Pakistanis call a "feudal" landholding family. The British knighted her grandfather, who owned great chunks of the province of Sindh.

Her life has been the stuff of Shakespeare. Her father, Zulfikar Ali Bhutto, was Pakistan's popular prime minister in the 1970s, until he was deposed and executed by General Zia.[102] Benazir Bhutto spent much of her subsequent life under house arrest or in exile, until she returned in triumph to Pakistan in 1988 to the cheers of crowds that numbered in the hundreds of thousands.[103] While she was prime minister one of her brothers was killed outside her Karachi mansion in a shoot-out with police. Another brother was mysteriously poisoned in France.[104] Her beloved husband was jailed in Pakistan on corruption charges in 1996.

All this history was going through my mind when I met Bhutto. She was dressed in a pink *shalwar kameez,* a designer veil fluttering around her face. Since Pakistan's current military government had pressed corruption charges against her, she now lived in exile in London and Dubai, making occasional trips to the United States to meet with supporters.

While I was talking with the former prime minister I could feel her mind operating on several levels as she assessed how best to get me on her team. She alternately charmed and cajoled, explaining that the corruption charges against her and her husband had been trumped up by the previous government.

I turned the subject of our conversation to bin Laden. "The first time I heard of Osama was in 1989 during a no-confidence vote against my government," she said. "Four parliamentarians came to me with briefcases of money. They had twelve and [a] half lakhs of rupees, about eighty to a hundred thousand dollars they had been given to vote against me. They said the money came from Saudi Arabia. I was shocked, because King Fahd was a supporter and had made a special effort to help my country. I sent a delegation to Saudi Arabia to ask why are the Saudis funding this." The reply, she said, was that " 'there is a rich Saudi individual who is doing this, Osama bin Laden.' I had never heard of him."

Bhutto blamed the head of Pakistan's military intelligence service, the Islamist General Hamid Gul, a supporter of Islamist militant groups whom she had recently fired, for engineering the bribery charges together with his friend bin Laden. "The international Islamist movement [that emerged out of the Afghan war] saw Pakistan as its base," she explained. "They saw my party as a liberal threat." On November 1, 1989, Bhutto narrowly survived the no-confidence vote.[105]

A few weeks later, on November 24, bin Laden's mentor Abdullah

Azzam was assassinated, a crime that remains unsolved. A car bomb planted at the entrance of the Saba-e-Leil Mosque in Peshawar exploded at midday as Azzam was going to Friday prayers. Also killed with him were two of his sons, Muhammad, twenty-three, and Ibrahim, fourteen.[106]

By the end of 1989 there was little reason for bin Laden to linger in Pakistan. He was persona non grata with the new Pakistani government, the Soviets had withdrawn from Afghanistan, and his closest jihad collaborator was dead. So for the first time in several years he returned to live in his native country, where he would take up other holy wars.

He was thirty-two.

CHAPTER 3

Blowback:
The CIA and the Afghan War

*Never think that those who were slain in the cause of God
are dead. They are alive and well provided for by the Lord.*
     —The Koran, 3:169

Were bin Laden and his Afghan Arabs a creation of the U.S. government? Various books and multiple news reports have charged that the CIA armed and trained the Afghan Arabs and even bin Laden himself as part of its operation to support the Afghan rebels fighting the Soviets in the 1980s. They argue, therefore, that the United States is culpable in the jihads and terrorism those militants subsequently spread around the world. As we shall see, those charges are overblown and are not supported by the evidence. However, the CIA certainly made tactical errors during the war, some of which encouraged the growth of anti-Western Afghan factions allied to Arab militants.

For the United States, the Soviet invasion of Afghanistan in December 1979 was an opportunity for a little payback: just as the Soviets had funded the North Vietnamese in their war against the United States, so now the Americans would finance the Afghan struggle against the Soviets. President Jimmy Carter's national security adviser, Zbigniew Brzezinski, put it succinctly: it was time, he said, "to finally sow shit in their backyard."[1] The CIA took the lead in arming the

Afghans, and from a strategic point of view that operation was a brilliant success. The last Soviet troops withdrew from Afghanistan on February 15, 1989. At CIA headquarters in Langley, Virginia, a little party was held in celebration.[2]

But were the CIA and the Afghan Arabs in cahoots, as recent studies have suggested? One author charges: "The CIA had funded and trained the Afghan Arabs during the war."[3] Another refers to "the central role of the CIA's Muslim mercenaries, including upwards of 2,000 Algerians in the Afghanistan War."[4] Both authors present these claims as axioms, but provide no real corroboration.

Other commentators have reported that bin Laden himself was aided by the CIA. A report in the respected British newspaper *The Guardian* states: "In 1986 the CIA even helped him [bin Laden] build an underground camp at Khost [Afghanistan] where he was to train recruits from across the Islamic world in the revolutionary art of jihad."[5] This defies common sense. American officials did not venture into Afghanistan during the war against the Soviets for fear of handing the communists a propaganda victory if they were captured. Bin Laden, meanwhile, had espoused anti-American positions since 1982, and thanks to the fortune derived from his family's giant construction business had little need of CIA money.[6] In fact, the underground camp at Khost was built in 1982 by an Afghan commander, with Arab funding.[7]

A source familiar with bin Laden's organization explains that bin Laden "never had any relations with America or American officials. . . . He was saying very early in the eighties that the next battle is going to be with America. . . . No aid or training or other support have ever been given to bin Laden from Americans." A senior U.S. official unequivocally says that "bin Laden never met with the CIA."[8]

While the charges that the CIA was responsible for the rise of the Afghan Arabs might make good copy, they don't make good history. The truth is more complicated, tinged with varying shades of gray. The United States wanted to be able to deny that the CIA was funding the Afghan war, so its support was funneled through Pakistan's military intelligence agency, Inter Services Intelligence agency (ISI). ISI in turn made the decisions about which Afghan factions to arm and train, tending to favor the most Islamist and pro-Pakistan. The Afghan Arabs generally fought alongside those factions, which is how the charge arose that they were creatures of the CIA.

Former CIA official Milt Bearden, who ran the Agency's Afghan operation in the late 1980s, says: "The CIA did not recruit Arabs," as there was no need to do so. There were hundreds of thousands of Afghans all too willing to fight, and the Arabs who did come for jihad were "very disruptive . . . the Afghans thought they were a pain in the ass." I have heard similar sentiments from Afghans who appreciated the money that flowed from the Gulf but did not appreciate the Arabs' holier-than-thou attempts to convert them to their ultra-purist version of Islam. Peter Jouvenal recalls: "There was no love lost between the Afghans and the Arabs. One Afghan told me, 'Whenever we had a problem with one of them we just shot them. They thought they were kings.' "

Moreover, the Afghan Arabs demonstrated a pathological dislike of Westerners. Jouvenal says: "I always kept away from Arabs [in Afghanistan]. They were very hostile. They would ask, 'What are you doing in an Islamic country?" The BBC reporter John Simpson had a close call with bin Laden himself outside Jalalabad in 1989. Traveling with a group of Afghan *mujahideen,* Simpson and his television crew bumped into a Arab man beautifully dressed in spotless white robes; the man began shouting at Simpson's escorts to kill the infidels, and then offered a truck driver the not unreasonable sum of five hundred dollars to do the job. Simpson's Afghan escort turned down the request, and bin Laden was to be found later on a camp bed, weeping in frustration. Only when bin Laden became a public figure, almost a decade later, did Simpson realize who the mysterious Arab was who had wanted him dead.[9]

In 1998 Milt Bearden wrote a well-received thriller, *Black Tulip,* in which a top CIA operative establishes a base inside Afghanistan that is used by a "handful of American officers."[10] This is, of course, a total fantasy. CIA officers did not travel into Afghanistan. Indeed, the CIA had relatively few contacts with Afghans. Vince Cannistraro was the staff director of the interagency group at the National Security Council that coordinated Afghan policy during the mid-1980s. Cannistraro says there were only six CIA officials in Pakistan at any given time, and they were simply "administrators" who made up the *entire* Agency operation in the country.[11]

Furthermore, a former CIA official told me that the Agency's officers in Pakistan seldom left the embassy in Islamabad and rarely even met with the leaders of the Afghan resistance, let alone with Arab militants. He recounted a story in which CIA officers had to literally beg to join a group of U.S. officials meeting with Afghan leaders in Peshawar in the mid-1980s.[12]

Brigadier Mohammad Yousaf, who ran ISI's Afghan operation between 1983 and 1987, explains with admirable clarity the relationship between the CIA and the Afghan *mujahideen*, or holy warriors: "The foremost function of the CIA was to spend money. It was always galling to the Americans, and I can understand their point of view, that although they paid the piper they could not call the tune. The CIA supported the *mujahideen* by spending the taxpayers' money, billions of dollars of it over the years, on buying arms, ammunition, and equipment. It was their secret arms procurement branch that was kept busy. It was, however, a cardinal rule of Pakistan's policy that no Americans ever become involved with the distribution of funds or arms once they arrived in the country. No Americans ever trained or had direct contact with the *mujahideen*, and no American official ever went inside Afghanistan."[13] A former CIA official told me: "As quartermasters we were okay."[14]

In short, the CIA had very limited dealings with the *Afghans*, let alone with the Afghan Arabs. And for good reason. There was simply no point in the CIA and the Afghan Arabs being in contact with each other. The Agency worked through ISI during the Afghan war, while the Afghan Arabs functioned independently and had their own sources of funding. The CIA did not need the Afghan Arabs, and the Afghan Arabs did not need the CIA. So the notion that the Agency funded and trained the Afghan Arabs is, at best, misleading. The "Let's blame everything bad that happens on the CIA" school of thought vastly overestimates the Agency's powers, both for good and ill.

However, in one strange episode, the CIA did help an important recruiter for the Afghan Arabs, the Egyptian cleric Sheikh Omar Abdel Rahman, who would eventually be convicted for his role in conspiring to blow up New York City landmarks such as the United Nations complex and the Holland Tunnel. Despite the fact that Sheikh Rahman was well known as the spiritual leader of Egypt's terrorist Islamic Group, he was issued a visa for the United States in 1987 and a multiple-entry visa in 1990.[15] The U.S. government said these visas were issued as the result of computer errors, or because of the various spellings of the sheikh's name. But at least one of the visas was issued by a CIA officer working undercover in the consular section of the American embassy in Sudan.[16] Whether this was a mistake or something more remains an open question.

A further connection between the CIA and the Afghan Arabs is an Egyptian-American, Ali Mohamed, who worked briefly as a CIA informant in the early 1980s and later worked for al-Qaeda. However, while these links are certainly interesting, they are only that. They hardly amount to an operation by the Agency to train and fund the Afghan Arabs.

This is not to say the CIA did not make a significant tactical error during the Afghan war by allowing all the decisions about the funding and prosecution of the conflict to be made by the Pakistanis. Letting the Pakistanis run the show made sense during the early years of the war—first of all to preserve the United States' ability to deny its role in the conflict, but also because the Pakistanis understood the facts on the ground better than anyone else. By 1985, however, President Ronald Reagan was very publicly meeting with Afghan military commanders, so "deniability" was no longer relevant; also, by then a wealth of information was available to U.S. officials about which Afghan commanders were effective and which were anti-American. At that point, the U.S. government and the CIA should have put pressure on the Pakistanis to distribute American aid in a manner that better reflected the interests of the United States.

That never happened. Instead, the Pakistanis continued to disproportionately fund the most Islamist factions, thereby contributing to a brutal civil war in Afghanistan. They also funneled hundreds of millions of dollars to anti-Western Afghan factions, which in turn trained militants who later exported jihad and terrorism around the world—including to the United States. Such an unintended consequence of covert operations is known, in spook parlance, as "blowback."

To understand how this blowback came about, one has to understand how the U.S. government became involved in the Afghan war. Six months before the Soviet invasion, the United States was already providing limited support to Afghans fighting the Soviet-leaning regime of President Nur Mohammed Taraki. On July 3, 1979, President Carter signed a presidential finding that authorized funding for the anticommunist guerrillas.[17] When the Russians invaded over Christmas of 1979 to install Hafizullah Amin, effectively a Soviet puppet, as president, it was a "watershed" in the Carter administration's attitude to the Soviets, according to then Carter aide Robert Gates, who would later go on to head the CIA.[18] "The Soviet invasion of Afghanistan is the greatest threat to peace since the Second World War," Carter fulminated. "It's a sharp escalation in the aggressive history of the Soviet Union."[19]

The Carter administration quickly put together a plan to ratchet up support for the *mujahideen.* The most important element of the plan was "plausible deniability." The CIA used Saudi and American funds to purchase weapons from China and Egypt so that no support could be traced to the United States.[20] No one wanted to hand the Soviets the propaganda victory of trumpeting the United States' deep involvement in supporting the *mujahideen.*

Afghanistan, a landlocked country, was surrounded at that time by countries whose regimes were hardly sympathetic to American interests: Khomeini's Iran, the USSR, and China. The only possible conduit to the rebels was through Pakistan. So the CIA's operation would be run through an all-important "cutout": Pakistan's ISI. American assistance to the Afghans began in 1980 at the relatively modest level of $20 million to $30 million a year, rising to $630 million a year by 1987. Over the course of the 1980s $3 billion was funneled to the Afghan resistance.[21]

By simply handing ISI some $3 billion of American taxpayers' money, the CIA also handed the Pakistanis complete control of how the funds were distributed.[22] That would turn out to be a rather expensive mistake. By the most conservative estimates, $600 million went to the Hizb party, headed by Gulbuddin Hekmatyar, an Islamist zealot.[23] Hizb was one of seven parties into which leaders of the Afghan resistance had organized themselves. These ranged from Hekmatyar's ultra-Islamist organization to moderate parties that favored the return of the Afghan monarchy. Hekmatyar's party had the dubious distinctions of never winning a significant battle during the war, training a variety of militant Islamists from around the world, killing significant numbers of *mujahideen* from other parties, and taking a virulently anti-Western line. In addition to hundreds of millions of dollars of American aid, Hekmatyar also received the lion's share of aid from the Saudis.[24]

To find out why the United States had subsidized Hekmatyar to such an extent, I went to see Graham Fuller, who was the Agency's bureau chief in Kabul until 1978 and later took charge of the CIA's long-range forecasting. Fuller speaks Chinese, Turkish, Russian, and Arabic, among other languages. His house is in a leafy suburb not far from CIA headquarters. Surrounded by mementos of his various foreign postings, Fuller explained in the measured tones of an academic: "For several years there was no real concern about the nature of the anti-Western jihad in Afghanistan. There was clearly the impression the *mujahideen* were anti-Soviet. The money was funneled through the Pakistanis. They had a mastery of *mujahideen* politics. Washington would have been crazy if they claimed they knew the *mujahideen*. But by 1984 it was clear that some of these groups were ideologically zealous. Hekmatyar was top of that heap. There were questions that he might be a Soviet agent. He spent a lot more of his time fighting other *mujahideen* than killing Soviets. He was a nasty guy. In the late seventies he was a Pakistani agent and the Pakistanis used him as an instrument. The Pakistanis felt he was effective, and he was 'their man.' "

Authoritative accounts of the Afghan war amplify the point that Hekmatyar was power mad and a creature of Pakistan, which has always sought to support sympathetic Afghans aligned with the Pathan tribal group that straddles the Afghan-Pakistan border. The historian Henry Bradsher charges: "His party was Leninist in both its dictatorial nature and its ruthless drive to achieve power in whatever amoral way was expedient."[25] Bradsher quotes Pakistan's dictator General Zia on Hekmatyar: "It was Pakistan that made him an Afghan leader and it is Pakistan who can equally destroy him if he continues to misbehave."[26] Another scholar of the war writes that Hekmatyar "consistently placed the long-term goal of Islamic revolution above resistance to the Soviets or to the Kabul regime. His militants were commonly engaged in fighting against fronts of all the other parties, for his most important strategic goal was securing the dominance of Hizb [Hekmatyar's party] over all the Islamic forces."[27]

Kurt Lohbeck, who covered the war for CBS News and was one of the few Western journalists permanently stationed in Peshawar, devastatingly summed up American delusions about Gulbuddin Hekmatyar: "The [U.S.] embassy . . . put the 'spin' on the Afghan story: Gulbuddin *was* the resistance. Which was simply not true. Gulbuddin had no effective fighting organization. He had not a single commander with any military reputation."[28] Indeed, Hekmatyar would play a starring role in a comprehensive *mujahideen* defeat, the disastrous siege of Jalalabad in 1989.[29]

If Hekmatyar did not excel at killing Russians, he did excel at killing Afghans. The Australian-American journalist Richard Mackenzie, who spent months at a time inside Afghanistan, was the first to report that Hekmatyar had slaughtered thirty-six men under the command of Ahmad Shah Massoud in northeastern Afghanistan in July 1989.[30] This massacre was then extensively covered by human rights organizations.[31] By 1990 a U.S. State Department report singled out Hekmatyar for killing fellow Afghans.[32] From 1992 onward, Hekmatyar would kill thousands of civilians in Kabul during his daily rocket attacks on the city, despite the fact that he had been given the title of prime minister in the *mujahideen* coalition government.

Hekmatyar's unsavory reputation and anti-Americanism were hardly secrets during the war against the Soviets. The historian David Isby recounts: "As early as 1981 Afghans from other resistance groups were coming to Washington and telling the stories of Gulbuddin's willingness to have people killed. They told this to government officials, to members of Congress, to anyone who would listen."[33] In 1985 the Congressional Task Force on Afghanistan heard testimony that Hekmatyar's group was "the most corrupt" of the Afghan parties.[34] That same year Hekmatyar visited the United States and pointedly refused to meet with President Reagan.[35] Saddam Hussein and Muammar Qaddafi both financed Hekmatyar, and Hekmatyar would go on to support Saddam Hussein during the Gulf War.[36]

Hekmatyar also operated as a sort of bin Laden alter ego, attracting Islamist militants to train with him from around the world. One such recruit was a Palestinian named Abu Mahaz, who told CNN in 1993: "We are terrorists, yes we are terrorists because it is our faith. Listen to this verse from the Koran: 'You should prepare whatever is within your reach in terms of power and horses to terrorize Allah's enemies.' "[37] Abu Mahaz took the position that all formerly Muslim lands, including Spain, should be returned to the fold of Islam.

Bin Laden and Hekmatyar worked closely together. During the early 1990s al-Qaeda's training camps in the Khost region of eastern Afghanistan were situated in an area controlled by Hekmatyar's party. Typical of the Arabs recruited by Hekmatyar were three Algerians, a Moroccan, and a Saudi interviewed by Kabul television in 1993. They said they had entered Afghanistan from Pakistan in early 1991[38] and were trained at a Hekmatyar base in eastern Afghanistan.

In 1993 I attended a press conference given by Hekmatyar at his headquarters south of Kabul. (One of the Afghan journalists at the event was later killed by Hekmatyar's men because stories he filed for the BBC were deemed insufficiently genuflectory.)[39] Hekmatyar was dressed immaculately in a black turban and white *shalwar kameez* that contrasted with his jet-black beard. Asked if there were any Arab volunteers among his group, Hekmatyar replied with a barefaced lie: "We have no training centers for foreigners and we are not willing to create problems for others."[40]

Was there an alternative to Hekmatyar, to whom American support might have been better directed? The answer is a resounding yes. The Afghan commander Ahmad Shah Massoud was a moderate Islamist and a brilliant general, who never received American aid proportionate to his battlefield exploits.[41] Richard Mackenzie, who spent more time with Massoud than did any other journalist, says: "He was conducting an Islamic revolution. He wasn't going to bring in Magna Carta, but he would have been a voice for fairness and a more democratic state in Afghanistan." (Massoud would be mortally wounded by two Arab assassins posing as television reporters on September 9, 2001, only forty-eight hours before the World Trade Center towers were destroyed—an ominous portent. Like the attacks on New York and Washington, the operation had Osama bin Laden's fingerprints all over it.)

Massoud's prowess on the battlefield was incontestable. He fought off nine Soviet offensives aimed to dislodge him from his stronghold in the northern Panjshir Valley, the fifth and sixth of which "were two of the biggest battles of the war."[42] The French scholar Olivier Roy explains that Massoud was able to transform the nature of traditional Afghan warfare, which was essentially tribal and primarily concerned with prestige and booty,[43] to create a mobile modern guerrilla force: "The Massoud model demonstrated its effectiveness: It conquered all northeast Afghanistan and fought the only real battles in the whole Afghan war, despite the hostility manifested against this system by the Pakistanis."[44] Massoud studied the tactics of Mao and Che to hone his skills, he "grasped the importance of the key elements of guerrilla warfare: surprise, organization, rapid concentration, and dispersal of forces," with the result that "his group rapidly established itself as the most effective in the country."[45] A 1992 editorial in *The Wall Street Journal* opined that Massoud was "The Afghan Who Won the Cold War."[46] It was Massoud, not Hekmatyar, who captured Kabul in April 1992 from the Afghan communist regime that took the place of the departing Soviets in 1989.[47] And it was Massoud's forces that finally took Kabul from the Taliban in the winter of 2001 while Hekmatyar, then in exile in Iran, called for continued anti-American attacks.

In 1993 I met with Massoud, a wiry, intense Tajik with a palpable inner strength that derived from the fact he had spent his entire adult life in battle. This was leavened by his interest in the mystical Sufi brand of Islam and a playful sense of humor. Asked whether he was a fundamentalist, he had a rather interesting answer. "In Islam there is no extreme and there is no fundamentalism. I do believe that Islam is a moderate religion, and I am a moderate Muslim."

Massoud was firm in his desire for the Afghan Arabs to return home: "The reality is the jihad is over in Afghanistan. We do not need armed Arabs going around our country. It is better for them to leave the country."[48] It is clear from this interview that Massoud would not have tolerated the use of Afghanistan by militant Arabs for jihad training, as did Hekmatyar and, later, the Taliban.

During the next decade Afghan Arabs would hijack commercial airliners and use them to destroy the World Trade Center in Manhattan and attack the Pentagon; they would kidnap Western tourists in Yemen, kill tourists in Egypt, foment terrorism in the Philippines, bomb two U.S. embassies in Africa, blow up an American military post in Saudi Arabia, train Somalis who may have killed American troops in Mogadishu, and tear Algeria apart in a brutal civil war. And this is only a partial listing of their handiwork. Clearly, American money should have been funneled to Massoud, who was not only the best general in the Afghan war but the Afghan leader whose policies were much more in keeping with American interests.

Given that Hekmatyar was a disaster for American policies and Massoud would have been infinitely preferable, why did the CIA not intervene with Pakistan's ISI to change the situation? The answer seems to be a combination of willful ignorance and a tendency to take the Pakistani assessment of the situation in Afghanistan at face value. Brigadier Yousaf certainly believed that Hekmatyar was the "toughest" *mujahideen* commander, but as we have seen there is little evidence to support this view.[49] Perhaps the Pakistanis started believing their own propaganda about Hekmatyar. The question is: Why did the CIA believe it, too?

In a 1993 interview, Robert Gates defended the Agency's Afghan policy in the confident tone of a high school debating champion: "Their approach [the Pakistanis] was that the assistance would be funneled to those groups that were fighting most effectively against the Soviets. A lot of them [the Afghan *mujahideen*] weren't people you'd invite home for dinner. The reality is that you had to make do with the strategic situation you found in Afghanistan." Milt Bearden, who ran the CIA's Afghan operation for the last three years of the war against the Soviets, told me: "You wouldn't want any of these guys marrying your daughter. . . . From our point of view Massoud was more independent than the others, to the point that he did only what he wanted. Hekmatyar himself was a darkly troubled man, but had a number of commanders who were reasonably effective."

If backing Hekmatyar was a disaster, the decision in 1986 to provide the *mujahideen* with American Stinger missiles turned the tide of the war against the Soviets (although the long-term consequences of that decision may prove less salutary to American interests). The Stinger is the most effective hand-held anti-aircraft missile in use, a "fire and forget" weapon that locks onto the heat radiated by helicopter and airplane engines.[50] Once the Stingers were deployed, the Soviets lost the total air superiority they had formerly enjoyed. As Massoud observed: "There are only two things the Afghan must have: the Koran and Stingers."[51]

Graham Fuller recalls that the decision to give Stingers to the Afghans was initially contentious in Washington, not so much because of worries that the missile technology would fall into the hands of the Soviets, but because there were real concerns that the Afghan conflict could mushroom into a wider U.S.-Soviet war: "The decision to give Stingers was controversial. It marked an escalation of the confrontation with the Soviets. John McMahon, the deputy director [of the CIA] was opposed to doing it. For him, geopolitical concerns were the most important. The Soviet war could be taken into Pakistan. He was less concerned about the technology giveaway."

Vince Cannistraro says there were also concerns at the Agency that the Afghans would not be able to handle the sophisticated Stinger. That worry would prove baseless. In 1986 and 1987, around nine hundred Stingers were supplied to the Afghans; the missiles would bring down 269 Soviet planes and helicopters by the end of the war.

However, some of the two hundred or so Stingers that remained unused against the communists have since fallen into the hands of the Iranians, the Taliban, and al-Qaeda itself.[52] At Kandahar airport in December 1999, I saw Taliban soldiers carrying two Stinger missiles. That al-Qaeda also has acquired the missiles is clear from the testimony of a witness at a 1995 terrorism trial in New York, who saw a Stinger at an al-Qaeda camp in eastern Afghanistan in the early nineties. Al-Qaeda tried, unsuccessfully, to ship some Stingers from Pakistan to Sudan in 1993, and in 1998 bin Laden announced at a press conference in Afghanistan that a number of his followers in Saudi Arabia had recently been arrested in possession of a Stinger. Before September 11, 2001, U.S. officials had been concerned about the possibility of a Stinger being employed against American troop transport planes in Saudi Arabia.[53] Now, of course, any future military operation in Afghanistan must consider the threat of Stinger attacks. It is not clear exactly how many Stingers al-Qaeda has today, but it is a safe bet that the group possesses a number of them.

Are those Stingers still operational? According to the conventional wisdom, the weapon's shelf life is limited. However, an official deeply involved in the CIA's operation to buy back the missiles in the 1990s says that is a myth propagated to depress interest in Stingers and lower their price. So far, Stingers left over from the Afghan war have been used only in conventional battles, not by terrorists. (In 1999, Massoud's forces used one to bring down a Taliban jet fighter.)[54] As a senior U.S. official points out, it is one thing to possess a Stinger in Afghanistan, quite another to use it against a target outside the country: "From a logistical point of view they are difficult to conceal, difficult to get through Customs. And then you have to be very sure of your intended target—exactly which plane you are shooting at and who is on the plane." There remains a healthy market for Stingers inside Afghanistan. In 1995 a cameraman I know surreptitiously shot footage of three Stingers for sale in Kabul.

The couple of hundred unaccounted-for Stingers are emblematic of the troubling legacy of the Afghan war against the communists, which ended up creating a transnational force of Islamist militants who have spread terrorism and guerrilla movements around the world. An immense blow to the prestige of the Soviet army, and ultimately to the Soviet edifice, the victory in Afghanistan was also significant for the Muslim world. Since Napoleon's armies invaded Egypt in 1798, the story of Muslim relations with the Western powers has been one of the inexorable decline of Muslim military power and the rise of the West, culminating in the British and French defeat of the Ottomans and colonization of much of the last Islamic empire after World War 1.[55]

So the victory against the communists in Afghanistan was an intoxicating moral victory: a superpower had been defeated in the name of Allah. It was an important lesson for the Afghan Arabs and for bin Laden himself, who applied it to his next holy war—against the United States.

CHAPTER 4

The Koran and the Kalashnikov:
Bin Laden's Years in Sudan

> *"They began issuing statements amongst themselves in the Sudan, calling the Americans infidels. . . . But, ladies and gentlemen, it was not just words. You will hear that bin Laden and his group began taking actions to prepare to do battle with his enemies, particularly the United States."*
>
> —Opening statement of a federal prosecutor in the
> Manhattan trial of four bin Laden associates,
> February 5, 2001

"**C**ome upstairs, I have something to show you," said a Middle Eastern dissident I was visiting in London in 1997. In his study he pulled out a videotape and popped it into his VCR. The footage, shot through the windows of a slowly moving car, showed some of the tens of thousands of Americans living in Saudi Arabia.[1] The camera panned to a sign announcing a housing complex for employees of Aramco, the oil company. Then the cameraman drove into the complex and zoomed in on an American woman pushing her child on a swing. In the next sequence, the cameraman overtook a U.S. army truck driven by a female soldier, who glanced nervously at the camera when she realized she was being videotaped. The tape was poorly shot, but fascinating in a voyeuristic way. It had no narration, but its message was plain: "Look at these infidels trespassing on our holy land."

Opposition to the longtime presence of Americans on the Arabian peninsula intensified dramatically after August 7, 1990, the day the first U.S. troops were dispatched to Saudi Arabia as part of Operation Desert Shield. The dying edict of the Prophet Muhammad had been "Let there be no two religions in Arabia"; now "infidels" of both sexes were trespassing on the holy land of the Arabian Peninsula.[2] For bin Laden, this was as transforming an event as the Russian invasion of Afghanistan had been a decade earlier. It is no coincidence that exactly eight years later, on August 7, 1998, his men blew up two U.S. embassies in Africa, the bombs going off almost simultaneously in two different countries—no mean feat of coordination.

Of course, bin Laden had been denouncing Americans well before he was forced to put up with them in the flesh. On his return from the Afghan war in 1989, he was quickly in demand as a speaker in mosques and homes, and one of his principal themes was a call for a boycott of American goods because of that country's support for Israel.[3] Hundreds of thousands of recordings of his speeches circulated in the Saudi kingdom.[4]

Ironically, bin Laden was sympathetic to the underlying cause of the U.S. presence in Saudi Arabia: the war against Saddam Hussein. He had embarrassed the Saudi regime much earlier by warning of the Iraqi leader's intentions.[5] "A year before Hussein entered Kuwait," bin Laden recalled, "I said many times in my speeches at the mosques, warning that Saddam will enter the Gulf. No one believed me. I distributed many tapes in Saudi Arabia. It was after it happened that they started believing me and believed my analysis of the situation."[6]

After Hussein's forces did invade the small, oil-rich state on August 1, 1990, and threaten the security of Saudi Arabia, bin Laden immediately volunteered his services and those of his holy warriors. The Saudi army and his own men would be enough to defend the Kingdom, he reasoned; after all, hadn't his own troops been instrumental in driving the Russians from Afghanistan?

The Saudis did not take this offer seriously. Despite the tens of billions of dollars they had spent on their own army, they turned instead for help to the U.S. government and then-President Bush, who had made his fortune in the oil trade and so understood exactly what was at stake in Iraq's invasion of Kuwait (whatever rhetoric was employed on the theme of a "New World Order"). Operation Desert Shield—later Operation Desert Storm—drew more than half a million U.S. soldiers to the Gulf. (One of them was Timothy McVeigh, who would go on to bomb the federal building in Oklahoma City in 1995, murdering 168 Americans—the most deadly terrorist incident in America until the 2001 attack on the World Trade Center.)

Bin Laden's opposition to the presence of American troops was echoed by two prominent religious scholars, Safar al-Hawali and Salman al-ʿAuda, who were subsequently jailed by the Saudis.[7] In a sermon delivered in 1991 al-Hawali observed: "What is happening in the Gulf is part of a larger Western design to dominate the whole Arab and Muslim world."[8] Bin Laden, whose credentials as a religious scholar are nonexistent, often cites al-Hawali and al-ʿAuda to justify his own pronouncements against the United States.

By the start of 1991, bin Laden was already talking of leaving Saudi Arabia for the ultra-Islamist state of Sudan, says Egyptian journalist Essam Deraz, who had spent three years on and off with bin Laden in Afghanistan. "I told him don't do it," Deraz says. "He was overenthusiastic, not a man of tactics." Deraz visited at the end of bin Laden's stay in Saudi Arabia and remembers that the multimillionaire was continuing to live the modest lifestyle he had adopted in Pakistan and Afghanistan: "The house was nothing. People were sleeping on the ground. His office was there and the other floors were for his family. I myself slept on the floor during my three-day visit."[9]

The groundwork for bin Laden's move to the Sudan had been in place for at least a year. To facilitate it, al-Qaeda's Jamal al-Fadl traveled from Pakistan to Egypt and Sudan on false documents; to avoid detection as an Islamist militant, he shaved his beard and packed cologne to make it appear that he was interested in women. Once in Sudan, where al-Qaeda had a cozy relationship with Sudanese intelligence, al-Fadl bought a farm north of the capital, Khartoum, for $250,000 and a salt evaporation farm on the coast near Port Sudan for $180,000. Both would be used by the group.[10]

The Saudi government was by now tiring of bin Laden's critiques of the regime and put him effectively under house arrest, his travel limited to Jeddah. But bin Laden had a plan of escape. He used his family connections with King Fahd to convince the government that he needed to leave the country to sort out some business matters in Pakistan. Arriving there in April 1991, he then sent a letter to his family telling them that he would not be able to return home. After some months in Afghanistan he arrived in Sudan, where he was warmly welcomed by Hassan al-Turabi, the leader of the country's National Islamic Front (NIF).[11]

The nominal Sudanese head of state, Brigadier Omar Hassan Ahmad al-Bashir, had staged a military coup to overthrow the previous civilian government in 1989; but it was al-Turabi, a brilliant Sorbonne graduate who aimed to create a purist Islamist state,[12] who was the real power behind the throne. He and bin Laden soon embarked on a conveniently symbiotic relationship. Bin Laden was allowed to operate freely in the Sudan and subsequently invested millions of dollars in the desperately poor country. Al-Qaeda purchased communications equipment, radios, and rifles for the NIF, while the Sudanese government returned the favor by providing two hundred passports to the group so that its members could travel with new identities.[13]

In Sudan, bin Laden lived a double life. On the one hand, he built up a business empire by investing in banks and agricultural projects and building a major highway. At the same time he organized training camps at which hundreds of his followers could be tutored in paramilitary tactics.

Bin Laden persuaded Saudi businessmen, including some of his brothers, to invest in the country. One of the businessmen bin Laden hoped to attract was his friend Khaled al-Fawwaz, who was given a tour of his various projects. "I visited the highway he was building," al-Fawwaz said. "He also took me to a large farm where he was doing experimental plantings of unusual trees. He wanted to encourage me to invest in Sudan. I was not convinced. I thought Sudan was difficult to invest in, because of their regulations. At that time I was in the food import-export business. Osama said: 'You should grow food in Sudan and then export it to Saudi Arabia.' "

According to al-Fawwaz, bin Laden continued to live without the creature comforts of a typical multimillionaire: "When I observed his house and his way of living, I couldn't believe my eyes. He had no fridge at home, no air conditioning, no fancy car, nothing."[14]

Bin Laden set up an extraordinary range of companies in Sudan, where al-Qaeda was almost literally Holy War, Inc. The first business was Wadi al-Aqiq, a trading company that had dispensation to ship anything it wanted. Other enterprises followed: another trading company, Ladin International Company; Al-Hijra Construction (owned jointly by bin Laden and the Sudanese government), which built roads and bridges and employed more than six hundred people; and the Al-Themar agricultural company, which had four thousand employees working at its one-million-acre Al-Damazine farms, which manufactured sesame oil and grew peanuts and corn.[15] According to the U.S. State Department, one of bin Laden's companies, Taba Investment, Ltd., "secured a near monopoly over Sudan's major agricultural exports of gum, corn, sunflower, and sesame products."[16] Taba also traded in sugar, bananas, canned goods, and soap. The Blessed Fruits company grew fruit and vegetables, while Al-Ikhlas produced sweets and honey. Bin Laden also set up a trucking company, Al-Qudurat; a leather company, Khartoum Tannery; a bakery; and a furniture-making concern.[17] He sank $50 million of his own money into the Al-Shamal Islamic bank in Khartoum.[18]

Al-Qaeda was as globally minded as any other international company. To facilitate business, the group maintained accounts at banks in Cyprus, Malaysia, Hong Kong, Dubai, Vienna, and London.[19] Al-Qaeda members bought trucks from Russia and tractors from Slovakia to be used for the group's companies, and went on business trips to Hungary, Croatia, China, Malaysia, and the Philippines.[20]

Bin Laden established a nine-room office on McNimr Street in Khartoum, later opening another office-residence in the Riyadh section of the city. Near the Blue Nile river, the group purchased four farms where bin Laden, an accomplished horseman, would spend weekends riding while his followers swam, played soccer, and picnicked. (Other than riding, bin Laden's only leisure activity is reading. He reads extensively in the areas of Islamic thought and current affairs.[21])

Most of the thousands of employees in bin Laden's vast array of businesses had no idea that al-Qaeda existed. That was a secret; to know of the group's existence you had to be a member. Salaries for al-Qaeda members ranged from $500 to a top rate of $1,200 a month, money that went a long way in one of the poorest countries in the world.[22]

At the end of 1993, bin Laden gave his first interview to a member of the Western press, Robert Fisk of Britain's *Independent*. Fisk recounts how Sudanese villagers lined up to meet bin Laden, stylishly dressed in a gold-fringed robe, to thank him for building a new highway from Khartoum to Port Sudan on the Red Sea, a distance of twelve hundred kilometers on the old road that was now shortened to eight hundred kilometers.[23]

Scott MacLeod, a correspondent for *Time* magazine, was also shown bin Laden's entrepreneurial side in early 1996: "At that time he was building the road to Port Sudan . . . and he owned a sunflower plantation and a tanning factory. And he was at great pains to show me all this. . . . I saw them making leather jackets for export to Italy out of goatskin and sheepskin. . . . And clearly he was trying to present the image that—'Look, I am a businessman.'"[24]

That was only partly true. In fact, bin Laden's five years in Sudan were a period of intense activity in his capacity as a political leader and the mastermind of paramilitary operations against American targets. The commercial operations proved a useful cover. In the early nineties, for example, a plane loaded with sugar flew to Afghanistan and returned to Sudan with a consignment of guns and rockets.[25]

Bin Laden told CNN in 1997 that one of his proudest achievements while he was based in Sudan was the role of his Afghan Arabs in the 1993 killings of more than a dozen American soldiers stationed in Somalia. Since he has repeatedly dismissed efforts to link him to attacks on American soldiers in Saudi Arabia in 1995 and 1996 and has denied any direct role in the bombings of the U.S. embassies in Africa in 1998, it is surprising that he should take credit, even tangentially, for this particular operation. While his exact role remains murky and has been questioned by some U.S. officials,[26] the State Department's coordinator for counterterrorism, Ambassador Philip Wilcox, told CNN in 1997: "We take [bin Laden] at his word." Prosecutors in New York would devote several paragraphs of their 1998 indictment of bin Laden to his alleged anti-American activities in Somalia.

A force of 28,000 American troops had been ordered to the country by then-President Bush in the first week of December 1992 as part of a U.N. mission to feed starving Somalis. The first of those troops, consisting of Navy SEALs and Marines in full battle gear, landed on the beaches of Somalia during the dark early-morning hours of December 9, only to be greeted by a phalanx of photographers and video crews from the world's press.[27] It was an inauspicious beginning for the Pentagon's mission, which began somewhat farcically and would end tragically.

Al-Qaeda saw the arrival of those troops—just two years after the United States had based thousands of soldiers in Saudi Arabia—as part of a strategy to take over ever larger chunks of the Muslim world.[28] So the *fatwa* committee of al-Qaeda issued calls to attack U.S. troops in Somalia, saying that they had to cut off "the head of the snake."[29] In late December, al-Qaeda affiliates in Yemen bombed two hotels housing American troops in transit to Somalia. (The bomb killed an Australian tourist but no Americans.)

The peacekeeping mission all too quickly turned into a war when U.S. troops became embroiled in the clan fighting that was consuming the capital, Mogadishu, and aggravating the famine. U.N. and American commanders determined that attacking Mohamed Aidid, the most powerful clan leader, was the best way to establish peace. They made Aidid the object of a massive manhunt, which would prove to be a costly mistake.

In 1993 one of bin Laden's military commanders, Muhammad Atef, traveled twice to Somalia to determine how best to attack U.S. forces, reporting back to bin Laden in Sudan. An al-Qaeda mortar specialist was also dispatched to the country.[30] By early 1993 Atef was providing military training and assistance to Somalis. On October 3 and 4, 1993 eighteen American soldiers were killed in an intense firefight in Mogadishu on a mission to try and snatch two of Aidid's lieutenants. At least five hundred Somalis were also killed.[31] During the battle, rocket-propelled grenades (RPGs) downed two American Black Hawk helicopters. A U.S. official told me that the skills involved in shooting down those helicopters were not skills that the Somalis could have learned on their own. In the definitive account of the Mogadishu battle, *Black Hawk Down*, the journalist Mark Bowden reports that Aidid's men were indeed trained by Arabs who had fought against the Soviets in Afghanistan and who taught the Somalis that the most effective way to shoot down a helicopter with an RPG was to hit the vulnerable tail rotor.[32] Within a week of the Mogadishu battle, the United States announced plans for its pullout.[33]

Given all the claims and counterclaims about bin Laden's role in Somalia, the most likely scenario is that his men did train Somali tribesmen opposed to the American presence. But it may never be clear who exactly these tribesmen were, and whether they actually fought against American soldiers. In the Manhattan trial of four bin Laden associates in 2001, testimony was offered that an al-Qaeda member, Mohamed Odeh, actually trained Somali tribesmen who were *opposed* to Aidid.[34] On the other hand, trial testimony also established that Haroun Fazil, later a key member of al-Qaeda's Kenya cell, was in Mogadishu in 1993 next door to a building that came under intense American helicopter fire.[35] In 1997, Fazil would also write a letter meant for the consumption of al-Qaeda's leadership: "America knows well that the youth who work in Somalia and who are followers of the Sheikh [bin Laden] are the ones who have carried out the operations to hit the Americans in Somalia."[36]

Bin Laden himself has been unambiguous on the subject. In Afghanistan in 1998 he introduced Hamid Mir, a Pakistani journalist, to a man he described as "my military commander in Somalia, the commander of my troops who fought against the American troops and he destroyed an American helicopter."[37] In 1999 Al-Jazeera television aired bin Laden's first television interview in Arabic, in which he again claimed his men had fought in Somalia: "Based on the reports we received from our brothers, who participated in the jihad in Somalia, we learned that they saw the weakness, frailty, and cowardice of U.S. troops. Only eighteen U.S. troops were killed. Nonetheless, they fled in the heart of darkness, frustrated after they had caused great commotion about the New World Order."[38]

What is undeniable is that bin Laden and his followers became increasingly radicalized during their time in Sudan. Essam Deraz says this was due in part to the presence around bin Laden of many angry young men who faced persecution or even death in their native Middle Eastern countries. Members of al-Qaeda were naturally suspicious of outsiders and extremely vigilant: an informant who penetrated the group in Sudan was shot.[39]

By 1991 there were somewhere between a thousand and two thousand members of al-Qaeda in Sudan, and within three years bin Laden had set up a number of military camps in the north.[40] Not everyone saw them; even L'Hossaine Kherchtou, an al-Qaeda member who visited Sudan often, had no glimpse of the intensive training.[41] The reason for al-Qaeda's discretion might have been that its members weren't content with conventional military training: they also turned their attention to more exotic weaponry. In 1993, the group paid $210,000 to acquire an airplane in Tucson, Arizona, that was then flown to Khartoum. This plane was intended to transport highly effective American Stinger anti-aircraft missiles from Pakistan to Sudan; however, the shipment never actually took place.[42]

Between 1990 and early 1993, some members of the group also undertook the massive task of writing the *Encyclopedia of the Afghan Jihad*. This multivolume series, thousands of pages long, details everything the Afghan Arabs learned in the jihad against the Soviets. Each volume is dedicated to participants in that holy war, although the only ones mentioned by name are the late Abdullah Azzam and bin Laden, "who did not cease to wage jihad and incite jihad to this present day."[43] The *Encyclopedia* contains eight hundred pages on weaponry, including how to use American Stinger missiles, and 250 pages on how to mount terrorist and paramilitary attacks.[44] A CD-ROM version of it went on sale in the bazaars of Pakistan in the mid-1990s.[45] And a similar how-to terrorism book, *Military Studies in the Jihad Against the Tyrants*, would be seized in Manchester, England, in May 2000 in the home of Anas al-Liby, who is a fugitive charged in the bin Laden terror conspiracy.[46]

Al-Qaeda also sought to acquire weapons of mass destruction. In the early 1990s Jamal al-Fadl went to an industrial area of Khartoum, Hilat Koko, where representatives of the group and a Sudanese army officer discussed the manufacture of chemical weapons. Al-Qaeda and the Sudanese army also cooperated in efforts to mount chemical agents on artillery shells.[47] Al-Fadl approached another army officer to inquire about purchasing uranium and was put in touch with an associate, who offered to sell him a consignment for $1.5 million. That man displayed what he said was uranium—in a cylinder about two or three feet long and six inches in diameter, apparently from South Africa—but al-Fadl dropped out of the negotiations and never found out if the group made the purchase. (He was given a $10,000 bonus for his efforts.[48])

Bin Laden has since made clear his posture on weapons of mass destruction: "We don't consider it a crime if we tried to have nuclear, chemical, biological weapons. . . . We have the right to defend ourselves."[49] Moreover, Mamdouh Mahmud Salim, a top official of al-Qaeda, is alleged to have sought nuclear weapons components for the group and approved efforts to "procure enriched uranium."[50] Al-Qaeda has also conducted grisly experiments on dogs that were injected or gassed with cyanide as a prelude to a possible use of the deadly agent against American targets.[51]

There is, however, as yet no evidence that al-Qaeda has ever "weaponized" any of the chemical and nuclear materials it has flirted with. The technical skills necessary are, at least as of this writing, beyond its scope.

In 1995 the de facto ruler of Sudan, Hassan al-Turabi, organized an Islamic People's Congress, during which bin Laden was able to meet with leaders of militant groups from Pakistan, Algeria, and Tunisia as well as the Palestinian Islamic Jihad and Hamas.[52] At the same time, al-Qaeda sought to forge alliances with the Iranian-backed Hezbollah, based in southern Lebanon. Despite their disputes over religious doctrine—Hezbollah is Shia, while bin Laden espouses a conservative Sunni Islam—the two groups buried their differences to make war against their common enemy, the United States. Al-Qaeda members traveled to Lebanon, where the group maintained a guesthouse, and, with Hezbollah, learned how to bomb large buildings.[53] Bin Laden, meanwhile, met with Imad Mughniyeh, the secretive, Iran-based head of Hezbollah's security service.[54] This was an important meeting: It was Mughniyeh who masterminded the suicide truck bombing of the Marine barracks in Beirut in 1983, which killed 241 American servicemen and precipitated a U.S. pullout from Lebanon within a few months.[55]

According to the plea bargain of Ali Mohamed, an al-Qaeda member who is now a U.S. government witness against the group, the Beirut model was one bin Laden hoped to follow: "Based on the Marine explosion in Beirut . . . and the American pull-out from Beirut, they will be the same method, to force the United States out of Saudi Arabia."[56] This shows a certain naïveté about American foreign policy. The United States had no compelling strategic interest in Lebanon, while Saudi Arabia sits on a quarter of the world's known oil resources—the very blood of the American economy.[57]

Al-Qaeda made several other important contacts with overseas groups while it was based in Sudan.[58] The group opened a satellite office in Baku, Azerbaijan; sent fighters to Chechnya, at a cost of $1,500 each; dispatched holy warriors to Tajikistan; trained members of the Filipino Moro Front; delivered $100,000 to affiliates in Jordan and Eritrea; and smuggled weapons into Yemen and Egypt. Iran shipped explosives to the group designed to look like rocks.[59]

In the early nineties the overseas conflict with the greatest import for al-Qaeda was the war in the former Yugoslavia between the Serbs and the largely Muslim Bosnians. While the Bosnian conflict never took on the dimensions of the Afghan jihad, between 1992 and 1995 hundreds of Afghan Arabs were fighting in Bosnia, particularly in the region around Zenica.[60] A Vienna-based charity linked to bin Laden, Third World Relief Agency, funneled millions of dollars in contributions to the Bosnians.[61] Al-Qaeda trained *mujahideen* to go and fight in Bosnia during the early nineties, and bin Laden's Services Office also maintained an office in neighboring Croatia's capital, Zagreb.[62]

During the time al-Qaeda was based in Sudan, the group forged alliances with a range of other militant organizations: Egypt's Islamic Group and Jihad Group; Algeria's Armed Islamic Group; the Libyan Fighting Group; a Yemeni group, Saif Islamic Jannubi; and the Syrian organization Jamaat e-Jihal al-Suri.[63]

As early as 1993, members of bin Laden's group started planning an attack on the American embassy in Nairobi. As bin Laden made clear in a later interview, Nairobi was targeted for particular reasons, among them the fact that "the brutal U.S. invasion of Somalia kicked off from there."[64] The Egyptian-American Ali Mohamed said he traveled to Nairobi in late 1993 to "conduct surveillance of American, British, French, and Israeli targets"—including the American embassy—in order "to retaliate against the United States for its involvement in Somalia." Mohamed then went to Khartoum, where bin Laden examined his surveillance files and photographs; he "looked at the picture of the American embassy and pointed to where a truck bomb could go as a suicide bomber."[65]

While al-Qaeda was based in Sudan, the group was riven with petty disputes about money and larger arguments about tactics—problems typical of any organization. In 1993, al-Qaeda members debated whether to bomb the U.S. embassy in Saudi Arabia after the arrest in New York of Sheikh Omar Abdel Rahman, the spiritual leader of the group's Egyptian members. This proposal was rejected because of the danger of killing civilians—scruples al-Qaeda would later abandon.[66]

No such constraints, however, were in place against attacks on American military targets in the Kingdom. On November 13, 1995, a car bomb went off outside the National Guard building, a joint Saudi-U.S. facility in Riyadh. The bomb, the first of its kind in the country's history, killed five Americans and two Indians.[67] In April of the following year, Saudi television broadcast the confessions of the alleged perpetrators.[68] Although the four men accused had probably been tortured, their statements have the ring of truth. (They had recognizable Saudi tribal names and accents; also, the Saudi government has no interest in encouraging the notion that it faces a violent domestic opposition.)[69] One of the bombers said he was influenced by the writings of bin Laden and Egyptian Islamist groups. Another explained that he assembled the bomb "according to my experience in explosives which I had during my participation in the Afghan Jihad operations."[70] Three of the four bombers had fought in the Afghan holy war, so it is fair to infer that they had contact with bin Laden's Service Office.[71] One of them, Muslih al-Shamrani, was a member of bin Laden's "Farooq" brigade in Afghanistan.[72]

In a 1999 interview with the Arabic television station Al-Jazeera, bin Laden underlined the connections between his rhetoric and the Riyadh bombing: "I admit I was one of those who cosigned the *fatwa* that urged the nation to engage in jihad. We did so a few years ago. Thanks be to God, many people responded favorably to our *fatwa*. Of these people were the brothers we regard as martyrs. . . . During interrogation they admitted coming under the influence of some of the statements and circulars we issued to the people."[73]

Unfortunately, further investigation of the Riyadh attack is impossible because the Saudis beheaded the alleged bombers before American investigators could interview them.[74] Case very much closed.

The next attack on American targets came on June 25, 1996. This was a far more serious affair. A bomb in a fuel truck parked outside the

Khobar Towers military complex in Dhahran set off a huge explosion that killed nineteen U.S. servicemen and injured hundreds of others. The blast was so powerful that it tore the front off the eight-story Khobar Towers building and was felt twenty miles away in the Gulf state of Bahrain.[75] The Saudi government blamed the attack on Iran or the Iranian-backed Shia from the Eastern Province of the country,[76] but the subsequent arrest of six hundred Afghan Arabs suggests that, at least initially, it believed bin Laden veterans might be responsible.[77] In June 2001, thirteen members of Saudi Hezbollah, a Shia group with ties to Iran, were indicted in the United States for the Khobar bombing.[78]

In his 1997 interview with CNN, bin Laden praised as "heroes" those behind the Riyadh and Dhahran bombings but denied any involvement himself: "I have great respect for the people who did this. What they did is a big honor that I missed participating in."[79]

At the same time that bin Laden was organizing military training for his men and plotting to attack American targets, he also was involved in a more strictly political effort to undermine the Saudi regime. He founded the Advice and Reformation Committee (ARC), which the U.S. government portrays as an extension of his al-Qaeda paramilitary operation but which seems more likely a legitimate outgrowth of a gathering opposition movement to the Saudi regime.[80] That movement coalesced around the Memorandum of Advice, a letter advocating a series of reforms and signed by prominent Saudi Islamists in the summer of 1992.[81] In July 1994 bin Laden appointed Khaled al-Fawwaz as director of the London office of the ARC. According to its London constitution, ARC was to "promote peaceful and constructive reform with regard to the way Arabia is governed using only legitimate means."[82]

In his London office al-Fawwaz told me: "The Advice and Reformation Committee, first of all, is not a new thing; it is simply a continuation of those reformers which have been working for decades. We thought that because individual reformers . . . are getting more and more harassed . . . so that's why we come up with this idea: Why don't we organize ourselves, why don't we unite ourselves together, so that we help those who get hurt or those who get badly treated by the [Saudi] regime, or at least help their families if something goes wrong?" Al-Fawwaz wanted to make one thing very clear to me: "I don't work for Osama, we are friends."[83]

ARC issued numerous communiqués. One, #17 of March 8, 1995, is a rambling indictment of the Saudi regime, criticizing it for a wide variety of sins. These include its use of "man-made laws" that are not part of *sharia*, Islamic law; the indebtedness of the nation; rising unemployment; the lavishness of the palaces built for the royal family; and the estimated $60 billion the government spent on the Gulf War in addition to the vast expenditures it had made on its own inefficient military.[84] The communiqué concludes by demanding the resignation of King Fahd.

Such critiques were anathema to the al-Saud, who have ruled Saudi Arabia as a family fiefdom for decades. By 1994 they had frozen bin Laden's assets in the country and stripped him of his citizenship. At this point bin Laden's family, at least officially, cut him off. His brother Bakr, who runs the family businesses, issued a statement to Saudi media in March 1994 expressing "regret, denunciation, and condemnation" of Osama's activities.

The Saudis tried to dissuade bin Laden from his campaign against them. Saad al-Fagih says, "I know personally of three delegations that went to the Sudan to ask him not to target Saudi targets. They told him: 'Your fight is with the United States, not with us.' " Bin Laden said that the Saudis "—sent my mother, my uncle, and my brothers in almost nine visits to Khartoum asking me to stop and return to Arabia to apologize to King Fahd . . . I refused to go back."[85]

The Saudis also used less subtle tactics. The al-Qaeda defector Jamal al-Fadl discussed with Saudi officials the possibility of assassinating bin Laden. In 1994, a group of men armed with AK-47s opened fire at bin Laden's house in Khartoum—an attempt probably engineered by the Saudis.[86]

While al-Qaeda was headquartered in Sudan, it remained active both in Afghanistan and Pakistan. Al-Qaeda maintained a guesthouse in the Peshawar suburb of Hayatabad, in a section known as Phase 4, from 1991 onward.[87] Across the border in Afghanistan, the group operated several training camps named Khalid ibn Walid, al-Farouq, Sadeek, Khaldan, Jihad Wal, and Darunta.[88]

L'Hossaine Kherchtou might seem an unlikely al-Qaeda recruit: he is a Moroccan who attended catering school in France. Nonetheless, in 1991 he traveled from Italy to Pakistan, first stopping at the bin Laden guesthouse *Beit al-Ansar* and then proceeding to Afghanistan, where he went through a rigorous training program that makes basic training for U.S. Army recruits look laughably rudimentary. At one in the morning on his first night in camp, Kherchtou was awakened by bursts of gunfire. It turned out to be not an attack but an exercise designed to keep the new recruits on their toes. ("Don't think you are going to sleep in this camp," he was told.) Then he was trained on a extraordinary variety of weaponry: the American M-16 rifle, the Russian AK-47 rifle and PK submachine gun, the Israeli Uzi submachine gun, and anti-aircraft guns. He also took classes on grenades and was taught how to use such explosives as C3, C4, and dynamite. Finally, he was trained in the use of various mines: antipersonnel mines, antitruck mines, and butterfly mines, which children sometimes mistake for toys. During this period, Kherchtou lost forty or so pounds. After his training, he returned to Peshawar, where he was inducted into al-Qaeda at one of its guest houses, *Beit al-Salaam*. It's a nice Orwellian touch: *Beit al-Salaam* means "house of peace."[89]

During the early nineties, the Pakistani government asked Arab militants like Kherchtou to register with the government. Many, of course, did not, but of those who did in the North-West Frontier Province that abuts Afghanistan, 1,142 were Egyptian; 981 Saudis; 946 Yemenis; 792 Algerians; 771 Jordanians; 326 Iraqis; 292 Syrians; 234 Sudanese; 199 Libyans; 117 Tunisians; and 102 Moroccans.[90] Those numbers indicate the relative contribution of different Middle Eastern countries to the Afghan Arabs.

Middle Eastern governments, particularly Egypt's, were increasingly disturbed by the use of Pakistan as a base for Islamist militants.[91] They pressured the Pakistanis to crack down on the Afghan Arabs, who were subsequently expelled from the country at periodic intervals. In March 1993 eight hundred were arrested.[92] In May of that year bin Laden paid the travel expenses for at least three hundred of them to join him in Sudan.[93] But the militants continued to operate in Pakistan; on November 20, 1995, they mounted a devastating truck bomb attack on the Egyptian embassy in Islamabad, killing fifteen and injuring eighty.[94] American prosecutors maintain that al-Qaeda, whose leadership is heavily Egyptian, was involved in the attack.[95] The bombing was similar to the later assault on the American embassy in Kenya: in both operations, a suicide bomber drove a vehicle packed with explosives, and grenades were thrown to distract security guards.[96] Six months before the attack on the Egyptian embassy, al-Qaeda members also tried to assassinate Egyptian president Hosni Mubarak while he was attending a conference in Addis Ababa, Ethiopia.[97]

The attack on the Egyptian embassy led the Pakistani government to arrest 150 Arabs, including the director of bin Laden's still functioning Services Office, the Palestinian Mohammed Yussuf Abbas, who later moved to Saudi Arabia. *Jihad* magazine, published by the Services Office, was also closed down at this time.[98]

By 1996 intense pressure had been placed on the Sudanese government by the United States and Egypt to expel bin Laden, who left Sudan to return to his familiar stamping grounds in Afghanistan.[99] The Sudanese government has since said that they offered to hand over bin Laden to the Saudi government, but that proposal was turned down. Forcing bin Laden to leave for Afghanistan would turn out to be a little bit like the German High Command sending Lenin to Russia during World War I: while the policy might have resulted in short-term gains for the Germans, it set the stage for the creation of Germany's most implacable enemy. So, too, in the case of bin Laden and Afghanistan. From Afghanistan bin Laden was—and is—able to function unimpeded, attracting Muslim militants to a country that is becoming the modern world's first jihadist state. There, in Afghanistan, he would pose a much greater threat than he ever did in Sudan.

CHAPTER 5

From the Peaks of the Hindu Kush:
The Declaration of War

> *"What is your understanding of what the Prophet Muham-
> mad would say about whether it is proper to drive a truck
> into a building and blow up everyone inside?"*
>
> > —Question by a federal prosecutor during the trial of
> > four bin Laden associates convicted of conspiring
> > to blow up two American embassies in Africa in
> > 1998
>
> *"If you study the life of Prophet Muhammad, peace and
> blessings be upon him, you will see the most gentle man. He
> would never allow innocent people to die, never. Never."*[1]
>
> > —Answer by the Muslim cleric Imam Siraj Wahhaj,
> > of Brooklyn, New York

When bin Laden arrived in Afghanistan in May 1996, accompanied by his three wives and many of his children, he was in a
sense coming home. He knew the place well, having traveled over its
rugged mountains and valleys on and off for more than a decade, and
he greatly admired the Taliban religious warriors who were gradually
taking control of much of the country.

The journey to Afghanistan also had a profound spiritual importance for bin Laden: it recalled for him the Prophet Muhammad's em-
igration, or *hijra*, from Mecca to Medina in the seventh century. The

Prophet and his followers left their native city because they were under intense pressure from their fellow Meccans, pagans who did not appreciate Islam's monotheistic message. From Medina, Muhammad waged war almost continuously for eight years until he retook Mecca from the unbelievers.[2] This was the model bin Laden planned to follow in his jihad against the West. And Afghanistan, in his mind, was the Medina of the twenty-first century.[3]

The Saudi exile first settled near the eastern town of Jalalabad, shuttling between various mountain hideouts in the area.[4] The Taliban's leader, Mullah Muhammad Omar, sent a delegation after his arrival to assure bin Laden that the Taliban would be honored to protect him because of his role in the jihad against the Soviets.[5]

In November 1996, Abdel Bari Atwan, the editor of the newspaper *Al-Quds Al-Arabi*, traveled to meet bin Laden at his base in a cave in the Afghan mountains. In his office in west London, Atwan recalled the visit: "It was not comfortable. His quarters were built in an amateurish way with the branches of trees. He had hundreds of books, mostly theological treatises. I slept on a bed underneath which were stored many grenades. I maybe slept for half an hour. I saw perhaps twenty to thirty people around him, Egyptians, Saudis, Yemenis, and Afghans. At night it was very cold, fifteen degrees below zero. I waited for two days to see him. He was familiar with my writings. I found him to be sincere, simple, not trying to impress. He never portrayed himself as an Islamic leader. He told me that the Saudi government had applied pressure on him. They offered him $400 million if he said the Saudi regime was an Islamic regime." To no avail, obviously.

"His followers really, really believe in him," Atwan told me. "They can see this millionaire, who sacrificed all those millions, and he is sitting with them in a cave, sharing their dinner, in a very, very humble way."[6]

From his new refuge in Afghanistan bin Laden issued a slew of ever more radical pronouncements, beginning with "The Declaration of Jihad on the Americans Occupying the Country of the Two Sacred Places" on August 23, 1996. This call to arms against the continued American military presence in Arabia featured an analysis of American policy in the Middle East since Franklin Roosevelt, attacks on the Saudi regime for its corruption and anti-Islamic policies, and a discussion of the views of Muslim scholars about the proper relations to non-Muslims across the centuries.

In the declaration bin Laden states: "The Muslims have realized they are the main target of the aggression of the coalition of the Jews and the Crusaders [his term for the West]. . . . The latest of these assaults is the greatest disaster since the death of the Prophet Muhammad (Peace be upon him)—that is the occupation of the country of the two sacred mosques—the home ground of Islam." Bin Laden explains that this contravenes a *hadith*, or saying, of the Prophet Muhammad, who said on his deathbed: "If Allah wills and I live, God willing I will expel the Jews and the Christians from Arabia."

At one point bin Laden, who is fond of a certain sort of morbid poetry, addresses an unusual ode to the then U.S. secretary of defense, William Perry:

> *O William, tomorrow you will be informed*
> *as to which young man will face your swaggering brother*
> *A youngster enters the midst of battle smiling, and*
> *Retreats with his spearhead stained with blood.*

Something may have been lost in the translation, but one gets the general drift.

Bin Laden concludes the declaration with a call to arms: "Our Muslim brothers throughout the world . . . Your brothers in the country of the two sacred places and in Palestine request your support. They are asking you to participate with them against their enemies, who are also your enemies—the Israelis and the Americans—by causing them as much harm as can be possibly achieved." Bin Laden signed his manifesto with a flourish: "From the Peaks of the Hindu Kush, Afghanistan."

This declaration of holy war against Americans, which was picked up by various media outlets and publicized around the world, was, according to an Arab journalist, written on an Apple Macintosh.[7] "Think different," indeed.

In early 1997, bin Laden gave his first television interview—the one that opens this book—to CNN from one of his hideouts near Jalalabad. He reiterated his calls for attacks on U.S. soldiers and said that he could not guarantee the safety of American civilians should they get in the way of those attacks. Shortly afterwards, bin Laden moved to the southern Afghan city of Kandahar, where Mullah Omar was based.

On February 22, 1998, bin Laden upped the ante considerably when he announced the formation of the World Islamic Front for Jihad against the Jews and the Crusaders. Cosignatories of the agreement included Ayman al-Zawahiri of Egypt's Jihad Group, bin Laden's most trusted lieutenant; Rifa'a Ahmed Taha of Egypt's Islamic Group; and the leaders of Pakistani and Bangladeshi militant organizations.[8] All were brought together under one umbrella for the first time.

Because the announcement of the inauguration of the World Islamic Front is the key text that set the stage for al-Qaeda's terrorist attacks, it is worth quoting at some length:

> Since Allah spread out the Arabian Peninsula, created its desert, and drew its seas, no such disaster has ever struck as when those Christian legions spread like pest, crowded its land, ate its resources, eradicated its nature, and humiliated its leaders . . . No one argues today over three facts repeated by witnesses and agreed upon by those who are fair . . . They are: Since about seven years ago, America has been occupying the most sacred lands of Islam: the Arabian Peninsula. It has been stealing its resources, dictating to its leaders, humiliating its people, and frightening its neighbors. It is using its rule in the Peninsula as a weapon to fight the neighboring peoples of Islam . . . The most evident proof is when the Americans went too far in their aggression against the people of Iraq . . . Despite major destruction to the Iraqi people at the hand of the Christian alliance and the great number of victims exceeding one million, Americans are trying once again to repeat these horrifying massacres as if they are not satisfied with the long blockade or the destruction. Here they come today to eradicate the rest of these people and to humiliate its Muslim neighbors. Although the Americans' objectives of these wars are religious and economic, they are also to serve the Jewish state and distract from its occupation of the Holy Land and its killing of Muslims therein. The most evident proof thereof is their persistence to destroy Iraq, the most powerful neighboring Arab state . . . All those crimes and calamities are an explicit declaration by the Americans of war on Allah, His Prophet,

and Muslims. . . . Based upon this and in order to obey the Almighty, we hereby give all Muslims the following judgment: The judgment to kill and fight Americans and their allies, whether civilians or military, is an obligation for every Muslim who is able to do so in any country. . . . In the name of Allah, we call upon every Muslim, who believes in Allah and asks for forgiveness, to abide by Allah's order by killing Americans and stealing their money anywhere, anytime, and whenever possible. We also call upon Muslim scholars, their faithful leaders, young believers, and soldiers to launch a raid on the American soldiers of Satan and their allies of the Devil."[9]

A CIA analysis pointed out: "These *fatwas* are the first from these groups that explicitly justify attacks on American civilians anywhere in the world."[10] A few months after the issuance of the *fatwa* I met with Khaled al-Fawwaz, bin Laden's London representative. Al-Fawwaz appeared genuinely surprised by it, in part because of the large number of people who had signed on, but also because of its call for attacks on all Americans. "It's not Islamic to kill civilians," he explained.

Al-Fawwaz's unequivocal statement suggests some serious questions we must ask: First, according to the Koran, what are the justifications for holy war? Then, can bin Laden's call for the expulsion of American troops from Arabia, his principal political goal, be justified by reference to the *hadith,* or sayings of the Prophet Muhammad? And, finally, is the killing of civilians permissible in a holy war and, if not, how does bin Laden justify such a campaign?

Various, sometimes conflicting, justifications for holy war can be found in the Koran. In one often quoted verse, Muslims are allowed to engage in a defensive war: "Permission to take up arms is hereby given to those who are attacked, because they have been wronged." Another suggests that Muslims are encouraged to engage in aggressive war against infidels: "But when the Sacred Months are past, then kill the idolaters wherever you find them . . ." Bin Laden cited this verse when he announced the formation of his World Islamic Front.[11]

By contrast, Jesus in the New Testament admonished his followers, "Whoever shall smite thee on the right cheek, turn to him the other also," and urged them to "Love your enemies." Of course, in practice,

Jesus' message has been largely ignored by Christians, who have enthusiastically slaughtered each other and "heathens" for two millennia.

Muhammad admired Jesus as one of the greatest of God's messengers, but he further distanced himself from the Nazarene by removing the distinction that Jesus had earlier made between the secular and the sacred: "Render unto Caesar the things which are Caesar's, and unto God the things that are God's." For Muhammad, the needs of God were automatically the needs of Caesar. Indeed, Muhammad's success as a prophet was inextricably entwined with his role as a political and military leader. Within a century of Muhammad's death, war and conversion combined enabled the Prophet's successors to preside over a vast empire that stretched from the African coast of the North Atlantic to northern India. It is to this golden age of Islam that bin Laden harks back.

Yet it is worth noting that Islam has had a long tradition of tolerance. (Indeed, the word *Islam* is related etymologically to the word *salaam*, which means peace.) When the philosopher Moses Maimonides fled Spain's twelfth-century persecution of the Jews, he sought refuge in Egypt, where he became Saladin's physician.[12] This pattern was later repeated by many European Jews, who escaped their ghettos for the relative freedom of the Ottoman Empire.[13]

Also, *jihad*, which sounds violent to Western ears, does not mean only holy war or war against an infidel enemy. The literal meaning is "effort" or "struggle," and the word often signifies battle against one's own moral shortcomings.[14] The Prophet Muhammad himself recognized the dual meaning of *jihad;* but to him "the great *jihad*" was the fight against one's own evil inclinations, "the little *jihad*" the war against the enemies of Islam.[15] In bin Laden's mind, these priorities are surely reversed.

What about the call to expel American troops from the Arabian peninsula? The answer, discomfiting to many Westerners, is that Muslim tradition *does* provide justification for bin Laden's call. Bernard Lewis, a professor of Middle Eastern history at Princeton University, points out that one of the Prophet's immediate successors, the Caliph Umar, issued a "final and irreversible decree" that Jews and Christians be evicted from the "holy land of Hijaz," the region where the holy cities of Mecca and Medina are located, based on the words of the Prophet: "Let there be no two religions in Arabia." Since then, according to Lewis, non-Muslims have been allowed to stay in other areas of Arabia only on a temporary basis. When Great Britain and France dismembered the Ottoman Empire after World War I, ruling over Iraq, Egypt, Sudan, Syria, and Palestine, they only "nibbled at the fringes of Arabia in Aden and the trucial sheikhdoms of the Gulf, but were wise enough to have no military and minimal political involvement in the affairs of the peninsula." [16] (Of course, that restraint may also have had something to do with the fact that before the discovery of oil Arabia was largely an inhospitable desert inhabited by warring tribes.)

Bin Laden can therefore rely on sayings of the Prophet as support for his stance that "the United States is occupying the lands of Islam in the holiest of its territories, Arabia." [17]

Dr. Saad al-Fagih, the London-based Saudi dissident, amplified for me the points made by Professor Lewis: "I don't think there is a sensible person who believes that the Americans should stay in Saudi Arabia . . . if you are a devoted Muslim, there is a religious obligation not to accept non-Muslims in military form staying in the country, especially the holy land."

Dr. al-Fagih has never advocated violence against Americans, but his view represents the commonly held perspective of many serious Muslims on this subject. As Yemen's former deputy prime minister Abdul Wahab al-Anesi put it: "The U.S. military forces are not liked or appreciated." A British diplomat in the region told me that he had a conversation with some of his American counterparts in 1998 in which he told them that their presence in Saudi Arabia was "quite clumsy and provocative and counterproductive." Akthar Raja, a London-based lawyer who specializes in defending Muslims, says: "Give back what is ours, leave Saudi Arabia. What if I sent a jihad group into the Vatican?" [18]

Of course, while many Muslims may be unhappy about the American troops posted in Saudi Arabia and about U.S. policies in the Middle East, only a tiny minority are committed to violence against American citizens. And there is much in the Koran to counter bin Laden's calls for violence against all Americans. For example, the Koran is explicit in the protections offered to civilians in time of war and commands tolerance for the "People of the Book," the very Jews and Christians against whom bin Laden has declared war. [19]

To understand why bin Laden makes the leap from opposition to

American policies to killing thousands of U.S. civilians, one must grasp that in his mind the United States has been equally violent in its treatment of Muslim civilians. On the al-Qaeda videotape circulating around the Middle East during the summer of 2001, bin Laden repeatedly returns to the theme of Muslim civilians under attack in countries from Israel to Iraq, for which he blames the United States. He rages over pictures of dying children in Iraq, saying, "More than a million [Iraqis] die because they are Muslims," and refers to President Clinton as a "slaughterer." For bin Laden it's quite simple: attacks against American citizens are necessary so that they can "taste the bitter fruit" that Muslims civilians have long tasted. Strange that this "holy" man's holy war should come down to simple lust for revenge.

On March 12, 1998, a conference of about forty Afghan *ulema*, or clergy, convened to examine the question of what to do about the American military presence in the Gulf. This was highly significant for bin Laden. Although he may be well read in the Koran, even his stoutest defenders would have to acknowledge that bin Laden is not a religious scholar and does not have the authority to deliver a *fatwa* on his own. The Afghan clerics concluded: "The Union of Afghanistan's scholars . . . declares Jihad according to Islamic law against America and its followers." At the end of April a similar *fatwa* was issued by a group of Pakistani clerics based in Karachi.[20]

Now bin Laden had the backing of dozens of religious scholars and the clerical cover to call for a real jihad. His aide, Muhammad Atef, faxed the group's contact in London, Khaled al-Fawwaz, and urged him to get the text of the Afghan *fatwa* placed in *Al-Quds Al-Arabi*, where it was subsequently published.[21]

Four days after the issuance of the Afghan *fatwa*, bin Laden released a letter that recapitulated the themes of his declaration of war. In it he underscored "the calamity of the Americans' occupation of the Arabian peninsula." Referring to Operation Desert Storm, he asked: "Why were American women soldiers brought in?"—to his mind, the ultimate insult. To further support his position, he cited a well-known medieval Muslim thinker: "Scholars have long agreed that fighting the infidel enemy is an obligation to every Muslim. . . . Sheikh ibn Taymiyyah said . . . after faith, nothing is more obligating than defending against the enemy who spoils the religion and the world." He concluded: "We call upon the Almighty Allah to visit His anger, disgust and concern on the American soldiers in the Gulf, their allies the Jews in Palestine, and all those hypocrites, to send who He has from the sky to kill them."

Further critical support for bin Laden's calls for the expulsion of American troops from Saudi Arabia came in June from a prestigious quarter: the imam of the Prophet's Mosque in Medina, Sheikh Ali al-Hudaifi. In addressing a large gathering at Friday prayers, the imam called for the withdrawal of American troops and criticized the United States. Audiocassettes of the speech were quickly circulated around the Muslim world, and booklets translating it appeared in Pakistan in both English and Urdu.[22]

Back in Afghanistan, on May 14, following tests by the Indian government of several nuclear devices, bin Laden issued a call for a Muslim nuclear weapon, "Dangers and Signs of the Indian Nuclear Explosion." Bin Laden wrote: "The world was awakened last Tuesday by the sound of three underground nuclear Indian explosions. . . . We call upon the Muslim nation and Pakistan—its army in particular—to prepare for the jihad. This should include a nuclear force."

On May 26 bin Laden held a press conference in eastern Afghanistan at al Badr, his camp named after a key battle fought by the Prophet Muhammad.[23] According to the Pakistani journalist Ismail Khan, bin Laden's entrance was theatrical. "I could see a plume of dust coming," he said,—and then I saw three cars coming, and these hooded guys escorting Osama. Then Osama came out of the car, and the moment he stepped out there was shooting, you know, frenzied shooting. And these guys firing RPGs, rocket propelled grenades, at the mountains." Khan counted twenty-four bodyguards.

Bin Laden sat at a table flanked by his senior adviser, Ayman al-Zawahiri, and his military commander Muhammad Atef. He began by noting that a number of his followers had been arrested in Saudi Arabia in January in possession of an American Stinger missile and a number of SA-7 surface-to-air missiles, a further indication that al-Qaeda had managed to secure some of the world's most effective hand-held anti-aircraft weapons.[24] Bin Laden then announced the inauguration of his World Islamic Front. Khan said that bin Laden concluded by implying there would be some sort of action by his group: "This thing still boggles my mind, you know, he spoke of some good news in the weeks ahead."

Nine weeks later two U.S. embassies in Africa were bombed.

Also attending the conference, said Khan, were two sons of the Egyptian militant Sheikh Omar Abdel Rahman, who is serving a life sentence in the United States for his role in the plot to blow up Manhattan landmarks. The two, Asadallah and Asim, both in their mid-twenties, told Khan they would follow in the footsteps of their father and "continue the jihad." The two sons distributed a laminated card with a picture of their father praying. The card, printed in Arabic, calls on all Muslims to attack Jews and Christians: "Divide their nation, tear them to shreds, destroy their economy, burn their companies, ruin their welfare, sink their ships and kill them on land, sea and air. . . . May Allah torture them by your hands."[25]

Another Pakistani journalist at the press conference, Rahimullah Yusufzai, was able to ask bin Laden some questions privately. Asked if his family was still supporting him, the Saudi exile gave the ambiguous answers: "Blood is thicker than water," and "I am rich in my heart."

Bin Laden's finances have long been a topic of great speculation. U.S. government officials have estimated that the bin Laden family companies are worth $5 billion. For three reasons—the companies are privately held; the family is secretive; and Saudi Arabia is one of the most closed societies in the world—this is just an informed guess. The picture is further complicated by the fact that, in addition to the main family company, the Saudi Binladin Group, there are other smaller family concerns in which just a few members of the family are invested.[26] The family now has several hundred members, and some of their businesses are intertwined with those of the al-Saud ruling family itself, which generally hides behind layers of nominees to disguise its interests.

In the early 1980s, the bin Laden family moved to settle the estate of patriarch Mohammed bin Laden.[27] A source close to the family says that Osama's share of his father's estate was $35 million.[28] However by 1996 American officials were estimating his total worth at $250 million, which suggests either that he made some very good investments, or that their figures were inflated.

What is certain is that bin Laden encountered money problems while he was living in Sudan. Telling evidence comes from testimony at the embassy bombers' trial in Manhattan in 2001. A former al-Qaeda member said that at the end of 1994, there was a "crisis . . . bin Laden saying there is no money and he lost all his money." This witness said that salaries for group members were cut.[29] In 1996, bin Laden's personal pilot approached his boss for money to renew his pilot's license and was turned down by because money was too tight.[30] The pilot was also told the group could not spare five hundred dollars to help his wife pay for medical care during a complicated pregnancy. And in a 1997 letter, a key member of al-Qaeda's Kenya cell complains that he would like to visit his ill mother, but "keep in mind we only have $500."[31]

The reasons for these money woes were twofold. First, the Saudis revoked bin Laden's citizenship in 1994 and subsequently froze his considerable assets in the Kingdom. Also, while living in Sudan, from 1991 on, bin Laden sank vast sums of money into road construction, an Islamic bank, and a variety of agricultural projects—substantial investments he had to leave behind when Sudan expelled him in 1996. A Middle Eastern source familiar with bin Laden's group suggests he lost as much as $150 million.

Nonetheless, bin Laden continued to have access to considerable sums after he left Sudan for Afghanistan in 1996. A Western diplomat in Pakistan told me that bin Laden gave the Taliban "millions for construction projects" in the Kandahar area, such as a large mosque, a dam, and agricultural projects.[32] During the nineties certain family members may have still funneled him money that rightfully belonged to him, from the estate of his father. Also, according to Middle Eastern sources and senior American officials, during this period he continued to receive a flow of donations from sympathizers, particularly Saudi and Gulf businessmen.[33] One such businessman may be Khalid bin Mahfouz, who is under house arrest in Saudi Arabia for allegedly transferring funds from the giant National Commercial Bank, owned by his family, to charities that are fronts for bin Laden.[34] Finally, al-Qaeda has benefited, and may continue to benefit, from money sent to Muslim humanitarian organizations, some of which is diverted to the group.[35]

Tracing al-Qaeda's funds is complicated by the fact that the organization does not use banks that charge interest, since "usury" is prohibited by the Koran. That rules out about 99.9 percent of the world's banks. It also means that attempts by the U.S. government to go after bin Laden's assets have been largely feel-good measures, with little impact on his finances. Nevertheless, within a week of the September 11, 2001, attacks President Bush announced new measures intended to freeze bin Laden's assets. The measures are no more likely to succeed than those taken by President Clinton three years earlier, following the embassy bombing attacks in Africa.

Bin Laden has, however, used banks that operate according to Islamic principles, such as the Dubai Islamic Bank, in the United Arab Emirates, one of the first banks in the modern world to operate without charging interest.[36] In 1999, U.S. officials traveled to the UAE to talk to the government about stopping bin Laden from using the bank for transferring his funds. The UAE government subsequently took steps "to clean up the bank and its reputation."[37]

How did funds get to bin Laden in Afghanistan, a country ravaged by more than two decades of war, when the nearest functioning bank was hundreds of miles away, in neighboring Pakistan? Some monies came by courier and others arrived through the venerable *hawala* system of interlocking money changers, which has operated for centuries all over the Middle East and Asia, handling sums both large and small, on a handshake and trust.[38] Hundreds of millions of dollars are transferred through this system every year and the funds are essentially untraceable.[39]

Although Afghanistan was largely cut off from the outside world under the Taliban, the moneychangers in the capital, Kabul, ran a surprisingly sophisticated operation. On a street running along the Kabul River, dozens of tiny shops did a thriving business, their proprietors sitting cross-legged behind vast bundles of afghanis. The money changers would make deals for just about any currency in the world except the Russian ruble, which they wouldn't touch. It isn't hard to imagine one of bin Laden's aides coming down to the money market to pick up some funds after placing a few satellite phone calls from Kabul's nearby central post office, a bustling place against which the U.S. government was unlikely to launch cruise missile attacks. (Indeed, in September 1998 I exchanged telephone calls and faxes with

Muhammad Atef, a top bin Laden aide, while I was in Peshawar and he was at the Kabul post office.)

Of course, a little bit of money goes a very long way in Afghanistan, which is so poor the World Bank no longer registers its economic indicators. And weaponry and explosives are not hard to come by in a country awash in both after more than two decades of war. The United States and Saudi Arabia pumped $6 billion into arming the Afghan resistance during the war against the Soviets, and when the communists fled the country a further vast trove of weapons started circulating. Every self-respecting Afghan man is armed.

And, as bin Laden has surely grasped, terrorism is by definition "asymmetrical warfare," which does not require huge sums of money. The estimated cost of the bomb that blew up underneath the World Trade Center in 1993, killing six and causing half a billion dollars worth of damage to one of the world's best-known buildings, was $3,000.[40] When an al-Qaeda-trained terrorist was dispatched from Pakistan in 1998 to foment terrorism in the United States, he was given all of $12,000 to do it with.

Given the complexity and sophistication of the operation, and the devastation it caused, even the attacks of September 11, 2001, cost a relatively small amount—an estimated $200,000 to $500,000. The conspirators kept their operating expenses to a minimum, staying at $40-a-night motels and eating at Denny's. Their only extravagances were the tens of thousands of dollars they spent on flying lessons and sessions on passenger-jet flight simulators. Al-Qaeda was able to leverage its relatively small investment into attacks that cost the United States an estimated $100 to $300 billion in damage to the economy.

Ultimately, however, the money question is a red herring. No amount of money could possibly persuade someone to fly a passenger jet at high speed into a large building. Nor can money buy the discipline exhibited by the men who attacked the United States on September 11; none of them bragged about their plans in such a way that they got caught and none were arrested for petty crimes that might have gotten them deported. A former senior CIA official who has supervised dozens of agents marveled at the conspirators' "competency." It is bin Laden's ability to attract recruits willing to martyr themselves that is the priceless commodity in his holy war, as underlined by the attacks on two U.S. embassies in Africa in 1998, which we will examine next.

CHAPTER 6

Investigation and Retaliation: The Embassy Bombings

> *A bomb outrage to have any influence on public opinion now must go beyond the intention of vengeance or terrorism. It must be purely destructive.*
>
> —Joseph Conrad, *The Secret Agent*

> *And ye shall know the truth and the truth shall make you free.*
>
> —An inscription in the lobby of the headquarters of the CIA, from the Gospel According to John

By 1998, the stage was set for bin Laden's most spectacular terrorist attack to date: the nearly simultaneous bombings of the American embassies in Tanzania and Kenya. Al-Qaeda members referred to the Kenya attack as the Holy Kaaba operation, after the site in Mecca that is the holiest in the Muslim world; the Tanzanian attack was code-named Operation al-Aqsa, after the mosque in Jerusalem that is Islam's third holiest site.[1]

On May 28 bin Laden gave an interview to ABC News in Afghanistan in which he made it clear that, because of the American military presence in Arabia, he was calling for the deaths of all Americans. "We do not differentiate between those dressed in military uniforms and civilians: they are all targets," he said, predicting a "black day for America."[2] By then the plots to bomb the American embassies in Africa would have been in their advanced stages.

The planning for the Kenya operation had taken five years. As early as 1993, an attack on the embassy in Nairobi had been on the drawing board. In 1995, a Jordanian member of al-Qaeda, Mohamed Odeh, moved from Pakistan to Mombasa, Kenya, to set up a fishing business—the same cover the bombers of the U.S.S. *Cole* would use several years later in Yemen. That cover story would explain a lot of coming and goings at odd hours, as well as shipments from other countries.[3] Odeh quickly married a local Kenyan girl.[4] Acquaintances describe him as a devout Muslim who prayed five times a day and whose only reading material was the Koran. He hated smoking and refused to watch television.[5]

But there was more to Odeh than a devout Muslim struggling to make ends meet with his young family. He had received extensive training in weapons and explosives in Afghanistan in the early nineties. As Odeh later told an FBI agent, his Kenyan cell used code words for important communications: "working" was *jihad,* "tools" were weapons, "potatoes" were hand grenades, and "goods" were fake documents.[6]

An indication of how seriously al-Qaeda treated the Kenya operation was the dispatch to Kenya of Abu Ubaidah al-Banshiri, a former Egyptian policeman who in the early nineties functioned both as bin Laden's number two and the military commander of the group. In the spring of 1996 al-Banshiri died in a ferry accident on Lake Victoria.[7]

To replace him, one of the leaders of al-Qaeda's Kenya cell, Haroun Fazil, was dispatched to Nairobi in 1997. Fazil was born in 1972 on the Comoros Islands off the coast of Africa. A slightly built man of five foot five, Fazil left the Comoros for Pakistan at the tender age of fifteen for religious training.[8] In 1994, at age twenty-two, he attended an Afghan paramilitary training camp, and subsequently moved to Kenya.[9] Fazil, now at large, is described by U.S. prosecutors as being "very good" with computers and fluent in Swahili, Arabic, French, and English. He is also a "serious, committed" Muslim whose wife goes completely covered.[10]

Once in Nairobi, Fazil shared a house with Wadih el-Hage, who served as bin Laden's personal secretary when the Saudi militant was living in Sudan and would be convicted for his part in the conspiracy to bomb the African embassies.[11] In May 1998 Fazil rented a villa in a quiet neighborhood of Nairobi, where the bomb would be assembled.

A month or so later, two al-Qaeda colleagues purchased a Nissan truck that would carry the device.[12]

Another conspirator in the Kenya bombing was Mohamed Rashed al-'Owhali, who, like bin Laden, comes from a wealthy, prominent, devout Saudi family.[13] He was born in 1977 in Liverpool, England, where his father was studying for an M.A. Al-'Owhali was brought up in a religious manner, in his teens devouring magazines and books about jihad, such as *The Love and Hour of the Martyrs* and the *Jihad* magazine published by bin Laden's Services Office. He attended a religious university in Riyadh and considered going to fight in Bosnia or Chechnya in 1996, finally opting for training in Afghanistan.[14]

When al-'Owhali reached the Khaladan training camp in Afghanistan, he was told that he should adopt an alias like everyone else. At a certain point he was granted an audience with bin Laden, who told him to train some more. He was instructed in the black arts of hijacking and kidnappings, with priority given to planning for attacks against American military bases and embassies and the kidnapping of ambassadors. He also learned how to organize security and gather intelligence. Al-'Owhali then volunteered to fight alongside the Taliban, who were at war with Afghanistan's former rulers in the north of the country. Distinguishing himself on the battlefield, he then moved on to a month of specialized instruction in "the operation and management of the cell." The cell, he was taught, was divided into sections—intelligence, administration, planning, and finally execution. He was also taught how to do a site survey of a target using stills and video.[15]

Al-'Owhali was now judged ready for a big job. Three months before the bombing, he was finally told his mission: to be a martyr in an anti-American operation in Africa. A video was shot of him, in which he declared himself a martyr on behalf of the "Army of Liberation of the Islamic Holy Lands."[16] He attended the May 26 press conference in Afghanistan, at which bin Laden spoke of "good news" in coming weeks. As a result of the threats bin Laden made at the conference, the State Department issued a warning on June 12 that noted: "We take those threats seriously and the United States is increasing security at many U.S. government facilities in the Middle East and Asia."[17] Significantly, the State Department warning did not mention Africa.

Al-'Owhali arrived in Nairobi on August 2, five days before the attack, just as the leaders of the Kenya cell were making their plans to leave the country for Afghanistan.[18] The conspirators gathered at the Hilltop Hotel, a seedy hostelry frequented by prostitutes, for their final meetings and preparations.[19] Al-'Owhali also met the man who was to be his fellow martyr in the suicide operation, a young Saudi known as Azzam whom he had known in Afghanistan.[20] On August 4, they both reconnoitered the embassy.[21] On August 5, two days before the bombings, a fax arrived at the Cairo office of *Al-Hayat* newspaper from Ayman al-Zawahiri's Jihad group, now effectively an arm of al-Qaeda.[22] The fax said that American interests would shortly be attacked because of help the United States had given in extraditing a key member of the Jihad group from Albania to Egypt in June.[23]

The bomb was set to explode the morning of Friday, August 7, between 10:30 and 11 A.M., so that observant Muslims, who make up approximately a third of the Kenyan population, would likely be worshipping at their mosques.[24] Azzam's job was to drive the vehicle to the embassy. Al-'Owhali's was to tell the security guard to open the drop bar at the embassy gate at the rear parking lot so they could get the vehicle as close to the target as possible.[25]

On the drive to their target, Azzam and al-'Owhali chanted religious poems to keep their motivation up. As they approached the security guard, al-'Owhali leaped out of the vehicle but forgot his pistol. And so, armed only with some homemade stun grenades, he shouted at the guard to open the gate and began tossing the grenades. Seeing that the gates remained closed but that Azzam had maneuvered the vehicle close enough to the embassy to complete the mission, al-'Owhali reasoned that remaining near the bomb was no longer the act of a martyr, but was simply suicidal. He ran away as fast as he could, a luxury not enjoyed by his many victims.[26]

To grasp the carnage unleashed by the bomb, a concoction of TNT and aluminum nitrate weighing several hundred pounds, which had been put together by "Abdel Rahman," an Egyptian explosives expert for al-Qaeda, one has to understand the area of Nairobi in which it was placed. The American embassy is on the intersection of two of the busiest streets of downtown Nairobi, a city of about two million. The nearby railway station ensures a constant stream of travelers and of vendors to service them, as well as a large number of buses going to and fro. And the bomb went off in the middle of the morning on a workday. It is as if the device had been placed near Manhattan's Grand Central Terminal on a Friday morning. Or at the World Trade Center.

At approximately 10:30, the giant bomb exploded.

"The lucky are blinded and the unlucky are dead," is how Patrick Fitzgerald, the U.S. government lawyer prosecuting the embassy bombers, put it in his summation of the case.[27]

Frank Pressley managed communications at the embassy. Shortly after ten that Friday morning, he was at a meeting discussing some problems with the fax machines. He looked out the window and could see some people running and hear what sounded like firecrackers—in fact, the grenades that al-'Owhali had just thrown. Then he heard a larger explosion, and "All of a sudden I was flying. . . . I think for a few seconds I kind of lost things. I hit a wall. . . . I noticed a ceiling had gone. I tried to stand up. It was difficult. I stood up and I just could not believe what I saw. I looked around and I saw like chunks of blood or red kind of meat on the walls. . . . I lost part of my jaw. I lost a large section of my shoulder . . . I looked down and I saw bone sticking out of my shirt . . . I saw some legs, a pair of just man's legs with pants on."[28]

Sammy Nganga, a fifty-three-year-old Kenyan, was in a building adjacent to the embassy. He heard two loud explosions and then found himself buried in rubble. He looked down at his legs and saw bones protruding from them. He could not walk and, buried under a pile of debris, he could not be rescued for two days. A woman entombed next to him was not so lucky. She died before she could be freed.[29]

That morning the American ambassador was not at her usual office in the embassy but attending a meeting at the neighboring Cooperative Bank building with Kenya's minister of commerce. The aptly named Prudence Bushnell, a veteran diplomat, had long been concerned about the security of the embassy, which because of its busy downtown location was threatened not only by terrorism but also by street crime. Bushnell had cabled Washington on December 24, 1997, pointing out the threat of terrorism and the embassy's extreme vulnerability because of its location and the lack of setback from the street.[30] She wrote another letter to the U.S. secretary of state, Madeleine Albright, in April 1998, reprising her concerns.[31]

Bushnell's worst fears were, unfortunately, confirmed. The morning of the bombing she heard one loud explosion followed by another enormous one, and suddenly she was "sitting down with my hands over my head." After the second explosion the only sound the ambassador could hear was the eerie rattle of a lone teacup. She pulled herself up to walk into the stairwell, where she found many frightened people making their long and uncertain way down to the ground floor. "Some people were praying, some other people were singing hymns. . . . This huge procession of people who were bleeding all over one another. There was blood everywhere on the bannister. I could feel someone bleeding on my hair and back."[32]

Pressley, Nganga, and Bushnell escaped the bombing with their lives but with wounds both psychic and physical. Two hundred and one Kenyans and twelve Americans were not so lucky. The *New York Times* reporter covering the trial of the bombers was moved to most un-*Times*-ian prose in recounting how prosecutors read a list of the people who died in the blast: "It is shocking how long it takes to read the names and ages and sex of 213 dead people. It takes twenty minutes, give or take a minute or two . . . a death poem chilling in its utter plainness."[33] Four thousand others were injured. The death toll would have been even worse if not for the courageous actions of the security guards who refused the terrorists access to the embassy's garage, which was their ultimate goal.[34] If they had got in there, a U.S. intelligence official told me, the building would have been "leveled." As it was the blast completely obliterated a five-story building next door to the embassy that housed a secretarial college, and wrecked a twenty-five-story bank building a little farther away.[35]

Nine minutes or so after the Kenya blast—and several hundred miles to the southeast—there was another explosion, outside another American embassy. This one was in Dar es Salaam, Tanzania. The planning for the Tanzania bombing had taken several months. Of the five men indicted for a direct role in that bombing, only Khalfan Khamis Mohamed is in U.S. custody.[36] Testimony at his trial provides the fullest account of how the bombing was organized.

Mohamed was born into a family of impoverished farmers on an island off the coast of Tanzania in 1973.[37] As a teenager, he moved to Dar es Salaam to work in his brother's grocery store. By the age of twenty-one, he had saved up enough money to travel to Afghanistan for training he hoped to use in a holy war, in Bosnia or Chechnya. Although Mohamed never got used to the bitter cold of the Afghan winter, he was given the gamut of training: religious indoctrination and tuition in the use of weapons, including surface-to-air missiles and explosives.[38] Mohamed was not called upon to go to Bosnia or Chechnya but was told to leave a contact number so he could be reached in Tanzania if he was needed. Returning to Africa in 1995, he started a fishing business, like Odeh, traveling up the coast of Somalia and Kenya.

Around the time bin Laden announced his declaration of war against Americans in the spring of 1998, Mohamed was approached by someone known as "Hussain" for help with a "jihad job." Mohamed seems typical of the type of person al-Qaeda will recruit to be a go-fer on the ground, once a terrorist mission is under way. Although he admired bin Laden as "a scholar and a leader," Mohamed had never met with him and learned about his calls for attacks on Americans only from the BBC and CNN.[39] Despite the fact that he had trained in Afghan camps run by al-Qaeda, he had never even heard of the group, demonstrating that to become a member required skills and aptitude a man like Mohamed did not possess.

The former CIA official Dr. Jerrold Post, who pioneered the psychological profiling of terrorists, testified in Mohamed's defense during the death penalty phase of his trial. Over the course of several meetings, Post came away with the following insights into Mohamed—insights that may well apply to many of al-Qaeda's less sophisticated recruits: "I saw this guy as extremely deferential to religious authority and someone who had a rather empty life outside of the mosque. In the mosque he was exposed to pictures of the brutalization of Muslims going on in Bosnia and Chechnya, and he was told he must help those suffering Muslims. He went to Afghanistan for training, not just military training, but also ideological conditioning, which meant that Mohamed was indoctrinated beyond his first inchoate ideas to help suffering Muslims."

Mohamed says he was not told by more senior members of al-Qaeda what the target of their attack in Tanzania might be. This is probably true, because al-Qaeda works on a cellular basis: you are only told what you "need to know." However, it defies common sense to think that Mohamed was not generally aware that the bomb would be used against an American target.

Being fairly low on the totem pole, Mohamed was assigned to arrange transportation of bomb components and to find housing where the bomb would be constructed, preferably a single-family house with high walls, a gate, and a compound area in a neighborhood where no one could see what was going on inside the house and yard. (This is exactly the same kind of house the bombers of the U.S.S. *Cole* would use two years later to build their bomb.) Mohamed was also charged with finding refreshments for his superiors, who favored Fanta, the sickly-sweet orange drink.

The bomb consisted of four to five hundred packets of TNT each the size of a soda can, ground up and then placed in wooden crates. Mohamed helped grind up the TNT used in the device.[40] The packets of TNT were attached by wiring to oxygen-acetylene cylinders to magnify the blast, and then to a hundred detonators linked to two truck batteries. Al-Qaeda's capable Egyptian explosives expert, "Abdel Rahman," who also built the Kenya bomb, constructed this complex device without the benefit of notes, shortly before the bombing.

A few days before the attack the four more senior members of the bomb-making cell, including "Hussain" and "Abdel Rahman," skipped town, a pattern seen in the Kenya bombing and later in the attack on the U.S.S. *Cole.* Mohamed's task was to help the man who would drive the suicide–truck bomb to the embassy, "Ahmed the German," in fact an Egyptian who did not speak the local language, Swahili. Mohamed rode the bomb vehicle, a refrigerator truck used to transport meat, some way to the embassy and then got out, letting Ahmed drive it the rest of the way.

The bomb went off at 10:39, nine minutes after the Nairobi explosion.

Embassy translator Justina Mdobilu remembered: "I suddenly saw what was like a flash of lightning for a split second and what sounded like a thunderstorm for fifteen seconds. I thought I was dreaming. When I looked around me people were bleeding." Elizabeth Slater, who worked in the information section of the embassy, recalled, "It went pitch black. Coming down the stairwell there were all kinds of body parts." When Slater emerged from the building she saw a security guard in a terrible state: "He didn't have any skin left. I just wished he would hurry up and die."[41]

The bomb killed eleven Tanzanians, several of them Muslim. No Americans died in the attack.

The Arabic-language television station Al-Jazeera aired an interview with bin Laden in June 1999 in which bin Laden exulted in the Nairobi embassy bombing: "Thanks to God's grace to Muslims the blow was successful and great. They deserved it. It made them taste what we have tasted during the massacres committed in [Lebanon and Israel.]"[42]

The man who walked into the immigration section of Karachi's bustling airport in southern Pakistan early on the morning of Friday, August 7, 1998, looked like any one of the thousands of arrivals from the Gulf who land there every day. Mohamed Odeh had taken a flight out of Nairobi the day before, changing planes in Dubai and flying on to Karachi. He must have felt a sense of relief.

But something was not quite right with Odeh's passport photograph. It showed a man with a beard, when Odeh had already shaved his off a few days earlier so that he would appear less religious.[43] A Pakistani source familiar with the scene at the airport says: "At first Odeh was waved through, but then a supervisor took a second look at the passport, which was a genuine Yemeni passport, but the photo was not a match. They took Odeh aside, and later, having heard on the BBC about the bombing, they asked him: 'Are you a terrorist?' Now, most people in that situation would say: 'Of course not,' but Odeh didn't say anything. When they asked him about the bombing he said he had been involved and he started trying to persuade the immigration officer it was the right thing to do for Islam. To which the immigration officer replied, 'Not in my country.' At which point Odeh was handed over to intelligence officers, to whom he made a full confession."[44]

Pakistan's then Minister of Information, Mushahid Hussain, smilingly told me: "For once our immigration authorities were very efficient . . . he was apparently interrogated by our security people and he did make a confession." That lucky break would become a key component of the largest overseas investigation to that date undertaken by the U.S. government, and would lead U.S. investigators quickly to the conclusion that al-Qaeda was behind the embassy bombings.

The same weekend that Odeh was arrested in Pakistan, members of America's über-elite were gathering several thousand miles to the west in Italy, to celebrate a potent merger of media and politics: the nuptials of Christiane Amanpour, CNN's intrepid international correspondent, and Jamie Rubin, long the debonair public face of the U.S. State Department and a close adviser and friend of Secretary of State Albright. The ceremony was to be held outside Rome, in the medieval village of Trevignano, which hugs the hills rising out of Lake Bracciano. It was an A-list gathering of the great and the good, including not only Albright but everyone from John F. Kennedy, Jr., and his wife, Carolyn Bessette, to the CEO of Time-Warner, Gerald Levin.

Suddenly news began circulating around the wedding party that something terrible had happened at two American embassies in Africa. Albright, who had just arrived in Rome, called Rubin at the rehearsal dinner to make her apologies, then returned posthaste to Washington. The wedding went ahead as planned: for once Rubin and Amanpour did not have to react to any news except for the fact they were now man and wife.

One of Rubin's close friends, Jordan Tamagni, then a speechwriter for President Clinton, remembers there was immediately much speculation during the wedding celebrations that bin Laden was behind the bombings, but also talk of the difficulty of "getting him," if indeed he was the culprit. Another guest was Michael Sheehan, who had worked for Albright when she was U.S. ambassador to the United Nations. Albright would soon tap Sheehan for the key job of coordinator of the U.S. State Department's Office of Counterterrorism. He was in some respects an unusual choice for an appointee in the Clinton administration: a Republican and a retired Army lieutenant colonel, who had served in Panama as a Special Forces team leader.[45] But Albright trusted Sheehan and believed that he would energize the counterterrorism program. One of the wedding guests remembers that Sheehan was certain the Saudi militant was behind the bombings, saying: "It's Osama bin Laden, and we'll find him."

For the next two years Sheehan would bring his considerable energy and intellect to bear on the effort to bring bin Laden to justice. But how could he be so sure, so soon, that bin Laden was behind the embassy bombings? Although bin Laden had not yet achieved his current infamy, he had been the subject of considerable interest to the U.S. government for years. His name had first surfaced in the investigation of the 1993 bombing of the World Trade Center building where, along with approximately one hundred others, he had been named as an unindicted co-conspirator—prosecutor-speak for "We don't know what to make of this guy's involvement but he seems to be implicated in some way." Bin Laden was however, still not on the radar screen of the Congressional Task Force on Terrorism, which in September 1993 published a list of several dozen "prominent figures in Islamist terrorism" from which bin Laden's name was conspicuously absent.[46]

During the 1995 trial of Sheikh Omar Abdel Rahman and nine others subsequently convicted in a plot to blow up New York City landmarks, U.S. prosecutors asked at least one of the witnesses if he knew of bin Laden. In 1996 a grand jury was empaneled in New York to investigate the Saudi militant, by the same U.S. Attorney's office that had successfully prosecuted the World Trade Center bombers. Assigned to investigate bin Laden were FBI agents who had investigated the first World Trade Center case. The initial charges against bin Laden were the relatively narrow ones, based on his public statements, of soliciting violence against American soldiers.[47]

The Central Intelligence Agency had also paid close attention to bin Laden for several years. To drive to CIA headquarters from Washington, D.C., you cross the Potomac River and turn on to the George Washington Parkway. Unlike most highways in the eastern United States, this is a road of extraordinary natural beauty, lush and heavily wooded, hugging the gently meandering contours of the Potomac. Within fifteen minutes you are in Langley, Virginia, where the CIA does little to announce its presence. You turn off the parkway and arrive at a security booth, where you are asked to show your driver's license. It helps if you have an appointment. Satisfied that you are not a communist or a terrorist, the beefy security guards let you proceed to the main building, which would look at home in the science park of a modern university.

The end of the Cold War required a radical rethinking of the CIA's modus operandi, and the Agency has now embraced new missions and a culture of relative openness. (A sign of the times is the well-appointed gift store on the ground floor of the Agency, where you can buy all manner of tchotchkes, such as CIA coffee mugs and key rings.) In the past decade the Agency has significantly expanded the resources it devotes to the wars on drugs and terrorism—colloquially known as "drugs and thugs." One of the beneficiaries of the expanding antiterrorism budget is the CIA's Counterterrorist Center (CTC), which was founded in 1986.[48]

Initially, analysts at the CIA believed that bin Laden was merely a "Gucci terrorist"—one who financed some acts of terrorism but had no larger operational role. After the first World Trade Center attack, their views changed. Because bin Laden's name kept cropping up in that investigation and later terrorist acts, such as the 1995 bombing of a facility housing American soldiers in Saudi Arabia, the CTC decided to form a separate unit devoted to tracking him. Unlike other such units, the bin Laden task force is allowed to act something like an overseas station of the CIA and does not have to consult much with the bureaucracy in Washington.

The CTC does more than analyze data about terrorists; the center is also staffed by officers of the CIA's Directorate of Operations, and information collected about bin Laden's network is used by operatives in the field to disrupt his organization's operations.

The CTC draws from many other agencies' areas of expertise in the course of its investigations. Most significantly, the CTC works closely with the FBI; for example, the official who ran CTC in recent years once worked at the Bureau. Given the history of animosity between the two organizations, this is a useful development. In addition to the FBI, an alphabet soup of other government agencies is represented within CTC, including the National Security Agency, which eavesdrops on telephone conversations around the globe; the Secret Service; the Federal Aviation Agency; the Department of Defense; the State Department; and the Bureau of Alcohol, Tobacco, and Firearms.[49]

Despite all these resources, developing information about bin Laden's network has proven difficult. In the 1970s and 1980s American agencies gathered intelligence about terrorists sponsored by states such as Syria, Libya, and Iran. Groups such as the Abu Nidal Organization (ANO) were highly structured and could therefore be analyzed in a systematic way. The bin Laden network is by contrast a loosely af-filiated transnational group with a more diffuse organizational struc-ture that makes it hard to penetrate—although the U.S. government has had some success in recruiting former al-Qaeda members as in-formants, an easier proposition than inserting a spy into its ranks. Fur-ther complicating matters is the strong religious orientation of bin Laden's followers. As one U.S. official told me. "In the old days I could have a drink with a secular terrorist—there is no way with the bin Laden guys. Also, those guys have a shared history and outsiders are viewed with suspicion."

Aside from the fact that the CIA and FBI had been investigating bin Laden for several years, there was another compelling reason that American officials immediately suspected al-Qaeda in the Africa bombings. They had been investigating a bin Laden cell in Kenya for over a year and had already received specific warnings of a possible at-tack on the Nairobi embassy. On August 21, 1997, almost exactly a year before the embassy bombing, an FBI agent accompanied by Kenyan police performed a search of Wadih el-Hage's house in Nairobi. They seized an Apple PowerBook and various address books and diaries. A computer technician made a "mirror image" of the com-puter's hard drive,[50] on which was found a letter from one of the lead-ers of al-Qaeda's Kenya cell. The letter described the existence of the cell and the author's awareness of bin Laden's call for attacks on Amer-icans—although the letter writer noted that, as yet, he and his confed-erates were unaware of their exact mission in Kenya, since they were simply "implementers."[51]

In addition, nine months before the Nairobi attack, an Egyptian named Mustafa Mahmoud Said Ahmed walked into the embassy and told intelligence officials there was a plan afoot to use stun grenades to divert the attention of embassy security guards so that a truck bomb could be driven into the underground parking garage of the embassy, precisely al-Qaeda's plans for attacking the building. Ahmed worked for a bin Laden company in Kenya, so he had some basis for his infor-mation.[52] Ahmed's warning was ignored, probably because of the sheer volume of credible threats against U.S. overseas installations that come in every day.

Besides the quick arrest of Odeh in Pakistan, a further break in the embassy bombing case was the decision by Mohamed al-'Owhali not to commit suicide in the Kenya attack. Instead, he checked himself into a local hospital, where he was treated for various minor injuries. On August 12, he was arrested by Kenyan officials for not having proper identification papers, and he was immediately handed over to FBI agents.[53] Over the course of a week of interrogations, al-'Owhali confessed to his role in the bombing.[54]

The arrests and confessions of al-'Owhali and Odeh pointed definitively to al-Qaeda's role in the embassy attacks—in effect, acts of war against the United States. American officials believed they deserved military retaliation. They dubbed that response Operation Infinite Reach, but it might just as well have been called Operation Infinite Overreach. Just as there had been attacks on U.S. embassies in two countries, there would be attacks against bin Laden-related targets in two countries. Tit for tat. Twice.

Infinite Reach underlines the strengths and weaknesses of intelligence-gathering about al-Qaeda, as well as the limits of certain types of military actions against bin Laden's network. (No doubt Bush administration officials have Operation Infinite Reach very much in mind as they embarked on what appears at this writing to be a long-range and multifaceted plan of action in response to the events of September 11.)

On the clear, hot morning of August 20, 1998, the White House press corps was on Martha's Vineyard, the holiday island off the coast of Massachusetts. President Clinton had three days earlier given his evasive testimony in the Monica Lewinsky case, and had apologized, sort of, to the American people for misleading them about his relationship with the young intern. The big story was done, and now Clinton was on the Vineyard for his summer break. The journalists expected nothing more than a quiet day, during which the Duffer-in-Chief might hit the links and later hang out with some of his celebrity friends—his usual vacation routine. So they sat down to watch a movie—which, in an almost too perfect case of art anticipating life, was *Wag the Dog*, in which a president concocts a fake war with a country no one knows about (in this case Albania) to distract the public's attention from some presidential hanky-panky.

At about one P.M., Clinton's spokesman, Mike McCurry, interrupted the journalists to say the president was going to make a national security announcement. Around two, a solemn Clinton announced to the assembled reporters that cruise missiles had been launched at bin Laden targets in Afghanistan and Sudan in retaliation for his role in the bombings of the two embassies in Africa.[55]

The president quickly flew back to the White House, where he addressed the nation from the Oval Office. "Our target was terror," he said, "Our mission was clear; to strike at the network of radical groups affiliated with and funded by Osama bin Laden, perhaps the preeminent organizer and financier of international terrorism in the world today. . . . Earlier today, the United States carried out simultaneous strikes against terrorist facilities and infrastructure in Afghanistan. Our forces targeted one of the most active terrorist bases in the world. It contained key elements of bin Laden's network and infrastructure and has served as the training camp for literally thousands of terrorists around the globe. We have reason to believe that a gathering of key terrorist leaders was to take place there today, thus underscoring the urgency of our actions. Our forces also attacked a factory in Sudan associated with the bin Laden network. The factory was involved in the production of materials for chemical weapons."

The strikes against bin Laden were highly unusual. The Clinton administration had previously launched attacks against places associated with Saddam Hussein and Slobodan Milosevic, but these were leaders of countries more or less at war with the United States. Now an *individual* and his followers were the subject of missile attacks directed at two sovereign nations where al-Qaeda had some presence.

In a nod to the 1976 executive order banning any U.S. government employee from conspiring or engaging in assassination, senior officials were careful to say that the attacks were designed to hit bin Laden's "infrastructure" and that he himself was not a target. But this was Jesuitical hair-splitting, given the president's own announcement that the strikes were timed to coincide with a supposed meeting of al-Qaeda's leaders.[56]

A senior Pakistani official told me that the United States gave Pakistan no warning that its airspace would be used for the cruise missile attacks on Afghanistan. This official said that American warships had been maneuvering near Pakistani waters and conducting missile tests as early as April. Shortly after the missiles were fired, an American general visiting Pakistan informed government officials about the strikes so that the Pakistanis would know that they were not under attack by India, their longtime enemy.

A senior U.S. official described the Clinton administration's actions during the days leading up to the strikes. Within a week of the attacks, by August 14, U.S. officials had determined that bin Laden was responsible for the embassy bombings and had formulated a plan of action.[57] President Clinton's advisers told him that they had cracked the case and that he had a few alternatives—to continue pursuing a legal case against the Saudi militant, to retaliate militarily, or to proceed down both tracks. The advisers also told the president that intelligence indications suggested another bin Laden attack in the works.[58] The advisers said they anticipated a conference of the bin Laden leadership in Afghanistan on August 20 and that he had no choice but to do the strike on the day of the meeting. Clinton, the official said, knew he was going to take criticism of the *Wag the Dog* variety, but decided to go ahead anyway.

At that point, the CIA and the Pentagon came up with a target list. The first target was the group of bin Laden camps in eastern Afghanistan. The camp complex, near the eastern town of Khost, consisted of six bases, known as al-Badr 1, al-Badr 2, al-Farooq, Khalid bin Walid, Abu Jindal, and Salman Farsi.[59] The whole complex could accommodate up to six hundred fighters.[60] The second was the alleged chemical-weapons plant in Khartoum, Sudan.

The Afghan camps were indeed being used by al-Qaeda for training, and had been for years.[61] In Pakistan, shortly after the strikes, I interviewed Saifullah Gondal, a student of Islamic law in Islamabad, who had attended one of the training facilities at Khost in 1992. Together with about a hundred other Pakistani students, he had taken a fifteen-day course consisting of religious instruction in the morning and weapons training in the afternoon. I was also shown photographs of military training (including the use of tanks) at the camp complex, taken by Pakistani journalists in 1997.

Twenty or so people were killed in the strike against the camps, among them not only Afghans but also Pakistanis.[62] Also among the dead were at least six of bin Laden's followers: three Yemenis, two Egyptians, and a Turk, a toll underlining the fact that the camps were used by a variety of different nationalities. Still, the operation was essentially a failure: at the time of the strike, bin Laden and other al-Qaeda leaders were elsewhere. So much for the intelligence that key terrorist operatives would be in the camp on August 20. (The faulty information probably originated from Pakistani government sources.)[63]

There were several reasons that al-Qaeda's leaders were not at the Khost camp complex. The evacuation of American diplomatic personnel from neighboring Pakistan and the evacuation of all foreigners from Kabul in the days before the attack had tipped off bin Laden's followers that something was afoot.[64] Moreover, Mohamed Odeh told an FBI agent that on August 6, 1998, a day before the bombings of the embassies in Africa, news came from Afghanistan that: "All [bin Laden's] people have been evacuated [because] we're expecting retaliation from the U.S. Navy."[65] The al-Qaeda leadership was savvy enough to realize that American retaliation would not come in the form of a Special Forces commando raid against their camps, nor in the form of U.S. Air Force bombing raids—both of which might incur the type of casualties the Pentagon hastened to avoid at the time—but in the shape of cruise missile attacks launched from American destroyers plying the Arabian Sea, hundreds of miles away.

And there was a final compelling reason that bin Laden was not in the camps at Khost. He had very publicly given a press conference at the Khost camp on May 26 and an extensive interview to ABC News in the same location two days later, nine weeks before the embassy bombings. Bin Laden is a fairly shrewd operator, so after spending five years planning the attacks on the U.S. embassies, just about the last place he would be likely to hang his turban is the site from which he had told the world about his plans to attack Americans. Indeed, as early as May 16 he told a Pakistani journalist that he had "information that Americans are planning to hit my bases so I am very careful."

An Afghan reporter working for a Western news agency arrived at the camp complex a day after the strikes and said it was a scene of utter destruction; all the buildings, including the camp mosque, had collapsed. Remaining at the complex were sixty or seventy men who had escaped death. In their rage, they turned on the reporter and smashed his satellite phone and cameras. At one point it seemed he might be executed, but he was saved by the intervention of a senior Taliban official.

Two or three of the American missiles that landed in Afghanistan did not explode, Afghan and Pakistani-based sources say that the Taliban sold one or more of the unexploded cruise missiles to Chinese officials who were interested in reverse-engineering them—that is, taking them apart to learn how they work. Taliban officials would not comment on the story, although they did not deny it.

After the cruise missile attacks, I interviewed Habib Ahmed, a nineteen-year-old Pakistani who was severely burned. I talked to him at his hospital bed in Peshawar, surrounded by his understandably irate friends and family. The young man described what it was like to be on the receiving end of fifty or so Tomahawk cruise missiles: "After evening prayer we were studying the Koran. When we finished we went to sleep. Then we heard a big noise. When we went out of the mosque we saw a missile attacking the camp. Many people were there. They were crying after they were injured. The Holy Korans were burned. We were very shocked by this."

Ahmed claimed that all he was doing at the camp was receiving Koranic instruction, although it hardly seemed necessary to travel to Afghanistan to study the Koran when there are literally thousands of religious schools in Pakistan. Ahmed said he attended Khalid bin Walid, a camp affiliated with both bin Laden and Harakat ul-Mujahideen, a Kashmiri militant group.

Although the strikes in Afghanistan did hit bin Laden's camps, the only casualties were locals and some low-level militants. And the camps themselves were made of the stone, timber, and mud typical of Afghan villages, making it easy to quickly rebuild them. Indeed, within two weeks of the strike, the Pakistani journalist Rahimullah Yusufzai visited the complex and reported: "Life is back to normal at the simply-built camps." [66]

Moreover, the notion that bin Laden could somehow be intimidated by cruise missile attacks shows a misunderstanding of his psychology. He and his immediate followers spent three years fighting the Soviets in Afghanistan, making a point of remaining on the front lines, under constant threat by helicopter gunships. Bin Laden appears to revel in his close calls with death, saying: "Once I was only thirty meters from the Russians and they were trying to capture me. I was under bombardment, but I was so peaceful in my heart that I fell asleep."[67] As his friend Khaled al-Fawwaz put it to me after the unsuccessful cruise missile attacks, for bin Laden and his men "this attack was not a big deal, they are very much used to SCUD missile attacks from the Russians. Those kind of people actually *enjoy* this kind of thing."[68]

If the attacks on the Afghan camps were essentially a dud, the strike on the alleged chemical weapons plant in Sudan was an intelligence fiasco, a dress rehearsal for the later inadvertent bombing of the Chinese embassy in Belgrade during the 1999 Kosovo war. Under a hail of a dozen or so cruise missiles, the al-Shifa plant was flattened, leaving a pile of smoking rubble and twisted girders. The Sudanese Information Minister had no problems quickly making connections of the *Wag the Dog* variety, going on television to denounce Clinton as a "proven liar" and a man "with more than a hundred girlfriends."[69]

A senior U.S. official defended the Sudan attack on the following grounds: bin Laden maintained personnel and companies in Sudan and had brokered discussions between Sudan and Iraq to improve military cooperation; the plant manager was living in bin Laden's former house; and the facility was under heavy guard by the Sudanese military. The CIA had sent an agent into Sudan who collected a soil sample at the plant that showed traces of the chemical agent EMPTA, which has no use other than as a precursor of the nerve gas VX. The official said that the chemical analysis of the sample was convincing, but it did not stand alone. For four years bin Laden had been trying to acquire chemical weapons. The official concluded, "for me the strike was a no-brainer."

That official's rationale reflects the administration's public assertions: that the plant made chemical weapons, was heavily guarded, was part of Sudan's military-industrial complex, and was tied to both Iraq and bin Laden.[70] All those assertions would turn out to be false or seriously flawed.

It is impossible to prove a negative, but the evidence suggests that the plant simply produced pharmaceuticals. At two separate laboratories, Tom Tullius, a Boston University professor of chemistry, analyzed thirteen soil samples taken from several different sites at the plant. Tullius turned up no evidence of EMPTA, although his tests did find traces of ibuprofen![71]

Sudan is an economic basket case, so the plant, which produced half of the country's medicines, was something of a showpiece and was regularly toured by visiting dignitaries and businessmen.[72] One of the visitors was Peter Cockburn, a British industrialist, who had stopped in several times in the months before the bombing and noticed nothing out of the ordinary. Furthermore, the plant was not heavily guarded and there were no "no-go" areas inside the plant.[73] Henry Jobe, the American chemical engineer who designed the plant, says it wasn't suitable as a "dual-use" facility making both medicines and chemical weapons. The German ambassador to Sudan wired Bonn after the bombing to tell his government that the United States had made a mistake.[74] A British newspaper headline put it rather nicely: "Whoops! What a Cock-up!"[75]

The charge that the plant was a bin Laden front is dubious. Salah Idris, who bought the plant for $28 million some months before the attack, says he has never met or done business with bin Laden. Again, it is impossible to prove a negative, but Idris hired the prestigious investigative firm of Kroll Associates to examine his claims. Kroll turned up only the following connection between Idris and bin Laden: Abdul Baset Hamza, a mutual business acquaintance in Sudan. Hamza was a colonel in the Sudanese military who was active in the construction and telecommunication businesses.[76]

There are further holes in the government's case. At the time of the attack, the U.S. government was not aware that Idris had bought the plant.[77] The previous owners of the plant had included the Baaboud family, a family of Hadrami-Yemeni origin, like the bin Ladens. The Baabouds had done some business with bin Laden, but that's hardly surprising since he was one of the biggest businessmen in Sudan during the early and middle 1990s.[78] The plant did indeed do business with Iraq, but only for veterinary medicines, a shipment of which the United Nations had approved in January 1998. In Khartoum, bin Laden rented a house owned by someone who became the general manager of the al-Shifa plant *after* the Saudi exile had been forced to leave Sudan.[79] This appears to be a coincidence: the Sudanese business elite is very small. Or it could mean something more sinister—*if* you accept the dubious premise that the plant was manufacturing chemical weapons.[80]

A careful study of the al-Shifa plant by a researcher at the Monterey Institute's Center for Nonproliferation Studies concluded: "it remains *possible* that at some point in time, a small quantity of a VX precursor chemical was produced or stored in Shifa or transported through or near it. However, the balance of available evidence suggests that the facility probably had no role whatsoever in CW [chemical weapons] development."[81]

Finally, a former United Nations official familiar with Iraqi weapons programs told me: "We were tracking Iraqi involvement in the military in Sudan. We had a watch list of Iraqis in Sudan in relation to this. If that plant was involved, we would have been watching it [and we weren't]." Curiously, the U.S. government showed a marked lack of enthusiasm for a possible U.N. investigation into whether the al-Shifa plant was producing chemical weapons at the same time that it was enthusiastically bombing Iraq for not cooperating fully with U.N. inspectors seeking to determine Iraq's chemical weapons capacity.[82]

Immediately after the attack, the U.S. government froze $24 million of Idris's money in an American bank on the grounds that he might have terrorist links, only to unfreeze the funds eight months later.[83] U.S. officials continued to maintain that this was not an acknowledgment that Idris was innocent of consorting with terrorists and producing weapons of mass destruction. Instead of issuing him the apology he seemed to deserve, they made further aspersions on his character (off the record, of course).[84]

Although the strikes were hardly a success, a Western diplomat based in Pakistan told me soon afterward that they had served a useful purpose because they showed "we have reach. They served as a marker—fuck with us and you have a major problem."

The attacks, however, had a major unintended consequence: they turned bin Laden from a marginal figure in the Muslim world into a global celebrity. When I visited Pakistan a couple of weeks after the U.S. strikes, two instant biographies about bin Laden were already on sale in the bookshops of Islamabad. Osama became a common name for newly born sons in Pakistan.[85] Maulana Sami ul-Haq, a corpulent cleric who runs what is probably Pakistan's largest religious academy, explained that the strikes had made bin Laden "a symbol for the whole Islamic world. Against all those outside powers who were trying to crush Muslims. He is the courageous one who raised his voice against them. He's a hero to us, but it is America that first made him a hero."

CHAPTER 7

The American Connection:
From Brooklyn to Seattle

> *"We have to be terrorists. . . . The Great Allah said, 'Against
> them make ready your strength to the utmost of your power
> including steeds of war, to strike terror [into the hearts of]
> the enemies of Allah and your enemies.' "*
>
> —Sheikh Omar Abdel Rahman, the spiritual leader of
> the Egyptian members of al-Qaeda, to his followers
> in Los Angeles, December 1992

In November 1986 Ali Mohamed enlisted in the U.S. Army for a three-year stint. His first assignment was to a supply company at Fort Bragg, North Carolina, headquarters of the U.S. Army's secretive, elite Special Forces. The crème de la crème of the U.S. military, these soldiers attend the John F. Kennedy Special Warfare Center for classes on such esoteric subjects as "psy-ops" (how to conduct psychological operations against an enemy); and it's a measure of Ali Mohamed's talent and dedication that within a year or so, as a sergeant, he was teaching seminars there himself.[1] Special Forces soldiers are dispatched to tackle the riskiest missions: During the Gulf War, its units went deep inside Iraq, where they guided American bombers to targets, and they were quickly deployed to Afghanistan to hunt down bin Laden following the Trade Center attacks.[2] So Fort Bragg is pretty much the last place in the world you'd expect to find a bin Laden operative. Yet Ali Mohamed, it turns out, was an indispensable player in al-Qaeda.

This is emblematic of one of al-Qaeda's most alarming achievements: its ability to stretch its tentacles into the heart of a variety of American communities and institutions. Indeed, over the last two decades the United States has proved one of al-Qaeda's most useful bases of operations, serving as a fund-raising, recruiting, and training ground and base for dozens of its members.

Ali Mohamed is a chilling illustration of how easily a "sleeper" bin Laden agent was able to penetrate one of the U.S. military's most secretive establishments and plot terrorist acts on American soil. More chilling still is that the trajectory of his life—from his birth in Egypt in 1952 to his arrest in the United States in 1998—is the template for those al-Qaeda recruits who burrowed deeply into their American communities, biding their time with extraordinary patience as they hatched their plans for the devastating attacks of September 11, 2001.[3]

Mohamed was a man of unusual worldliness. After attending high school in his Egyptian hometown of Alexandria, he went on to the military academy in Cairo; he then spent thirteen years in the Egyptian army between 1971 and 1984, rising to the rank of major.[4] While in the army he also studied psychology at the University of Alexandria, receiving a B.A. in 1980.[5]

At some point in the early eighties he proffered his services as an informant to the CIA, the first of his several attempts to work for the U.S. government. The Agency was in contact with him for a few weeks but broke off relations after determining he was "unreliable."[6] That would turn out to be a masterful understatement, as Mohamed was already a member of Egypt's terrorist Jihad group.[7]

After being discharged from the Egyptian army in 1984, Mohamed engaged in what American political operatives call opposition research—a job in the counterterrorism department of EgyptAir.[8] The following year he moved to the United States, where he was unemployed for several months before landing a job as a security officer with American Protective Services in Sunnyvale, California. During this period he married Linda Sanchez, an American medical technician. His marriage and enlistment in the Army would speed the process of acquiring American citizenship—a valued prize for al-Qaeda members. And a U.S. passport, he told a colleague at the Special

Warfare Center, would enable him to travel freely around the Middle East.[9]

Mohamed's record at Fort Bragg reveals a man of considerable intelligence and versatility. In addition to his native Arabic, he spoke English, French, and Hebrew, and he found time in his off-duty moments to pursue a Ph.D. in Islamic studies.[10] He was clearly a committed soldier: he enrolled in paratrooper training, received a commendation for "exceptional performance" on his physical fitness test, and won a badge for his expert use of the M-16 rifle.[11] His superiors were impressed, noting in his record that his personal conduct was "beyond reproach" and that he was both "consistently accomplished" and "totally responsible."

Mohamed's teaching career at the Special Warfare Center was a consequence of his familiarity with the Middle East. As an assistant instructor, he helped the seminar director prepare classes about the region's politics, history, culture, and armed forces.[12] His supervisor, Norvell De Atkine, remembers Mohamed as "a good soldier, quite intelligent. If we had a lecture on Islam, rather than me give it, I would have him teach that particular class."[13] Mohamed also translated military briefings from English into Arabic and vice versa, and made a series of videotapes about the Middle East for use by students at the Special Warfare Center. According to his military record, he also gave an "outstanding" class on Spetsnaz, the elite Soviet Special Forces units then deployed in Afghanistan. That was because his expertise was based on personal experience: he'd used a leave from the Army to fight alongside bin Laden's men in Afghanistan.

In the videotapes Mohamed prepared for his classes, he appears neatly dressed in a dark business suit, blue shirt, and black tie. One's first impression is that he seems intense and intelligent, a commanding presence at six foot one and 190 pounds.[14] The second is that his views on the Middle East, delivered in accented but fluent English, were hardly in sync with U.S. policies.

On one videotape his supervisor, De Atkine, asks Mohamed, "Why is Israel a threat to the Arab world? I mean, it only has, like, three million people"—to which Mohamed replies, "Actually, it's not the three million people. Actually Israel is trying to enlarge."

"Do you really believe that, Ali?" De Atkine asks.

"I believe in it because Israel is a major threat for our existence in the area,"[15] says Mohamed, adding, "We do not accept no peace . . . No international conferences. Nothing, no compromises."[16]

Four of Mohamed's superior officers say that he made no secret of his deeply felt Islamist beliefs and even claimed to have trained militants in Lebanon.[17] But his opinions did not bother his supervisor. "He told me pretty near the same things that I had heard from my time in the Middle East—almost eight years—that I heard every day, which was that American policy is dead wrong," said De Atkine.[18]

Lieutenant Colonel Robert Anderson, Mohamed's overall boss, did find some of his beliefs disturbing. Anderson recalled being particularly struck by a conversation with Mohamed about the Egyptian president Anwar Sadat, who had been assassinated in 1981 for making a peace deal with Israel. "I told him that I thought that Anwar Sadat was a true patriot for Egypt," Anderson said. "With a very cold stare, he said to me, 'No, he had to go, he was a traitor.' "[19] Indeed, Anderson says, Mohamed told him that he had belonged to the same army unit as Sadat's assassin.[20]

Anderson was further troubled by the fact that Mohamed used his leave to make an unauthorized trip to Afghanistan in 1988 to fight against the Soviets. "For him to go to Afghanistan as a United States soldier, he would have had to have the approval of his commander, and of course we would not approve that," Anderson noted.[21] When Mohamed returned bearing trophies, among them a tactical map, "He also brought back a Russian Special Forces belt and gave it to me," said Anderson. "He told me that he had personally killed the Russian soldier that had the belt on."[22] Anderson told me that he was sufficiently concerned about Mohamed's political views and unauthorized travel to take the unusual step of filing two intelligence reports on the subject.[23] But no one ever followed up, and a Fort Bragg spokesperson says the reports cannot be located.[24]

Anderson is convinced that Mohamed could have gotten into the U.S. and arrived at Fort Bragg only if someone at the CIA or State Department had signed off on his visa: "I can't imagine in my wildest dreams how this would happen, other than with assistance," he said.[25] The CIA will only acknowledge its brief contact with Mohamed in the early eighties, before his arrival in the United States. *The Boston*

Globe, however, reported that Mohamed did in fact benefit from a visa waiver program for intelligence assets.[26] If this is true, the CIA must have hoped—ironically enough—to use him as an informant someday.

Mohamed received an honorable discharge from the U.S. Army in 1989, but his involvement in military matters did not end. While engaged in what appeared to be a pedestrian existence (running an import-export business), he was living a life of high intrigue. Mohamed traveled back and forth to the war zones of Afghanistan, and, in the United States, gave courses on basic military tactics to Islamist militants based in New York.[27]

Those militants were associated with the Alkhifa Refugee Center, in Brooklyn, which was incorporated as "Afghan Refugee Services, Inc.," in December 1987 to "provide for the needs and welfare of Afghan people particularly the refugees due to the Soviet invasion."[28] However, Nejat Khalili, an Afghan-American who was an active fundraiser for Afghan refugees in the eighties, said in 1993 that he had never heard of the Alkhifa center.[29] In fact, during its six years of operation, Alkhifa—the name means "the struggle" in Arabic—had little to do with either Afghans or refugees. Instead, it was the recruitment hub for U.S.-based Muslims seeking to fight the Soviets. As many as two hundred fighters were funneled through the center to Afghanistan.[30]

One of Ali Mohamed's Alkhifa-based friends was El Sayyid Nosair, an Egyptian-American who was later convicted of weapons charges in the assassination of the Jewish militant Rabbi Meir Kahane at a Manhattan hotel in 1990.[31] Mohamed had taught Nosair field-survival tactics and how to handle weapons.[32] After the Kahane assassination, police retrieved a trove of U.S. Army documents from Nosair's New Jersey apartment given to him by Mohamed.[33] Some were marked "John F. Kennedy Special Warfare Center, Special Forces Airborne." The documents, neatly translated into Arabic, dealt mostly with military training, but also included memorandums concerning the disposition of American military units in the Middle East. Also recovered from Nosair's apartment were Arabic bomb-making manuals and Arabic writings that referred, somewhat elliptically, to plans to attack the World Trade Center.[34] Unfortunately, investigators did not get around to translating those documents until after the World Trade Center was bombed in 1993.[35]

At the same time that Ali Mohamed was providing weapons train-ing in the New York area to some of the other militants who fre-quented the Alkhifa center, he was racking up frequent flyer miles for al-Qaeda—making trips to Egypt, Saudi Arabia, Kenya, Tanzania, Uganda, United Arab Emirates, Morocco, Sudan, Pakistan, Af-ghanistan, and Somalia.[36] He traveled wherever he was needed. In 1991, he went to Afghanistan to arrange for bin Laden's transfer to Sudan.[37] In September 1992, he was again in Afghanistan, training commanders of al-Qaeda in the eastern Khost area.[38] He also taught al-Qaeda members a range of surveillance techniques, from how to operate hidden cameras to how to read maps and blueprints—tech-niques they practiced on bridges and stadiums.[39] In 1993, using his leather import-export business as a cover, Mohamed went to Kenya, where he scoped out the U.S. embassy in Nairobi and reported back to bin Laden. After an assassination attempt against bin Laden in Sudan in 1994, Mohamed traveled to Khartoum to train his body-guards. That same year, bin Laden sent Mohamed to Djibouti to sur-vey French military bases and the American embassy for possible attacks.[40]

Between 1992 and 1997, when he wasn't flying around the world attending to his jihad duties, Mohamed lived in Santa Clara, Califor-nia. The woman who owned his apartment described him as unfail-ingly polite, with nothing about him that was out of the ordinary. In 1997, Mohamed and his wife moved to Sacramento, where he joined Valley Media, a wholesaler of recorded music and videos, as a com-puter network support specialist.[41] A search of his Sacramento house in August 1998 yielded documents on assassination techniques, the surveillance of military and government targets, the planning of ter-rorist operations, and the use of explosives.[42]

Incredibly, while performing missions for al-Qaeda. Mohamed con-tinued to apply for work in U.S. government agencies. In 1993, he ap-proached the FBI for a job as a translator, and in 1995 sought security clearance to work as a guard at a company doing classified work for the Department of Defense.[43] In his interview for the FBI job, he appar-ently teased the Bureau with his inside knowledge, telling agents that bin Laden's group aimed to overthrow the Saudi government. In an-other FBI interview, in 1997, he admitted that he had trained bin

Laden's bodyguards. During phone calls with an FBI agent in August 1998, Mohamed said he knew who had carried out the embassy bombings in Kenya and Tanzania but would not provide their names.

In September, 1998 Ali Mohamed's double life came to an abrupt halt when he was arrested on suspicion of being part of al-Qaeda's conspiracy to kill Americans.[44] Although apparently a member of bin Laden's inner circle, he was not, as it turned out, sufficiently zealous to martyr himself for the cause, opting for a plea agreement rather than a life in prison protecting al-Qaeda's secrets. Exactly what sort of game Mohamed was playing remains unclear—as do, for that matter, his larger motivations. Perhaps he was simply attracted to intrigue and derring-do, which, working for both bin Laden and the U.S. military, he certainly had. Whatever the case, he might ultimately prove to be the best witness yet against the top man himself: Ali Mohamed links bin Laden directly to the embassy bombings in Africa.

Meanwhile, Muslims active at Brooklyn's Alkhifa center were openly referring to it as "the Services Office," which was the name of the organization bin Laden had funded in Pakistan to provide support for those fighting the jihad in Afghanistan—and which had evolved into al-Qaeda.[45] The Brooklyn organization had become bin Laden's main American branch and a hub for outposts in Atlanta, Chicago, Connecticut, and New Jersey. (In all, recruitment for the Afghan jihad took place in twenty-six states.)[46] Bin Laden's mentor, Abdullah Azzam, the charismatic cofounder of the original Services Office, was a frequent visitor, raising money and recruiting men in lectures at the mosque next door. He can be heard in a 1988 video telling a crowd of several hundred that "blood and martyrdom are the only way to create a Muslim society."[47]

The Alkhifa Center seemed an unlikely jumping-off point to Paradise, located as it was on a gritty stretch of Brooklyn's Atlantic Avenue in a dingy three-story building above the unfortunately named Fu King Chinese restaurant. But it was certainly a lively place. From its inception in 1987, it was run by Mustafa Shalabi, a devout Muslim from Egypt who had been trained as a chemist before moving in 1980 to New York, where he started an electrical contracting business.[48]

One of Shalabi's aides at the center was the future al-Qaeda member Jamal al-Fadl, who arrived in the United States in 1986 on a student visa and swiftly married an American woman.[49] Another was Mahmud Abouhalima, one of the 1993 World Trade Center bombers.

Shalabi was instrumental in helping the militant Egyptian cleric Sheikh Omar Abdel Rahman get settled in the United States in 1990, leasing a house for him in the Bay Ridge area of Brooklyn.[50] That would prove a mistake: As soon as the sheikh began to preach at the mosque adjoining the center, the two men clashed over how to spend Alkhifa's money.[51] "When the Soviets withdrew [from Afghanistan in 1989] there was still some money left over," explained the Egyptian academic Saad Eddin Ibrahim, whose first cousin married Shalabi in the mid-eighties. "Shalabi, a very principled guy, said we now have to consult with the people who donated the money [about what should be done with it]. Rahman was very unhappy about this because he wanted to support other causes, and that's where the tension began."

Sheikh Rahman wanted the money to go to the cause dearest to his heart, the Egyptian jihad, while Shalabi wanted to keep funneling it to groups vying for control of Afghanistan. Eventually, Sheikh Rahman began preaching that Shalabi was a "bad Muslim," and signs appeared in New York–area mosques accusing him of financial mismanagement of the center.[52]

Those accusations appear to have been Shalabi's death sentence: on March 1, 1991, someone entered his Coney Island, "gated community" (where visitors had to be buzzed in by a security guard) and his apartment (the door of which was not forced) and fatally stabbed him.[53] The murder remains unsolved.

Not surprisingly, some in Brooklyn's Muslim community and in Shalabi's family believe he was murdered by a member of Sheikh Rahman's circle. Ibrahim told me that although his cousin would not at first meet with the FBI, she later revealed that her husband had received threats from followers of Sheikh Rahman. Shalabi had sent his wife and three-year-old daughter back to Egypt and was himself making plans to travel to Pakistan a day or so before he was killed.[54]

The Alkhifa center was taken over by bin Laden loyalists, among them Wadih el-Hage, who had arrived in New York from Tucson the day before Shalabi's murder.[55] Another al-Qaeda member who happened to be an American citizen, el-Hage was born in Lebanon in 1960 into a Catholic family but converted to Islam before moving to the United States.[56] In 1978, he settled in Lafayette, Louisiana—a slight, bearded, shaggy-haired urban planning student at the University of Louisiana.[57] According to one of his professors, el-Hage wasn't particularly vocal about his political beliefs.[58] But during the eight years that it took him to finish his degree, he would be drawn to the Afghan jihad, traveling to Peshawar to work for a Saudi charity, the Muslim World League.[59] Jamal Ismail, then a student at Peshawar University, remembers el-Hage as a "very quiet person, with a very thin, weak body, who didn't seem to be militant."[60] Because of a withered right arm, he took no part in fighting.

In 1985, el-Hage married April Ray, an American convert to Islam, in Tucson, Arizona.[61] "She was so beautiful, he was happy," remembers his mother-in-law, Marion Brown, a nurse who had also converted to Islam. After el-Hage signed the marriage contract there was a feast for several dozen guests. But life would get harder. Brown recalls el-Hage fondly as "a devoted husband, a wonderful father, and a wonderful son-in-law," but says that despite his degree in urban planning, he was able to find only menial jobs—at a Dunkin Donuts, as a custodian, and as a cabdriver.

Within a year of their wedding, Wadih and April had a son, the first of seven children, and moved to Quetta, a city in the southwestern deserts of Pakistan that bears a passing resemblance to Tucson. Brown also moved to Pakistan, working as the matron of a hospital in Quetta for a year and a half. El-Hage, she says, was working for Abdullah Azzam, and would travel into Afghanistan with consignments of books for children.[62]

Between 1987 and 1990, el-Hage made several visits to Brooklyn's Alkhifa Center and briefly ran it after Shalabi's killing. There he met with three of the men later convicted of conspiring to blow up Manhattan landmarks.[63] In 1993, his name surfaced in the World Trade Center bombing case when one of the bombers told investigators that he had tried to buy guns from el-Hage.[64] By then, el-Hage was already in Sudan, working as bin Laden's personal secretary.

Between 1996 and 1997, el-Hage traveled between Arlington, Texas, where he worked at Lone Star Tires as a manager, and Nairobi,

Kenya.[65] A friend in Texas, Sam Alasad, says: "The only thing I knew about him is that he was doing charity work in Africa—where exactly, how, and what, we didn't discuss because it never came up." El-Hage did set up an organization with the awkward but direct name of Help Africa People, which ran a malaria vaccination program.[66] He also dabbled, not very successfully, in the import-export business, trading in gems, coffee, and even ostrich meat.[67] A photo entered into evidence at his trial shows him riding an ostrich, not something I had previously thought was possible or even desirable.

According to American prosecutors, el-Hage was doing much more than selling tires, riding ostriches, and working for charities. He was setting up al-Qaeda's Kenya cell while sharing a house with Haroun Fazil, who (as described in chapter 6) is accused of playing a key role in the bombing of the U.S. embassy in Nairobi. Although el-Hage was not charged with a direct role in the Kenya bombing, he was accused of perjury on the basis of misleading statements he made to the grand jury investigating bin Laden, and of being part of al-Qaeda's conspiracy to kill Americans. He was found guilty of all the counts against him in June 2001.

The 1993 World Trade Center bombing looks increasingly like a dress rehearsal for al-Qaeda's devastating attack on the Twin Towers eight years later. Several of the 1993 plotters had ties to the Alkhifa Center. As mentioned above, bomber Mahmud Abouhalima, who fought in Afghanistan in 1990, possibly with al-Qaeda, was an aide to Shalabi.[68] And the man who might have been behind Shalabi's murder, Sheikh Omar Abdel Rahman, who is affiliated with al-Qaeda, was convicted of being a part of the conspiracy to bomb the Trade Center. On the al-Qaeda videotape that appeared on the Internet in the summer of 2001, bin Laden refers to Sheikh Rahman as a "hostage" in American prison. He says of the cleric, "We hear he is sick. The Americans are treating him badly."

Ramzi Yousef, the operational leader of the Trade Center attack, appears not to have frequented the Alkhifa center, but he had close ties to al-Qaeda members. When he flew to New York from Peshawar in September 1992, a few months before the bombing, he was accompanied by

Ahmad Ajaj, who was immediately arrested at Kennedy Airport on immigration charges.[69] Discovered in Ajaj's possession was an explosives manual, the title of which was mistranslated as "The Basic Rule" when it was entered into evidence at the Trade Center trial. *The New York Times* later correctly retranslated it as "Al-Qaeda, The Base."[70]

A further interesting connection between Yousef and bin Laden is Yousef's uncle, Zahid Sheik, who was the regional manager of Mercy International Relief, a charity based in Peshawar, during the mid-1990s.[71] At the same time, Mercy International Relief's Nairobi branch worked closely with al-Qaeda, issuing identity cards to bin Laden and Ali Mohamed.[72] After a police raid on Wadih el-Hage's house in Nairobi in 1997, eight boxes of his personal papers were stored at the charity's office in the city.[73] Moreover a reliable Pakistani magazine, *The Herald,* reported in 1993 that Zahid Sheik ran the Islamic Coordination Council.[74] The Council was established by bin Laden's mentor Abdullah Azzam, to coordinate the activities of twenty charities in the city.

"Ramzi Yousef can be traced back to Afghanistan," said Vincent Cannistraro, who ran the CIA's Counterterrorist Center between 1988 and 1990. He added that, once in the U.S., Yousef recruited a group of "useful idiots" to help him with the World Trade Center operation, and it was these "idiots" who were left holding the bag when Yousef quickly decamped. (Interestingly, this was the same modus operandi employed by the al-Qaeda masterminds of the African embassy bombings and the attack on the U.S.S. *Cole.*)

After the 1993 bombing Yousef disappeared for two years, traveling to Thailand, the Philippines, and Pakistan, where he stayed in a bin Laden guesthouse in Peshawar, *Beit al-Shuhadaa* ("House of the Martyrs").[75] Al-Qaeda member (and Alkhifa Center regular) Jamal al-Fadl testified at the embassy bombings trial that he saw Yousef at the group's Sadda training camp on the Pakistan-Afghanistan border sometime between 1989 and 1991.[76] Located in the Khumram Agency, a tribal area of Parachinar (a region of Pakistan that juts into Afghanistan), the camp was presided over by Abdul Rasool Sayyaf, the Afghan leader closest to bin Laden.[77] Yousef would later tell an FBI agent that he spent six months in a camp in Afghanistan learning how to make bombs and went on to become an instructor in the use of explosives.[78] He also used Casio watches in his bombs as timing devices—a signature of al-Qaeda.[79]

While living in the Philippines in the early 1990s, he made contact with an Islamist terrorist group, Abu Sayyaf (named for the above-mentioned commander), which had been funded by bin Laden's brother-in-law Muhammad Khalifa. According to a U.S. official, Yousef and Khalifa were both in the Philippines at the same time, although Khalifa denies knowing Yousef.[80]

One of Yousef's terrorist partners in the Philippines was Wali Khan Amin Shah, who trained in Afghanistan under bin Laden.[81] Indeed, bin Laden remembered Amin Shah fondly in an interview with ABC News. "He is nicknamed the Lion," bin Laden said. "We were good friends. We fought together in the same trenches against the Russians."[82]

Unfortunately for Yousef, Filipino police accidentally stumbled onto his trail in 1994, when an explosives experiment he was conducting in his small apartment in Manila went awry. With smoke pouring out of his apartment, he was forced to flee, leaving behind his computer—from which experts who decrypted its hard drive were surprised to learn of detailed plans to blow up eleven passenger jets and assassinate Pope John Paul II.[83] Yousef would be captured a year later by FBI agents in Islamabad, Pakistan; among his possessions was the address of a bin Laden guesthouse.[84] Another member of Yousef's crew was Abdul Hakim Murad, a Pakistani who had trained as a commercial pilot in the United States. Murad told Filipino investigators that in addition to the plots to assassinate the Pontiff and bomb numerous American jets, he planned to crash a plane into CIA headquarters in Virginia.

The connections between Abu Sayyaf and Yousef were further underlined in April 2000 when the group kidnapped fifty people from schools on one of the southern islands of the Philippines and demanded the release of Yousef from his American prison, where he is now serving a 240-year term.[85]

A full accounting of al-Qaeda's U.S.-based members and associates is beyond the scope of this book. But a few are worth mentioning for their particulars—and how they have lived their lives among the infidels.

You wouldn't expect to encounter a bin Laden associate at Disney World, but that was the one-time employer of American citizen Ihab

Ali.[86] Educated in the U.S., Ali worked in Orlando, Florida, in a variety of dead-end jobs: at the Magic Kingdom, a Sheraton hotel, a Wells Fargo bank, and driving a taxicab.[87] In 1989, he traveled to Peshawar to aid in the jihad against the Soviets.[88] Four years later, he helped to purchase a U.S. airplane, which was flown to al-Qaeda in Sudan.[89] Ali learned to fly at a flight school in Norman, Oklahoma. He moved to Kenya in the mid-nineties, working as a pilot for al-Qaeda and corresponding with Wadih el-Hage.[90] He was detained in 1999, and has apparently refused to cooperate with authorities on religious grounds.[91] But his training as an al-Qaeda pilot must make him the subject of intense scrutiny in the wake of the September 11 attacks.

Another American-bred bin Laden recruit is Raed Hijazi, who was born in California in 1969, of Palestinian heritage.[92] While a student at California State University in Sacramento, Hijazi adopted a militant form of Islam, traveling to bin Laden's training camps near Khost in eastern Afghanistan. After a stint in Boston as a cabdriver in 1997, he abruptly left for Jordan, where he acquired bomb-making materials for a plot to attack tourists visiting Christian holy sites in Amman during the celebrations of the new millennium.[93] Jordanian investigators foiled the plan: Hijazi was arrested in Syria in October 2000 and extradited to Jordan, where he was convicted on charges of terrorism in 2002.[94]

Unidentified at this writing are several African-American members of al-Qaeda. An Al-Qaeda pilot, L'Hossaine Kherchtou, testified at the embassy bombings trial that there were "some" African-Americans with the group when it was based in Sudan during the mid-1990s. And the Pakistani journalist Hamid Mir was introduced to two African-Americans when he visited bin Laden in Afghanistan in May 1998.

T he deadly terrorist attacks of September 11, 2001, were not al-Qaeda's first attempt to bring holy war to American soil. According to U.S. officials, bin Laden's network plotted to start New Year's 2000—the new millennium—with a series of bombings.

The American plan fell apart at a U.S. border crossing in Washington State on December 14, 1999, when Ahmed Ressam, a thirty-three-year-old Algerian, was arrested on a ferry arriving from Canada.[95] As Ressam's car rolled out, U.S. Customs Inspector Diana Dean pulled him over and noticed that in spite of the December chill his hands were shaking and he was sweating.[96] Ressam got out of his car and began running away from customs agents, unsuccessfully trying to commandeer another vehicle.[97] The agents found 130 pounds of explosives in his car. A search of Ressam's apartment in Montreal yielded a map of California with circles around three airports: Los Angeles, Long Beach, and Ontario.[98] Immediately after Ressam's arrest, officials speculated that he might have been intending to attack West Coast landmarks such as the TransAmerica building in San Francisco or the Space Needle in Seattle. (Ressam had booked himself a motel room not far from the latter.)[99] Concerns about an attack on the Space Needle led Seattle officials to cancel its millennium celebrations.[100]

For a year and a half after his arrest, Ressam remained resolutely silent about his intended target. But after he was convicted of terrorism in April 2001 and found himself facing a possible sentence of 130 years, he began cooperating with authorities, telling them he had planned to bomb Los Angeles International Airport. U.S. officials have linked this plot to contemporaneous efforts by al-Qaeda to bomb a U.S. warship in Yemen and various targets in Jordan.[101]

Ressam had taken a circuitous route to becoming an international terrorist. After graduating from an Algerian high school in 1988, he worked illegally on the island of Corsica, picking grapes and doing painting jobs in a tourist resort. In 1994, he moved to Montreal, where he survived on welfare payments and by stealing suitcases from tourists and engineering credit card frauds. Despite his life of petty crime, Ressam was a regular worshipper at Montreal mosques.[102]

In 1998 he traveled to Afghanistan to al-Qaeda's Khaldan camp, meeting first, in Pakistan, with Abu Zubaida, a Palestinian whom American and British officials describe as the chief recruiter for bin Laden's training facilities and the coordinator of the failed millennium plot to bomb tourist sites in Jordan.[103] Once in camp, he spent several months with a polyglot group of Arabs, Germans, Swedes, French, Turks, and Chechens. (Mohamed Rashed al-'Owhali, the would-be suicide bomber in the Kenya embassy attack, and the Jordanian-American Raed Hijazi would also attend the same camp in the late nineties.[104]) Ressam received the usual al-Qaeda tutorials on a variety of weapons and explosives, graduating to specialized classes on electronic circuitry for bombs. He was also taught how to attack airports, railroads, and military installations, and trained in the subtler arts of assassination. One method was to smear on a doorknob toxins sufficiently powerful to enter the bloodstream and kill the unwitting victim.[105] Lectures were offered on previous terrorist operations: the failures, such as an abortive attempt to assassinate Egyptian President Hosni Mubarak in Ethiopia in 1995; and the successes, such as the 1983 truck bombing of the U.S. Marine barracks in Beirut.[106]

Around this time, al-Qaeda experimented with cyanide in the hope it could be introduced into the air intakes of U.S. government buildings. Ressam's camp confederates orchestrated ghastly trials in which they injected the poison into canines, on one occasion putting a dog in a box with a mixture of cyanide and sulfuric acid. (Unsurprisingly, the dog expired within minutes.)[107]

At the camp, a cell of Ressam's fellow Algerians agreed that, after their training, they would meet up in Canada, an agreeable base because of the relative ease with which one can enter the United States from it.[108] Once in Canada, they would rob some banks and use the money for terrorist operations against American targets. Other militants at the camp were planning similar attacks in Europe, the Gulf, and Israel.[109]

In February 1999, Ressam returned to Montreal with $12,000 from an al-Qaeda official, a bomb-making manual, and a supply of hexamine, a booster material for explosives.[110] During the summer, Ressam and an associate contemplated bombing an Israeli target in Canada, but by the fall their plans had changed: they decided to attack a target inside the United States.[111] During this period, Ressam was also the point person for Algerians in Montreal seeking training in bin Laden's camps in Afghanistan; his contact was al-Qaeda's Abu Doha, an Algerian living in London.[112] (In July 2001, American prosecutors charged Abu Doha with playing a key role in al-Qaeda. When British police searched his apartment they found notes about bomb-making materials that matched the mixture of explosives in Ressam's car, as well as a number of fake passports.[113])

Ressam spent much of November and early December 1999 in Vancouver, holed up in a hotel, constructing four timing devices from Casio watches—multiple backups in case any of them shorted out. He also bought or stole bomb-making materials—urea, nitric acid, and sulfuric acid—from local fertilizer stores and manufactured small quantities of RDX and HMTD, highly potent explosives that would boost the force of the device.[114] Ressam then loaded his supplies into a rental car for the trip to Victoria, British Columbia, where he would catch the ferry to Washington State. Worried that the vibrations of the long car journey from the Canadian border to Los Angeles might inadvertently detonate the explosives, he planned to take a train to L.A. once he reached the United States.[115]

Luckily, Ressam never made it past the border crossing. His arrest probably averted a catastrophic bombing of Los Angeles' busiest airport during the Christmas tourist season.

The arrest of this al-Qaeda training camp veteran is further proof of the prominent role played by Afghanistan, to which thousands, perhaps tens of thousands, of others like him have traveled to learn the art of holy war. While Ressam was making his final preparations for the L.A. attack, I was heading for Afghanistan to investigate why the Taliban continued to allow bin Laden and al-Qaeda to operate with seeming impunity, and why they continued to tolerate the existence of a dozen or so training camps in which the next generation of Ressams were honing their deadly skills.

CHAPTER 8

True Believers:
The Taliban and bin Laden

> *Things fall apart; the center cannot hold;*
> *Mere anarchy is loosed upon the world,*
> *The blood-dimmed tide is loosed, and everywhere*
> *The ceremony of innocence is drowned;*
> *The best lack all conviction, while the worst*
> *Are full of passionate intensity.*
>
> —W. B. Yeats, "The Second Coming"

Maulvi Hafeezullah, an official in the Taliban's Foreign Ministry, attacked the pile of chocolate doughnuts with gusto. Between mouthfuls of what may have been the only Taliban-sanctioned indulgence, he sputtered, "We will never hand over bin Laden. The U.S. has made a monster out of one man. We can unleash a 'heroin bomb' to match your nuclear bomb." This was a nod to the fact that Afghanistan, under the Taliban, had been recently cited by the United Nations as the world's leading producer of opium, the raw material of heroin.[1]

I was in Afghanistan in December 1999 to talk to senior members of the Taliban and learn more about their movement—as well as why they harbored bin Laden and other Islamist militants of his ilk. They continued to do so despite pressure from the United Nations, which had just imposed sanctions on the country.

Given the far from amiable relations between these religious warriors and the United States, it is ironic that the State Department had initially seemed to welcome them when they took over Kabul in 1996. Although its expression of support was hardly effusive, the United States said publicly that there was "nothing objectionable" in the Taliban's version of Islamic law.[2]

This tepid support can be explained on several grounds, the first of which was simple ignorance. The United States, which had closed its Kabul embassy for security reasons in 1989, had little idea who the Taliban were.[3] (On a visit in 1993 I found the embassy a shuttered concrete monolith, with weeds the size of small trees sprouting from its walls—an apt metaphor for the sad state of the U.S.'s Afghan policy. On September 27, 2001, the embassy was torched and gutted by Taliban protesters chanting "Long live Osama." It was finally reopened in December 2001.) And the State Department, which relied heavily on the Pakistanis for information on Afghanistan, was willing to embrace any group that looked as if it might bring some degree of stability to the country. U.S. officials were hardly unaware that Unocal, a giant American energy firm, was competing to build a multibillion-dollar pipeline through Afghanistan that would link oil and gas fields in Central Asia with ports on the Indian Ocean—a desirable plan, as it would steer the pipeline clear of Iran.[4] Unocal's cause was advanced by powerful players like Robert Oakley, the former U.S. ambassador to Pakistan, who sat on its board.[5] The Taliban seemed likely to provide a secure environment in which the Unocal pipeline might finally move ahead. There was also hope that the Taliban would take a hard line on drugs, as its early pronouncements seemed to indicate.[6]

By 1997 American illusions about the movement had evaporated. On a visit to Pakistan, Secretary of State Madeleine Albright declared: "I think it is very clear we are opposed to the Taliban because of their despicable treatment of women and children, and their general lack of respect for human dignity."[7]

The easiest way into Afghanistan is via neighboring Pakistan, one of only three countries in the world that initially chose to recognize the holy warriors who controlled most of the country. (Saudi Arabia and the United Arab Emirates had also recognized the Taliban.) Pakistan's Islamist parties and its powerful spy agency, Inter-Services Intelligence (ISI), were instrumental in the Taliban's rise to power.[8] That's not to say that the movement owed its existence to Pakistan. It was truly an indigenous band of religious students who, seemingly out of nowhere, seized the southern city of Kandahar in 1994. But, as the Taliban gained territory, Pakistan's military-religious complex quickly put its money on what looked like a winning horse in the civil wars that continued to rack the country. General Naseerullah Babar, the interior minister in Benazir Bhutto's government, was an adviser to the Taliban in its early days, as was Fazalur Rahman, the leader of one of Pakistan's religious parties.[9]

In 1998, a U.S. official based in Pakistan surprised me when he estimated that up to ten thousand of the Taliban's thirty thousand soldiers were from Pakistan—an astonishing 20 to 40 percent. Telling examples of Pakistan's influence: to telephone Afghanistan, you went through a Pakistani exchange; and the fuel that powered the Taliban's motorized units and tanks had to transit Pakistan.

One muggy fall day in 1999, I walked over to Pakistan's chancery on Washington's Embassy Row to apply for a visa. The visa application process is usually a strikingly accurate foretaste of the country you are about to visit. (A harrowing two-day wait for a visa at the Indian consulate in Paris, along with about a hundred other people packed into a tiny, sweltering room, all too readily springs to mind.)

The Pakistani chancery is housed in a once grand mansion desperately in need of a coat of paint and new carpeting. Waiting outside the press attaché's office I spotted a man who looked vaguely familiar. I went over and told him I was looking for the press attaché. Looking dejected, he said: "I had that job until yesterday, but now I've been fired." It was then I remembered his name, Malik. I had applied to him for a visa to Pakistan a year before and had received a disquisition on the likelihood of militant Islamists taking over the country. Instead, it was the army that had just taken charge—and given Malik the jackboot.

It had been an old-school coup straight out of some 1950s CIA handbook. On October 12, 1999, soldiers closed the nation's airports and seized the national television station, which began to broadcast a continuous loop of listless folk dancing.[10] An announcement was made that the new leader would shortly address the nation. In the middle of the night, General Pervez Musharaf appeared in his well-pressed uniform and read a stilted two-minute statement to the effect that for the fourth time in its five-decade history the army was again in charge: "The armed forces have moved in as a last resort to prevent further destabilization," he said.[11] The coup was met with near universal applause.[12] Pakistan's "democratic" politicians had systematically looted the country for years.[13] Pakistanis were fed up, and a return to military rule seemed to be the only option left.

It was a "soft" coup by Pakistan's often bloody standards. Sure, there had been arrests—of Prime Minister Nawaz Sharif and some of his ministers—but this was a far cry from the eighties military regime of General Zia ul-Haq, a man whose resplendent uniform, slicked-back hair, luxuriant mustache, and heavily lidded eyes ringed with dark circles made him look like the caudillo of a 1930s banana republic.[14] General Zia had charmed some American journalists and politicians, who chose to ignore the fact he executed potential rivals with relish and ruled with an iron fist.

The 1999 power grab by Pakistan's army was good news for the Taliban and, by extension, for bin Laden. During the eighties, Zia had packed the army with Islamists, who played an important behind-the-scenes role in the Taliban's spectacular rise to power and were immune to Western entreaties to pressure the Taliban to expel bin Laden.[15]

Back at the Pakistani consulate, I asked Malik what he was planning to do with his life. Mournfully he replied, "It's probably not the best time to go back: I could get thrown in jail. I really don't know what I am going to do. I am a career civil servant. I have two children. I am taking this philosophically because there is nothing else I can do." Pointing to an imposing desk, he said, "I used to be sitting there, but now I am sitting here," gesturing to the visitors' couch.

I reminded him of our conversation the year before and his fears that Islamists would take over his country. "It's still possible," he said. "A lot of the officers in the army are Islamists. The new leader, General Musharraf, may be secular minded, but he too can be overthrown. The problem with these military coups is that every time one happens the roots of democracy get further weakened."

Despite the fact that Malik had just been fired and was only at the chancery to sign some documents hastening his own departure, he said he would inform the new press attaché that I had come by and make sure I was taken care of. This was so typically Pakistani: the desire to be hospitable whatever the circumstances.

As I flew to Islamabad I reflected on the interesting similarities between Pakistan and Israel. Both countries had been founded on religion—one as a homeland for Muslims of the Indian subcontinent, the other for Jews of the Diaspora. Both were midwifed by Britain after World War II, as the British washed their hands of an empire over which the sun never set but which they could no longer afford. Pakistan had even suffered its own little-known holocaust, the murder of perhaps a million Muslims fleeing India for the newly created country.[16] Both felt encircled fighting repeated wars with their neighbors, and both had acquired nuclear weapons to enhance their security. And in both, religious parties exercised far greater power than their small showings at the polls would indicate.

I landed in Pakistan during Ramadan. Pakistanis from every walk of life were observing one of the five pillars of Islam: the fast from dawn to dusk that marks the holy month. Three channels on my hotel television were broadcasting the same live feed from Saudi Arabia, showing hundreds of thousands of men circumambulating the Kaaba, Islam's holiest site, a cuboid several stories tall containing the Black Stone sacred to both the pre-Islamic Arabs and the world's Muslims.[17]

It was December and mornings were chilly, but by midday the sun had warmed the velvet breezes that blew the turning leaves off the trees. By two in the afternoon most offices had closed and the streets were largely empty. Just before sunset, there was a huge upsurge of traffic as drivers manic with hunger raced to wherever they were taking *iftar*, the meal that broke their fast. The streets would then fall eerily silent for an hour as everyone remained indoors, single-mindedly stuffing themselves.

Despite the Ramadan observances, Pakistan does have a secular side. On sale at my local bookshop were Western magazines with legends like "Oral Sex: How to Really Enjoy it" and "Seven Ways to Give

Your Man More Pleasure," My television featured Asian MTV, which played a heavy rotation of a simpering Indian V.J. who read letters from her teen fans about how much they adored her, as well as cable channels showing films starring Pamela Anderson and her decolletage.

Nevertheless, Pakistan remained a country where the idea of women's honor was paramount. On my second day in Islamabad I dropped into an ice cream shop in one of the poshest areas of the city. Several tables away a woman chatting with her husband immediately pulled her veil over her face and kept it there for fifteen minutes until I had left. I also paid a visit to the U.N. Club, one of the few places foreigners socialize in Islamabad. On the notice board was a list of rules for conduct around the swimming pool, among them the deliciously understated: "Topless for women is not an option."

For fear of attacks by Islamist militants, the club closed at 10:30 P.M. each night. The fear was not paranoia. In mid-November 1999, a series of well-coordinated rocket attacks on the U.S. embassy, the U.N. compound, and the American cultural center had been launched by unidentified terrorists who apparently objected to the imminent imposition of sanctions on Afghanistan for continuing to harbor bin Laden.[18] By sheer luck, no one was killed. The club manager told me, "The U.N. security officer says any future attacks are likely to come after eleven at night, so I am probably going to have to cancel the New Year's party, as it won't be much of a party if we have to shut it down at ten-thirty."

The unidentified terrorists represented only a small percentage of those willing to defend bin Laden: at the time he enjoyed a cultlike status there. "I think he is more popular than any political leader in Pakistan," said Hamid Mir, the editor of an influential Urdu newspaper. For Pakistani magazines, a cover story on bin Laden was a surefire way to sell copies. One such piece, in the weekly *Wujood,* had a lurid and patently absurd account of 150 Palestinian commandos, trained in Israel and the United States, standing by to snatch or kill the Saudi exile.[19]

Bin Laden's ideas resonated deeply with certain members of the Pakistani clergy—who, as we have already seen, issued a *fatwa* in 1997 that echoed his calls for the removal of U.S. troops from Saudi Arabia.[20] Furthermore, leaders of Pakistan's religious parties outdid one another to threaten violence against Americans if attacks were made on the Saudi exile.[21] One such call was issued by the well-known Muslim scholar Mufti Mizam-ud-din Shamzai, who decreed a boycott of Western goods, adding: "Because America is in a war with Muslims, under Islamic *sharia* [law], the shedding of American blood is permissible."[22] A convention of Islamists outside Peshawar in spring 2001 attracted hundreds of thousands of Pakistanis to whom bin Laden was simply a hero. Giant posters of him were hung at some of the convention's booths, and participants at the meeting followed a policy of boycotting American-made goods.[23]

Nowhere was bin Laden more popular than in Pakistan's *madrassas*, religious schools from which the Taliban drew many of its recruits. During the early 1980s General Zia ul-Haq supported *madrassas* along the Afghan-Pakistan border to serve as recruiting grounds for those who participated in the holy war against the Soviets.[24] Graduates emerged with little understanding of the world, but had learned much of the Koran by rote and showed an impressive zeal for jihad. During the nineties, *madrassas* sprang up all over Pakistan. In 1997, in Punjab province alone, there were more than 200,000 students at the *madrassas*, which have supplied tens of thousands of recruits to the Taliban—men who are a latter day version of Christianity's medieval monk-warriors, the Knights Templar.[25]

Perhaps the most famous *madrassa* is the Jaamiah Darul Uloom Haqqania, located outside Peshawar and headed by Maulana Sami ul-Haq. ("Maulana" is a senior religious title.) Maulana ul-Haq presides over 2,800 students, mostly from Pakistan, but also including hundreds from Afghanistan and dozens from the Central Asian republics of the former Soviet Union.[26]

I met with Maulana ul-Haq in a villa in a quiet suburb of Peshawar. Until then I had pegged him as not much more than a jovial village mullah who had somehow lucked into his headmaster's position. And indeed he was a gregarious, hearty bear of a man, who smiled often beneath his full beard. But he was a lot more important than his appearance suggested. He had the money and clout to fly himself and his entourage around Europe. He was part of an interesting nexus that connected Islamist parties in Pakistan to the Taliban. Maulana ul-Haq was the leader of a faction of the hard-line Jamiat-e-Ulema Islam

(JUI), at one time representing the party as a senator. And his school had educated as many as eight cabinet-level members of the Taliban.[27] He was also an ardent admirer of bin Laden, whom he had met when the Saudi militant was based in Peshawar in the 1980s. (One of ul-Haq's aides told me that he had enjoyed the CNN interview with bin Laden, adding that he had watched it in a passenger lounge at an airport outside Paris.)

Maulana ul-Haq told me how his school had grown from modest beginnings: "My father, Maulana Abdul, was a teacher in an important religious school in India. After the partition [of India and Pakistan in 1947] he came here . . . and started a small school." Ul-Haq explained that students paid nothing because the school was supported by wealthy Muslims, which was part of the attraction for the thousands of destitute Afghans who had been educated there.

Dusk was approaching and Maulana ul-Haq gathered his entourage to go outside in the garden to say their evening prayers. I have always found watching a group of Muslim men at prayer a moving experience. The act of collective worship woven into the fabric of daily life is something we have almost entirely lost in the West. Millet's nineteenth-century drawing of French peasants stopping their work in the fields to say the Angelus is a scene from a very foreign country now.

When Maulana ul-Haq had finished his prayers, I asked him what he thought of bin Laden. He answered: "I do not think he has any aggressive thoughts. He is not a saboteur; nor is he a terrorist. . . . God has gifted us with blessings like oil and gas, but it seems as though Americans want to take everything. I think his answer is that America is being unfair to us." Ul-Haq went on to say that just as the Russians had sent an army into Afghanistan and bin Laden had fought them, bin Laden was now fighting the American army that had arrived in his native Saudi Arabia.

Toward the end of our chat, I asked Maulana ul-Haq whether he believed that the social policies the Taliban had introduced into Afghanistan might also be introduced into Pakistan. This was a concern for more secular-minded Pakistanis, who had seen a gradual "Talibanization" of regions along their borders with Afghanistan, where Islamist groups such as the Tehrik-e-Taliban had banned television and implemented Taliban-style punishments such as amputation.[28] In the Malakand tribal area, for example, local mullahs had declared the rule of *sharia*.[29] This Islamist mood was spreading across Pakistan with a proliferation of extremist groups such as the Sipah-e-Sahaba, which was behind the killings of hundreds of minority Shia.[30] Although most Pakistanis condemned such terrorist activities, polls showed they were receptive to Islamist ideas. One poll, commissioned by the respected magazine *Newline* in 1998, found that 57 percent of Pakistanis favored *sharia* "in letter and spirit."[31] In a desperate attempt to shore up his flagging popularity, the then prime minister, Nawaz Sharif, had even proposed revising Pakistan's constitution to make *sharia* Islamic law, the sole law of the land.[32]

Ul-Haq took a moment to consider my question about Pakistan's future, then spoke passionately: "The Taliban are becoming popular here because people are sick and tired of corruption. There is no democracy here, no basic rights. People are being crushed under this corrupt system. And America does not want us to change this system peacefully. If America doesn't let us change our economic, political and judicial system . . . then there will the same reaction [that has taken place in Afghanistan]."[33]

Back in my hotel room in Islamabad. I looked up the latest State Department travel advisory about Afghanistan. The following passages were typical: "Americans remain vulnerable to politically and criminally motivated attacks and violence, including robbery, kidnapping and hostage-taking. The estimated 5–7 million landmines scattered throughout the countryside pose a danger . . . The Department of State urges Americans who decide to remain in Afghanistan in spite of this Warning to exercise extreme caution, monitor their security situation closely and make plans for responding to a sudden deterioration in security conditions."[34] "Sudden" struck me as a nice touch.

The following morning I was awakened at dawn by the muezzin's call to prayer. After consuming a guilt-inducing breakfast, served by a waiter who I knew was observing the Ramadan fast, I went to the Afghan embassy. Black-turbaned Taliban officials sat at desks piled with visa applications. I sat down next to one whose card identified him as "Engineer Abdul Khabir Hotaki, Third Secretary."

"What can I do for you?" he asked curtly in English, without looking up.

I told him I wanted a visa for Afghanistan. he asked for what purpose, and I told him I was writing a book about Islamist movements.

"Who else are you writing about?"

I mumbled something about Egyptian militant groups and bin Laden.

Now Hotaki looked at me with a penetrating gaze. "But these groups are anti-American," he said.

I smiled blandly as Hotaki continued. "Your publisher needs to send us a letter specifically requesting your visa to Afghanistan," he explained. "After that it will take ten days, maybe two weeks, to be approved."

On the duly appointed day I went to pick up my visa. "Thirty dollars for the visa," said the man behind the window.

"Can't I pay in rupees?" I asked.

"Dollars only."

The Taliban were no fans of the United States, but they understood the power of the greenback.

As I waited for the visa to be issued, I read a list of rules addressed to journalists planning to visit Afghanistan. First you had to register with the Foreign Ministry. Then you could stay only at the Intercontinental Hotel, in Kabul, and you had to use a government-provided "guide" and driver (who were to be paid in dollars, of course). Finally, "The filming and photography of living objects is strictly prohibited." The First Amendment did not appear to be a feature of *sharia* law.

With a smile, the visa official handed me my passport back with the stamp of the Islamic Emirate of Afghanistan.

"Now you can go."

Before setting off for Afghanistan, I visited Rahimullah Yusufzai, the Peshawar bureau chief of *The News* and a stringer for *Time*, the BBC, and ABC News. Rahimullah's unprepossesing office was usually full of visiting journalists, local politicians, and supplicants of every variety, all looking for help or advice and all of whom he greeted with unfailing humor and patience. He was a devout Muslim, invariably breaking off conversations if it was time to pray, and he was imbued with two qualities lacking in many journalists: modesty and generosity.

Rahimullah was the first college graduate from his village, and on Fridays he would return to hear petitions or sort out disputes. I was always puzzled as to when he got work done, but his output was prodigious.

Rahimullah eased his lanky frame out from behind his cluttered desk and greeted me with his customary warmth. We were both eager to talk about the recent coup in Pakistan: one of the first to be arrested had been the information minister, Mushahid Hussein, who some considered to be the real brains behind the now deposed government of Nawaz Sharif. I had interviewed Hussein in the past and had come away liking him: He was smart and open and actually cracked a few jokes—qualities not found to excess in Pakistani politicians. His ease with the media could be explained by his previous job as a newspaper editor, where he had once been Rahimullah's boss. Rahimullah said the military had trumped up some charges against Hussein because "he is very smart, and he knows how to organize a media campaign against the military government."

The military had also tried to recruit prominent Pakistanis to assist their government; Rahimullah had been approached about sitting on an important policy panel. He had made it clear that he could not accept such a position.

We also talked of the Taliban, to which Rahimullah had unrivaled access, not only because he was one of the best journalists in Pakistan but also because he is from the Pathan tribal group, as is the Taliban leadership. In fact, Rahimullah is one of the few journalists to have interviewed its reclusive leader, Mullah Omar. Rahimullah described a man who avoided foreigners like the plague and who operated the Taliban treasury in a manner reminiscent of a twelfth-century English monarch. "Mullah Omar has a box in his room; he takes a key out of his pocket, opens the box, and takes out wads of money," which he then distributed to whoever needed it.

Rahimullah confirmed my sense that the Taliban were not necessarily the ardent fans of bin Laden that their public statements had suggested, "I have privately heard some criticism," he said. "They say sarcastically, 'Even after the war [against the communists] we are required to look after bin Laden.'" Other observers of the Taliban pointed out that there had been splits between the hardliners and the moderates, who wanted more contacts with the West and for whom bin Laden was a headache.[35]

Rahimullah wished me well on my trip, and, with mounting excitement, I set off for Afghanistan. I traveled the same route I had taken two years before to meet bin Laden, and once again stayed at the Spinghar Hotel in Jalalabad, where I was the only guest. I remembered the desk clerk from my previous trip. He had grown an impressive beard in the interim, no doubt to ingratiate himself with the local Taliban leadership. For the privilege of staying at his zero-star hotel, the clerk charged me the outrageous fee of eighty dollars a night—a sum that approximates the yearly income of the average Afghan. He later visited my room wondering whether I had any "spare" dollars or pounds, as he "collected" foreign currency. Chutzpah, Taliban-style.

The next morning I started off for Kabul. Happy families, Tolstoy wrote, are all alike, and each unhappy family is unhappy in its own way; the same might be said of the family of nations. And by just about any indicator, Afghanistan is not a happy nation. According to a guidebook from the seventies, the trip from Jalalabad to Kabul should take two and a half hours.[36] Today it takes closer to seven; two decades of war have pounded the road into little more than a stony track broken up by enormous craters. This has generated a small-time industry for boys and old men, who shovel heaps of gravel into the potholes in the expectation of small tips thrown out the windows of passing cars.

As we entered Kabul we passed streets that looked like Dresden after the firestorms of World War II, or Grozny after the Russians had destroyed it for the second time. It's not surprising that when children in Kabul play war games, they don't make the "bang, bang" sounds that most American kids make. Instead, they say "tac, tac"—the sound of the incoming fire with which they have grown up.

Ramadan in Kabul: by comparison, Lent in Savonarola's Florence was party central. In a country where millions were going cold and hungry, the faithful were fasting. As at the Spinghar Hotel, I was the only guest in the grim, cavernous, and incongruously named Intercontinental. That made me popular with the hotel staff, who dogged me like hyenas scenting fresh blood. One night a young waiter came to my room with a sad tale. He said he was the only wage earner in his family, working at a building site during the day and at the hotel at night to support them. "I have only four dollars a month for my family. I can't feed them. It's Ramadan. I would not tell a lie." This situation was that of most Afghans, even professionals like doctors, who typically earned six dollars a month. I gave the waiter the equivalent of twenty dollars. He embraced me, saying: "Don't tell anyone here about this."

Vestiges of former eras lingered in the hotel lobby—signs for the ballroom, directions to the bar, and advertisements for Intourist vacations in the Soviet Union. But that was all a long time ago. In Kabul, curfew started at nine. By eight the streets were deserted except for the young Taliban soldiers who stood at every traffic circle, carefully checking passing vehicles. Some wore black kohl eyeliner, which gave them a look at once feline and fierce. Women, meanwhile, were banned from using cosmetics.

The Taliban had imposed their ultra-purist vision of Islam on much of the country. Men were not allowed to shave or trim their beards. Women had to wear the all-enveloping *burqa* and stay at home unless accompanied by a male relative. The Taliban's edicts were enforced by the religious police of the poetically named Ministry for the Promotion of Virtue and the Prevention of Vice, who raced around in pickup trucks looking for malefactors to beat with sticks.[37] Such policies reached their apogee of absurdity in an ordinance ordering homeowners to paint their windows black so that no one might accidentally see the faces of women inside.[38] In neighboring Iran—the target of much criticism for its supposed misogyny—women are allowed to work, vote, and run for political office.

The Taliban have defended their shrouding and confinement of women by saying these were simply the cultural norms of Afghan culture. What they didn't acknowledge is that these were really the social norms of the Pathan ethnic group, which made up a little under half of the population of Afghanistan and pretty much the entire top leadership of the Taliban movement.[39] In neighboring Pakistan, where there is no legal compulsion to wear the *burqa,* women in Pathan areas nonetheless generally avail themselves of the garment. A proverb sums up the status of Pathan women: "Women belong in the house or the grave."[40]

It is important to understand the thinking behind confining women to their homes. For the Taliban this was not taking away their rights, as it was understood in much of the rest of the world, but rather *giving* women their full rights as they understand those rights under *sharia* law. As the Taliban governor of Herat put it: "We have given women their rights that God and his Messenger have instructed, that is to stay in their homes and to gain religious instruction in *hejab* [seclusion.]"[41]

For the other ethnic groups in Afghanistan, largely Tajiks, Hazaras, and Uzbeks, and the inhabitants of the larger cities, particularly Kabul, the Taliban-Pathan policies were imports from another culture.[42] Even in the 1960s, Kabul was already a somewhat cosmopolitan city. A Japanese visitor in 1967 wrote: "With their well-tailored suits and Italian-style shoes the men might have been government employees in any western European city. . . . The women, too, wore well-cut suits and high-heeled shoes and—to the surprise of many of our group—no *chadris,* as the voluminous, shroud-like veil that Muslim women wear is called in this part of the world."[43] At that time, Kabul was a required stop on the overland trail to India. Hippies would while away weeks sampling the local hashish, and well-off Pakistani women would vacation there, wearing miniskirts and partying in a fashion not permissible in their own country.

The peculiar worldview of the Taliban is, however, more than just the culture of the Pathans. So extreme a movement could only have emerged in a country that had undergone the traumas of two decades of war. The Taliban reminded me a little of the Khmer Rouge, which had emerged, largely unheralded, out of the forests of Cambodia in 1975 in the aftermath of a devastating proxy war between the Soviet Union and the United States and had imposed on the Cambodians its Maoist version of paradise. Unlike the Khmer Rouge, the Taliban did not create a totalitarian regime that murdered a million of their own citizens. But they shared the same absolute certainty about how to create paradise on earth. The Khmer Rouge called this paradise the Year Zero. The Taliban called it the rule of *sharia,* and were convinced that once it was properly implemented Afghans would become virtuous and the perfect society would be created. Minor details—such as a program of governance that would get Afghanistan back on its feet after two decades of war—were of little interest to the Taliban. While five million or so Afghans, a quarter of the population, faced "serious food shortages," the Taliban were preoccupied with abstruse matters such as what sort of distinguishing clothing should be worn by the country's minuscule Hindu population.[44]

And the Taliban's version of *sharia* often conflicted with the teachings and life of Muhammad. For example, the Prophet's first marriage—a very happy one—was to the wealthy merchant Khadijah, an older, urbane woman of the world who employed him in her booming business. In stark contrast, the Taliban had decreed that women should neither work, nor be educated, nor even be seen by anyone outside their immediate families.[45]

In fact, the Koran demands that *both* sexes take reasonable steps to guard against sexual temptation: "Enjoin believing men to turn their eyes away from temptation and restrain their carnal desires . . . Enjoin believing women to turn their eyes away from temptation and to preserve their chastity." The verse does goes on to instruct women to dress modestly: "not to display their adornments (except such as are normally revealed); to draw their veils over their bosoms and not to display their finery except to their husbands, their fathers, their husband's father, their sons, their step-sons, their brothers, their brother's sons, their sister's sons, their women-servants, and their slave-girls, and children who have no carnal knowledge of women."[46] These injunctions are put into practice in many different ways across the Muslim world, from the simple veils of many Pakistani women to the all-enveloping robes worn by the women of rural Yemen.

Although the Taliban was often seen as monolithic, it had in fact been split between hard-liners and those who want to engage more with the outside world. Indeed, during 1999 there was a quiet, underground shift away from one of the Taliban's defining policies: banning education for girls and work for women. Erik de Mul, who coordinated the various U.N. agencies in Afghanistan, characterized the shift as informal and described the places where it occurred—primarily rural areas of Afghanistan—as a "twilight zone." The Taliban tended to regard the major cities as "occupied territories," Sodoms and Gomorrahs that needed to be punished for past transgressions, and so enforced their edicts more harshly there.

The change was most profound in the area of girls' education. In 1999, the Swedish Committee for Afghanistan, one of the largest aid organizations in the country, reported that at the six hundred schools they supported, there were now thirty thousand girl students and, astonishingly, that "there are parts of rural areas in Afghanistan today, where there are more girls in schools than ever before in Afghan history."[47] And U.N. officials said that even in Kandahar and Kabul a number of private schools had opened since 1998 and were now educating thousands of girls. One such school, in Kabul, was discreetly located off an alley in a private house where a husband-and-wife team had set up a makeshift classroom. They were paid fifty dollars a month by a Western charity to teach twenty or so girls how to write, do arithmetic, and learn foreign languages.[48]

The Taliban were reluctant to acknowledge these changes officially; no individual wanted to weaken his Islamist credentials by appearing too "liberal." And the shift in Taliban policy should not be exaggerated: education for girls still ended at the age of twelve.

In 1999 there were other shifts as well. The Taliban had come to realize that they could no longer both forbid that women be treated by male doctors *and* bar women from practicing medicine, so small numbers of female nurses and doctors were now working in city hospitals. In Herat, the World Food Program (WFP) was supporting a three-year medical education program for more than a hundred women, approved by local authorities in May 1999. A WFP official said such a project simply could not have been embarked on before. In Kandahar, a group of male doctors told me that the bar on treating women had been lifted.

And in the late nineties there were even small opportunities for women to work. Since 1997, the WFP had opened forty-nine bakeries in Kabul and the northern city of Mazar-e-Sharif run entirely by Afghan women, mostly widows who would otherwise have been destitute.[49]

Still, the Taliban's human rights record remained dismal. For a unique perspective on the issue, I paid a visit to Isaac Levi, Kabul's last Jew, who lived in a rambling, rundown house that seemed uninhabited except for the one squalid room that was his living quarters. A long white beard and a gray astrakhan hat framed Levi's face. He had been born in Herat about sixty years before, spending the past twenty-five in Kabul. When I arrived, he bustled about finding pillows to make me comfortable. He was preparing rice in an electric cooker so that he would have food ready for the Sabbath, which was the next day.

I asked what he planned to do for the holy day. "I will pray to Almighty God," he said, seeming both anxious and sad.

Before the Soviet invasion in 1979, there had been as many as sixty Jewish families living in Kabul, Levi said. His children, four sons and a daughter, had since moved to Israel. He described himself as a rabbi who had taken custody of the last remaining Torah in the city. But in May 1999, "I was arrested and beaten for practicing sorcery," he told me. "I spent forty-nine days in Pol-e-Charki prison," a grim dungeon a few miles from Kabul. The Ministry of the Interior had taken possession of his precious Torah.

I asked Levi why he chose to remain in Kabul. "This house belonged to my father and other members of the Jewish community," he said. "If I leave, the house will be seized by the Taliban. I have an obligation to maintain the place."

On the question of how he supported himself, he was evasive, saying that as a clergyman he would pray for people's headaches to disappear. (My interpreter later told me that Levi was often visited for palm readings.) The rabbi wrapped things up after about fifteen minutes, observing that he did not want neighbors on his street reporting that he was meeting with foreigners.[50]

Isaac Levi's story is hardly an aberration. Amnesty International accused the Taliban of killing thousands of Hazara Shias after taking Mazar-i-Sharif in August 1998, and a U.S. State Department report issued in spring 2000 said the Taliban had committed "numerous serious human rights abuses." According to the report, some of the worst abuses occurred in their prosecution of the war in the north against the nation's former rulers, where the Taliban summarily executed civilians, forcibly relocated populations, burned homes and crops, and used forced labor.[51]

I was curious to see firsthand the Taliban's human rights practices and decided to pay an unannounced visit to the Pol-e-Charki prison. I was greeted warmly at the gate by the assistant commander, Mullah Khan Jan, who explained that he had only had his job for the past month. The cheerful mullah, who allowed me to tour the facility at will, seemed more like a candidate to play Father Christmas at a suburban mall than a prison official.

In the main courtyard I found hundreds of prisoners milling about.

Despite the generally wretched conditions, none seemed to be suffering from any obvious ill-treatment. The prison held a total of 1,800 inmates, divided into four categories: "political"; "prisoners of war" from the anti-Taliban Northern Alliance; common criminals; and those picked up by the Vice and Virtue police. The first two categories made up the vast majority. I talked to one of the political prisoners, who said he had been incarcerated for eleven months. He believed that his sentence would likely be indefinite. I also spoke to one of the fifteen prisoners in the Vice and Virtue section, an older man who said he had been beaten and had spent two and a half months in the prison for drinking.

The small number of Vice and Virtue prisoners suggested that the Taliban's real war against the forces of the former government, known as the Northern Alliance, had forced the cultural war to the back burner. This was confirmed in numerous small ways during my trip. Everywhere I went I saw people playing soccer and boys flying kites, both of which had been banned by early Taliban edicts. I often heard forbidden Hindi music in taxis. I saw more unaccompanied women on the streets than I had on the 1997 trip. Although these were hardly momentous changes, they did indicate a softening, perhaps in response to the political reality that many Afghans did not favor the Taliban's brand of neo-fundamentalist Islam.

On one subject, however, the Taliban remained immovable: Osama bin Laden. This was clear from my first appointment in Kabul, with the minister of planning, Qari Din Mohammad Hanif. The designation "Qari" meant that the minister had memorized the entire Koran, a prodigious feat he had begun at age nine and completed by the time he was twelve. This qualification, however, was unlikely to help him in the task of rebuilding his country. A vivid sign of the country's poverty could be seen in the minister's office: my freezing breath. Resources were scarce; the entire ministry possessed only four computers. (Afghanistan would clearly not be in need of a contingency plan for the looming Y2K problem.) On Hanif's table sat a paperweight from Central Asia Gas Pipeline Ltd., a grim token of that now defunct multibillion-dollar enterprise.

"We are a wounded people," announced the minister, incensed at the sanctions that the United Nations had recently placed on Afghanistan for continuing to harbor Osama bin Laden. "We need salve for the wounds—instead they have rubbed salt in them." The prices of basic foodstuffs, he said, had doubled since the sanctions had been imposed, and the afghani had lost more than 10 percent of its value. Pressed about bin Laden, he continued, "The subject is brighter than the sun. We have to respect tradition. He is not a terrorist, he is a holy warrior. The West only accuses him. We have a hospitable tradition. He is our guest. It is the tradition of our people."

Indeed, the Taliban leadership subscribed to the ancient and elaborate Pathan tribal code of conduct, *pukhtunwali*.[52] Pukhtunwali puts an enormous premium on two concepts: *malmastiya,* "the obligation to show hospitality to all visitors without any hope of renumeration or favor," and *nanawati,* the offering of asylum.[53] The leading modern authority on Afghanistan defines the obligation of *nanawati* this way: "to fight to the death for a person who has taken refuge with me no matter what his lineage."[54] A report in a Pakistani newspaper in 1998 explained how the tribal code of protection is still very much alive: "In recent times, a tribal elder agreed to suffer the demolition of his fort-like house rather than hand over a wanted man to the governor."[55] The Taliban found handing over bin Laden as unimaginable as a Christian priest in the Middle Ages would have found it to hand over someone who had sought sanctuary in his church.

The hardest line I heard was from Maulvi Hafeezullah of the Foreign Ministry, who, unprompted, embarked on a fifteen-minute diatribe against the U.S. policy on bin Laden. "We like the people of the U.S.," he said. "We want to tell Albright, Clinton, and Cohen you are jeopardizing your future interests in this region. . . . These sanctions have turned Afghans who were not necessarily pro-Taliban and have brought them closer to the government. . . . We can live on grass, we don't need Pepsi. Obviously now that we are cornered we have to fight back." Hafeezullah pointed out that during World War II, when Afghanistan came under pressure from the Allies to hand over several hundred Germans living in the country, the request was denied. "These were not even Muslims," he said, "and we did not hand them over."

The Taliban's decision-making process had all the transparency of

Leonid Brezhnev's Politburo, but one thing was certain: the last word on policy belonged to Mullah Omar, the man who led the band of religious students that seized the city in 1994 and who went on to consecrate his leadership by literally wrapping himself in the Cloak of the Prophet, one of Afghanistan's holiest relics, publicly displayed only three times in the past century.[56] A recluse who rarely gave interviews, Mullah Omar lived in a gaudy compound in Kandahar—making that city, not Kabul, the spiritual heart and political capital of the Taliban. He held no official position in the government, but, as *Amirul Momineen,* "Commander of the Faithful," Mullah Omar was the highest authority this side of paradise. And the highest authority had made his verdict plain: "Handing [bin Laden] over, for us," he has said, "is as difficult as leaving a pillar of Islam."[57]

Beyond his status as an honored guest, bin Laden was a valued ally of the Taliban, having contributed money and men to its cause for years. He gave the Taliban $3 million at a critical moment in 1996 as the religious warriors geared up to take Kabul.[58] An Afghan journalist working for the Associated Press told me he witnessed a "kind of division" of bin Laden's troops—perhaps as many as three hundred men—fighting alongside the Taliban on the front line north of Kabul in the winter of 1997. They were well equipped, and even had tanks at their disposal.[59] By 1999 four hundred Arabs under bin Laden's leadership—the 055 Brigade—were fighting against the anti-Taliban forces, the Northern Alliance.[60]

Not surprisingly, one of the people most familiar with the capabilities of bin Laden's forces was the Northern Alliance's foreign minister, Dr. Abdullah. Dr. Abdullah met me in the lobby of Washington's posh Mayflower Hotel for tea in late September 2000. The 055 Brigade, he said, had fought in the areas around Kabul but had moved north; via radio intercepts, his intelligence team had identified two bin Laden aides directing troop operations in the Kunduz area. "They are good fighters," he said. "Not *tactically* good, but their morale is exceptionally high." He explained that bin Laden's troops preferred suicide to capture and recounted a grisly tale of how his forces had discovered the bodies of four Arabs near the town of Charikar in 1999. They had used their last grenade to blow themselves up.

At the time of our meeting, Dr. Abdullah was the alter ego of the military commander of the Northern Alliance, Ahmad Shah Massoud. They made an unlikely pair: Massoud, the soldier, in battle fatigues and the dun woolen cap of his native Panjshir Valley; Dr. Abdullah, the professional diplomat, in his well-tailored blue jacket (with a natty red handkerchief), starched white shirt, and silver cuff links. But appearances were deceptive: Dr. Abdullah had seen his share of carnage. Trained as an eye surgeon in Kabul in the early eighties, by 1985 he had joined Massoud's forces in the Panjshir and set up a medical clinic. During the mid-eighties, the Soviets had launched some of the most devastating attacks of the war on Massoud's forces in the Panjshir, and Dr. Abdullah's clinic was busy—too busy. It is difficult to look for any length of time into eyes that have a focused intensity—not the intensity of the neurotic, but that of a man who has seen too much.

After Panjshir, Dr. Abdullah joined the resistance full-time, working first as Massoud's secretary, rising over the years to foreign minister. With Massoud's assassination on September 9, 2001, Dr. Abdullah is now playing a critical role in the American effort to garner intelligence about bin Laden and in the planning of potential military operations against him and the Taliban.

Exactly how close were bin Laden and the shadowy Mullah Omar? There were widely circulated rumors of a marital alliance between their families: perhaps bin Laden had married one of Omar's daughters. Every Taliban official I spoke to denied this. (In 2000, bin Laden married the fourth and last wife allowed to him under Islamic law; she is a Yemeni.)

The Taliban and bin Laden have not enjoyed perfect relations. While he was their guest and they were not eager to hand him over to the United States, he had also been a headache for the movement's leadership, who did not appreciate his repeated calls for violence against Americans that had complicated their already difficult quest for international recognition. According to one report, the Taliban even struck a deal with Saudi officials in the early summer of 1998 to send bin Laden to a Saudi prison, but it fell apart after the bombings of the American embassies in Africa and the subsequent U.S. missile strikes on Afghanistan.[61]

The tensions between bin Laden and his Afghan hosts came to a head in February 1999. According to the *Al-Quds Al-Arabi* newspaper, Mullah Omar snubbed bin Laden, keeping him cooling his heels for a couple of hours when he came to offer his respects during the Eid celebration marking the end of Ramadan. Mullah Omar had been annoyed by bin Laden's public threats against the United States at the end of December 1998.[62] *The New York Times* even carried a histrionic report that there had been a possible exchange of gunfire between Taliban soldiers and bin Laden's bodyguards.[63] Afghan officials denied this, but said they had asked bin Laden to suspend his political and military activities in February 1999, confiscating his satellite phones and providing him with a ten-man guard to observe his movements.[64] After that bin Laden stopped giving interviews to the world's media. (Instead, his lectures and public appearances were videotaped by the media arm of al-Qaeda and given to Arab outlets for wider dissemination.)

In June 2001, Mullah Omar said that any *fatwas* by bin Laden were "null and void," as he did not have the religious authority to issue them.[65] There was less to this than meets the eye, because Afghan clergy had already issued *fatwas* supporting bin Laden's positions on such matters as the presence of American troops in Saudi Arabia.

If the Taliban had shown little sustained interest in bringing bin Laden to heel, they had shown even less interest in cracking down on the training camps that continued to operate in Afghanistan in the late nineties. Indeed, weapons used for those camps were purchased from the Taliban.[66] An Afghan journalist told me he had talked to Pakistanis from religious schools in Peshawar, Quetta, and Lahore who had arrived in Kabul in the fall of 1999 for military training. (The Pakistanis were the most visible of a polyglot group of Chechens, Kashmiris, Uzbeks, Tajiks, Bangladeshis, Egyptians, Algerians, Libyans, Yemenis, Chinese Uighurs, Burmese, and even African-Americans.)[67]

On the basis of information drawn from my interviews with U.S. officials and Pakistani and Afghan sources, I counted a dozen or so training camps operating in Afghanistan in 2000. A U.N. official who regularly visited the country said that one camp of Arab and Chechen fighters was located twenty kilometers south of Jalalabad, an area where bin Laden had operated on and off for years.

In his September 2000 interview Dr. Abdullah identified four principal camps for the militants of the Islamist Internationale. One, near Khost, was leveled by the American cruise missile attacks in August 1998 but subsequently rebuilt. The second, in the Jalalabad area, near Hadda, had been used by bin Laden's group. The third was south of Kabul in Charasayab and had once been the base of Gulbuddin Hekmatyar. I had visited this base in 1993 and it was ideally suited for training purposes, with an extensive complex of barracks already set up. The fourth camp was in Uruzgan, in south-central Afghanistan.

By 1999, Pakistani officials, who rarely criticized their Taliban protégés, had become concerned about the training camps: graduates were increasingly implicated in the deadly Shia-Sunni conflicts that were leaving a trail of hundreds of bodies across Pakistan.[68] A week before he was toppled by General Musharraf's coup, Prime Minister Nawaz Sharif declared: "We have with us solid evidence that there exist training camps in Afghanistan which are training terrorists and sending them into Pakistan to kill our people."[69] In June 2000, Pakistan's military government gave the Taliban a list of eighteen camps believed to be training Pakistani militants, and the Taliban actually closed two camps near Kabul—although local residents said that the militants had simply moved north to fight against the Northern Alliance.[70]

In sum, most of the Taliban's military training camps continued to function despite the denials of Foreign Minister Wakil Ahmed Muttawakil, who told CNN in January 2000, less than accurately, "We don't need any camps or any other people to be trained. They have been automatically closed." As the Taliban had failed to close those camps, American airpower and Afghan manpower would eventually do the job for them.

Despite signs of moderation in the late nineties, by 2001 the Taliban was increasingly in the grip of its hard-liners. Early in the year, Mullah Omar ordered the destruction of all the statues in the country on the basis that representations of the human form are un-Islamic. Accordingly, Afghanistan's extraordinary trove of thousands of Buddhist relics, a legacy of the time when the country was a fount of Buddhist culture, were systematically pulverized. Those actions provoked horrified condemnation in both the West and the Muslim world, particularly when it was announced that the plan also called for the destruction of two massive Buddhas standing over a hundred feet high. Carved out of cliffs in central Afghanistan, the Buddhas dated from the third and fifth centuries and were one of the country's premier tourist attractions in the 1970s. In March 2001, Taliban soldiers, who had already disfigured the statues in past years, were dispatched to finish the job once and for all with artillery and explosives.[71] Then, in an eerie echo of Hitler's Nuremberg Laws, Afghanistan's Hindus were ordered to wear yellow clothing and identify their houses with a yellow sash. They were also told that they could no longer live with Muslims.

The Taliban also made it increasingly difficult for international aid agencies to work in their devastated country. In August 2001, the government arrested twenty-four aid workers, both Afghans and Westerners, including two Americans, on charges that they were proselytizing for Christianity, a crime punishable by prison or expulsion for the Westerners and death for the Afghans.[72]

After the September 11 attacks, the Taliban continued to insist that they would not hand over their ally bin Laden. It seemed as if their revolution had entered its Jacobin phase with no Thermidor in sight. But after holding most of Afghanistan for five years the Taliban movement was largely destroyed by the end of 2001. On October 7 the United States began intensive bombing raids on key Taliban command and control sites and the Northern Alliance launched an artillery barrage north of Kabul. Many commentators, including myself, presumed that the Taliban would put up stiff resistance, but the Taliban did not understand the new kind of war they were fighting. They assumed that the United States would fight the same kind of war that the Soviets had fought in Afghanistan, sending in large numbers of static ground forces that they could hit with guerrilla raids. Instead, the Taliban came under withering and precise U.S. bombing raids directed by Special Forces on the ground, which damaged the Taliban's will to fight. Many Taliban commanders switched sides for money or because they could see which way the wind was blowing. On November 10 the first major Taliban city, Mazar-e-Sharif, fell to the Northern Alliance, followed in quick succession by Herat and Kabul.

With the capture of Kandahar on December 7 the Taliban was finished as a viable movement. However, senior Taliban leaders, including Mullah Omar himself, have either melted into the Afghan countryside or crossed the border into Pakistan. Those leaders will surely present a lingering problem to the new government in Afghanistan and American and European forces stationed in the counry.

CHAPTER 9

The Holy Warriors of Yemen:
The Bombing of the U.S.S. *Cole*

Faith is Yemeni, wisdom is Yemeni.
                    —Yemeni proverb

*"The heads of the unbelievers flew in all directions, and their
limbs were scattered. The victory of Islam had come, and the
victory [we scored] in Yemen will continue."*

                    —Osama bin Laden speaking about the bombing of
                    the U.S.S. *Cole* on an al-Qaeda recruitment
                    videotape, 2001

On the sweltering, slightly overcast morning of October 12, 2000, two Yemeni men drove their Nissan truck to a beach near the southern port of Aden and unloaded a small boat, which was packed with somewhere between five hundred and seven hundred pounds of explosives.[1] They knew that the window of opportunity to pull off their mission was narrow, since the warship U.S.S. *Cole* would take only a few hours to refuel. Handing a twelve-year-old boy a tip to watch their vehicle, they pushed off to sea for the fifteen-minute trip to where the vast destroyer was berthed.[2]

The bombers had the presence of mind to stand up and wave at the crew on the deck of the warship before detonating the charge that would deliver them, they believed, to Paradise.[3] Back on earth, the blast blew a forty-by-sixty-foot hole in the reinforced steel hull of the

Cole, killing seventeen American sailors, injuring thirty-nine others, and inflicting a quarter-billion dollars' worth of damage on the ship.

No terrorist group had attacked a U.S. naval warship before, so the bombing was an enormous shock to the Pentagon. It probably shouldn't have been. During the nineties, Yemen had attracted an international cast of Muslim militants who found its weak central government and remote mountainous regions a congenial place to train—and to launch attacks on American and British targets.[4] (After 9/11 the Yemeni government made a determined effort to crack down on al-Qaeda cells in the country. The jury is out, as of this writing, about how successful that effort has been.)

For the trip north of the capital, on a road known as Kidnapper's Alley, the government had thoughtfully provided me an armed escort: a Toyota pickup with a heavy machine gun bolted to its floor and half a dozen Yemeni soldiers in orange and brown desert fatigues. My first problem in Yemen was getting rid of them. Only when I ditched my bodyguards could I continue on to visit Sheikh Muhammad bin Shajea, a tribal leader who presides over a vast, desolate swath of territory from his desert fortress on Yemen's northern border with Saudi Arabia's Empty Quarter. He was one of the Yemenis I hoped would shed some light on their nation's most infamous son.

At Sa'da we waved good-bye to the soldiers, who probably assumed we were going to visit a local tourist site, and were suddenly joined by a couple of bin Shajea's gunmen. After they had unceremoniously jumped into our vehicle, we drove east for dozens of miles, a journey through barren, rock-strewn hills where we saw not another living being.

That is, until two shots rang out above our heads. Bin Shajea's lead gunman, a dead ringer for Omar Sharif circa *Lawrence of Arabia*, leaped out of our van, his well-oiled Kalashnikov at the ready. He was joined by my driver, who had his own rifle and pistol handy for such eventualities. A battered orange pickup screeched to a halt beside us and out jumped three hard-faced young men, weapons drawn. A huge shouting match ensued. The young men later claimed they were interested only in getting a ride for one of their friends and meant us no harm—on balance, a rather lame story. My translator said he was sure they'd planned to kidnap us but had given up on encountering real opposition.

Whatever the truth, this was a severe breach of tribal etiquette. The leader of the young gunmen offered Omar Sharif his weapon as recompense, an offer declined on the grounds that the matter would then have to be taken up by their respective sheikhs and could develop into a major hassle. In these parts, major hassles are settled with artillery.

It seemed a fitting way to start my trip to the interior of Yemen, a country with a rich history of kidnappings and terrorism. The uncertain government control of Yemen's more remote regions is compounded by the fact that the country has suffered a series of civil wars pitting communists against nationalists and Islamist militants. A legacy of those wars, the last of which was fought in 1994, are the estimated sixty-five million weapons distributed among a population of eighteen million.[5] You do the math.

A somewhat silly movie, *Rules of Engagement*, released a few months before the *Cole* bombing, stars Samuel L. Jackson as a heroic Marine officer unfairly charged with the massacre of Yemeni civilians. The movie opens with a scene of a huge mob of Yemenis, some secreting automatic weapons, who besiege and then storm the American embassy in San'a. Obviously, this was a Hollywood construct: In reality the American embassy in Yemen is not housed in a crumbling old palace with a huge public plaza conducive to enraged demonstrations, but is set far back from the street and surrounded by walls and hardened guardposts. There is, however, a grain of truth in the picture of the unsettled Yemeni populace that *Rules of Engagement* paints. A day after the *Cole* attack, a bomb went off at the British embassy, knocking down an exterior wall and blowing out windows. Because the device went off at six in the morning, no one was injured.[6] In January 2001, a plane carrying the American ambassador to Yemen was hijacked by a self-described pro-Iraqi activist, who was subsequently overpowered. Because of terrorist threats in June 2001, FBI agents investigating the *Cole* attack were pulled out of Yemen and the American embassy was closed for all but essential purposes. Yemeni police arrested ten militants, believed to be affiliated with bin Laden, who were equipped

with bomb-making materials, grenades, and maps of the area surrounding the U.S. embassy.[7]

Despite its lawless history, Yemen has become something of a
tourist destination because of the charm of its inhabitants and its extraordinary medieval cities. Old San'a is a maze of centuries-old brown
mud-brick mini-skyscrapers decorated with white stucco, rising as
high as twelve stories like so many impossibly tall gingerbread cakes
piped with sugar icing. On the uppermost floor of any house is the
mafraj, arguably the most important room, reserved for the afternoon
qat-chewing sessions that are the principal leisure activity of Yemeni
men. The bitter, green-leafed *qat* provides a mild euphoria that stimu-
lates convivial conversation.[8]

On the labyrinthine lanes below are scenes that Hieronymus Bosch
would have painted if he had made it this far south; smithies making
nails over open fires; men turning wooden dagger handles on lathes or
sharpening blades to fine points in a cloud of metallic dust; hawkers
bellowing the names of their wares to the throngs on the cobbled
streets; blinkered camels powering giant wooden mortars that crush
seeds for sesame oil; shops illuminated by candlelight selling ancient
muskets and flintlock pistols inlaid with pearl; and spice sellers offering fist-sized chunks of amber-colored myrrh and piles of granulated
frankincense.

Men amble around in outfits that in other locales would seem odd.
For example, you'll often see a formal Western business jacket worn
over a skirtlike undergarment held together by a belt with a *jambiya*—
a massive curving dagger that must surely present its wearer with logistical problems in sitting down. I had seen pictures of Yemeni men
in this garb in my guidebook but had assumed it was the kind of getup
favored by national tourism boards rather than actual inhabitants. Not
so. My translator, who was moonlighting from his job as a Web master
at a newspaper, wore a beautifully embroidered, century-old belt that
held both his dagger and his pager.

I arrived at the beginning of Ramadan, when the first sighting of
the sickle moon signals the start of the month of fasting, memorializ-
ing the revelations of the Koran to the Prophet Muhammad. As dusk
deepened, the sonorous tones of competing muezzins rose from every
mosque—*"Allah akbar, Allah akbar"*: God is great, God is great. As

the sun set, a mob of men who had been fasting all day besieged a food store, shoving money at the proprietor and emerging with paper bags that contained unidentified tasty morsels. Their wives waited patiently at some distance from the crowd.

During the holy month, Yemen turns the clock upside down. Businesses adhere to an unusual schedule, opening in the afternoon and closing as late as three A.M. I was surprised to find downtown San'a at midnight to be as lively as Manhattan. In a shopping mall awash in marble, groups of black-robed Yemeni women sipped Pepsi, resting from their labors at the holy trinity of Bally, Boss, and Baskin-Robbins. At one in the morning, the band in my hotel restaurant cranked out the hits. The chorus of one of their songs sounded like "Rastafari, Rastafari, sinsemilla, sinsemilla"—although this is unlikely. Invoking a God other than Allah is not encouraged in Yemen. And, with all the *qat* they chew, Yemenis are in little need of other herbal remedies.

All night long bug-eyed men hurried down the streets of San'a, their cheeks bulging with baseball-sized wedges of *qat*, masticating furiously, as if rushing off to a Bugs Bunny look-alike convention. When I first tried *qat*, it seemed like chomping on a lump of sodden, bitter grass. Once I got past the taste, however, I found *qat* produced a combination of the heightened sharpness that follows a double espresso with the generalized bonhomie imparted by a martini. No wonder every Yemeni male from the prime minister on down is an ardent advocate of the "chew."

Although it was only six weeks after the bombing of the *Cole*, people smiled and waved at me as I strolled the streets of the old city. But directly opposite my hotel was an overpass on which the single word "Osama" had been sprayed in red letters—a reminder of the purpose of my visit.

While Yemen is the poorest country on the Arabian Peninsula, the streets of San'a are choked with Mercedes and Toyota Land Cruisers: *somebody* is making the riyals.[9] And Yemen can genuinely claim to be an emerging democracy. Its president since 1978, Lieutenant General Ali Abdallah Salih, has instituted a fascinating type of political system that, for want of a better term, might be called despotic democracy. As in most Middle Eastern dictatorships and monarchies, portraits of the president are ubiquitous, but there is also a parliament that wields

a modicum of power and in which groups of various persuasions—
including the Islamist-tribal Islah party and the smaller nationalist and
socialist parties—are represented. Yemen is generally reckoned to be
among the most democratic of Arab countries; this is flattery of only
the mildest sort.[10]

Yet it was precisely Yemen's relative freedom that fostered the
growth of jihadist groups in the nineties. Yemenis were among the
principal recruits to bin Laden's group during the Afghan war against
the Soviets; at the end of that war, in 1989, they returned to Yemen in
vast numbers, bringing with them compatriots from countries like
Syria, Jordan, and Egypt, men who would have faced arrest in their
own native lands.[11] In 1991, a camp for the Afghan Arabs was set up in
the mountains of northern Yemen, near the town of Sad'a.[12] Bin
Laden, meanwhile, financed a training facility in Yemen's southern
Abayan province.[13]

The first time the Afghan Arabs struck at American military targets
in Yemen was December 1992, eight years before the U.S.S. *Cole* attack, when bombs exploded outside two hotels in Aden. As noted earlier, about a hundred American servicemen were billeted there on
their way to Operation Restore Hope, the doomed American mission
to feed starving Somalis that was interpreted by al-Qaeda as part of a
U.S. scheme to increase its military presence in Muslim nations.[14]

The bombs went off outside Aden's poshest hotels, the Mövenpick
and the Goldmohur, killing a tourist and a hotel worker but no Americans. A U.S. law enforcement official told me that bin Laden was behind the attacks, but there was little chance of prosecuting the case
because of a lack of forensic evidence.[15] Within days of the hotel
bombings, the Pentagon announced it would no longer use Yemen as a
support base for its Somalia operation. Bin Laden made a veiled reference to those attacks in his interview with CNN: "If the U.S. thinks
and brags that it still has this kind of power even after all these succes-
sive defeats in Vietnam, Beirut, Aden, and Somalia, let them go back
to those places." Would that the United States had taken this warning
to heart.

According to a Western diplomat in Yemen and a senior Yemeni official, the man who directed the hotel bombings was Tariq al-Fadhli,
the son of the deposed sultan of Abayan, a region near Aden.[16] In

1967, the socialists of southern Yemen ousted the British, who had ruled the city-state of Aden for more than a century. Al-Fadhli's father, stripped of his sultanate, moved to Saudi Arabia, and Tariq al-Fadhli was brought up in Jeddah.[17] For about two years during the eighties, he fought in Afghanistan against the communists.[18] There he met bin Laden, with whom he had "good relations."[19] After the Soviet withdrawal from Afghanistan in 1989, al-Fadhli returned to Yemen as the leader of the Afghan Arabs, which was more a collection of like-minded militants than a formal organization.[20] Bin Laden funded their holy war to rid Yemen of the socialist government of southern Yemen.[21]

Following the 1992 hotel bombings, authorities sent an armored brigade to arrest al-Fadhli in his stronghold, a fortress in the Maraqasha mountains near Aden; he eventually surrendered under murky circumstances.[22] Also allegedly linked to those bombings was another Afghan war veteran, al-Fahdli's second-in command, Jamal al-Nahdi.[23] In both their cases the Yemeni government seems to have developed amnesia: al-Fadhli became a member of the president's personally selected consultative council, and his sister is married to General Ali Muhsin al-Ahmar, a member of President Salih's family; al-Nahdi is a businessman in San'a and a member of the permanent committee of Yemen's ruling party.[24]

The hotel bombings were the first sign that bin Laden and his Afghan Arabs meant business in Yemen. According to the U.S. indictment against him, from 1992 onwards bin Laden's al-Qaeda group issued *fatwas* that called for attacks on American military targets in the country.[25]

The twists and turns in Yemen's political fortunes during the mid-1990s worked to the advantage of the Afghan Arabs. Until 1990, Yemen was divided into two countries, the Yemen Arab Republic in the north and the Marxist People's Democratic Republic of Yemen in the south. (An axiom of political theory: any combination of the words "People's" and "Democratic" in a country's name indicates the ruthless repression of both the people and democracy.) The post-1990 union was always uneasy; in 1994, north Yemen went to war against the socialist south. Sheikh Abdul Majid al-Zindani, a prominent Islamic scholar, future founder of the Islamist Islah party, and a major recruiter for the Afghan jihad (U.S. officials also identify him as an ally of bin Laden's), mobilized the Afghan Arabs for the war against the south.[26] They didn't need a lot of prodding: here was another happy opportunity to attack the godless communists. Ten thousand civilians were killed in the course of the war, and when the Afghan Arabs swept into the southern capital of Aden they burnt down the country's only brewery.[27] The victorious northern Yemen government was grateful to the holy warriors and doled out government jobs in the newly reunified country.[28]

After the war, leaders of the Afghan Arabs like Sheikh al-Zindani and Tariq al-Fadhli were gathered into President Salih's national unification government. To some extent, the "big tent" strategy has worked. Saeed Thabit, a journalist and spokesman for Sheikh al-Zindani, holds a view of the American military presence on the Arabian peninsula that is worlds away from bin Laden's sweeping declarations. "Do the Americans enter Mecca?" Thabit asked me. "If they do not there is no problem with the Americans. The only holy places are Mecca and Medina." Thabit also stressed that the Islah party was committed to democracy, which made it unpopular with the Afghan Arabs and other Islamists. As we talked, an unveiled young woman walked in and out of his office—to me, the most telling sign that Islah had traveled a long way from the neo-fundamentalism of the jihadists.

That perception of Islah was reinforced by Abdul Wahab al-Anesi, a former deputy prime minister of Yemen, with whom I met in a reception room in one of the party's offices. Around the floors were red cushions and pillows on which to recline. The high white stucco walls were topped by arched windows of stained glass—mosaics of blues, reds, yellows, and greens. Al-Anesi wore an exquisitely tailored gray overcoat and vest over his white robes. His manner was thoughtful as he pointed out that Islah ("Reform") did not have the word Islam in its name: "Yemen is a Muslim nation, and no one can claim it is the sole party of Islam." He emphasized that, unlike other Islamist groups, Islah is committed to Yemen's multiparty system: "Democracy," he said, is the "secure frame for Yemen."[29]

While some Yemeni jihadists did indeed hang up their holy war gear in the mid-nineties, a substratum of Afghan Arabs had no such intention. Consider the links that continued to flourish between the holy warriors in Yemen and those in Afghanistan during the late nineties. In 1999 Julie Sirrs, a former intelligence analyst for the Pentagon, interviewed a number of POWs held by the anti-Taliban Northern Alliance. Among the prisoners were two Yemenis who had come to Afghanistan to fight for a few months and were planning to return home with battle skills sharpened.[30] The Yemenis volunteered that they were "willing to go anywhere to kill Americans."[31] When the United States attacked bin Laden's camps in eastern Afghanistan in 1998, three Yemenis were among the dead.[32]

In 1997, bin Laden even seriously contemplated moving his base of operations from Afghanistan to his ancestral homeland, sending envoys to a gathering of powerful tribal leaders to work out the specifics. He had already told *Al-Quds Al-Arabi* that Yemen's armed tribesmen, mountainous terrain, and "clean air you can breathe without humiliation" were the reasons he was considering the move.[33] One of the Yemeni tribal leaders consulted about bin Laden's arrival was Sheikh bin Shajea, whom I was on my way to interview.

After our aforementioned encounter with the hitchhikers-cum-kidnappers, we drove on towards bin Shajea's fortress. The rocky track gave way to flat, white desert that abruptly turned into the orange-tinged dunes of the Empty Quarter. Finally, we arrived at a lookout tower and, beyond that, bin Shajea's compound, which consisted of a mosque and several villas for the various wives with whom the sheikh has sired twenty sons and twenty daughters. No business could be conducted before sitting down to a vast spread of lamb, chicken, salads, soups, and a dessert of Yemeni honey (supposedly an aphrodisiac) slathered over a dome of pastry, all of which the sheikh insistently heaped on my plate. Sitting with us were perhaps twenty or so of the sheikh's retainers and bodyguards, smartly turned out in gray pin-striped jackets, white robes, and red-and-white checkered head-dresses, who set aside their various weapons before tucking into the feast that broke their Ramadan fast.

We then repaired to bin Shajea's *divan*, or meeting room; it was the length of a football field and its ceiling was punctuated by crystal chandeliers. "I am important here," the sheikh was quick to point out, "and the president is important in San'a." Bin Shajea is so important that he can conduct his own private wars with little fear of government inter-

ference. At the time of our meeting he was in the midst of an eight-
een-month dispute with another tribe—a dispute that was being settled with mortars, rockets, and a variety of cannons. Eighty lives had
already been lost.[34]

The sheikh told me he had met with bin Laden a couple of times in
Saudi Arabia before the latter was forced to move to Sudan in 1991; he
said he respected bin Laden as a "religious scholar" and "Saudi opposition figure." But, he added emphatically, he had little patience with his
calls for holy war. For emphasis, the sheikh had the mildly disconcert-
ing habit of taking my hand in his and squeezing it.

Bin Shajea explained he was one of a group of about twenty tribal
sheikhs who met with emissaries from bin Laden in San'a in early
1997. *Squeeze*. The meeting with the envoys, two Saudi and two
Yemeni clerics, lasted three hours. The clerics asked for adequate protection for bin Laden and an area in which he could operate, specify-
ing a preference for the mountainous regions of Yemen's northwest,
on its border with Saudi Arabia. They did not offer any cash incentive
for the deal. *Squeeze*. The sheikhs replied: "We consider you Yemeni,
we are not rejecting you, but we ask you that you suspend any political
or military activities directed against other countries." After that, bin
Shajea told me, they never heard back from bin Laden. *Squeeze,
squeeze*.

Despite bin Shajea's professed tolerance, there has been a growing
anti-American sentiment in Yemen. One expression of this was the
December 1998 kidnapping of sixteen Western tourists near Aden.[35]
The victims included twelve Britons, two Australians, and two Americans; a nurse, a postal worker, several university lecturers, a teacher,
and an executive of the Xerox Corporation. All had set out for a vacation over the Christmas holidays.[36]

Kidnapping is something of a cottage industry in Yemen: between
1996 and 2000, kidnappers seized 150 hostages, 122 of them foreigners, and in the course of these relatively civilized affairs, the hostages
were well treated and the kidnappers sought either cash or redress of
some local grievance.[37] But in the 1998 incident, this almost quaint,
nonviolent tradition was shattered. The group responsible, the Islamic
Army of Aden (IAA), had trained with al-Qaeda, and after an intense
two-hour firefight with security forces, four hostages and three kid-

nappers lay dead.[38] (Memo to self: in the event of a kidnapping, never be "rescued" by a Third World army.)

The story of the IAA provides a fascinating window on the jihadist groups based in Yemen and their connections both to officials in the Yemeni government and to militants outside the country. It's also a cross between a Gilbert and Sullivan farce and a Shakespearean tragedy, infused with a healthy dose of Kafka.

First, let us meet the villain of the piece. The man who directed the kidnapping was thirty-two-year-old Zain al-Abdine al-Mihdar, better known as Abu Hassan.[39] (Khalid al-Mihdar, a member of Abu Hassan's tribe, and possibly a relative, would play an important role in the September 11, 2001, attacks on the United States.) Abu Hassan fought in Afghanistan alongside bin Laden and founded the Islamic Army of Aden sometime in 1997.[40] While the IAA was never much of an army, it began issuing communiqués in 1998 praising the bombings of the U.S. embassies in Africa.[41] When he was finally tried for kidnapping the western tourists, Abu Hassan referred to his hostages as the "grandchildren of pigs and monkeys" and averred that if his pistol had not jammed he would have killed more of them.[42]

The other key figure is Egyptian Abu Hamza, whom the Yemeni government has labeled the éminence grise of the IAA.[43] If this were indeed Shakespeare, Abu Hamza would be the Fool who wanders in and out of the drama making observations either absurd or pertinent or both. The Yemeni government says he is the mastermind of the IAA, but Abu Hamza styles himself merely their "media adviser."[44]

He is not to be found in Yemen but thousands of miles to the north, in London, where he is the imam of the Finsbury Park Mosque, just up the road from the stadium of the legendary London soccer team Arsenal. Serious Arab opposition figures regard Abu Hamza as a self-publicizing joke, for he is neither a profound scholar of Islam nor an important political figure.[45] But jokes can sometimes turn deadly serious.

I visited Abu Hamza in November 1999 at his modern mosque, which sits at the end of a row of modest nineteenth-century houses. In the front hall was a notice pleading for donations to the Muslims in Chechnya: "The Russians are bombing our brothers, using chemical weapons." There were tapes for sale on a long trestle table. A couple of titles caught my eye: *Why Jihad?* and *Never Feel Sorry for Wicked*

America, both by Abu Hamza. Young men streamed in from the rain-swept, blustery London streets.

It seems that the only politically correct bad guy in movies these days is a bug-eyed Arab terrorist ready to blow up the world, but no Hollywood screenwriter would have dared to dream up a baddie as outlandish as Abu Hamza. He is a huge man, dressed in the typical Afghan outfit of *shalwar kameez* and brown woolen cap. The first things you notice are that one of his eyes sits motionless in its socket, and that when he gestures he does so with arms that are stumps, the result of a mine explosion in Afghanistan. To those stumps he some-times attaches a hook, which gives him the sinister aspect of a Bond villain. The effect is hardly dispelled by his calls for a jihad against the enemies of Islam, delivered in sound-bite-ready English. No wonder he is in the Rolodex of every talk-show booker in London.

Because we were surrounded by a small group of his acolytes, I decided not to inquire about reports that his first job in England was as a bouncer at a nightclub in London's Soho sex district.[46] Nor did I ask about the welfare payments he draws from the British govern-ment that he so despises. The *New York Times* reporter John Burns, visiting the mosque six months earlier, had had a gun pulled on him by an Algerian follower of Abu Hamza, so it seemed prudent not to annoy the lads. But I did ask the man himself to tell me—in general—about his life.

Abu Hamza was born Mustafa Kamal in Alexandria, Egypt, in 1958, and left for England in his twenties to study civil engineering at Brighton University.[47] (He graduated in 1986.) While a student, he met Sheikh Omar Abdel Rahman, the spiritual leader of Egypt's jihad movement. Abu Hamza described the blind sheikh, now jailed in the United States for his role in plots to blow up New York City land-marks, as "a good example—he shines for us now." In the early eight-ies, he married a Western woman, from whom he is now divorced; the union produced a son, Mohammad, of whom more shortly. In 1987 Abu Hamza met with the chief recruiter for the Afghan jihad, Abdul-lah Azzam, while performing the hajj pilgrimage to Saudi Arabia. He described Azzam as "one of the big sparks of jihad in our time."

Inspired by the Afghan holy war, Abu Hamza spent much of the pe-riod between 1989 and 1993 in Afghanistan. There he settled in the eastern town of Jalalabad, where he became chief engineer of the surrounding Naranghar province, building houses and de-mining the heavily mined countryside. "In 1993 I had my accident," he said. And so he returned to London to start "teaching at this mosque" and set up his organization, Supporters of Sharia (SoS), with other veterans of the Afghan war.[48]

SoS took the position that jihad is a compulsory obligation for all but the elderly, the blind, and women.[49] Discussion groups on its Web site made this clear. In one query someone asked: "My primary purpose for meeting the Taliban . . . is to join the jihad or at least acquire the training for this purpose. What would be the approximate cost in U.S. $s to stay with the Taliban for at least one year?" To which a reply came: "Just apply for a Pakistani tourism visa which lasts 90 days. . . . From there try to find a good Muslim Arab who should help get you to Afghanistan. . . . I can't imagine your overall spending to be more than $2,000." Another posting details the account numbers of banks in Pakistan to deposit funds for Harakat-ul-Mujahideen, a Kashmiri terrorist group tied to bin Laden that hijacked an Indian Airlines jet in December 1999.[50]

In his office at the North London mosque, Abu Hamza told me he spent the mid-nineties going back and forth to Bosnia to aid the Muslims being slaughtered in the tens of thousands by Serbs hoping to create an "ethnically pure" Yugoslavia. He spent much of his time in Zenica in central Bosnia, where hundreds of other Arabs drawn to the jihad were based.

In the late nineties he turned his attention to Yemen. "I tried to raise the voices of Islamists in Yemen," he said, "The United States was trying to build a base there.[51] We were in touch with mujahldeen from Afghanistan living in the north and south of Yemen. There was a lot of warning that military action was going to happen. I knew some Yemenis who were going back and forth." During this period, Abu Hamza appeared on a satellite channel broadcast all over the Middle East and called for the killings of "nonbelievers" in Yemen.[52] It is these contacts with Yemeni militants, including Abu Hassan, that have led the Yemen government to cast Abu Hamza as the mastermind of the Islamic Army of Aden.

Also arriving in Yemen in late 1998 was a group of second-generation British Muslims of Asian and Middle Eastern parentage, several of whom had ties to Abu Hamza. One was his son, Moham-mad, another his son-in law, and another was the press officer for Abu Hamza's SoS group.[53] These eight Britons, between seventeen and thirty-three years of age, grew up in the Midlands or the London area. Most had gone to school for courses in business studies, computers, or accounting, and those who had jobs were in unexceptional lines of work such as insurance.[54] In short, they could not have been more or-dinary and unthreatening. The Aden Eight, as they came to be known, said they'd gone on vacation to Yemen either to visit family members or to pick up some Arabic.[55]

But a routine traffic stop by a Yemeni cop near Aden on December 24, 1998, brought to light a far more interesting tale.[56] Inside the car were three of the eight men, who tried to speed away but were quickly arrested.[57] Their arrests led the Yemeni government to a house in which they found a trove of items not normally associated with a quiet vacation: mines, rocket launchers, computers, encrypted communica-tion equipment, and a variety of audiocassettes and videos from Abu Hamza's SoS organization.[58] The Yemeni government contends that the Brits were linked to Abu Hassan's IAA and that some of their num-ber were planning a veritable festival of Christmas bombing attacks in Aden—on an Anglican church, on the British consulate, on an Ameri-can de-mining team, and on the Mövenpick hotel (bombed six years before by bin Laden's group).[59] A Western diplomat in Yemen told me that some of the Brits met with Abu Hassan before their arrest—cer-tainly an unusual choice for an Arabic tutor.[60]

The British government's official position is that the Aden Eight, five of whom were sentenced to serve between three and seven years in Yemeni jails, did not receive a fair trial—not least because Yemen's president announced their guilt before the proceeding.[61] Defense lawyers for the eight men say they were in some cases tortured into making false confessions.

Whatever the truth of this tangled tale, the Christmas Eve arrests of the Brits would quickly have tragic consequences.

It was a little before midday on Monday, December 29: for another group of Western tourists, a day for driving through the deserts and mountains of Yemen's hinterland; for a group of kidnappers armed with bazookas, RPGs, and Kalashnikov rifles, a day for taking revenge for the capture of their recently jailed brother militants.[62] The kidnappers, about twenty in all, could see the convoy of Toyota Land Cruisers making its way along the open plain on the road toward Aden.[63] The militants could see that the passengers in the convoy were all *kufr*, infidels, and prayed that as many of them as possible were Americans. Their leader, Abu Hassan, was determined to secure the release of his British comrades.[64]

In one of the Land Cruisers was Mary Quin. A vice president of the Xerox Corporation from Rochester, New York, she was in Yemen to visit its unusual medieval cities. "We were supposed to drive about three hundred kilometers that day," she told me. "We were driving along in five Toyota four-wheel-drive vehicles on a desert road just past a market town when a pickup truck pulled up between two of our vehicles. The first indication that something was wrong was gunshots. I thought, 'This is not going to be a normal day.' We didn't understand what was happening. Guys with guns surrounded the vehicles and took us off across the desert. We drove for about twenty minutes, until we got to a ravine."

Quin, a no-nonsense business executive with a Ph.D. in materials science, estimated that there were eighteen kidnappers: a hard-core group that was anxious and tense (including one man with a satellite phone), and a group of local village guys along for the ride.[65] "Only one of the terrorists in the group spoke English," she said. "He told us that we were being kidnapped because the Yemeni government had arrested some of their English comrades." The kidnappers said they were also protesting the recent Operation Desert Fox, when over the course of seventy hours beginning December 17 the United States had launched more than four hundred cruise missile attacks and dropped more than six hundred bombs on Iraqi targets.[66] Quin's captor told her: "You are not responsible for the bombing of Iraq, but your governments are." She said it was clear that the hostage-takers were unhappy that the tour group included only two Americans.

The ordeal had its lighter moments. Quin recalled, among them a Monty Python–esque discussion with one of the kidnappers about the difference between "sauce" and "gravy." But the following day would prove anything but amusing.

"Almost exactly twenty-four hours after we had been kidnapped, we suddenly realized we were being rescued," she said. "It was very chaotic—guns were fired and grenades were thrown. We were getting shot at for two hours." Quin said her training as a scientist helped her to assess the situation from a logical point of view and kept her calm. "We were forced to be human shields," she said. "I grabbed the barrel of the gun of one of the kidnappers, who had been shot, and we had a tug-of-war over his AK-47 and I ripped it out of his arms." The grit she'd gotten from her native New Zealand emerged when she kicked and stomped the kidnapper on the head "with some relish."

The Yemeni government, which had never in dozens of previous kidnappings launched a rescue attempt, had forgotten to mention its plans to Western diplomats in Yemen.[67] (The diplomats presumably would have discouraged the effort, being aware that such operations are hardly a specialty of the Yemeni army.) The scale, it turned out, had been large: more than two hundred Yemeni troops in an all-out assault on the kidnappers' hideout. The Yemeni government maintained that the kidnappers had fired first—an account that the surviving hostages hotly dispute.[68]

During the shoot-out, Abu Hassan told his lieutenant, Osama al-Masri, a member of Egypt's Jihad group—by now effectively part of al-Qaeda—to kill a woman, any woman.[69] Unfortunately, al-Masri died in the battle, so investigators could not explore his links to Egypt's Jihad group and to bin Laden. The two had earlier that year issued a joint communiqué calling for the deaths of all Americans.

Killed in the botched rescue operation were three Britons and an Australian, men and women of character, including Dr. Peter Rowe, an iconoclastic physics lecturer at Britain's Durham University whose impatience with university politics was in inverse ratio to the love he had for his students.[70] His wife, Claire Marston, also a university professor, was critically wounded. Ruth Williamson, a gentle Scottish health-care worker, was executed by one of the hostage takers.[71] Also killed was Margaret Whitehouse, an English primary-school teacher who, forced to act as a human shield, went to her death "as though she were going on a Sunday walk" and died in front of her husband.[72]

Abu Hassan and two other defendants went on trial in January 1999. Abu Hassan did not deny his guilt: he explained that after the kidnapping his self-styled army planned to assault British and American targets in

Aden, throwing in an attack on a church for good measure, on the principle that "two religions cannot unite and a church bell cannot sound on the Arabian peninsula."[73] His admission did no favors for his British Muslim buddies languishing in Yemeni jails—those were precisely the bombing plans with which they were later charged.

The most pressing question remains: Was there a relationship between Abu Hassan and Islamist elements in the Yemeni government? Tantalizing glimpses of such collusion came out during the kidnapping trial, among them the testimony of a driver employed by the tour company. He testified that Abu Hassan had made a satellite phone call to General Ali Muhsin al-Ahmer, a relative of President Salih who is reported to have met with bin Laden in Afghanistan in the eighties.[74] Why would Abu Hassan take time out from his kidnapping efforts to chat with a member of the president's family? Another of the drivers testified that Abu Hassan used his satellite phone to call an unidentified person—presumably in charge of the operation—to say, "We got the goods that were ordered: sixteen hundred cartons marked British and American," a not very coded reference to the sixteen tourists. And a local tribal leader who had tried to mediate with Abu Hassan testified that the kidnappers told him, "We have contacts at a very high level."[75] Abu Hassan was certainly running up his satellite phone charges: he also called Abu Hamza in London to tell him that he "did not expect the Yemeni government to deal with this matter in the same way it deals with other kidnappings."[76] The solution to the mystery died with Abu Hassan, who was executed almost exactly a year before the bombing of the U.S.S. *Cole*.

In a coincidence that did not bode well, December 1998 was also the month in which protracted negotiations between the United States and Yemen to allow U.S. warships to refuel in Aden were finally concluded.[77] Even more ominously, Mohamed al-'Owhali, one of the bombers of the U.S. embassy in Kenya in August 1998, had already told U.S. investigators that the bin Laden group planned next to attack an American ship in Yemen.[78] Coming from a source in a position to know (al-'Owhali had traveled from Yemen to Afghanistan to meet bin Laden, and then to Kenya, in the months before the embassy bombing), it was a statement that ought to have set off more alarms than it evidently did.[79] Just as al-'Owhali had warned, an altogether more disciplined group of Islamist militants than Abu Hassan's were gathering in Aden in 1998, well into preparations for attacking a far more ambitious target than a group of tourists.[80]

Their leader was Mohammed Omar al-Harazi, an Afghan fighter who, like bin Laden, was of Yemeni origin but born in Saudi Arabia.[81] A U.S. investigator privy to the interrogations of the Yemeni suspects in the *Cole* attack told me that after bin Laden's group had pulled off the Nairobi embassy bombing, al-Harazi informed members of the Yemen cell that "our next target is a U.S. Navy warship."[82]

At first, the militants contemplated using rocket-propelled grenades but they abandoned those plans, the investigator said, because an "RPG would not produce the effect they wanted." It was then that they turned to the idea of a bomb-laden boat. The bombers would employ C4, a high-explosive material manufactured by a relatively small group of countries including the United States and Iran. A former U.S. intelligence official told me the waterproof C4 used in the *Cole* attack might have been manufactured in Tennessee in the mid-seventies.[83]

American vessels had been refueling in Aden on an informal basis even before the United States signed the December 1998 deal with the Yemeni government, so the plotters had had plenty of time to probe the warships' defenses with seemingly innocuous *houris*, the narrow fishing boats that zip around Aden's harbor like so many gnats.[84]

To understand the success of the *Cole* bombing, one must grasp the geography of the port of Aden. It's one of the world's outstanding natural harbors, a series of white-sand inlets over which loom craggy cliffs; a sea of the deepest blue recedes into the distance, where giant oil tankers are anchored. The harbor is made up of two curling peninsulas that embrace the bay like lobster claws. On one is Little Aden, an area of tidy, modest houses, many built by the British, who seized Aden in 1839 only to relinquish it in 1967. On the other peninsula are Aden proper and the main harbor, which the British called Steamer Point.

The bombers used quiet, out-of-the-way Little Aden to build their bombs and conduct tests on the motor for the boat. They constructed a wall of corrugated metal about fifteen feet high around the perimeter of a house so they could do their business unseen.[85] On the Steamer Point peninsula, they rented another house on a hill with an unobstructed view of the tanks where the American ships refueled.[86]

As they traveled back and forth between their bomb factory in Little Aden and their observation post in Steamer Point, the bombers would have passed a huge compound prominently marked "Bin Ladin International Ltd.," a branch of Osama's family's construction business. The bin Laden family was rebuilding Aden's airport, which was heavily damaged, in part by the Afghan Arabs, during the 1994 civil war. If the bombers had had a sense of humor, this might have prompted a wry chuckle.

The first attempt to sink an American warship came on January 3, 2000—the holiest day of Ramadan, "the night of power" when Muhammad received the first verses of the Koran.[87] The religious significance would hardly have escaped the bombers: dying on this day is said to be a sign of Allah's grace. But no one was to die. The boat loaded with hundreds of pounds of explosives was launched from a beach off Little Aden and promptly sank.[88] Although the bombers had told their neighbors they were fish merchants, they clearly had no idea how to distribute cargo aboard a boat.[89] Their target, the destroyer U.S.S. *The Sullivans*, steamed away from Aden, the crew unaware of how narrowly they had avoided catastrophe.

Richard Clarke, the U.S. national coordinator for counterterrorism, told *The Washington Post* that the attack on *The Sullivans* was to have taken place at roughly the same time that a group of Jordanian militants with ties to bin Laden planned to bomb the Radisson hotel in Amman, and an area of the Jordan River associated with St. John the Baptist frequented by groups of American tourists.[90]

Around the same time that this failed terrorist spectacular was taking shape, Osama bin Laden and other leaders of his group were gathered at a religious school in Kandahar, Afghanistan. Their meeting was videotaped by the aptly named Jihad Media, and the tape is of interest to U.S. investigators for several reasons. First, a visibly aged bin Laden, his beard streaked with white, is wearing a *jambiya*. In the dozens of pictures that exist of him, he had never before been seen to wear a Yemeni dagger. Second, bin Laden's chief lieutenant, Ayman al-Zawahiri, the leader of Egypt's Jihad, says: "Enough of words, it is time to take action against this iniquitous and faithless force [the United States] which has spread its troops through Egypt, Yemen, and Saudi Arabia."[91] Finally, it was around this time that bin Laden married his fourth wife, a Yemeni from Abayan province.[92] The symbolism surely pleased him.

On the tape Bin Laden says: "On this blessed night we pledge . . . to expel the Jews and the Christians from the sacred places [the Arabian peninsula.]" The reference to the "blessed night," in my opinion, suggests that the tape was recorded during the month of Ramadan, perhaps even on January 3 as the Yemen plotters were finalizing their plans to attack *The Sullivans*. As I have said, bin Laden prepares his attacks with an eye to the calendar. He also likes to signal subtly his group's next action. In May 1998, he had held a press conference in Afghanistan to say that there would be "good news in the coming weeks." Nine weeks later, bombs devastated the two U.S. embassies in Africa.

In January, after their boat had ignominiously sunk, the Aden bombers briefly skipped town, returning later to fine-tune their plans.[93] This time there would be no failures. Mohammed Omar al-Harazi visited Aden before the *Cole* attack to provide money and training; then, according to a senior Yemeni official, he left for Afghanistan after the attack's successful outcome.[94] He did not lack for company. "Numerous people immediately left Yemen for Afghanistan" at the same time, according to the congressional testimony of Ambassador Michael Sheehan, the U.S. coordinator for counterterrorism.[95]

Those who remained in Aden to die were the two suicide bombers. The first went by the alias of Abdullah al-Musawah, obtaining a fake I.D. in that name in 1997 from Lahej, an Islamist stronghold not far from Aden.[96] His real name was Hassan Saeed Awad al-Khamri and he was a Yemeni in his late twenties—from Hadramawt, like bin Laden.[97] In a photograph Khamri used to register the boat that would deliver the bomb he stares out unsmilingly from behind glasses and a heavy beard.[98] The other suicide bomber has yet to be identified but is also believed to have been a Yemeni who had settled in Saudi Arabia.

There were other alleged conspirators. Jamal al-Badawai, who has reportedly admitted to having trained in bin Laden's camps in Afghanistan, is charged by the Yemenis with running errands and purchasing equipment for the bombers.[99] Also charged by the Yemenis was the hapless Fahd al-Qoso, who they say was paged in the Steamer Point observation house with the code "101010"—a signal to videotape the bombing of the *Cole*.[100] He apparently fell asleep and missed his cue.[101]

The sailors who died in the explosion were mostly from small-town America, places like Woodleaf, North Carolina; Rex, Georgia; Kingsville, Texas; and Portland, North Dakota.[102] The oldest was only thirty-five, and some were still teenagers. Marc Nieto, a twenty-four-year-old from Fond du Lac, Wisconsin, who worked on the *Cole*'s enormous engines, was one of the victims. He had only two weeks left in his six-year naval career and had proposed to his girlfriend, Jamie DeGuzman, also a sailor on the *Cole*, as they steamed toward Yemen.[103] Nieto's mother said: "He had goals to the sky and he was going to achieve those goals. He was just starting his life"—as were the sixteen other young men and women who were killed for the crime of serving in the armed forces of the country they loved.

Half a mile from where the *Cole* was berthed, Abdul Aziz Hakim was working in his family's bookshop, as he had done most days since 1946.[104] The shop is cluttered with a musty collection of books and magazines redolent of Aden in the 1960s, when it was one of the world's busiest ports and a proud outpost of the British Empire. Moldering back issues of *Commando* magazine featuring Nazis shouting "Surrender or die, English pig dog" jostle with books on etiquette asking: "For day parties—bridge or whist for example—is it just one table of friends, or is it to be a grander affair with two or more tables?" The shock wave from the *Cole* explosion blew out the windows in Hakim's solid stone Victorian building. Two miles away, a cabdriver in the Malla neighborhood said he was sure it was an earthquake.

As had happened in the 1993 bombing of the World Trade Center and the 1995 attack on the Oklahoma City federal building, the first confused reports suggested that the *Cole* explosion might have been some sort of accident. The Yemeni government stuck with this line several days past its sell-by date, reluctant to admit the possibility of terrorism. On the other hand, U.S. officials in Washington awakened in the early morning by the news had—at least unofficially—few doubts about the real nature of the explosion.[105] Within four days, the case was transferred to the jurisdiction of the New York office of the FBI, which by virtue of its investigations of the World Trade Center and African embassy bombings had a vast repository of knowledge about Islamist terrorism.[106] Dispatched to Yemen were FBI agents who had tracked bin Laden for years.[107]

When I visited Aden a couple of months after the *Cole* attack, I checked into the Goldmohur hotel, the same one bombed eight years before by bin Laden's followers. Since that bombing, which destroyed the fourth floor, the Goldmohur had been beautifully renovated. As I approached the hotel, which sits on a peninsula on the Bay of Aden, I was puzzled to find my cab checked by two security teams. When I arrived I understood. The easily defensible peninsula had been selected as the base of operations for American officials investigating the *Cole* blast. In the lobby, a young woman wearing a "New York Subway Series" baseball cap was talking to a heavyset middle-aged man with the unmistakable air of an FBI agent. Accidentally getting off the elevator on the wrong floor, I was greeted by a Marine in full battle dress.

The Fortress America approach of the investigators was indicative of the very real threat that they might be targeted by Yemeni militants. The inquiry had gotten off to a rocky start, not only because of a culture clash between the FBI, arguably the world's most highly skilled investigative agency, and Yemen's police force, whose own forensic techniques often run to torture, but also because of an assumption by some U.S. officials that Yemen would give them carte blanche to investigate the case.[108] This demonstrated a fundamental misunderstanding of the neighborhood in which they were working. In 1995 and 1996, after American military installations in Yemen's northern neighbor, Saudi Arabia, were bombed and twenty-four U.S. Army personnel killed, the Saudis swiftly beheaded four suspects in the 1995 case, and were minimally cooperative with American investigators in the 1996 case.[109] In Yemen, President Salih would have to deal with the political reality that the Islah party controls 20 percent of the seats in parliament and that many Yemenis are opposed to any type of American military presence in their country.

Former deputy Prime Minister al-Anesi's reaction to the bombing was typical of many Yemenis': "There was no justification for the *Cole* bombing. I was shocked and surprised. But the U.S. bears a great degree of responsibility for the incident for the way the U.S. deals with issues in the Middle East. It is not just Palestine and its stand on Israel, but the totality of the U.S. policies. The U.S. military presence is not liked. . . . Since America is going to continue this policy, it will see a lot of things like this."

A week after the bombing of the *Cole*, Louis Freeh, the Elliot

Ness–like director of the FBI, arrived in Yemen and praised the cooperativeness of the Yemenis. At a press conference, he explained that the *Cole* blast was the result of "an explosive device on a water-borne delivery vehicle." One of the assembled hacks shouted out: "You mean—a bomb on a boat," to general hilarity.[110]

At first, U.S. agents received only poorly translated and heavily edited transcripts of interviews with the sixty or so suspects and hundreds of witnesses rounded up by the Yemeni police.[111] By the end of November, however, the two governments had signed an agreement allowing American agents to sit in on interrogations and submit follow-up questions. This was about as good an arrangement as could be expected, but results were at best spotty. Seven months later, in June 2001, the remaining FBI agents in the country pulled out, not only because of terrorist threats but also because of continued disputes with the Yemenis about how to conduct the investigation.[112]

How had the U.S. government let things get so out of hand? After all, the deal to refuel in Yemen was inked *after* the United States had heard from a highly credible source that an attack on an American warship in the area was in the works.

In April 1999, the State Department issued its annual "Patterns of Global Terrorism" report. The section on Yemen is instructive. It acknowledged that Yemen had taken steps to force foreign extremists to leave the country, but also pointed to the Islamic Army of Aden's recent kidnapping of Western tourists.[113] A year later, in the next "Patterns" report, the section on Yemen gave credit to its government for signing "a number of international antiterrorist conventions" and "incremental measures to better control its borders, territory, and travel documents," but went on to say that the "government's inability to exercise authority over remote areas of the country continued to make the country a safe haven for terrorist groups." Those groups included Egypt's Islamic Jihad, the group that, according to the New York indictment of bin Laden, had "effectively merged" with al-Qaeda in 1998.

Clearly the Pentagon officials and the American envoy to Yemen, Barbara K. Bodine, a former counterterrorism official who signed on to the Aden refueling agreement, were hardly unaware of the contents of the indictment against bin Laden. Nor were they ignorant of the contents of the State Department's own terrorism reports. So it is fair to ask: *What in the world were they thinking?*

Here is the case for their defense: First, Aden is a superb natural harbor, the best in a radius of hundreds of miles. Its location on the Red Sea and thus the Suez Canal is why the British held it for over a century. In the seventies and eighties, when southern Yemen was a socialist state, the Soviets used it to refuel their ships. Second, the United States was hoping to enlist Yemen's help in the fight against terrorism and draw the country, an ally of Iraq, into the Pax Americana.

Hauled before Congress after the *Cole* explosion, General Anthony Zinni, a formidable commander who headed U.S. forces in the Middle East and Asia, took full responsibility for the Aden refueling decision. When I called him at his Virginia home a few days after the bombing, he was a model of politeness: "We needed a refueling point down there," he explained. "There were no perfect options. We checked out the security situation in Aden and the problems were lower than in other possible refueling places like Jeddah and Djibouti. We don't have enough oilers to refuel the individual ships, so we need ports."

The decision to refuel in Aden claimed the lives of seventeen young Americans, caused $240 million in damage to one of the U.S. Navy's most advanced destroyers, and signaled the United States' impotence in the face of what defense experts call asymmetrical warfare—a fancy term for David killing Goliath.[114] According to a former CIA official, "The Aden refueling decision was a political calculation that was obviously misplaced. The U.S. tried to use the carrot approach with the Yemeni government, an $80 million contract." But Aden, he went on, was a "security nightmare, with so many terrorist groups around. It was very easy for them to watch and plan. U.S. ships were docking there fairly frequently." Another former U.S. intelligence official who visited Aden says, "I understand what the U.S. government was doing was trying to get closer relations with the Yemenis, but it was a very bad idea, as this was not a friendly country."

Beyond the fact that Yemen was a haven for terrorist groups and that the Aden port was far from secure, one has to understand the thinking of the men behind the bombing. Those who carried out the attack believe, like bin Laden, that the presence of American "infidels" in the holy land of the Arabian Peninsula is a crime against God. American officials might have felt that Saudi Arabia was dangerous for this reason and not have understood that, to the jihadists, Yemen is just as sacred.

And Yemen is likely to continue attracting militants in search of jihad training if the government continues to allow, or is unable to stop, them. I paid a very brief visit to a religious school that U.S. officials believe has functioned as a training camp for those militants. The school is a few miles from the northern city of Sa'da in the village of Dammaj. As it was early in the morning during Ramadan, when the students and staff were sleeping, I was able to make a quick tour of the place unimpeded. My Yemeni translator and driver were extremely nervous and opted to remain in the car.

Dammaj is a little world unto itself. That world revolves around a large, whitewashed auditorium (the site of prayers and lectures) from which there radiates a warren of one-story rooms (where the students live). The school is ecumenical only in the nonreligious sense: it attracts students from around the world, including more than thirty from Britain (particularly Birmingham), several from the United States, and others from Germany, France, Algeria, Libya, Turkey, Indonesia, Russia, and India—in addition to thousands of Yemenis.[115] "American Taliban" John Walker Lindh attempted to study at Dammaj on a trip he made to Yemen in 1998, however, it is not clear if he was successful in this endeavor.[116]

Sheikh Moqbul al-Wadai'i, the now deceased cleric who presided over Dammaj, propounded a strict Salafi view of Islam—similar to the ultra-purist views of the Taliban—denouncing television and radio, jobs for women, and democracy.[117] He shunned publicity; he gave his only interview to an English-language weekly, *The Yemen Times*, in July 2000, taking pains to point out: "We do not intend to fight any religion." The sheikh also denied reports that graduates of his academy had gone on to fight in holy wars in Afghanistan, Kashmir, and Chechnya, insisting that his school harbors no "terrorist or radical cells."[118]

This public profession of pacifism was somewhat at odds with the miasma of violence that attached itself to the sheikh and his school. Shortly before Moqbul talked to *The Yemen Times*, a British student, sixteen-year-old Hosea Walker, was shot to death at Dammaj in what was described as an accident.[119] In 1998, while the sheikh was giving a sermon at one of his mosques in San'a, a bomb went off, killing two people and injuring some of his followers, including two Americans and a Canadian.[120] Around the same time, one of the sheikh's bodyguards was assassinated. And it is hard to square Sheikh Moqbul's love of peace with the *fatwa* he sent to the extremist Indonesian Muslim group, Laskar Jihad, in March 2000: "The Christians have fanned the fires of conflict . . . where they have massacred more than 5,000 Muslims. That is why you, honorable people of one faith, must call all to total jihad and expel all the enemies of Allah."[121] Moreover, Yemeni sources says guns are commonplace at Dammaj. In his *Yemen Times* interview, the sheikh conceded: "Students get their own guns and weapons on a personal basis."[122]

The investigation of the U.S.S. *Cole* attack had essentially ground to a halt by the summer of 2001. For its part, the Yemeni government had arrested the half-dozen or so men directly implicated, and felt that was as far as it was prepared for the investigation to go. The FBI, on the other hand, wanted to expand the investigation to include members of Yemen's government, a leader of the *Islah* party, and an army general related to President Salih. Unsurprisingly, the Yemeni government had little appetite for such a wide-ranging inquiry. A Yemeni newspaper editor observed: "It was clear from the start that the accessories to the attack would be tried and executed, but the people inside Yemen who financed it, and used their power to facilitate it, would never be brought to book."[123]

It is still not clear exactly what bin Laden's role in the *Cole* explosion was, but the glee he took in the attack is undeniable. In Afghanistan in January 2001, at the wedding celebration for one of his sons, bin Laden declaimed an extraordinary poem about the *Cole* to hundreds of cheering guests: "A destroyer, even the brave might fear. It inspires horror in the harbor and the open sea. She goes into the waves flanked by arrogance, haughtiness and fake might. To her doom she progresses slowly, clothed in a huge illusion. Awaiting her is a dinghy, bobbing in the waves."[124]

Neither the Clinton nor Bush administrations took any military action against al-Qaeda following its attack on the *Cole*. Bin Laden must have surely felt that the United States would tolerate almost any provocation.

Earlier, I described my visit to Hadramawt in some detail. To see the region is to understand the conservative religious culture that Osama bin Laden's father passed on to his youngest son. To reach the bin Ladens' ancestral village, I traveled through Wadi Doan, a hundred-mile-long valley in which the road is not much more than a rocky path. Even seventy years after Osama's father, Mohammed bin Laden left this valley to find his fortune in Saudi Arabia, black-robed women flit like wraiths down the alleys of the towns, avoiding eye contact with foreigners. Out in the fields, women harvest crops while completely swathed in black, wearing distinctive conical hats made of straw. Attempts to photograph Hadrami women produced such a volcanic explosion of rage by my local driver that I abandoned the enterprise.

The bin Laden village is tucked into the shade of honey-colored cliffs that tower above the valley floor by a couple of thousand feet. It is a compact place, filled with laughing children who wander the streets between the high-walled mud-brick houses. The village is called al-Rubat Ba'eshn, named after a Sufi saint, Said Mohamed Ba'eshn, who is buried in the mountains above the town. Wherein lies a nice irony: the villagers of al-Rubat embrace Sufism and venerate the graves of long-dead saints, a form of worship that bin Laden himself abhors as idolatry. And the inhabitants of al-Rubat, despite their abject poverty and deeply conservative way of life, reject bin Laden's brand of zealotry.

While bin Laden declaimed poetry extolling the *Cole* explosion, al-Rabat's amiable mullah, who runs a school out of the old bin Laden family compound, told me, "We are against this holy war. The *Cole* attack does more to harm to Yemen's reputation than America's reputation. We feel sorry for the American boys and girls. They are our guests." He finished this peroration with an invitation for me to "come to Islam."

The last word on the subject should go to one of bin Laden's few relatives still left in al-Rubat. Khaled al-Omeri is a thirty-year-old cousin who owns a cramped food shop on Bin Laden Street. Al-Omeri ducked direct questions about his most famous relation, but when asked about his view on jihad—a word that, as I've said, means not only holy war but any kind of religious struggle—he pointed proudly at his three-year-old son and said, "This is my jihad."

CHAPTER 10

The Global Network:
Around the World in Eighty Jihads

"We talk about the bin Laden organization, but it is really a bin Laden alliance. It is unusual to find Palestinians and Yemenis. Sudanese and East Asians in the same alliance. He is the glue between groups that have little in common with each other, for instance the Kashmiris and Egypt's Islamic Jihad."

—U.S. official, Washington, 1998

When Ahmed Ressam, the would-be bomber of Los Angeles International Airport, stepped off the ferry from Canada at Port Angeles, Washington, on a blustery day in December 1999, and was nabbed by alert Customs agents, U.S. investigators had little inkling that the arrest would prove a turning point in their understanding of al-Qaeda's scope— of the networks that stretched across three continents and dozens of countries. They learned that al-Qaeda planned a New Year's 2000 terrorism spectacular spanning the globe: not just an attack on LAX but on tourist sites in Jordan and a U.S. warship in Yemen. The plots were foiled by a combination of good police work and the plotters' incompetence; and law enforcement officials would ultimately arrest affiliates of al-Qaeda in England, Spain, Germany, Italy, and Syria.[1] But against this success stood the sobering realization that now, on the brink of the new millennium, al-Qaeda had truly gone global.

A recent book about globalization posits a new class of world citizen: the "cosmocrats," who are as comfortable in London or Hong Kong as in their hometowns in, say, Ireland or Nigeria.[2] You may have encountered a cosmocrat in your travels: the management consultant who thinks nothing of going to a meeting in Baku and then, the next day, a wedding in Oxford; or the English World Bank executive, married to a Russian, who spends six months a year shuttling between Poland and Colombia. The cosmocrats value academic excellence and often have multiple degrees from an array of prestigious universities. What counts isn't family background but talent and drive.

There's an interesting parallel here with bin Laden's organization, which is as much a creation of globalization as a response to it. The network was formed in the crucible of an international conflict between the Soviet Union and Afghanistan—a war that also drew in Pakistan, the United States, and Saudi Arabia, along with Muslims from all over the globe. Islamic leaders have always cherished the idea of the *umma*, the world community of Muslims. It's a notion that predates globalization by more than a millennium and is considerably stronger than its counterpart, "Christendom," which probably lost its allure around the time that Henry VIII decided to look for a second wife.

Bin Laden's network—which also values technical proficiency, albeit of a rather specialized kind—is as cosmopolitan as the cosmocrats'. Consider the range of places in which it has principally operated: Sudan, Egypt, Saudi Arabia, Yemen, Somalia, Afghanistan, Pakistan, Bosnia, Croatia, Albania, Algeria, Tunisia, Lebanon, the Philippines, Tajikistan, Azerbaijan, Kenya, Tanzania, Kashmir in India, and Chechnya in Russia.[3] Al-Qaeda has also attracted followers in the United States—in New York, Boston, Texas, Florida, Virginia, and California; and in the United Kingdom—in London and Manchester. Bin Laden adherents have been arrested in places as disparate as Jordan, Seattle, France, Uruguay, and Australia.[4]

In the months that followed the African embassy attacks, U.S. intelligence detected bin Laden's followers targeting American embassies in Albania, Tajikistan, Azerbaijan, Uganda, Ivory Coast, Senegal, Mozambique, Liberia, Gambia, Togo, and Ghana.[5] David Carpenter, the head of the U.S. State Department's Office of Diplomatic Security, testified before Congress that American diplomatic facilities around the world received 650 "credible threats" from bin Laden's network in the six months following the embassy bombings.[6] According to a U.S. counterterrorism official, "credible threats" can be signaled by suspicious videotaping of an embassy, intelligence gathered from telephone surveillance, the presence of a terrorist in a particular city, or information from a "drop-in" informant.

In 2001 al-Qaeda plotted to attack American embassies in Yemen, Bangladesh, and India.[7] The bin Laden operative behind the Indian plot was Mohammed Omar al-Harazi, who was also the operational leader of the cell that bombed the U.S.S. *Cole*. In July 2001, Indian police arrested two men in New Delhi with six kilos of RDX, a high explosive. The men confessed that they had been planning, sometime in the coming months, to blow up the busy visa section of the American embassy, and that they were acting under instruction from a bin Laden lieutenant they knew as Abdul Rahman al-Safani, an alias for al-Harazi.[8] At the end of August, Indian police charged bin Laden and five others, including "al-Safani," of plotting to bomb the American embassy. That plan had been two years in the making.[9]

Al-Qaeda members are bona fide world travelers. During the 1990s, a top official of the group, Mamdouh Mahmud Salim, went to Turkey, Dubai, Azerbaijan, Afghanistan, Pakistan, Sudan, Malaysia, the Philippines, and China.[10] When he was arrested in 1998 in the town of Bruneck, Bavaria, he said he was in Germany to buy cars.[11] The Lebanese-American Wadih el-Hage shuttled between Louisiana, New York, and Pakistan during the eighties; in the nineties, he lived in Arizona, Sudan, Kenya, and Texas and made side trips to Afghanistan, Germany, and Slovakia.[12] Al-Qaeda's global scope is further underlined by calls made from bin Laden's satellite phone, a notebook-computer-sized device purchased from a New York–based company in 1996 for $7,500. Over the next two years, hundreds of calls were placed from that phone to London, Sudan, Iran, and Yemen, and dozens to Azerbaijan, Pakistan, Saudi Arabia, and Kenya.[13]

No book could fully cover all the countries in which al-Qaeda has operated, but I'd like to examine a few of particular interest. Foremost is Egypt, which has played a central role in the development of bin Laden's organization and which continues to be alert to his influence—so much so that my December 2000 fact-finding trip almost ended at the Cairo airport.

"What is this?" asked the customs inspector, holding up a sheaf of Arabic papers that he had triumphantly excavated from my bag.

I opted for the honest approach, as he could clearly read the offending material. "That's Osama bin Laden's declaration of war against Americans," I said in the most casual tone I could muster. I went on to explain that it was research material for a book I was writing and that I had no plans to hand out copies to any of bin Laden's adherents—for whom the declaration would hardly be news, anyway.

"Where did you get it?" the inspector asked, in vaguely menacing tones. "Was it from Yasser al-Sirri?"

Now I was getting into deeper waters. Yasser al-Sirri is a London-based Egyptian dissident accused of attempting to assassinate Egypt's prime minister in 1993.[14] (A young girl was killed in the botched attempt.[15]) In the unlikely event that al-Sirri ever decides to return to his native country, he can choose from a menu of unappealing sentencing options: imprisonment for twenty-five years, hard labor for fifteen, or—most likely—execution.[16]

"No, it wasn't from al-Sirri."

The inspector then escorted me down a corridor into a back office, clearly not for a nice cup of tea with members of Egypt's ubiquitous tourism police. From behind a vast desk, a plainclothes security officer asked me, not unpleasantly, "Have you ever met with Yasser al-Sirri?"

Now this was an excellent question, which would require some finessing; I had indeed spent several informative hours with al-Sirri. Volunteering this was clearly not going to abbreviate my chat with the secret police, but a further search of my bag would probably turn up his phone number. I opted for the full Clinton:

"I have talked to him on the phone," I said.

After a certain amount of hemming and hawing, the security officer evidently decided to take me at my word. He said I could go, then shook my hand.

Why, I wondered, was al-Sirri an obsession with these people? He is a slightly built, balding man in his late thirties who ran—very publicly—an outfit called the Islamic Observation Centre, which issued press releases critical of Egypt's government and provided information about Islamist militants. But it was a strictly small-bore operation, and al-Sirri has no following either inside or outside Egypt.[17] (Al-Sirri was arrested in London in late 2001 because the assassins posing as journalists who killed Afghan leader Ahmad Shah Massoud used accreditation from his Islamic Observation Centre.)

If I was taken aback by the focus on al-Sirri, I could well understand the country's vigilance about Islamist militants. For the last quarter-century, the Egyptian Jihad group has been engaged in an all-out war on the state. From the early nineties, it has worked hand-in-glove with bin Laden. The U.S. indictment against bin Laden says that al-Qaeda "effectively merged" with Jihad in 1998, but that's a little misleading, since the Egyptian group might well have been the more valuable property. While bin Laden became the public face and moneybags of al-Qaeda, its key members are Egyptian and its ideology and tactics are based on Egyptian models. The argument can be made that a group of Egyptian jihadists took over bin Laden's organization rather than the other way around.

It's not surprising that the ideology and tactics of al-Qaeda come from Egypt, long the cultural cockpit of the Arab world.[18] Cairo's al-Azhar University has been a leader in Islamic thought for centuries; and during the fifties and sixties, President Gamal Abdel Nasser was the fount of modern pan-Arabism. The leading ideologue of the jihadist movement, Sayyid Qutb, graduated from a teacher training college in Cairo.[19]

One cannot underestimate the influence of Qutb on the jihadist groups in Egypt and, by extension, on bin Laden. A journalist and critic, Qutb visited the United States as a student between 1948 and 1951 and was "appalled by the racism and sexual permissiveness." He returned to Egypt with "an uncompromising hatred of the West and all its works" and promptly joined the Islamist Muslim Brotherhood, which by the 1940s was already a significant mass movement with perhaps half a million members and which opposed the regime of President Gamal Abdel Nasser, who took over in a 1952 coup.[20] The slogan of the brotherhood was resounding and unambiguous: "The Koran is our constitution, the Prophet is our Guide. Death for the Glory of Allah is our greatest ambition."

Between 1954 and his execution in 1966, Qutb would spend over a decade in Nasser's hellish jails. While in prison, he wrote *Signposts,* in effect a blueprint for destroying Nasser's regime—and, by implication, any regime deemed un-Islamic. For Qutb, the Nasser state was *jahiliyya,* belonging to the pre-Islamic world of paganism and barbarism. Why? Because Nasser had created a society "in which Islam is not applied." It was therefore *kufr,* infidel. Qutb also interpreted jihad as more than just the inner struggle to purify oneself or a war in self-defense. Jihad must be used "to establish the reign of God on earth and eliminate the reign of man." The execution of Qutb elevated him to martyrhood; his writings were subsequently devoured by Islamists.[21] The Saudi dissident Saad al-Fagih describes Qutb's writings as the "most important" for the militant Islamist movement.[22]

The thrust of Qutb's writing was plain: Egyptian officials were infidels and the only way to remove them was with action, not words. This is the same chain of logic that bin Laden applies to the Saudi regime. (Such reasoning requires a selective reading of Islamic texts. The Prophet Muhammad himself said, "To insult a brother-Muslim is sinful, to kill him is unbelief.")[23]

The history of the Egyptian militant groups that have implemented Qutb's blueprint for jihadist action is complicated, full of the internal disputes and shifting alliances typical of extremist organizations. I will sketch them only broadly. In the 1970s and 1980s, the Al-Gama'a al-Islamiyya, the Islamic Group, started a campaign against "corrupt" elements in Egyptian society, burning down video stores, robbing jewelry shops owned by Copts (the Christian minority which makes up about 5 percent of Egypt's population), and killing tourists.[24]

In 1973 Ayman al-Zawahiri, then a medical student, founded (together with an electrical engineer and an army officer) a sister organization to the Islamic Group. This was the Jihad group, which was devoted more narrowly to overthrowing the Egyptian state and so confined its attacks to government officials and buildings.[25] Unlike the Islamic Group—which functioned semi-openly, collecting money in mosques and doing charity work—the Jihad group operated with the high degree of secrecy that would later characterize al-Qaeda.[26]

In early 1981, the Islamic Group and Jihad joined forces for their most successful operation to date, the assassination of Egypt's president Anwar

Sadat.[27] The militants had already concluded that Sadat was an "infidel," but when he struck a peace deal with Israel—sealing the agreement by shaking the hand of Israeli prime minister Menachem Begin in front of President Jimmy Carter on the White House lawn in 1979—he effectively signed his own death warrant.[28] The historic image was hailed around the world as signaling a new era of peace, but it enraged Egypt's militants; Sheikh Omar Abdel Rahman, the spiritual leader of both the Jihad and Islamic groups, gave his blessing to the assassination.[29] On October 6, 1981, a twenty-four-year-old army lieutenant named Khalid Islambouli sprayed Sadat with machine-gun bullets as the president was reviewing a military parade.[30] Islambouli then exclaimed, famously, "I have killed Pharaoh, and I do not fear death."[31]

In the year following Sadat's assassination, hundred of militants were tried for their roles in the plot and other subversive activities.[32] Sheikh Rahman was arrested, but acquitted after it was found that he had been tortured during the interrogation.[33] Al-Zawahiri was sentenced to three years in prison.[34] The investigation of Jihad revealed much that was unsettling to the Egyptian government: "rigorous arms and explosives training, studies of the behavior and routines of key government figures, and research of the layout of strategic installations"—just the type of training and planning that would years later characterize al-Qaeda's operations.[35]

Once out of jail, al-Zawahiri relaunched Jihad as the "Vanguards of Conquest," a nom de guerre it has continued to employ on occasion.[36] In the mid-eighties, al-Zawahiri, along with many Egyptian militants, traveled to Pakistan to lend his support to the Afghan *mujahideen.* Militant groups were distracted by that jihad until the Soviet withdrawal, and religiously inspired violence in Egypt abated until the Afghan veterans began returning to the country in 1990.[37]

Astonishingly, al-Zawahiri visited the United States twice during the early nineties, fund-raising for Jihad, which by that point was effectively part of al-Qaeda.[38] He was accompanied by Ali Mohamed, the former U.S. Army sergeant who was by then advising al-Qaeda on military matters.

Jihad attempted unsuccessfully to assassinate Egypt's interior minister in 1993 and the prime minister in 1995. It had more success with a truck bomb, which devastated the Egyptian embassy in Islamabad in 1995.

During the early and mid-nineties, Egypt's militants also killed police officers, Copts, and tourists—an estimated 1,200 people.[39] The violence culminated in 1997 with the grotesquely bloody massacre of fifty-eight tourists and four Egyptians in Luxor, the site of several well-known pharaonic monuments.[40] The terrorists hunted down their victims like dogs, shooting, knifing, and mutilating them, dancing with elation as they went about their bloody work.[41] Popular revulsion against the violence of the jihadist groups reached its zenith with the Luxor massacre. Leaders of the Islamic Group, realizing they were alienating any shred of popular support they once held, announced a cease-fire with the government in 1998—a move that al-Zawahiri has emphatically rejected.

The profound impact of al-Zawahiri on bin Laden's thinking has become increasingly clear, and some of have suggested that this little-known physician is more important to al-Qaeda than bin Laden himself.[42] Like the late Abdullah Azzam before him, al-Zawahiri has influenced his younger partner to become ever more radical. During their rare public appearances, al-Zawahiri sits beside bin Laden, a cerebral, taciturn man in his early fifties, his face framed by heavy glasses, a beard, and a white turban. He speaks English very well and sometimes has acted as bin Laden's interpreter.[43]

For insight into al-Zawahiri, I went to Saad Eddin Ibrahim, a well-known Egyptian sociologist who studied Islamist militants in Egypt in the late seventies. He told me he had met al-Zawahiri while the latter was a young man just beginning his jihadist career. "Very intelligent, very quiet," Ibrahim said. "He comes from a good family, related to the Egyptian aristocracy; his father was a famous physician. He seemed poised and articulate—but quiet."

After Ibrahim, my next stop on the trail of al-Zawahiri was Montasser al-Zayyat, who continues to act as the Islamic Group's unofficial spokesman. He was ill and my appointment was canceled, but I did have the experience of sharing his waiting room with a woman dressed not only in the head-to-toe covering of the *hejab* but, in a mark of ultra-fundamentalist zeal, black gloves—items of apparel that are hard to imagine the Prophet recommending in the searing heat of Arabia. The afternoon free, I decided to look in on the Jews and Copts whom some of al-Zayyat's client base had, in the past, felt it their religious duty to attack. Around the corner from his office was the Art Nouveau synagogue of Shaar ha Shamayim, built in 1905, which would not be out of place in an upscale arrondissement of Paris. The effect of the exterior was marred by a gaggle of heavily armed, bulletproof-vested police, but the inside was, if anything, more depressing: there was only a single old woman—one of two or three hundred Jews left in Cairo, she said. I asked if there would be a Sabbath service this night, and she said no: there was no rabbi so there was no service. The medieval churches across town in Coptic Cairo had fared better: ablaze with candles honoring icons of St. George, they were carefully tended by older parishioners and even the occasional priest.

On my next visit, al-Zayyat was still nursing a bad cold but agreed to talk about al-Zawahiri and the history of the militant groups. A heavy-set, bearded man in his late forties whose past defense of Islamist militants has not endeared him to certain elements of Egyptian society, al-Zayyat once narrowly escaped with his life when a bomb exploded in his car.[44] He assumes, he said, that all his phone conversations are bugged.

The first thing al-Zayyat did for me was to clarify the terms of the 1998 cease-fire agreement, spelling out that it was a "not a peace agreement" but simply "a cease of armed operations." In July 1997, before the Luxor massacre, leaders of the Islamic Group had approved the idea of a cease-fire, which was ratified by the group's *shura* council in March 1998. Al-Zawahiri and Rifia Ahmed Taha both opposed the action and, because of their continued support for violence and bin Laden, were asked to resign from their respective leadership roles in the Jihad and Islamic groups.[45]

And al-Zawahiri himself? "A very clever surgeon," said al-Zayyat, with a smile. "When you meet him you do not think that he has anything to do with violence. He is very quiet, very calm, doesn't talk much. He thinks deeply." Nonetheless, al-Zawahiri's words have had a powerful effect. It was in the course of treating the *mujahideen* during the Afghan war, al-Zayyat said, that al-Zawahiri converted a certain rich young Saudi "from primarily a donor of money into a holy warrior." He emphasized that al-Zawahiri is "bin Laden's mind."

That view was confirmed by multiple sources, among them Hamid Mir, the Pakistani journalist who has written an Urdu-language biography of bin Laden, and Abdel Bari Atwan, the editor of *Al-Quds*

Al-Arabi. The latter told me that it was al-Zawahiri who was most in-strumental in bin Laden's embrace of violence.

On the al-Qaeda recruitment tape that circulated in the summer of 2001, al-Zawahiri made one of his rare public statements. "One of the crimes of America," he said, "is that she claims she is the protector of democracy and protector of religions. We have in the Arab world not followed Islam. In Egypt they put a lot of people in jails—some people sentenced to be hanged. And in the Egyptian jails, there is a lot of killing and torture. All this happens under the supervision of America."[46]

Al-Zawahiri is not the only Egyptian who has played an important role in al-Qaeda. There was also the military commander of the group, Muhammad Atef, a former Egyptian police officer, one of whose daughters married bin Laden's son Mohammed in early 2001. (Atef was killed in an American bombing raid near Kabul in November 2001.) During the early and mid-nineties, bin Laden's right-hand man was the former Egyptian army officer Abu Ubaidah al-Banshiri. Another military advisor to al-Qaeda was the Egyptian-American soldier Ali Mohamed, now imprisoned in the United States. Mohammed Shawki Islambouli, the brother of Sadat's assassin, is part of al-Qaeda.[47] So is the explosives expert who constructed the bombs used in the attacks on the two American embassies in Africa, as is the operational leader—known as Saleh—of those bombings; and the co-signer of bin Laden's *fatwa* to kill Americans in 1998, Rifia Ahmed Taha.[48] Two sons of Sheikh Omar Abdel Rahman, the spiritual leader of the Egyptian Islamic Group, are also prominent within al-Qaeda.[49] One of the sons, Ahmed, was captured by the Northern Alliance in November 2001 and was handed over to American custody.[50]

On February 3, 1999, a hundred or so Islamic militants accused of terrorism went on trial in Cairo, including, in absentia, al-Zawahiri and that vexing author of press releases, Yasser al-Sirri.[51] Also indicted were al-Zawahiri's younger brother, Mohamed, an engineer, and Mustafa, the brother of al-Qaeda's Ali Mohamed. The latter was sentenced to five years.[52] The al-Zawahiris were sentenced to death.[53]

Al-Sirri, as I've mentioned, lives in Britain, which is the next stop on this global tour. Despite a flurry of recent arrests (many of them instigated by the United States), Arab militants who face prison or death in their native country have made their homes in London. Among them is Abdel Abdel-Bary, a lawyer who represented Jihad in Egypt and worked closely with al-Zawahiri.[54] In 1991, Abdel-Bary also helped in the defense of El Sayyid Nosair—a key member of the group of terrorists based in New York in the late eighties and early nineties—for his role in the assassination of Rabbi Meir Kahane in Manhattan.[55] In July 1999, Abdel-Bary was arrested on charges that he was part of bin Laden's conspiracy to kill Americans.[56] Also arrested was Egyptian Ibrahim Eidarous, who American prosecutors say arrived in London from Azerbaijan in 1997 to head the London cell of Jihad.[57] The charges against Abdel-Bary and Eidarous largely revolve around their handling of faxes claiming responsibility for the embassy bombings in Africa—activities that, on the face of it, do not seem criminal.

Khaled al-Fawwaz, who arranged our CNN interview with bin Laden, was also jailed by British police in late September 1998.[58] I phoned him, on a tip, in the middle of the arrest; when I arrived at his house, the man who answered the door was a forensic technician dressed in a reflective silver bodysuit, complete with a helmet and visor. He resembled nothing so much as an astronaut who had improbably touched down on Khaled's quiet suburban street.

I had grown to like and respect Khaled and am still perplexed by his arrest. He had admitted that bin Laden was his friend and that together they had set up the Saudi opposition group called the Advice and Reform Committee. But he had always expressed surprise at bin Laden's calls for attacks on Americans: although he stopped short of condemning them, he wouldn't condone them either. As I noted earlier, he also said that it was "un-Islamic" to target civilians. He made these statements to me and to other journalists, and I believe that they represent his genuine beliefs.[59]

It's true that there are damaging aspects of the U.S. case against Khaled. Phone records show him to have been in regular contact with al-Qaeda at times when bin Laden was issuing calls for violence against Americans, and Khaled did play a role in disseminating those calls to the media. In the mid-nineties, Khaled set up a car-importing business in Kenya, on the board of which sat Abu Ubaidah al-Banshiri, at the time al-Qaeda's military commander; Khaled was later identified by a U.S. government informant in Kenya as an al-Qaeda member.[60] He is also alleged to have paid for photographic expenses incurred by Ali Mohamed when the latter cased the American embassy in Nairobi in 1993.[61]

I believe that an innocent construction can be put on Khaled's actions. His contact with al-Qaeda was a consequence of being bin Laden's unofficial media spokesperson, and it's a slippery slope when you start prosecuting the messengers. The car-importing business that Khaled set up in Kenya was just that, and when it failed it was shut down.[62] As for paying for Ali Mohamed's expenses in Nairobi, there's no proof that Khaled even knew why Mohamed was in town. The informant who told the government that Khaled was a member of al-Qaeda might simply have been wrong. During the embassy bombing trial, the lead prosecutor, Patrick Fitzgerald, identified Khaled as having run a training camp in Afghanistan, but Khaled insisted to me that he had never even gone there (although his eldest brother had).

Of course, even if these innocent explanations are true, American conspiracy laws are written so broadly that Khaled could still be judged guilty of being part of the plot to kill Americans. For the moment, he, Eidarous, and Abdel-Bary are in British jails and might or might not be extradited to the United States.

Also based in Britain was al-Qaeda member Anas al-Liby, who lived in the northern city of Manchester until he skipped town in 1999 ahead of raids on his house by British police, who would have almost certainly arrested him. Al-Liby, who is described as a computer expert, trained al-Qaeda members in Afghanistan in surveillance techniques in the early nineties. In the mid-nineties, al-Liby tended to al-Qaeda's computer needs in Sudan.[63] He and Ali Mohamed traveled to Nairobi in 1993 and used the apartment of an al-Qaeda member to develop the aforementioned surveillance pictures of the American embassy, the first step in the five-year plan to bomb it.[64] When police searched his modest house, they found a 180-page manual called *Military Studies in the Jihad Against the Tyrants.*[65] The manual covered such topics as how to conduct terrorist operations, how to counterfeit currency, and how to organize safe houses.[66]

London has also attracted a wide range of other Islamist militants in the past decade, many of whom were inspired by bin Laden's actions and rhetoric. One of the most flamboyant is Sheikh Omar Bakri Muhammad, a Syrian who styles himself the judge of his own *sharia* court. On a disconcertingly balmy evening in April 2000, I wandered the streets of Walthamstow, in east London, looking for the hall where Sheikh Bakri was mounting a conference entitled "Osama bin Laden and Terrorism." I knew I was getting closer when I saw banners proclaiming JIHAD AGAINST THE PIRATE STATE OF ISRAEL.

The meeting was in a nondescript community hall, inside which a group of men were prostrating themselves in prayer. The hardcore went for a military-chic look. Some wore kaffiyehs and combat jackets; others, the woolen cap that marked them as veterans, would-be or otherwise, of the Afghan holy war. A few sported the photographer's vest that network correspondents affect when they want to signal that they're in a war zone. But most of the audience was dressed in the unremarkable fashion of students, cabbies, and small-business owners. I counted about 250 men and, somewhat surprisingly, more than a hundred women, a few completely covered but most wearing simply head scarves. It was a polyglot crowd of Arabs, Africans, and Asians.

As a group of men set up video equipment to screen scenes from Russia's bloody blitzkrieg in Chechnya, a young man showed me pamphlets with titles such as "Jihad in America?" On the walls of the hall, posters announced CLINTON: THE MOST WANTED TERRORIST and JEWISH OCCUPIERS: KILL THEM WHEN YOU SEE THEM. A sign on the wall showed a Star of David with a skull and crossbones slapped on top of it.

A hush fell over the room as Sheikh Bakri, charismatic with his walking stick and well-pressed black cleric's garb, made his way to the stage. "We are not here to promote Osama bin Laden, though we support him," he began. But, he asked rhetorically, "Who is a terrorist? Who defines what is wrong and what is right?" As the audience listened raptly, Sheikh Bakri continued, "We recognize the leadership of bin Laden, though we have not met with him . . . this man who sacrificed his life for Islam . . . a man who is a multimillionaire."

Next, a tall, muscle-bound young man dressed in a T-shirt and camouflage pants took the microphone. Identifying himself as the director of security for Sheikh Bakri's organization, he explained in a heavy Cockney accent that military training in Britain "is in itself not illegal."

Sheikh Bakri has said that he has recruited hundreds of British Muslims for holy wars in Chechnya and the troubled region of Kashmir.[67]

Al-Qaeda has looser but still strong connections with other jihadist organizations around the world, among them Kashmiri groups based in Pakistan. The stakes are high in this conflict: India and Pakistan have twice gone to war over the beautiful region of mountains and lakes, and leaders on both sides have made saber-rattling comments about nuclear weapons.[68] The CIA assesses the Kashmir situation as the most likely trigger of a nuclear exchange anywhere in the world. Since 1990, more than fifty thousand people have died in the conflict, which every day brings fresh news of a bombing attack by militants or reprisals by Indian soldiers.[69] In July 2001, a summit meeting in New Delhi between India and Pakistan foundered acrimoniously on the Kashmir issue.[70]

The ties between al-Qaeda and the Kashmiri terrorist group Harakat ul-Mujahideen (HUM) became clear in late August 1998, when the United States rained cruise missiles on al-Qaeda's military training camps in Afghanistan. Most of bin Laden's followers had vacated the camps before the strikes, but of the twenty or so militants who died, nine were from HUM.[71] And HUM is just one of the dozen or so Pakistani Kashmiri groups who seek to push India out of Kashmir. An offshoot of HUM kidnapped six Western tourists in Kashmir in 1995.[72] A HUM offshoot would later be implicated in the murder-kidnapping of American journalist Daniel Pearl in January 2002.[73]

In December 1999, I became more closely acquainted with HUM's terror tactics when I covered its notorious hijacking of an Indian Airlines jet. The plane had been seized in Katmandu, Nepal, and had hopscotched across Asia and the Middle East, landing in India, Pakistan, Dubai, and finally Kandahar, where the hijackers proceeded to negotiate for the release of Kashmiri militants and a Pakistani cleric, Maulana Masood Azhar, held in Indian prisons.[74] (The HUM offshoot that kidnapped some Western tourists in Kashmir in 1995 had several times demanded the release of Azhar, a central figure in their organization.[75])

When I learned of the plane's whereabouts I was in Kabul, interviewing a Taliban minister about bin Laden. An assignment editor at

CNN told me to get down to Kandahar ASAP; this was advertised as a nightmarish twenty-hour journey by car. The cab I took was driven by a genial, black-turbaned mullah who had fought the Soviets and was an early recruit to the Taliban, although that didn't stop him from singing along to a banned Hindi music cassette. We passed through mountainous desert regions and the occasional adobe village in which the only signs of modernity were the loudspeakers on the roofs of the mosques. The journey lasted a spine-jarring sixteen hours, with only a half-hour break for the cleric-cum-taxi-driver to break his Ramadan fast at a roadside restaurant where forty or so men, mostly Taliban fighters, waited punctiliously for the sun to drop behind the mountains. They began with dates, followed by a huge repast of nan bread, lamb in a yogurt-and-carrot hot sauce, and a Kabuli pilau of rice, thinly sliced orange peel, raisin, and lamb. The bill for three, tip and soft drinks included, was two dollars.

Then we drove through the night, south toward Kandahar, arriving at the airport on the morning of December 27. The tension was extraordinary, as the hijackers had just issued a three-hour ultimatum. Annoyed at having dealt only with a low-level Indian diplomat, they demanded to speak to senior Indian officials, threatening otherwise to execute some of the 155 passengers. They had already stabbed an Indian man who was returning from his honeymoon in Nepal: he bled to death in his seat over the course of two hours.[76]

As the deadline neared, the hijackers threatened to kill two Western passengers. The Taliban's foreign minister, Wakil Almad Muttawakil, told them via radio that a high-level delegation from Delhi was on its way to Kandahar, and he emphasized that if any of the passengers were harmed he would order his troops to storm the plane. Minutes before the deadline was to expire, a convoy of about eighty grim-faced, heavily armed Taliban commandos surrounded the jet. The deadline came and went without incident.

On the plane, Jeanne Moore, a California psychotherapist in her early fifties who treats severely disturbed children, was fortunately unaware that the hijackers had threatened to execute Western passengers. But she knew that they were dangerous men; early in the ordeal, she had received a sharp blow to the head with a gun butt when she made a slight noise, and she had heard one of the hijackers, known as

"Doctor," beating up a couple of passengers. She told me she would never forget the sound of the blows.

At a certain point, the men had rounded up all the foreigners (those who weren't Indian or from Nepal) and taken them to the front of the economy cabin. They took the passengers' passports, which is when they discovered that Moore was an American. The hijackers were alternately brutal and chatty. Moore was able to strike up something of a dialogue with one known as Burger, discussing English grammar and syntax and even the Monica Lewinsky affair. She reasoned that "any kind of camaraderie" would help. She used techniques she employs with the kids she counsels: "Establish rapport, but never get in their face."

From the control tower, Foreign Minister Muttawakil kept up a constant round of negotiations. On Tuesday, he persuaded the hijackers to drop some of their initial demands, including the exhumation of the corpse of a Kashmiri militant buried in India and a ransom of $200 million. He argued that those conditions were "un-Islamic." The Taliban also kept a fair amount of psychological pressure on the hijackers to come to an agreement. Every night, as the temperature in the deserts around Kandahar dipped below freezing, soldiers huddled around campfires in a perimeter around the Airbus. The red glow of the fires softly illuminated the jet.

The U.N. representative for Afghanistan, Erik de Mul, paced the grounds of the airport, wearing a trilby hat and greatcoat, chain-smoking. A patrician Dutchman, he was there to advise the Taliban; he told reporters that they were handling the negotiations in a mature and sensible manner.

It was hard, meanwhile, for Moore to keep track of what day it was: the cabin was kept dark and the passengers spent most of the time with their heads between their legs or blindfolded. And she had little idea where they were, although she'd made some educated guesses. Four or so days into the hijacking, she helped a female passenger who "was stricken with terror and was pleading for an ambulance. The power had just gone off and it was getting stuffier by the instant." Moore got the woman into the cockpit and for the first time was able to get a look around. Outside the windows were groups of bearded, armed men wearing turbans. *Welcome to the Islamic Emirate of Afghanistan.*

"I could feel the pressure on the hijackers," Moore told me. "They had had no sleep. They told me they didn't mind dying. I told Burger he should rotate his men so that some of them could get some rest, because they had grenades, and the alternative was the whole plane would blow up."

Negotiations continued through Wednesday, by which time the hostages were in bad shape. They had been on the plane for five days and their diet had consisted of bread, rice, and beans. The toilets on the plane overflowed and stank; the plane's engines had been running for days and now kept breaking down—which meant no heat or air conditioning.[77]

On Thursday, December 30, the Taliban made another show of force. This time, an armored personnel carrier rolled onto the tarmac, and a tank took up a position on a hillock a quarter-mile away. Again a convoy of commandos surrounded the plane, and a pickup truck carrying Taliban soldiers bearing two Stinger anti-aircraft missiles made a slow tour of the jet. On the plane, Moore remembered the hijackers telling the passengers: "Do not make a sound. Do not move."

Muttawakil characterized the troop movements as routine security measures, but the message was clear: end the crisis or we will attack the plane. It would have been a bloodbath, as the Taliban did not have units like the U.S. Delta Force or the British SAS, capable of carrying out "surgical" hostage rescues.

On Thursday night the final deal was struck. The Indians agreed to release Azhar and two other militants held in India: Mushtak Ahmed Zargar, leader of Al-Umar, a lesser-known Kashmiri group, and Ahmed Omar Sheikh, a British citizen, whose family is Pakistani and who is a graduate of the London School of Economics.[78] (Two years later Sheikh would allegedly orchestrate the kidnapping of American journalist Daniel Pearl in Karachi, Pakistan.) Muttawakil summoned reporters on Friday morning and said a deal had been made but that the actual release of the passengers would be an extremely delicate and potentially dangerous situation.

(I would learn only later that bin Laden had played a key, behind-the-scenes role in the negotiations between the Taliban and HUM, urging the hijackers to cut the best possible deal for themselves.)

In the afternoon, a jet carrying Foreign Minister Jaswant Singh of

India and the militants released from Indian jails touched down at the airport. In an elaborately choreographed operation, the hijackers stepped out of the plane and, assured that their comrades were indeed at Kandahar, allowed the hostages to board four passenger buses standing by to take them to a jet headed back to New Delhi. Moore was the last off the plane. Weakened and suffering from a virus, she was helped into a wheelchair.

After the release, Foreign Minister Singh, a tall, silver-haired diplomat dressed in a well-pressed gray Nehru suit, convened a press conference in a lounge at the airport. Singh made a brief announcement to the effect that the Indian government had *not* given in to the terrorists. This spectacular whopper was delivered with the utmost seriousness, as if sufficient gravitas would make it true. An Australian reporter, true to his nation's tradition of bluntness, had the temerity to challenge this line. Singh ignored him and, with his entourage, swept grandly out. In fairness, his government had been under extraordinary pressure to resolve the crisis. The pleas of the hostages' families to get their loved ones back home were the only story in the Indian media during the hijacking drama.

Shortly after the crisis, Indian prime minister Atal Bihar Vajpayee publicly speculated that Pakistan had orchestrated the hijacking. Pakistani media, meanwhile, suggested that it had been masterminded by the "hidden hand" of Indian intelligence. Those absurd theories are excellent illustrations of the fact that, on the subject of Kashmir, common sense all too often takes a vacation on the Indian subcontinent.

The operation was a fabulous success for the hijackers. Not only did they secure the release of their fellow militants, but the Taliban allowed them to escape, almost certainly to Pakistan. A senior U.S. official tagged it a "successful murder-hijacking."

To learn more about HUM and other radical Kashmiri groups, I decided to visit the town of Muzzafarabad, which is near the border separating Pakistan's Azad or "Free" Kashmir from Indian Kashmir, and which functions as the operational headquarters of most of the militant groups.

To get to Muzzafarabad from Islamabad, I enlisted the services of

Ilyas, a twenty-five-year-old cabdriver and a member of Pakistan's tiny Christian minority. Before we left, I stopped off at the Information Ministry, where an official gave me the required pass for Muzzafarabad. (The town is off limits to the casual visitor.) He told me that there had been a drought for the past few months and that everyone had been praying for rain over the Eid holiday, which marks the end of Ramadan. Those prayers were about to be answered.

We took the road out of Islamabad toward the compact hill town of Muree, which the British had used as a retreat from the burning heat of India's summers. The Victorian Holy Trinity church that graces Muree's main street would not look out of place in Sussex. As we climbed into the heavily wooded hills, we saw signs announcing the presence of peacocks and mountain lions. Ilyas cranked up the stereo, which featured some pretty dodgy rap songs he liked, along with Cher's weirdly compelling "I Believe." I was fond of Ilyas, which was good as we were about to bond pretty heavily. We passed another sign, this one warning LANDSLIDE AREA. By now a fine rain was falling and in the mountains ahead I could see mists forming. When we reached Muree a marker at a crossroads told us we were at 6,500 feet. The rain turned to snow.

Ilyas suddenly announced: "Mr. Peter, sir, I have driven in snow before, but never falling snow like this."

He promptly slalomed into a pickup truck, smashing our bumper.

I told Ilyas not to worry, I'd pay for the damage, and we gingerly proceeded, past the entrance to the Muree Golf Club, which loomed incongruously out of what was now a blinding blizzard. The road was littered with car wrecks, but going back on this narrow mountain pass would have been as foolhardy as going forward. Then, as if on cue, we did a long, slow skid toward a stone embankment and ended up wedged between a metal guard rail and a stone wall, inches away from a sheer drop of a hundred feet into a grove of snow-covered pines.

"Next time we bring chains," offered Ilyas.

Right now we needed help. A bus lumbered by and a group of Kashmiri men leaped out and pushed us back into the middle of the road. Ilyas was fairly shaken, observing that, "God and Jesus Christ saved us today." I agreed that our appointment with death had at least been been postponed, to which Ilyas responded: "These Englishers who do not believe in God. What do they believe? That the world just runs automatically?"

We drove very slowly along the snow-packed mountain road through little towns dominated by green-roofed mosques. Locals huddling under the eaves of buildings laughed gleefully as they took in our sorry, smashed-up cab. As we began to descend towards Muzzafarabad, the weather slowly lifted. We crossed over a river and came to a checkpoint where soldiers scrutinized our pass and waved us on.

As we drove into Muzzafarabad, a damp, scraggly town that sits on a series of hills wreathed in mist, I noticed signs welcoming home the recently freed Kashmiri militants and offering greetings to the great *mujahideen*. After a quick bite at our hotel, we immediately struck out for HUM, which had its base of operations in a white-walled villa in a suburban neighborhood. A phalanx of jeeps and pickup trucks was parked outside. Inside, perhaps a dozen young men armed with AK-47s milled about. One took me to a senior official, a burly man in his late twenties dressed in a camouflage jacket and a brown woolen hat. The official—who pointedly asked to remain anonymous—ushered me into a room lavishly decorated with pictures of tanks, machine guns, and RPGs. There he launched into what would become the standard icebreaker during my meetings with Kashmiri militants: a blow-by-blow disquisition on the history of the Kashmiri conflict.

Here's the abridged version: Kashmir, a Utah-sized region split between India and Pakistan, has been fought over since the two nations gained independence from Great Britain in 1947. Half of Kashmir lies on the Indian side of the border, but the majority of Kashmiris are Muslims and wish to secede from predominantly Hindu India. These secessionist sentiments have been further fanned by the Indian army's frequent human rights violations. Over the past five decades, India and Pakistan have fought two full-blown wars, in 1947 and 1965, over Kashmir. After the war in 1947, the United Nations established a cease-fire agreement and also set up the border region that divides Pakistan's "Azad" Kashmir from Indian Kashmir. The United Nations also called for a referendum on the future of Kashmir, which the Indian government has never, understandably, allowed to proceed: Kashmiris would overwhelmingly vote for independence.[79]

The latest flare-up began in the late eighties—partly out of frustration over Indian-rigged elections and partly because the end of the war against the Soviets in Afghanistan freed up a cadre of holy warriors for another jihad.[80] HUM was founded in 1985 as an Afghan *mujahideen* group under the name Harkat-ul-Ansar. In 1997, after the U.S. State Department put Harkat-ul-Ansar on its list of terrorist organizations, the group changed its name to Harkat-al-Mujahideen. (The HUM official I spoke with claimed this was just a coincidence and that the name change was prompted by an internal dispute.)

In May 1999 a combined force of Pakistani soldiers and several hundred Kashmiri militants—including members of HUM—seized strategic mountain positions in the Kargil region in Indian-held Kashmir and fought off Indian assaults for two months. In October, General Pervez Musharraf, who had presided over the Kargil operation, toppled the government of Prime Minister Nawaz Sharif, which had ignominiously retreated from Kargil.

When I asked the HUM official whether his group was responsible for the Indian Airlines hijacking he would not answer directly. But his sympathies clearly lay with the hijackers, if only because they had brought renewed attention to the Kashmir issue. He also denied that the group had any links to bin Laden—which was odd, since the leader of HUM, Fazil Rahman, had only a year before publicly announced that HUM fighters had been killed in the American cruise missile attacks on bin Laden's camps in Afghanistan. The HUM official was more candid about the group's future plans, noting that it had recently formed *fidayeen*—martyr squads—to send into India on suicide missions.

HUM isn't the only group assembling such squads. Another is Tehrik-e-Jihad, the leader of which lives not far from HUM's headquarters on another quiet Muzaffarabad street. Salim Wani, whom I met several hours after my visit to HUM, is a charismatic forty-year-old father of three who speaks perfect English. Unlike the anonymous HUM official, Wani was dressed not in military fatigues but in a simple jogging suit with a wool shawl draped around his shoulders for warmth. He received me in a room decorated with carpets and a few chairs. Over tea and cakes he told me how he came to be a Kashmiri militant.

Born on the Indian side of Kashmir, Wani attended Kashmir University in Srinagar, where he majored in economics. In 1988, he joined Kashmiri college students in anti-Indian protests. The government responded with a severe crackdown, and Wani fled to Pakistan. "My house was gutted, my father was interrogated seven times," he said. "After that, I had no choice but to turn to armed struggle." Wani joined a loose federation of militants known as the United Jihad Council, set up in 1990. At first, he said, the movement was ineffective. "But by 1996 we began to operate more effectively, sharing weapons and men." In 1997, Wani founded Tehrik. "We conduct operations against Indian outposts," he explained. "We started with firecrackers and petrol bombs, but over time we started capturing armaments from the Indians and learned how to use their tactics and wear their uniforms." Before I left, Wani urged me to get in touch with an uncle in Virginia and convey his best wishes.[81]

A key question is to what extent groups like Tehrik and HUM are aided by the Pakistani government. Western diplomats in Pakistan told me the militants received weapons and operational support funneled through ISI, Pakistan's military intelligence agency.[82] The HUM official said that his group received only "diplomatic, moral, and political" support from the Pakistani government. Whatever the case, the openness with which these groups operate shows that Pakistan did not stand in their way.

Consider Lashkar-e-Taiba, the largest Pakistan-based Kashmiri militant group, which maintains offices in Islamabad. Like other Kashmiri groups, Lashkar sent hundreds of militants to battle the communists in Afghanistan. On my arrival at Lashkar's office I was greeted by its spokesman, Abdullah Muntazir, a diminutive twenty-four-year-old whose thick beard makes him appear much older. Muntazir said that many of Lashkar's activities are aimed at whipping up Pakistani public opinion against India. The group supports some 2,200 "preaching centers" that disseminate information about Indian atrocities. At its yearly rallies, hundreds of thousands of Pakistanis show up.[83]

But Lashkar's fight isn't just rhetorical. After joining the group at age eighteen, Muntazir said, he was sent to a three-week training course in Afghanistan, where he learned, among other things, to handle anti-aircraft guns, AK-47s, pistols, and RPGs. After that he went to the Pakistani side of Kashmir for three months of "graduate training" in such skills as raiding buildings and ambushing vehicles. Muntazir has participated in only one operation, a failed attempt to mine an Indian supply trail.

Calls for a holy war against India fall on fertile soil in Pakistan—not just in Azad Kashmir, but all over the country. Maulana Masood Azhar, the cleric freed in the Indian Airlines hijacking, appeared in Pakistan a week or so after his release and addressed rapturous crowds in the southern city of Karachi and his hometown of Bahawalpur. Surrounded by gun-toting bodyguards, he called for a jihad to emancipate Kashmir. In February 2000, Azhar announced the formation of a HUM splinter group, Jaish-e-Mohammed (JEM), which has subsequently attempted to assassinate senior Indian officials and carried out several bombing attacks in Indian Kashmir. JEM's several hundred armed supporters are mostly Pakistanis and Kashmiris but also Afghans and Arabs. American officials believe JEM received financial support from bin Laden.[84]

During the war against the Taliban in late 2001 the Pakistani government distanced itself from the Kashmiri militant groups, arresting key leaders and two thousand of their followers, an effort that intensified following the murder-kidnapping of American journalist Daniel Pearl in January 2002.

Thousands of miles from Kashmir, bin Laden is also linked to a decades-old Islamist insurgency in the largely Catholic islands of the Philippines. Approximately 5 percent of the Philippines' more than fifty million inhabitants are Muslim, most of them found on the second largest island, Mindanao, but many scattered around hundreds of smaller islands in the south. Since 1972, various Islamic groups have waged guerrilla wars against the central government in the name of an independent state, and tens of thousands have died.[85]

Two of the highest-profile groups are the powerful Moro Islamic Liberation Front—which trained with al-Qaeda in the early nineties but signed a cease-fire agreement with the Philippine government in the summer of 2001—and the much smaller Abu Sayyaf, which split off from the Moro Front in 1991.[86] The latter group was founded by Abdurajik Janjalani, who adopted the name Abu Sayyaf—"Bearer of the Sword"—as a tribute to bin Laden's ally Abdul Rasool Sayyaf, with whom he fought during the Afghan war against the communists.[87] Abu Sayyaf consists of a core group of about two hundred fighters and is estimated to have made tens of million of dollars since it began a campaign of kidnapping in 1993.[88] Among the Western tourists kidnapped was American Guillermo Subero, who was on a diving trip in the country. In June 2001, the group announced that Subero had been beheaded.

As I wrote in the chapter on al-Qaeda's American operatives, the 1993 World Trade Center bomber Ramzi Yousef trained at a camp run by Abdul Rasool Sayyaf and would later plan terrorist acts with Abu Sayyaf. He and the bin Laden veteran Wali Khan Amin Shah collaborated with Abu Sayyaf in 1994 on a plan to blow up eleven passenger jets and to assassinate Pope John Paul II on his visit to the Philippines.[89] Those plots were foiled when an explosives experiment in Yousef's Manila apartment backfired; he left behind a laptop that detailed the entire operation. Since the arrest of Yousef by the FBI, Abu Sayyaf has repeatedly demanded his release from an American prison.[90]

Another Abu Sayyaf ally is Mohammad Jamal Khalifa, who is married to one of bin Laden's two full sisters and was a key recruiter in Jordan for bin Laden's Services Office in Pakistan during the Afghan war. In the early nineties, Khalifa oversaw a rattan-furniture-making business in the Philippines and married a Filipina, one of his four wives.[91] He also helped to finance Abu Sayyaf.[92] In 1994, a Jordanian court convicted him on terrorism charges and sentenced him to death, but by then he had successfully applied for a visa to the United States at the American consulate in Jeddah, listing one of the bin Laden family companies as his address.[93] He was arrested in San Francisco in December 1994 and was subsequently deported to Jordan, but the terrorism charges against him were later dismissed.[94]

Khalifa's lawyer in the United States told me in 1997 that his client had indeed given money to Abu Sayyaf, but for "humanitarian work"—not an entirely plausible explanation since, unlike Lebanon's Hezbollah, Abu Sayyaf has few activities apart from kidnapping and bombing.[95] Khalifa now lives in Jeddah and says of his infamous relative: "Bin Laden is one of my twenty-two brothers-in-law and I do not condone his terrorist activities. In fact, the whole family has cut ties with him, no communication whatsoever because we are aware of what he has been doing and we don't agree with his illegal activities."[96]

Bin Laden's followers are also active in southern Russia, in the brutal wars that have torn apart Chechnya since 1994.[97] Of course, the Chechens have battled the Russians since the mid-nineteenth century. Leo Tolstoy, who served in an artillery regiment in the Caucasus, paints a compelling picture of the Chechens in *The Cossacks:* "No one spoke of hatred for the Russians. The feeling which the Chechens felt, both young and old, was stronger than hatred."[98] A century and a half later, nothing much has changed.[99] The Russians tried to subdue the unruly Chechens in two wars, one that lasted from 1994 until 1996, and another that has gone on sporadically from 1999 until now.

One of the most feared soldiers in this war goes by the nom de guerre Khattab and is said to have developed a "father-son" relationship with bin Laden while fighting the Soviets as a teenager in Afghanistan. Other details of his past have been murky. Press accounts have referred to his Middle Eastern origins; U.S. government officials and Saudi dissident sources say that Khattab—the name comes from one of the Prophet Muhammad's successors—is a Saudi, born around 1970 in the al-Khobar area of northeastern Saudi Arabia, and that his family name is al-Suwailem.[100] In photographs, he glares sullenly at the camera, his face framed by black dreadlocks, a heavy beard, and a beret. He is dressed in the well-worn camouflage of the professional guerrilla.

What we do know is that Khattab has devoted most of his adult life to killing Russian soldiers in Afghanistan, Tajikistan, and Chechnya, and that he has helped to impart a more radical vision of Islam to Chechen commanders—who, at the outset of the war, were Muslim mostly in name only.[101]

In August 1999, Khattab and the Chechen commander Sail Basayev launched an attack against Russian troops in neighboring Dagestan, provoking the second Chechen war. On a videotape made around that time, Khattab says: "I don't know how many Russian troops are there. Every day columns pour in. . . . I just know that many will be killed, many will be taken prisoner, and there will be much blood."[102] Khattab added to his fearsome reputation when a series of bombs blew up apartment buildings across Russia in September 1999, killing nearly three hundred people, attacks which authorities blamed on him and his partner in holy war, Basayev.

In 1999 Khattab maintained a camp in the Chechen village of Serzhenyurt, where he provided military training principally to Chechens and Dagestanis, but also to Islamist militants from other countries, according to U.S. officials. He now commands up to a thousand soldiers, of which as many as two hundred come from the Middle East, Pakistan, and Afghanistan.[103]

The subtitle of this chapter is "Around the World in Eighty Jihads"— and, to borrow an old adage, what goes around comes around. The global nature of al-Qaeda and its affiliated groups is now mirrored by the global effort to contain them in the wake of the September 11, 2001, carnage. The once proud—perhaps too proud—United States is eagerly drawing on the resources of other countries, from Russia to Yemen to the Philippines, all of which have their own reasons for cracking down on Islamist militant groups that threaten their security. It is safe to say that bin Laden, who has tens of thousands of allies all over the world, now has hundreds of millions of enemies as well.

In the past al-Qaeda has carried its holy war from its base in Afghanistan to countries around the world. Now the world has carried that war back to al-Qaeda.

AFTERWORD

The Endgame

Shareef don't like it
Rock the Casbah
Rock the Casbah

> —from "Rock the Casbah," The Clash

"I am just a poor slave of God. If I live or die, the war will continue."

> —Osama bin Laden on a videotape which aired on
> December 27, 2001

BIN LADEN

> —Brand name stamped on bags of heroin sold in
> New York City in 2002

As I was completing this book in August 2001, at the beginning of a new century, the United States seemed secure. If bin Laden and his network posed a threat to that security, then Americans could seemingly rest easy at night: in most years they had a better chance of being killed by a snake than by a terrorist. The Cold War and its threat of nuclear annihilation had vanished like a barely remembered dream, and the pervasiveness of American cultural and military power made the United States much like the Roman Empire during its golden age, with no Goths or Vandals in sight.

On September 11, that complacency was exploded. The vandals were among us now, responsible for the deaths of thousands of Americans. Suddenly the blithe days of dot-com billionaires, Puff Daddy's legal problems, and Gary Condit's evasions about the missing Chandra Levy had disappeared like a delightful mirage. And the stunning attacks had come without warning: the most significant failure in the history of American intelligence-gathering. "American Taliban" John Walker Lindh, a hapless twenty-year-old Californian, had ended up fighting with the Taliban and meeting bin Laden in Afghanistan. Meanwhile, American intelligence agencies—funded to the tune of thirty billion dollars a year—were somehow unable to replicate Lindh's feat and found themselves utterly surprised by al-Qaeda's assaults on the "homeland."

After the attacks the airwaves quickly filled with blathering bloviators, who called this an attack on "the American way of life," the very idea of the United States and its culture. While such statements might have provided psychological satisfaction to those who made them, they shed more heat than light on the motivations of bin Laden and his followers.

If you have read this far then presumably the question you are hoping will be answered is: Why is bin Laden doing what he is doing? To attempt an answer, we have to refrain from caricature and instead attend to bin Laden's own statements about why he is at war with the United States. Bin Laden is not some "AY-rab" who woke up one morning in a bad mood, his turban all in a twist, only to decide America was the enemy. He has reasons for hating the United States, and if we understand those reasons, we will have a glimmer of insight into what provoked the terrible events of September 11.

In all the tens of thousands of words that bin Laden has uttered on the public record there are some significant omissions: he does not rail against the pernicious effects of Hollywood movies, or against Madonna's midriff, or against the pornography protected by the U.S. Constitution. Nor does he inveigh against the drug and alcohol culture of the West, or its tolerance for homosexuals. He leaves that kind of material to the American Christian fundamentalist Jerry Falwell, who opined that the September 11 attacks were God's vengeance on Americans for condoning feminism and homosexuality.[1]

Judging by his silence, bin Laden cares little about such cultural issues. What he condemns the United States for is simple: its policies in the Middle East. Those are, to recap briefly: the continued American military presence in Arabia, U.S. support for Israel, its continued campaign against Iraq, and its support for regimes such as Egypt and Saudi Arabia that bin Laden regards as apostates from Islam.

Bin Laden is at war with the United States, but his is a political war, justified by his own understanding of Islam, and directed at the symbols and institutions of American power. The hijackers who came to America did not attack the headquarters of a major brewery, movie studio, or Coca-Cola, nor did they attack Las Vegas or the Supreme Court. They attacked the Pentagon and the World Trade Center, preeminent symbols of the United States' military and economic might. And that fits the pattern of previous al-Qaeda attacks on U.S. embassies, military installations, and warships.

Some commentators have suggested that the 9/11 attacks were in some way the result of the socioeconomic inequities that exist between the West and the Muslim world. Such a notion fails all sorts of common sense tests: if the attacks were really about the poverty of Islamic countries, the hijackers should have been destitute Africans or Afghans—not scions of the Egyptian and Saudi middle class. Moreover, the leaders of al-Qaeda tend to come from the elite of the Middle East.

Having determined that bin Laden's war has little to do with either economic or cultural issues and everything to do with religion and the politics of the Middle East, were the attacks the opening barrage in what Harvard professor Samuel Huntington famously predicted would be a "clash of civilizations"? "Cultural communities are replacing Cold War blocs," he wrote, "and the fault lines between civilizations are becoming the central lines of conflict in global politics."[2] In Huntington's view, the tectonic plates of Islam would grind up against the plates of Christianity and Hinduism, while within Christendom the Orthodox would war with the Catholics. Such clashes, he predicted, would be the future ruptures of history.

Huntington singled out Islam itself as the "Dark Force" in tomorrow's world. Consider the following: "The Muslim propensity toward violent conflict is also suggested by the degree to which Muslim societies are militarized."[3] And this: "Some Westerners, including President Bill Clinton, have argued that the West does not have problems with Islam but only with violent Islamist extremists. Fourteen hundred years of history demonstrate otherwise."[4] Huntington has also written, "Islam has bloody borders"—a charge I am sure the Bosnian Muslims would second.[5]

Huntington correctly points to an "Islamic resurgence" in the twentieth century, but he mistakenly conflates this resurgence with violence. In this he resembles those American journalists, imprisoned in their secular-liberal prism, who blame the Christian fundamentalist revival in the United States for the assassinations of abortion clinic doctors; the Christian revival is a movement of millions, while the violence at abortion clinics is the work of a handful of zealots.

Superficially, bin Laden seems to fit into the "clash of civilizations" thesis. After all, he revels in attacks on American targets. But a closer look shows that his rage is as much directed against one of the most conservative Muslim states in the world—Saudi Arabia—as against the United States. And for all his denunciations of the Jews, al-Qaeda has so far never attacked an Israeli or Jewish target.[6]

In addition, treating "Islam" as a monolith defies common sense. There are as many Islams as there are Christianities. They range from the Muslim engineering students at M.I.T. who have set up their own prayer rooms; to the clerics in Yemen who are participating in elections; to the Iranian women who are creating an emerging Islamic feminism; to the Tablighi Jamaat, a nonviolent Muslim missionary movement of millions barely known in the West; and to the Taliban religious warriors in Afghanistan who destroyed the country's ancient Buddhist statues in the name of Allah.[7]

Even in the former Yugoslavia, Huntington's Exhibit A, where two hundred thousand died in the wars of the nineties among Orthodox Serbs, Bosnian Muslims, and Catholic Croats, his analysis works only to a point. As has been well documented, it took a Milosevic to ignite the Yugoslav wars, just as it took a Hitler to unleash the Final Solution. Yes, once these events were in motion, "ordinary" Germans and "ordinary" Serbs (and Croats and Muslims) took enthusiastically to the task of killing their neighbors. But "age-old hatreds" are not sufficient explanations for warfare and genocide. Political changes are key. Germany under Bismarck was not a bad place to be Jewish, just as Yugoslavia under Tito was not a bad place to be Muslim.

The clash of civilizations, however, is a seductive theory to explain the post-Cold War world. The test of such a theory is its applicability to a wide number of situations, and certainly Huntington can point to a wealth of examples: a bloody war in Sudan between its Islamist regime and animist and Christian rebels; continued wars between the Russians and Chechens; the Muslim insurgency in the Philippines; Arab versus Jew in Israel; and now, perhaps, the events of September 11.

But a myriad of conflicts around the globe have run inconveniently counter to the world according to Huntington. The bloodiest genocide of the nineties was not between civilizations but tribal groups when the Hutus of Central Africa massacred eight hundred thousand Tutsis. In Somalia, the West's humanitarian intervention in 1992 was a sideshow to a decade of brutal clan warfare in that overwhelmingly Muslim nation. The ongoing civil war in Colombia, which has displaced millions and killed tens of thousands, has devolved from a battle between leftists and rightists into a brutal competition for control of the cocaine trade.

Even examples that seem, at first blush, to confirm the idea of a clash of civilizations become more complicated when one takes a deeper look. In Kashmir it seems that Muslims, with the aid of Pakistan, are fighting to free themselves from the yoke of Hindu India; but on closer inspection, most Kashmiris are engaged in a nationalist struggle for independence and are opposed both to Indian rule and to the militant Islamists from Pakistan and elsewhere who have come to their aid.[8]

A more accurate predictor of post-Cold War rivalries, then, is good old nationalism, as could be seen in Kosovo. In 1999, the Kosovars, who are Muslim more in name than practice, specifically rejected the "help" of outside Islamists, not wanting to complicate their struggle for independence.[9] Kurds in Iraq and Turkey have struggled for decades to achieve greater independence from their fellow Muslim Turks and Iraqis.

A further predictor of conflict is what Michael Ignatieff, borrowing from Freud, calls the "narcissism of minor differences"—wars fought between culturally similar neighbors, like so many conflicts in Africa today.[10]

Another predictor is power politics as usual—for instance, Saddam Hussein's land grab to seize Kuwait from his brother Arabs in 1990, and the subsequent alliance of Western states and almost all of the Muslim states to dislodge him. Hussein's attempt to garb himself in the raiment of Islam in order to rally the Muslim world behind him during the ensuing Gulf War would have been pathetic if it had not been so breathtakingly cynical. Muslims were well aware that Hussein was ruthlessly and ecumenically secular, exterminating Muslim opponents whether they were militant Islamists, Kurds, Shias, or the Marsh Arabs of southern Iraq.

The Gulf War was unpopular in the Arab "street," yes, but Syria, Saudi Arabia, Egypt, Qatar, Bahrain, Kuwait, and Oman all sent troops for Operation Desert Storm.[11] Indeed, Saudi and Egyptian *ulema* (clergy) issued statements calling the war against Iraq a holy war.[12] Leaders of Muslim nations did not want Iraq to become the strong man of the Middle East, whatever rhetoric they may have employed to disguise the truth that they preferred the United States in that role.

Huntington used the 1980s war against the Soviet Union in Afghanistan as a prime example for his thesis, describing it as "a civilization war because Muslims everywhere saw it as such and rallied against the Soviet Union."[13] Fair enough. But the Afghanistan argument, once launched, turned into a hot-air-seeking missile that would circle back to blow up his own theory. The Soviets withdrew from Afghanistan in 1989. Since then the country has been torn apart by multiple civil wars pitting Afghan against Afghan, Islamist against Islamist, Shia against Sunni, Tajik against Pathan. Hundreds of thousands have been killed.[14] *The clash of acquaintances,* anyone?

Bin Laden himself hoped to provoke a clash of civilizations. A month after the attacks on Washington and New York an Arab journalist asked him: "What do you think of the so-called 'war of civilizations'? You keep repeating 'crusaders' and words like that all the time. Does that mean you support the war of civilizations?" Bin Laden replied: "No doubt about that: The book [the Koran] mentions this clearly. The Jews and the Americans made up this call for peace in the world. The peace they're calling for is a big fairy tale. They're just drugging the Muslims as they lead them to slaughter. And the slaughter is still going on."

However, bin Laden's plan to spark a global contest between the "believers" and the "infidels" turned out to be a damp squib. With the attacks on Washington and New York—the ultimate "propaganda of the deed"—bin Laden hoped to ignite anti-American sentiment in Muslim countries that would bring down their governments and replace them with Taliban-style theocracies. Sandy Berger, President Clinton's national security advisor, has perceptively observed that "bin Laden's ultimate 'twin towers' are Pakistan and Saudi Arabia."[15] However, the largest pro-Osama rally in Pakistan after 9/11 was in Karachi, a city of twelve million people, and it amounted to fifty thousand demonstrators at most.[16] For its part, the Pakistani government moved aggressively in early 2002 to jail thousands of Islamist militants and expel thousands of foreign religious students from the country. The "Talibanization" of Pakistan referred to in chapter eight is seemingly in the process of being rolled back. Moreover, the United States did not engage in a wide-ranging war against Muslims, but essentially a police action against al-Qaeda and its Taliban allies in Afghanistan, a campaign that has largely been conducted by the Afghans themselves.

While the clash of civilizations has not materialized there is certainly a wide gulf of misunderstanding between the Muslim world and the United States. A major poll conducted by Gallup after 9/11 tells the story. In a survey of nine Muslim countries containing about half of the world's Muslim population the poll found half of the people questioned had unfavorable opinions of the United States, while a quarter had favorable opinions. Of those surveyed, two-thirds saw the September 11 attacks as morally unjustified, but nearly 80 percent said the U.S. military action in Afghanistan was also unjustified. And the poll found an astonishing 61 percent did not believe Arab terrorists carried out the attacks on New York and Washington![17]

This finding is especially perplexing because no one seriously contests the fact that the hijackers were from Saudi Arabia, Egypt, Lebanon, and the United Arab Emirates. Moreover, bin Laden and his aides made a series of well-publicized statements after 9/11 which left al-Qaeda's role in the World Trade Center attacks in little doubt. Bin Laden *himself* has identified the hijackers as Middle Easterners;

indeed from his statements it seems he may have even known some of them personally.

The first such statement surfaced on October 7, 2001—the very night the United States launched its initial cruise missile attacks and bombing raids on Taliban and al-Qaeda targets. The world was treated to the indelible image of bin Laden sitting on a rocky outcrop flanked by his senior aides—"looking as untroubled as if he were on a camping trip," as *The New York Times* memorably put it—while Tomahawk cruise missiles rained down on his terrorist training camps and the military facilities of his Taliban allies. At the very moment that tens, perhaps hundreds, of millions of people around the world were glued to the grainy green nightscope picture of the bombing raids in Afghanistan, the world's most wanted man popped up in the middle of the coverage to revel in al-Qaeda's success. "America is struck by God Almighty in one of its vital organs. So that its greatest buildings are destroyed. Grace and gratitude to God. America has been filled with horror from north to south and from west to east," he intoned. It was a supremely confident performance and a perfect illustration of Holy War, Inc. in operation—utilizing the satellite uplinks of the world's television networks to beam a global message of holy war. Few political messages in history have been broadcast so widely.

Six days later bin Laden's spokesman, a heretofore obscure Kuwaiti teacher named Suleiman Abu Ghaith, warned on another videotape seen around the world that Muslims in the United States and Great Britain should not take plane flights or live in high buildings.[18] Then in mid-October the Arabic language television network Al-Jazeera conducted an exclusive interview with bin Laden but declined to air it, saying the interview was not "newsworthy." As a journalist I found this puzzling. This was after all the only television interview that bin Laden had given after 9/11 and was therefore the interview "get" of the past decade. For reasons that Al-Jazeera has never convincingly elucidated, the network sat on the interview. CNN obtained a copy of the interview and aired it in February 2002 without the consent of Al-Jazeera. What follows are the portions of the interview in which bin Laden explains it is defensible to kill civilians; that there is such a thing as "good" terrorism, and admits his intellectual authorship of 9/11. Judge for yourself if these statements are newsworthy:

AL-JAZEERA CORRESPONDENT: Dear viewers, welcome to this much-anticipated interview with the leader of the al-Qaeda organization, Sheikh Osama bin Laden. Sheikh, the question that's on the mind of the people around the world: America claims that it has proof that you are behind what happened in New York and Washington. What's your answer?

. BIN LADEN: America has made many accusations against us. Its charge that we are carrying out acts of terrorism is unwarranted. . . . If inciting people to do that is terrorism and if killing those who kill our sons is terrorism then let history be witness that we are terrorists. . .

AL-JAZEERA CORRESPONDENT: How about the killing of innocent civilians?

BIN LADEN: We kill the kings of the infidels, kings of the crusaders, and civilian infidels in exchange for those of our children they kill. This is permissible in law and intellectually.

AL-JAZEERA CORRESPONDENT: So what you are saying is that this is a type of reciprocal treatment. They kill our innocents, so we kill their innocents.

BIN LADEN: So we kill their innocents, and I say it is permissible in law and intellectually. . .

AL-JAZEERA CORRESPONDENT: How about the Twin Towers?

BIN LADEN: The towers are an economic power and not a children's school. Those that were there are men that supported the biggest economic power in the world. They have to review their books. We will do as they do. If they kill our women and our innocent people, we will kill their women and their innocent people. . . . Not all terrorism is cursed; some terrorism is blessed. . . . America and Israel exercise the condemned terrorism. We practice the good terrorism, which stops them from killing our children in Palestine and elsewhere.[19]

A videotape of a November 2001 meeting between bin Laden and a Saudi supporter was discovered by U.S. officials in Afghanistan and was released to the media the following month. On the tape we see the private bin Laden kicking back with his fawning cronies. Bin Laden is in good humor, chuckling softly as he discusses the Trade Center attack: "We calculated in advance the number of casualties from the enemy. . . . We calculated that the floors that would be hit would be three or four floors. I was the most optimistic of them all. Due to my experience in this field [construction] I was thinking that the fire from the gas in the plane would melt the iron structure of the building and collapse the area where the plane had hit and all the floors above it only. This is all that we had hoped for." Bin Laden goes on to observe: "We had notification since the previous Thursday that the event would take place that day [Tuesday.]"[20] On the tape bin Laden also mentions the names of several of the hijackers, including Mohammed Atta, the ringleader.[21]

On December 27, 2001 Al-Jazeera and CNN broadcast what may turn out to be bin Laden's final public statement. Bin Laden again mentions Atta and alludes to the fact that the other hijackers were Saudis. Referring to the "blessed attacks" on the Trade Center, bin Laden says the havoc they wreaked in the United States revealed its "fragile" nature.[22]

All of bin Laden's statements received wide dissemination around the world, yet in the Middle East a commonly held view remains that the Trade Center attacks were not the work of Arab terrorists, but the work of—you guessed it—the Jews. This was deduced from the supposed fact that 4,000 Jews did not show up for work on the day of the attacks. Mohammed Atta's father, a lawyer in Cairo, told reporters that the attacks were probably the work of Israeli intelligence.[23] I encountered this conspiracist mindset when I was reporting on the bombing of the U.S.S. *Cole* in Yemen, where otherwise seemingly sane and intelligent Yemenis assured me that it had been the work of the Israelis.

One commentator has aptly described this conspiracy culture of the Middle East as "the deeply rooted conviction that virtually every significant occurrence is caused by some external conspiracy."[24] Indeed it was partly a result of this culture of conspiracy that bin Laden was able to convince a transnational coalition of Arabs that the myriad problems of their home countries were somehow all the fault of the United States, rather than the incompetence and corruption of their various governments, most of which are authoritarian kleptocracies.

Charles Hill, a former U.S. diplomat, observes in *The Age of Terror: America and The World After September 11,* that it is the *political* failures of Arab governments which have incubated the religious terrorists:

"There is a single approach to the political ordering of society. . . . Power is held by a strongman, surrounded by a praetorian guard. . . . Those close to political power gain; the weak are disregarded. . . . Every regime of the Arab-Islamic world has proved a failure. Not one has proved able to provide its people with realistic hope for a free and prosperous future. The regimes have found no way to respond to their people's frustration other than a combination of internal oppression and propaganda to generate rage against external enemies. Religiously inflamed terrorists take root in such soil. Their threats to the regimes extort facilities and subsidies that increase their strength and influence. The result is a downward spiral of failure, fear and hatred."[25]

The distortions of the body politic in the Middle East are mirrored by the distortions of the body economic. Closed markets and an over-reliance on oil revenues have produced painfully skewed economies. If you subtract oil revenues from the GDP of the six countries that make up the Persian Gulf states their total output is equal to that of Finland.[26] Limited economic opportunities and the effective disenfranchisement of the population of the Middle East propel many towards Islamism. Islamism is attractive for several reasons: it is a political doctrine which emerges naturally from the cultural fabric of Muslim countries; its slogan "Islam is the solution" proposes a simple fix to all of society's problems, and it appears to promise a brighter future than the mirages of pan-Arab nationalism and socialism, which were the orthodoxies of the Middle East in past decades.

Within Islamism a tiny minority have traveled from Islamist politics to Islamist terrorism. Why do they make that journey? This is the subject of some debate. Some have proffered a psychological explanation: that belonging to a terrorist group satisfies some personal inadequacy. That argument can surely be made about a person belonging to any group whether it is the Shriners or al-Qaeda and does little to illuminate the motivations of al-Qaeda's members. Another perhaps more useful explanation is that terrorism is seen by its practitioners as a rational choice to bring certain political goals nearer and a short cut to transforming the political landscape. Israel's future prime minister, Menachim Begin, and his Irgun group conducted a campaign of terrorism against British targets in Palestine after World War II to hasten the British withdrawal from the country—a strategy that proved successful.

Bin Laden also made a strategic decision to use terrorism to bring about his political goals. The 1998 attacks on the American embassies in Africa were modeled after the attack on the U.S. Marine barracks in Lebanon in 1983 which precipitated the withdrawal of American troops from that country. Bin Laden hoped his campaign of terror against the United States would achieve his longtime political aim of removing American troops from Saudi Arabia.

And, astonishingly, bin Laden may get his wish because a significant reevaluation of the longtime marriage of convenience between the United States and the House of al-Saud has been one of the less predictable outcomes of 9/11. After the attacks American journalists began to focus on the fact that the source of much of the world's Islamist extremism is in fact Saudi Arabia. Imagine for a minute that fifteen of the nineteen hijackers had been Iranian instead of Saudi (as they in fact were). Imagine, too, that the Taliban received diplomatic and economic support not from Riyadh but from the regime in Tehran, and that bin Laden enjoyed the backing of Iranian clerics, charities, and businesses rather than their Saudi counterparts. Does anyone doubt that if any of the above were true, the United States would have already taken aggressive actions against Iran? The U.S. government has long characterized both Iran and Iraq as states that sponsor terrorism, yet there is not a scintilla of proof that either country had a hand in 9/11 or indeed any operational role in al-Qaeda.

That is not the case with the Saudis who, in an effort to shore up their own legitimacy as the custodians of Islamic orthodoxy, have financed militant Islamist movements around the world. This policy of backing Islamist groups that also happen to be virulently anti-Western has now borne disastrous results, from Afghanistan to Manhattan. The post 9/11 revaluation of the U.S.-Saudi alliance has precipitated a highly ironic outcome: bin Laden's call for the withdrawal of American troops from Saudi Arabia has since been echoed by American officials. Senator Carl Levin, who heads the Senate Armed Service Committee, told reporters in January 2002: "We need a base in that region, but it seems we should find a place that is more hospitable . . . I don't think they want us to stay there."[27] That same month President Bush's chief of staff, Andrew H. Card Jr., told CNN that the United States was interested in "reducing the U.S. footprint" in Saudi Arabia and that it would "happen over time."[28] Off the record, of course, senior Saudi officials have also suggested that the United States has "overstayed its welcome."[29] American military commanders have drawn up contingency plans to withdraw the 5,000 U.S. servicemen who remain in Saudi Arabia.[30]

The diminishing importance of the Saudi-American alliance is also underlined in two other significant developments: first, that Russia and Venezuela are competing to supplant Saudi Arabia as the leading exporter of oil to the United States,[31] and second, that every Middle Eastern country is in some way cooperating with the U.S. in its fight against al-Qaeda. Even countries like Jordan and Yemen, which were sympathetic to Saddam Hussein during the Gulf War, are aiding the American-led coalition. Most Middle Eastern governments are implacably opposed to al-Qaeda and its affiliates; they are well aware that they, too, are targets of bin Laden's campaign of violence. And their antipathy to the radical jihadist organizations that seek to overthrow them appears to be shared by their people; as support for extremist organizations declines, Islamist groups that are willing to work within the existing political framework have become increasingly powerful in countries across the Middle East.

The journalist Genevieve Abdo argues that the roots of this less confrontational Islamist movement can be found in groups such as Egypt's professional unions and that the movement has already made strides towards securing real influence.[32] Abdo's thesis is amplified by another journalist, Anthony Shadid, who shows that the moderate Islamist movement has become progressively more important not only in Egypt but also in Jordan and Iran.[33] (That said, the reverse is taking place in Israel and the Palestinian Authority, where the collapse of the peace process has empowered hardliners on both sides of the conflict.)

Yemen is also seeing the development of a democratic Islamist movement. The Islamist *Islah* party, which wins around 20 percent of the seats in parliament, includes elements of the Islamist Muslim

Brotherhood, which a decade ago would not have participated in elections. Now Islah works as a responsible political actor within Yemen's tentative experiment in multiparty democracy.[34]

The development of Islamist movements working within a democratic framework should not be surprising. There is nothing inherently "antidemocratic" in Islam, and there are Muslim concepts, such as *shura* (consultation with the people), that fit rather neatly into a democratic framework.[35] What are elections, if not consultations with the people? Just as Franco's fascism, seventeenth-century Europe's divine right of kings, and the eighteenth-century American innovation of the separation of church and state all emerged from Christian societies, any number of political models is possible in an Islamic environment. The proof lies in Indonesia: With more than two hundred million inhabitants, it is one of the world's largest democracies and the world's largest Muslim country.[36]

If the advocates of political Islam have failed to create viable Islamist states in countries such as Sudan and Afghanistan, and if countries in the Middle East are seeing the emergence of less confrontational Islamist groups, what then is the significance of Holy War, Inc., the most radical Islamist strain?

To help answer that question, let us consider the history of an analogous group: the Assassins, a radical Muslim sect of the eleventh and twelfth centuries that may have been the first group in history to use terrorism systematically as a means of destroying its enemies. The Assassins directed their campaign of terror from remote mountain fortresses in the region that is now part of Syria and Iran. Assassins were dispatched to bump off enemies of the group, principally leaders of the reigning Sunni political order and also a smaller number of Christians. Myths grew up around the Assassins, particularly in the West, where it was believed that the Assassins smoked hashish before they went off on their murderous missions. (Eight centuries later, in a distant echo of the Assassins, al-Qaeda's Mohamed Atta would go on a drinking binge days before guiding American Airlines flight 11 into the North Tower of the World Trade Center.) Medieval Western sources also thought that the Assassins were led by a mysterious leader, the Old Man of the Mountains, who had created a cultlike group of murderers.[37]

There are obvious parallels between the Assassins and al-Qaeda. The first is al-Qaeda's choice of a base, mountainous and remote Afghanistan, far from the reach of the powers it is attacking. The second is the use of terrorism to achieve its aims. Bin Laden and company have focused less on acts of assassination—although they did try to kill Hosni Mubarak in 1995—than on acts of mass destruction, but it is terrorism all the same. Although the Assassins were a splinter group of the Shia minority in the Muslim world, and bin Laden preaches a neo-fundamentalist Sunni Islam, in practice, both groups are opposed to the Sunni establishment and the West. And, like the Old Man of the Mountains, bin Laden has achieved an almost mythic status. While the Assassins certainly terrorized their enemies, in the long term they were not able to conquer even one city, and after a period of two centuries they disappeared. Will al-Qaeda follow the Assassins into the history books as a footnote, albeit a very bloody one? Or might its holy wars achieve something more?

That will, of course, depend on how well the American-led coalition deals with al-Qaeda as a whole. I am writing this six months after the Trade Center attacks. Since then al-Qaeda has had some significant setbacks; Afghan manpower and American firepower brought about the defeat of the Taliban, and Afghanistan is now run by Hamid Karzai's largely pro-Western government. This is significant because it means that al-Qaeda no longer has an entire country to use as its headquarters. Indeed al-Qaeda became so important in Taliban-run Afghanistan that it was more like a "country sponsored by terrorists as opposed to a state that sponsored terrorism" according to Zalmay Khalilzad, the Afghan-American who is leading the U.S. government's efforts to rebuild the shattered country.[38]

The defeat of the Taliban has important *long-term* implications because it does two things: it puts al-Qaeda's leadership on the run and it closes down the group's training camps in Afghanistan. Without the organizational skills of men like bin Laden and Ayman al-Zawahiri, both of whom have been involved in planning paramilitary actions for decades, and the Afghan terror training camps, the group's ability to mount spectacular terrorist operations will diminish over time. There are other places in the world where pockets of al-Qaeda still exist, such as Yemen and Chechnya, but nothing on the scale of what bin Laden created in Afghanistan. And that is of vital importance because it was the Afghan training camps that turned raw recruits with a general and inchoate antipathy to the West into cells of skilled operatives capable of building devastating bombs or carrying out complex operations such as the September 11 attacks.

Will the death or capture of bin Laden spell the end of al-Qaeda? It is possible that bin Laden is already dead. The U.S. government is performing DNA testing of the remains of al-Qaeda fighters to determine if that is the case.[39] If he is alive, he is certainly not in good health; the last known videotape of bin Laden which aired in December 2001 showed a man who has aged enormously in the past year. At the time of the taping, bin Laden was forty-four, but he looked like a man two decades older. During the course of his half-hour appearance on the tape, bin Laden did not move the left side of his body at all, suggesting that he has sustained some injury to it.

Assuming bin Laden is alive—and that is a reasonable assumption until there is conclusive evidence otherwise—how easy will it be to find him? The short answer is that it will likely be difficult. Afghanistan is a country the size of Texas, and bin Laden knows it intimately. He started building extensive underground complexes for his men there in the early eighties and will use them to hide. His core group consists of several hundred men with intimate knowledge of the terrain, who are battle hardened, highly motivated, and willing to die for their *emir*. They are also armed with RPGs and a variety of submachine guns, and are well trained in the use of a variety of explosives and mines. Moreover, a determined adversary who knows his own neighborhood can evade even the most intensive manhunt. Somali warlord Mohamed Aidid was the subject of a massive manhunt by thousands of U.S. troops in Mogadishu during 1993 and was never caught.

The initial hunt for bin Laden and his followers was hampered by a desire to limit American casualties. In the Tora Bora region in eastern Afghanistan in late 2001 the operation against al-Qaeda was conducted largely by Afghan groups with the aid of some American Special Forces. This operation was not a success, as hundreds of al-Qaeda members slipped across the border into Pakistan. A radically different approach characterized the tactics of anti-al-Qaeda operations in early 2002 near Gardez in central Afghanistan, involving more than a thousand U.S.

ground troops acting in concert with Afghan troops.[40] This approach has been more efficacious in rooting out the al-Qaeda forces in the area, a combined force of Arabs, Pakistanis, Chechens, and Uzbeks.

Bin Laden will eventually be captured—or more likely killed, as he has repeatedly said that he is willing to die in this struggle. His death would deal a blow to al-Qaeda. Others down the chain of command might hate the United States as much or more, but it was bin Laden's charisma and organizational skills that created his transnational terrorist concern. In death, bin Laden will certainly become a martyr for his immediate followers. But the most obvious statement you can make about martyrs is that they are dead, and that would immediately make bin Laden less potent. Bin Laden's al-Qaeda occupies the space that exists somewhere in between a cult and a genuine mass movement. Cults usually disappear with the deaths of their leaders: think of Jim Jones or David Koresh. So too will "Bin Ladenism" eventually join what President Bush has called "history's unmarked grave of discarded lies."[41]

Whatever bin Laden's fate, in the short term al-Qaeda is far from out of business. President Bush has said that tens of thousands of men were trained in the group's Afghan camps. Most of those trainees only received basic military training and only the best of those recruits would have gone on to more advanced terrorist training and eventual induction into al-Qaeda. Nonetheless, several thousand al-Qaeda members are scattered in sixty countries around the globe, and U.S. intelligence officials believe that Holy War, Inc. will probably devolve into local "franchises": truly a Hydra-headed monster. Indeed since 9/11 there has been a blizzard of operations by al-Qaeda and affiliated groups around the world. A Pakistani group tied to al-Qaeda attacked the Indian parliament on December 13, 2001, killing seven people, and putting enormous strains on the already testy relations between India and Pakistan. That same month an al-Qaeda plot to bomb the British, Israeli, Australian, and American embassies in Singapore was averted by arrests in Malaysia. In January 2002 a Pakistani group with ties to bin Laden kidnapped American journalist Daniel Pearl in Karachi, and al-Qaeda operatives planned to car bomb the U.S. embassy in Yemen. Abu Sayyaf, a Filipino terrorist group which has had historical ties to al-Qaeda, continues its kidnapping campaign of European and American tourists. In March 2002, Pakistani militants attacked a Protestant church in Islamabad with grenades, killing five people, including two Americans.[42]

Europe has been a fertile operational theater for al-Qaeda cells in past years. Following the Trade Center attacks those cells sought to unleash a campaign of terror against a wide range of European targets. In September 2001 Belgian police discovered two suspected al-Qaeda cells operating in the country; the same month, French police averted a plan to attack the American embassy in Paris; the following month, Bosnian authorities discovered a plot to attack the U.S. embassy in Sarajevo; and in late December, British citizen Richard Reid allegedly attempted to bomb an American Airlines aircraft en route from Paris to Miami.[43]

And the threat from al-Qaeda has not abated within the United States itself. The chairman of the Senate Intelligence Committee, Senator Bob Graham, told CNN in February 2002: "The estimate is that there are one hundred or more al-Qaeda operatives inside the United States, some of whom have been here for a considerable period of time."[44]

A further disturbing fact: one of al-Qaeda's defining characteristics is *patience*. The group first started plotting the 1998 bombing of the U.S. embassy in Kenya in 1993; the attack on the U.S.S. *Cole* in Yemen was two years in the making; and the cell of Trade Center plotters that formed around Mohammed Atta in Germany started meeting in 1998. It is quite possible that another catastrophic anti-American attack was in the pipeline before 9/11 and may only surface a year or two from now.

One can only hope that the arrest of an estimated one thousand al-Qaeda members around the world and the capture or killing of hundreds of al-Qaeda fighters in Afghanistan will avert such an attack. Among the dead is the group's military commander Muhammad Atef, the alleged planner of the Trade Center attacks. Abu Zubaida, a Palestinian who had supplanted Atef as the group's operational commander, was captured in Pakistan in March 2002. The Taliban Foreign Minister Wakil Muttawakil turned himself in to American authorities in February 2002 and may have useful information about al-Qaeda. However, in addition to bin Laden, key leaders of the group remain at large, such as Ayman al-Zawahiri. Moreover, during the winter of 2001 hundreds of al-Qaeda fighters based in Afghanistan slipped over the border into neighboring Pakistan and Iran.[45]

A further worry is that al-Qaeda had an intense, if amateurish, interest in developing or acquiring weapons of mass destruction (WMD), an interest sparked ironically by the concerns of the U.S. government that terrorist groups might deploy such weapons. An al-Qaeda internal memo notes that: "we only became aware of them [biological and chemical weapons] when the enemy drew our attention to them by repeatedly expressing concern that they can be produced simply."[46]

Bin Laden's own statements have always been the best predictor of his future actions and on this subject his words are chilling and unequivocal: "We don't consider it a crime if we tried to have nuclear, chemical, biological weapons." In his only newspaper interview since 9/11 bin Laden told the Pakistani journalist Hamid Mir: "I wish to declare that if America used nuclear and chemical weapons against us, then we may retort with chemical and nuclear weapons." Mir asked bin Laden: "Where did you get those weapons from?" Bin Laden ducked the question, but let us briefly review what is known about al-Qaeda's efforts to acquire WMD.[47]

As we have seen, in the late nineties al-Qaeda operatives conducted chemical weapons research using cyanide gas on animals. Four Moroccans arrested in Italy in February 2002 seemed to be putting that research into practice with a plot to poison the water supply of the American embassy in Rome with a cyanide-like compound. Al-Qaeda also explored the possibility of deploying biological weapons: diagrams of a balloon dispersing anthrax were discovered at an al-Qaeda safe house in Kabul, and CIA director George Tenet testified before Congress in February 2002 that documents discovered in Afghanistan "show bin Laden was pursuing a sophisticated biological weapons program."[48]

And it is possible that al-Qaeda has acquired materials for a crude "radiological" weapon. As discussed in Chapter 4, during the early nineties the group made determined efforts to secure uranium of the type that could be used in a nuclear bomb. While in Afghanistan, bin Laden met with pro-Taliban Pakistani nuclear scientists.[49] The U.S. government continues to analyze materials gathered at al-Qaeda bases in Afghanistan and has yet to find any radioactive materials, although that analysis is ongoing. The consensus within the government is that al-Qaeda probably has acquired some radioactive material, not of the kind that could be used in nuclear weapons, but of the type that could be deployed in what is known as a "dirty" bomb. Such a bomb consists of conventional explosives married to radioactive matter. If a dirty bomb was deployed its effect would be primarily to induce panic by contaminating an area of several city blocks. Al-Qaeda was also contemplating attacks on American nuclear power plants; diagrams of those facilities were found in Afghanistan, and U.S. intelligence picked up discussions between terrorism suspects after 9/11 that indicated that they would try to attack U.S. nuclear power facilities.[50]

In early 2002 the Bush administration expanded its war against al-Qaeda and affiliated groups, sending American servicemen to Georgia, Yemen, and the Philippines. And in a further expansion of the "war on terrorism" President Bush identified an "axis of evil" that includes Iraq, Iran, and North Korea. This is an odd formulation as these nations hardly constitute an axis. Indeed, Iraq and Iran are implacable enemies, having fought a brutal war during the 1980s which killed a million people. And describing Iran as "evil" has undermined the reformist camp in the Iranian government and generated vast anti-American rallies in a country where the United States was becoming increasingly popular.[51]

One thing, however, is clear about the axis: the U.S. government will take its war to Iraq; the question is only when and in what manner. It must be well understood why the United States is doing this. It is *not* because Iraq has engaged in anti-American terrorism; the terrorism that Saddam Hussein has inflicted has been primarily against his own people, for instance unleashing chemical weapons attacks against Iraqi Kurds. The reason that the U.S. will conduct further military operations against Hussein is his continued flouting of U.N. resolutions about allowing weapons inspectors to inspect his WMD sites. This is not only a legitimate use of force under international law, it is also prudent because Hussein is a vile dictator who has murdered hundreds of thousands of his own people; invaded his neighbors; has long pursued an aggressive WMD program; and has deployed chemical weapons against his enemies in the past. Hussein armed with nuclear weapons is not an attractive concept. In early 2002 a debate was raging in Washington whether to topple Hussein, an undertaking that might involve hundreds of thousands of U.S. ground troops, or to pursue some less ambitious plan. At a minimum, a Pentagon official told me, U.S. Special Forces will go into Iraq as part of an operation to take out sites where WMD are manufactured.[52]

When can we finally declare victory in the "war" on terrorism? There will obviously be no formal declaration of victory, but a kind of victory will be achieved when the threat from terrorism reverts to the status quo of pre-9/11, where terrorism was an irritant for American policy makers, but not the major national security concern. There will continue to be terrorist attacks against American targets as there were in the 1980s because there will always be groups opposed to U.S. policies. But those attacks will not be of the scale, complexity, and deadliness of al-Qaeda's operations. Until then, the United States will remain engaged in a strange kind of "war": one that is neither Cold nor hot; one where civilian casualties will probably outnumber military casualties; and a war that a Pentagon official told me may take as "long as a decade."[53]

In the meantime we can only hope that an enduring legacy of 9/11 will be the creation of a stable Afghanistan and the return of peace to a country that has suffered through more than two decades of war. And perhaps an Afghanistan that is at once Western-oriented yet profoundly Muslim will be a harbinger of a new era of reconciliation between the great civilizations of the West and the Islamic world.

As the great Jewish prophet—recognized by Muslims and Christians alike—observed two thousand years ago: "Blessed are the peacemakers, for they shall be called the children of God."

ACKNOWLEDGMENTS

W hen I sat down to write this book, I had the notion that it was just me and my keyboard. Nothing could have been further from the truth. No book is an island, as these acknowledgments make clear. I apologize to anyone I have inadvertently left out.

Thanks to all the academics, journalists, and other sources who made this book possible. Many of them are mentioned in the notes. I would like to acknowledge the enormous intellectual contributions of Gilles Kepel, Olivier Roy, Malise Ruthven, Bernard Lewis, Ahmed Rashid, Barney Rubin, Mamoun Fandy, and Karen Armstrong, all of whom informed my thinking about the jihadist movement. I would also like to acknowledge the reporting of *The New York Times,* specifically of Benjamin Weiser, Judith Miller, and John Burns, and the reporting of *The Washington Post*'s Vernon Loeb and Pamela Constable.

This book was a collaboration with a great number of people. Many people kindly gave of their time to be interviewed, and most of them are credited by name in the text. Others wished to remain anonymous. Thank you all.

I was lucky enough to have worked at CNN from 1990 to 1999 and have benefited enormously from the incredibly hardworking and professional staff at what is, by an order of magnitude, the best news network in the world.

I would particularly like to thank Pam Hill and John Lane, my long-time bosses at CNN, who indulged my interest in the Afghan Arabs and bin Laden at a time when these were not the stories they have since become. Pam and John were the ideal bosses in every respect. Thanks also to Peter Arnett, Peter Jouvenal, and Richard Mackenzie for an excellent trip to Afghanistan in 1993. Richard has continued to be a rich source of knowledge about the country, and a great friend. In 1997, I returned to Afghanistan with Peter Arnett and Peter Jouvenal to interview bin Laden. Without my companions there would have been no interview. Also at CNN, Henry Schuster and I collaborated on numerous bin Laden stories. Anyone who knows Henry knows he is one of the best reporters and producers in the business. He gave this book a thorough reading, and it has benefited from his insights and observations. Phil Hirschkorn of New York's CNN bureau repeatedly helped me with his encyclopedic knowledge about bin Laden and his associates.

Others at CNN, too, helped me report on the Afghan Arab/bin Laden phenomenon: Josh Gerstein, Steve Daly, Amy Kasarda, Valerie Shead, Brian Rokus, Julie Powell, and Alphonso van Marsh. At CNN I worked on a variety of bin Laden-related stories and segments with Jim Connor, David Ensor, Nancy Ambrose, Wolf Blitzer, Christiane Amanpour, Tom Dunlavey, John King, Beth Lewandowski, Chris Plante, Owen Renfro, Greta Van Susteren, Judy Woodruff, Roger Cossack, Nancy Lane, Paul Varian, Pam Benson, Marty Kramer, Nancy Peckenham, Jim Polk, Richard Griffiths, Christian "Fuzz" Hogan, Frank Sesno, Kathryn Kross, Rick Davis, Marianna Spicer-Brooks, Bud Bultman, Kelli Arena, Eileen O'Connor, and Kevin Bohn. Thanks also to Pierre Meilhan, Kimberly Arp-Babbit, Kim Buckwalter, Rick Perera, Amos Gelb, Sarah Shepherd, Kathy Slobogin, Brian Barger, Andy Segal, Ted Rubenstein, David Lewis, Ken Werner, Graham Messick, Ken Shiffman, Steve Turnham, Vaughn Morrison, Cliff Hackel, Jeff Milstein, Grace Wharwood, Robert Zuill, Brian Todd, Christian Hudson, Sam Feist, Bob Kovach, Kathy Benz, Gail Chalef, Pat Reap, Rebecca Bloch, Cameron Baird, Debbie Berger, Christina Kelly, Kim Abbott, Carol Buckland, and John Gilmore. Mike Maltas has long been a colleague and a friend.

Keith McAllister and Steve Cassidy very kindly employed me at CNN for periods when I was writing this book. Sean Kelly, one of the best video editors in the business, converted many of my bin Laden stories into watchable television. Thanks to Nic Robertson for the time we spent at Kandahar airport and for time since, discussing Afghanistan. Thank you, Rym Brahimi, for an excellent overview of Yemen before my trip there. Thanks to Pat Kloehn, Joe Murphy, Krystal Mabry, Kim Linden, and Rob Brickhill for much practical support over the years. I shared an office for several years with Bill Smee, one of CNN's most talented producers, and a more delightful office mate is hard to imagine. Thanks also to John Fielding, one of the great reporters in the business and now part of our family. Thank you, Paul Julian, for your advice over the years.

A special thanks to the talented journalist Nurith Aizenman, who many years ago at CNN worked on the early reporting of this book. Nurith also edited several of my bin Laden-related stories for *The New Republic,* and is a great friend. She brought her eagle editor's eye to this book from the proposal stage to the final editing and had many judicious and creative ideas about the material. David Edelstein, another fluid writer, was very generous with his time and also significantly improved the manuscript.

Many friends were supportive in the years I spent reporting and writing the book: Jonna Pattillo, Trish Enright, Jordan Tamagni, Cindy Balmuth, Lyndsay Griffiths and Mark Sands, Paul Berczeller, Eric Hilton, Farid Ali, Abdul Jewayni, Jenny Rees Tonge, Jean Gordon, Linda Burstyn, Nicky Kentish-Barnes, Rupert Smith, William Sieghart, Michael "Hutchy" Hutchinson, Scott Anger, Lou Hennessy, Scott Dunbar, Dominic Simpson, Nick Restifo and Maria Ionata, Ioana Beju, Saied Azali, Mark Hager, Tamara Hadji Linderman, Pauline Case, Patti Munter, Reuel Gerecht, Steve Emerson, Robert Noel, Ramin Bakhtiari, Tim and Amanda de Lisle, Piers and Tanya Thompson, Gavin and Kitty Wilson, Adam and Rosie Gardner, Paddy and Catherine Gibbs, Simon and Jemma Mayle, Henry Shukman, Aram Roston, Paul Leonard and Daryl Kerrigan, Liz Keirnan, Sol Levine, Katty Kay and Tom Carver, Ed Vulliamy, Julian Borger, Tom Hardart, Virginia Shore, Shaun Waterman, Neil Barrett, Bob Baer, Larry Johnson, Katie Kerr and Arif Lalani, Concepcion and Bernd Debusmann, Susan and Peter Millership, Omar Samad and Hassina Sherjan, and Rich Byrne. Tom Rhodes and Deborah Lee put up with my multiple visits to their New York apartment and provided much encouragement. Nancy Bagley kindly introduced me to her friend Benazir Bhutto. Thanks also to Chris Clifford.

My family was an immense support. My sister Katherine put me up in London on numerous occasions while I was reporting there and was always ready to help me out. My sister Margaret was a great help, particularly during the time she and her wonderful children Charlie, Bella, and Brendan lived with me while I was in the early stages of writing. Thank you, Mum, for all your myriad emotional and practical support over the years, the help on the French translations, and for the final line in the book. Thank you, Dad, for manning the fort at home in the extraordinarily busy weeks spent completing this book, and for all your valuable ideas about the manuscript.

I would like to acknowledge the late Stephan Dammann, an inspirational history teacher, and Fr. Leo Chamberlain, O.S.B., who between them propelled me toward New College, Oxford, to read history under the auspices of Eric Christiansen and Dr. Penry Williams. Also thanks to Fr. Francis Dobson, O.S.B., who first introduced me to American politics. These five gentlemen were my formative intellectual influences.

A number of friends also gave me very valuable feedback on the manuscript: Mathew Campbell, John Micklethwait, and Andy Marshall. Thanks also to Joe Reap of the Office of Counterterrorism at the State Department and to Bill Harlow and Mark Mansfield at the CIA's Office of Public Affairs.

Thanks to Ferial Demy for her help with the Arabic translations and to Dr. Virginia Schubert for her help with French translations.

Without the insights of Dr. Saad al-Fagih, Abdel Bari Atwan, Rahimullah Yusufzai, Ismail Khan, and Jamal Ismail, I would not have been able to write this book.

In Afghanistan and Pakistan, thanks to Khalid Mafton, Pamela Constable, Chanel Khan, Mark Wentworth, Amir Shah, Mohamed Bashir, the staff of the Chez Soi guesthouse, Jason Burke, Khaled Mansour, and Rory McCarthy. Also thanks to George Case and Barney Thompson for the trip to Pakistan in 1983 to make a film about the Afghan refugees and to Tom Jarriel and Janice Tomlin for a trip in 1989 to report for ABC News on the legal status of women in Pakistan.

In Yemen, I was lucky enough to join forces with John Burns, who has long been one my journalistic heroes; much help came from Mohammed al-Asadi, Khaled Hammadi, Faris Sanabani, and Ian Henderson. Thanks also to the staff of the Taj Sheba hotel in San'a. Reem Nada provided invaluable reporting and translating skills both in Yemen and in Cairo.

Thanks to Paul Golob for acquiring this book for The Free Press and for his encouragement over the years. Thanks also to those at the Free Press who speeded this book to publication: Martha Levin, Dominick Anfuso, Carol de Onís, and Brian Selfon, who made himself indispensable. Thanks to Carisa Hays for her sage advice about publicizing the book and to her assistant Courtney Fisher. Thanks to Elisa Rivlin for a painless legal review. Jolanta Benal did a superb job of copyediting. Thanks also to Maris Kreizman.

Thank you to Carsten Oblaender, Andreas Gutzeit, Vicky Matthews, and Dave McKean at Storyhouse Productions, and Diana Sperrazza at National Geographic television.

At *The New Republic*, thanks to Peter Beinart and Sarah Blustain. At *The Daily Telegraph*, thanks to Stephen Robinson. At the *Times*, thanks to Bronwen Maddox and Damian Whitworth. At *The Sunday Times*, thanks to Bob Tyrer. At the *Washington Times*, thanks to Helle Bering. At *Vanity Fair*, thanks to Graydon Carter, Wayne Lawson, Vicky Ward, Mary Flynn, and Chris Garrett. At *Foreign Affairs* thanks to James F. Hoge Jr., Gideon Rose, and Jonathan D. Tepperman. At *The Washington Post* thanks to Chris Lehmann. And thanks to Bruce Hoffman, one of the world's leading authorities on terrorism and the editor of *Studies in Conflict and Terrorism*.

Thanks to Ion Trewin, Michele Hutchison, and Katie White of Weidenfeld & Nicolson.

Thanks also to the trustees of the Leonard Silk journalism fellowship who provided an invaluable cash infusion at a critical moment as I was completing the book. I am especially grateful to Bernice and Mark Silk. A particular thank-you to Jason Renker of the Century Foundation, who shepherded my application and was very helpful about keeping me up to speed about developments.

The Johns Hopkins University School of Advanced International Studies (SAIS) Pew fellowship program provided an office and stipend that allowed me to get the book finished. Thank you to the wonderful people at the Pew program: John Schidlovsky, Louise Lief, Jeff Barrus, Denise Melvin, and colleagues David Lamb and Stephen Glain.

Also at SAIS, Marty Tillman put me in touch with my two very capable research assistants, first Kyle Stelma, who provided invaluable help, and later Erin Patrick, who brought a keen editorial eye and amazing research skills to the process, and then worked literally around the clock helping finish up the manuscript, while still working at her busy day job. Wrestling a thousand unruly footnotes into shape would turn out to be as problematic a task as meeting bin Laden. Thank you, Erin.

Thanks to Amanda Patten at Touchstone who ably shepherded this new edition of the book through the editing process, and thanks to her assistant Elizabeth Bevilacqua. Thanks also to London King.

Also thanks to the New America Foundation which provided me with a congenial home to work on this edition. Thanks to Ted Halstead, Steve Clemons, Sherle Schwenninger, and Hannah Fischer. Thanks also to John Mangin who was extremely helpful as the researcher for this edition.

My literary agency, Janklow & Nesbit, was vital to all phases of this project. Tif Loehnis performed major surgery on my inchoate proposal, provided a great deal of moral and editorial support, and became a great friend. When Tif moved to London to set up Janklow's office there, Tina Bennett took over and gave me enormous help and sage advice, right up to the point that she was about to deliver her first child, William. After Tina went on maternity leave, Tif again took the helm. Tif and Tina are simply the best in the business, and wonderful human beings to boot. Also at Janklow & Nesbit, Bennett Ashley was very helpful with the many contractual issues that arose. Thanks also to Richard Morris, Svetlana Katz, Carl Parsons, Laura Summerhays, and Maria Gallagher. Thank you, Cullen Stanley, for the stellar job on the foreign rights.

This book simply would not have happened without its original editor, Rachel Klayman. Rachel's extraordinary focus and discipline made up for my own lacunae in these areas, and she brought a keen intellect and rapier wit to the editing process. Rachel devoted an extraordinary number of hours to finalizing the book, in the process putting everything else in her busy life on hold. To a very large degree, this is also her book.

And, finally, thank you, Marcie McGallagher, for your love and support.

NOTES

Prologue: How to Find the World's Most Wanted Man

1. John L. Esposito, *The Islamic Threat, Myth or Reality?* (New York: Oxford University Press, 1992) pp. 49–50.
2. Dr. Saad al-Fagih, interview by PBS's Frontline, transcript at *www.pbs.org/wgbh/pages/frontline/shows/binladen/interviews/al-fagih.html*.
3. Western diplomat, interview by author, Islamabad, Pakistan, September 1998.
4. Kathy Gannon, "Taliban Decrees Rain Down on Kabul Residents," AP Worldstream, March 28, 1997.
5. Ibid.
6. Ahmed Rashid, *The Taliban, Islam, Oil and the New Great Game in Central Asia* (New York: I. B. Tauris, 2000), p. 115.
7. Sir Olaf Caroe, *The Pathans* (Karachi, Pakistan: Oxford University Press, 1990). In a chapter entitled "The Passing of Alexander," Caroe suggests that Alexander himself took a route winding through the Katagala Pass in Swat, in what is now Pakistan's Northern Territories.
8. *Newsline*, Pakistan, May 1993; John Ward Anderson, "Fortress Fit for King, or Trafficker: Accused Pakistani Drug Baron Flaunts Enclave Near Khyber Pass," *Washington Post*, April 29, 1993.
9. Ilyas Moshin, Secretary of the Pakistan Narcotics Control Board, interview with author, Islamabad, Pakistan, August 1993.
10. Rahimullah Yusufzai, interview by author, Peshawar, Pakistan, August 1993.
11. John F. Burns, "Afghan Capital Grim as War Follows War," *New York Times*, February 5, 1996.
12. Kamal Matinuddin, *The Taliban Phenomenon, Afghanistan 1994–1997* (Pakistan: Oxford Pakistan Paperbacks, 1999), p. 12.

13. G. Whitney Azoy, *Buzkashi: Game and Power in Afghanistan* (Philadelphia: University of Pennsylvania Press, 1982), p. 2.

14. The Pakistani journalist Rahimullah Yusufzai, who has probably spent more time with the Taliban leadership than any other journalist, says he has heard the story of the battling warlords from many Taliban sources.

15. Matinuddin, op. cit., p. 223.

16. Michael Griffin, *Reaping the Whirlwind: The Taliban Movement in Afghanistan* (Sterling, Virginia: Pluto Press, 2001), pp. 40–42.

17. Rahimullah Yusufzai in *The News on Friday*, Islamabad, Pakistan, March 5, 1995.

18. Suzanne Goldenberg, "News Focus: 'He Knelt, Aimed His AK-47 at the Shoulder Blades and Fired. The Condemned Man Toppled Over,'" *The Guardian*, September 26, 1998.

19. Ibid.

20. It is interesting that Saudi Arabia is the only country in the world to have the ruling family's name embedded in its name.

21. Al-Qaeda recruitment videotape, summer 2001; accessed at *www.moonwarriors.com.* on August 14, 2001.

22. Reuters Newswire, "Israelis Deliberately Shelled Post, UN Says," May 4, 1996; Marjorie Miller, "U.N. Report Disputes Israel on Shelling," *Los Angeles Times,* May 8, 1996.

23. Osama bin Laden interview by Abdel Bari Atwan of *Al-Quds Al-Arabi* newspaper, Afghanistan, November 1996.

24. Osama bin Laden interview with Al-Jazeera television, aired June 10, 1999. Transcript at *www.terrorism.com/terrorism/binLadinTranscript.shtml.*

25. Benjamin Weiser, "Defense in Terror Trial Cites U.S. Sanctions Against Iraq," *New York Times,* June 5, 2001; "A Deal? Iraq and the U.N." *The Economist*, January 27, 1996.

26. Osama bin Laden interview with CNN, Afghanistan, aired May 10, 1997.

Chapter 1. While America Slept

1. FBI press release, September 14, 2001, *www.fbi.gov/pressrel/pressrel01/091401hj.htm.*

2. Ibid.

3. According to the U.S. Weather Service, about seventy-three people per year are killed by lightning strikes. Lightning safety information at *http://205.156.54.206/om/wcm/lightning/overview.htm.*

4. Telephone interview with Christine Mohan, senior manager public relations, New York Times company, March 21, 2002.

5. Abdel Bari Atwan, editor of *Al-Quds al-Arabi* newspaper, telephone interview by author, August 13, 2001.

6. General Mike Hayden, interview with *60 Minutes II,* CBS, aired February 13, 2001.

7. George J. Tenet, director of the Central Intelligence Agency, testimony before Congress, February 2, 2001; John Goldman, "Second Bin Laden Defector Tells of Targeting Bomb Site," *Los Angeles Times,* February 22, 2001.

8. Benjamin Weiser, "Informer's Part in Terror Case is Detailed," *New York Times,* December 22, 2000.

9. Abdul Wahab al-Anesi, interview by author, San'a, Yemen, December 2000.

10. See Ali Mohamed section in Chapter 7, "The American Connection."

11. Mary Anne Weaver, *A Portrait of Egypt: A Journey through the World of Militant Islam* (New York: Farrar, Straus & Giroux, 1999), p. 258.

12. "Truebes aus der Quelle-CS1," *Der Spiegel,* Issue 43, October 19, 1998.

13. Osama bin Laden, interview with Al-Jazeera television, aired June 10, 1999. Transcript at *www.terrorism.com/terrorism/BinLadinTranscript.shmtl.*

14. *U.S.A. v. Usama bin Laden,* 98 Cr. 1023 (SDNY), Indictment.

15. Ibid., Testimony of Jamal al-Fadl, February 16, 2001.

16. Alan Cullison and Andrew Higgins, "Files Found: A Computer in Kabul Yields a Chilling Array of al-Qaeda Memos," *The Wall Street Journal.* December 31, 2001.

17. See *www.pbs.org/wgbh/pages/frontline/shows/binladen/upclose/computer.html.*

18. *U.S.A. v. Usama bin Laden,* Testimony of FBI Agent Stephen Gaudin, March 7–8, 2000.

19. Osama bin Laden interview with Rahimullah Yusufzai, ABC News, aired January, 1999. Transcript at *abcnews.go.com/sections/world/Daily News/transcript_binladen1_990110.html.*

20. *American Heritage Dictionary,* (Boston: Houghton Mifflin, 2001).

21. Sources used in determining countries include: *U.S.A. v. Usama bin Laden* indictment and Testimony of Jamal al-Fadl, February 6, 2001,

22. Sources used in determining nationalities include: *U.S.A. v. Usama bin Laden,* Testimony of Jamal al-Fadl, February 6, 2001 and Testimony of Ahmed Ressam, July 3, 2001 (bin Laden is Saudi; al-Fadl is Sudanese; L'Hossaine Kherchtou is Moroccan); Hamid Mir, interview by author, Islamabad, Pakistan, September 1998; sources familiar with the bin Laden organization; Ismail Khan, interview by author, Islamabad, Pakistan, September 1998.

23. Bin Laden interview with Rahimullah Yusufzai, ABC News, January 1999.

24. Al Venter, "America's Nemesis: Usama bin Laden," *Jane's Intelligence Review,* October 1, 1998.

25. Andrea Mitchell, NBC News, December 8, 1998.

26. Laurie Mylroie, *Study of Revenge: Saddam Hussein's Unfinished War Against America* (Washington, D.C.: AEI Press, 2000), p. 234.

27. Yossef Bodansky, *Bin Laden: The Man who Declared War on America* (Roseville, California: Forum Press, 1999), p. 3.

28. Ibid., p. 101.

29. Ibid., p. 152.

30. Adam Robinson, *Bin Laden: Behind the Mask of the Terrorist* (New York: Arcade, 2002), pp. 78–79, 89, 267, 276.

31. Arnaud de Borchgrave, interview by *The Washington Times*, March 21, 2000.

32. There is some controversy about who exactly Yousef is: see Mylroie for further explanation. Sources used for this description include Brian Duffy, "The Long Arm of the Law," *U.S. News & World Report*, February 20, 1995; Romy Tangbawan, Associated Press, February 13, 1995.

33. Benazir Bhutto, interview by author, New Jersey, March 2000.

34. U.S. State Department White Paper, August 1996.

35. Simon Reeve, *The New Jackals* (Boston: Northeastern University Press, 1999), p. 87.

36. Doug Struck, Howard Schneider, Karl Vick, and Peter Baker, "Borderless Network of Terror," *Washington Post*, September 22, 2001.

37. James Risen and David Johnston, "A Day of Terror," *The New York Times*, September 12, 2001.

38. Neil MacFarquhar, "Father Denies 'Gentle Son' Could Hijack Any Jetliner," *New York Times*, September 19, 2001.

39. Sheila MacVicar, CNN, September 24, 2001.

40. U.S. counterterrorism official, interview by author, Washington, D.C., September 29, 2001.

41. Susan Wells, "Terrorists Among Us," *Atlanta Journal and Constitution*, September 16, 2001.

42. Justin Blum and Dan Eggen, "Crop Duster Thought to Interest Suspects," *Washington Post*, September 24, 2001.

43. Rick Weiss and Justin Blum, "Suspect Made Inquiries About Cropduster Loan," *Washington Post*, September 25, 2001.

44. Bob Woodward, "In Hijacker's Bags, a Call to Planning, Prayer and Death," *Washington Post*, September 28, 2001.

45. Source familiar with bin Laden organization, interview by author, August 14, 2001. I was able to download the entire tape with links available at *www.moonwarriors.com*.

46. See *www.msanews.mynet.net/Scholars/Laden/*.

47. See *azzam.com*.

48. See *azzam.com/html/storieskhalladmadani.htm*.

49. Strobe Talbott and Nayan Chanda, eds., *The Age of Terror: America and the World After September 11* (New York: Basic Books, 2001), p. xi.

50. Mary Quin, interview by author, Washington, D.C., June 2001.

51. Mary Quin interview.

52. *U.S.A. v. Ahmed Ressam*, Case # CR 99-666-JCC, testimony of Jean Louis Brugiere, April 2, 2001: John F. Burns and Craig Pyes, "Radical Islamic Network May Have Come to U.S.," *New York Times*, December 31, 1999.

53. See *www.qoqaz.de/home.htm.*

54. See Chapter 9.

Chapter 2. The Afghan Jihad: The Making of a Holy Warrior

1. Osama bin Laden, CNN interview, Afghanistan, aired May 10, 1997.

2. Dilip Hiro, *Holy Wars: The Rise of Islamic Fundamentalism* (New York: Routledge, 1989), p. 111.

3. Osama bin Laden, interview by al-Jazeera television, aired June 10, 1999. Transcript at *www.terrorism.com/terrorism/BinLadinTranscript.shtml.*

4. The trees are tapped for their sap. The best frankincense is produced by the Luban tree. For a good account of the incense trade in south Arabia, see Freya Stark, *The Southern Gates of Arabia* (London: John Murray, 1936), pp. 1–7.

5. Nabil al-Habshi, interview by author, Hadramawt, Yemen, December 2000.

6. Jack Kelley, "Saudi Money Aiding bin Laden: Businessmen Are Financing Front Groups," *USA Today,* October 29, 1999. The article alleged that al-Amoudi has financed bin Laden's activities, a charge al-Amoudi's holding company, MIDROC, says was false. See also Mark Potts et al., *Dirty Money: The Inside Story of the World's Sleaziest Bank* (Washington, D.C.: National Press Books, 1992), p. 204. The bin Mahfouz family purchased 20 percent of the Bank of Credit and Commerce International, which was used by everyone from drug traffickers to the CIA to funnel money to the Afghan rebels. Phil Griffin, telephone interview by author, April 1997.

7. Nabil al-Habshi interview, December 2000.

8. Andrew Cockburn, "Yemen," *National Geographic Magazine,* April 2000.

9. Bin Laden interviews by Al-Jazeera, June 1999. Abdul Aziz founded the Saudi Kingdom in 1932; see Hiro, op. cit., p. 116.

10. Stark, op. cit., p. 111.

11. Khaled al-Omeri (bin Laden cousin), interview by author, al-Rubat, Yemen, December 2000.

12. Village mullah, interview by author, al-Rubat, Yemen, December 2000.

13. See *www.saudi-binladin-group.com/history.htm.*

14. Nabil al-Habshi interview, December 2000.

15. Saud resigned on November 2, 1964. See Hiro, op. cit., p. 120.

16. Said K. Aburish, *The House of Saud* (New York: St. Martin's Griffin, 1996), p. 200.

17. Ronald Kessler, *The Richest Man in the World: The Story of Adnan Khashoggi* (New York: Warner Books, 1986), p. 29.

18. Jack Kelley, "U.S. Finds bin Laden an Elusive Target: Even If He's Located, Catching Terrorist Will Be Complicated," *USA Today,* March 1, 2001; bin Laden interview by Al-Jazeera, June 1999.

19. Bin Laden interview by Al-Jazeera, June 1999.

20. Source close to bin Laden family, telephone interview by author, August 2001.

21. Khaled al-Omeri interview, December 2000.

22. Abdel Bari Atwan; interview by author, September 1998; "Bin Laden Honors Cole Attack," Reuters, March 2, 2001, reprinted in *The Seattle Times*.

23. Malise Ruthven, *Islam in the World* (New York: Oxford University Press, 2000), p. 223; Karen Armstrong, *Jerusalem: One City, Three Faiths* (New York: Knopf, 1996), p. 413.

24. Bin Laden interview by Al-Jazeera, June 1999.

25. Ibid.

26. Ibid.

27. Victor Henderson, interview by author, San'a, Yemen, December 2000.

28. See *www/saudi-binladen-group.com*.

29. Jerry Urban, "Feds Investigate Entrepreneur Allegedly Tied to Saudi," *Houston Chronicle*, June 4, 1992.

30. Ibid; Daniel Golden, James Bardler, and Marcus Walker, "Bin Laden Family is Tied to U.S. Group", *Wall Street Journal*, September 27, 2001.

31. Bill Minutaglio, *First Son* (New York: Three Rivers Press, 2001), p. 199.

32. Richard A. Oppel, Jr., and George Kuempel, *Dallas Morning News*, November 16, 1998.

33. Source close to the family, interview by author, September 2001.

34. U.S. official, interview by author, Washington, D.C., 1997.

35. Multiple interviews with satellite office, public relations firms, and law firms, conducted by author between 1997 and 2001.

36. See *www.saudi-binladin-group.com/bgi-exec.htm*.

37. U.S. official, interview by author, April 1997.

38. From a job posting from SBG at *www.hronline.com/forums/ohs/9903/msg 00378.html*, August 1999.

39. IPR Strategic Business Information, July 12, 2000; *www.saudi-binladen-group.com/news.htm*; Middle East Online, *www.middle-east-online.com/English*, April 24, 2001; Agence France-Presse, "U.S. Troops in Saudi Arabia to Get Housing Built by bin Laden Construction," September 14, 1998; Rowan Scarborough, "Air Force Barracks Is Built by bin Laden's Family Firm: Military Promises Security Sweep Before Operation," *Washington Times*, September 15, 1998.

40. See *www.saudi-binladin-group.com*.

41. Source close to bin Laden family, telephone interview by author, August 2001.

42. The fourth he married in 2000 in Kandahar, Afghanistan. She is Yemeni.

43. Bin Laden interview by Al-Jazeera, June 1999.

44. Gilles Kepel, *Muslim Extremism in Egypt* (Berkeley, Calif.: University of California Press, 1993), pp. 61, 64, 66.

45. Syed Qutb, *Signposts on the Road* (Mumbai, India: Bilal Books, 1998), p. 19. (*Signposts* is also sometimes translated as *Milestones*.)

46. Ibid., pp. 21, 62, 71.

47. Hiro, op. cit., p. 128.

48. Ibid., pp. 128–32.

49. Robert D. Kaplan, *Soldiers of God: With the Mujahidin in Afghanistan* (Boston: Houghton Mifflin, 1990), pp. 11, 227.

50. Rob Schultheis, *Night Letters: Inside Wartime Afghanistan* (New York: Crown, 1992), p. 155.

51. Helsinki Watch Asia, *To Die in Afghanistan* (Washington, D.C., December 1985), pp. 8–9.

52. G. A. Henty, *To Herat and Cabul: A Story of the First Afghan War* (republished by Saeed Jan Quereshi, Peshawar, Pakistan: Saeed Book Bank, 1983), p. 280.

53. Peter Hopkirk, *The Great Game: The Struggle for Empire in Central Asia* (New York: Kodansha, 1992), pp. 261–269.

54. Hamid Mir, interview by author, Islamabad, Pakistan, September 1998; bin Laden interview by author and Arnett, March 1997. "Ali," interview by author, Afghanistan, March 1997; Khaled al-Fawwaz, interview by author, London, March 1997; Essam Deraz, interview with author, Cairo, Egypt, December 2000; bin Laden interview by author and Arnett, March 1997.

55. Hamid Mir interview, September 1998; bin Laden interview by Al-Jazeera, June 1999.

56. Bin Laden interview by Al-Jazeera, June 1999.

57. Ruthven, op. cit., p.48.

58. Deraz interview, December 2000; *U.S.A. v. Usama bin Laden,* 98 Cr. 1023 (SDNY), Indictment, p. 3.

59. *U.S.A. v. Usama bin Laden,* Testimony of Essam al-Ridi, February 14, 2001.

60. Bin Laden interview by Al-Jazeera, June 1999.

61. Deraz interview, December 2000.

62. Hamid Mir interview, September 1998.

63. Hezbi Party, *Mujahideen Monthly,* Peshawar, Pakistan, January 1990; see *http://azzam.com/html/storiesabdullahazzam.htm.*

64. Mary Anne Weaver, *A Portrait of Egypt: A Journey Through the World of Militant Islam* (New York: Farrar, Straus & Giroux, 1999), p. 91. Rahman graduated in 1971.

65. *Nida'ul Islam Magazine,* July–September 1990. See *www.islam.org.au/articles/index2.htm.*

66. Gilles Kepel, *Jihad, Expansion et Declin de l'Islamisme* (Paris, Gallimard, 2000), p. 146.

67. Ibid.

68. See *www.crosswinds.net/nzzhsoszy/pakistan/index/ind0004.html.*

69. *U.S.A. v. Usama bin Laden,* Testimony of FBI Special Agent John Anticev, February 27, 2001.

70. Kepel, op. cit., p. 147.

71. Khaled al-Fawwaz interview, March 1997.

72. Weaver, op. cit., pp. 90, 170–171.

73. Olivier Roy, *Afghanistan: From Holy War to Civil War* (Princeton, N.J.: Darwin Press, 1995) p. 85

74. Jamal Ismail, interview by author, Islamabad, Pakistan, September 1998.

75. Hiro, op. cit., p. 262.

76. Michael Griffin, *Reaping the Whirlwind: The Taliban Movement in Afghanistan* (Sterling, Virginia: Pluto Press), p. 20; Hiro, op. cit., p. 312.

77. Jamal Ismail interview, September 1998; Khaled al-Fawwaz interview, February 1997.

78. Milt Bearden, interview by author, Washington, D.C., September 2000.

79. Mark Urban, *War in Afghanistan* (London: Macmillan, 1988), p. 244. The total number of guerrillas that would be operating on any given day would therefore not be below 35,000 and not above 175,000. Milt Bearden told me the maximum number of mujahideen at any given time was 250,000, but that figure includes mujahideen fighters who cycled through Pakistani refugee camps to see their families, or had to return to their native villages for harvesting, and so on.

80. Barnett R. Rubin, *The Fragmentation of Afghanistan: State Formation and Collapse in the International System* (New Haven: Yale University Press, 1995), p. 196; Kepel, 2000, p. 144.

81. Vince Cannistraro, interview by author, Washington, D.C., August 2, 2001.

82. Rubin, op. cit., p. 197.

83. Weaver, op. cit., p. 93.

84. Kepel, op.cit., p. 14: "Le jihad afghan a une importance cardinale dans l'évolution de la mouvance islamiste à travers le monde . . . Il supplante, dans l'imaginaire arabe, la cause palestinienne et symbolise le passage du nationalisme à l'islamisme."

85. Khaled al-Fawwaz interview, February 1997.

86. Deraz interview, December 2000.

87. Essam Deraz, Khaled al-Fawwaz; "Ali," a medic who served with bin Laden for three years; Jamal Ismail; and Saad al-Fagih, in separate interviews by the author, all concur.

88. Deraz interview, December 2000.

89. Jamal Ismail interview, September 1998.

90. Ibid.; Khaled al-Fawwaz interview, March 1997.

91. Judith Miller, *God Has Ninety-nine Names: Reporting from a Militant Middle East* (New York: Simon & Schuster, 1996), p. 113.

92. Essam Deraz, *Osama bin Laden Narrating the Greatest Battles of the Pro-Afghani Arabs* (Cairo, Egypt, 1991).

93. Deraz interview, December 2000.

94. Bin Laden interview by author and Arnett, May 1997.

95. Deraz, op. cit.

96. See *http://azzam.com/html/storiesabulmundhirshareef.htm.*
97. Jamal Ismail interview, September 1998.
98. *U.S.A. v. Usama bin Laden,* Testimony of Jamal al-Fadl, February, 2001.
99. Ibid.
100. Benazir Bhutto biography, People's Party of Pakistan, *www.ppp.org.pk/biog raphy.html.*
101. Hiro, op. cit., p. 302: the plane crash occurred on August 17, 1988.
102. Bhutto biography (see note 100, this chapter).
103. Ibid.
104. Mohammad Yousaf and Mark Adkin, *The Bear Trap: Afghanistan's Untold Story* (Lahore, Pakistan: Jang Publisher's Press, 1993), p. 11.
105. Mark Fineman, "Bhutto Survives No Confidence Vote," *Los Angeles Times,* November 2, 1989.
106. *Mujahideen Monthly,* Peshawar, Pakistan, January 1990.

Chapter 3. Blowback: The CIA and the Afghan War

1. Kurt Lohbeck, *Holy War, Unholy Victory: Eyewitness to the CIA's Secret War in Afghanistan* (Washington, D.C.: Regnery Gateway, 1993), p. 43.
2. Richard Mackenzie, "When Policy Tolls in a Fool's Paradise," *Insight* magazine, September 11, 1989.
3. Simon Reeve, *The New Jackals: Ramzi Yousef, Osama bin Laden and the Future of Terrorism* (Boston: Northeastern University Press, 1999), p. 55.
4. John Cooley, *Unholy Wars: Afghanistan, America and International Terrorism* (Sterling, Va.: Pluto Press, 1999), p. 195, see also pp. 83, 85, 86, 204.
5. Luke Harding, "Comment and Analysis: Chasing Monsters: The Americans Helped Create the Terrorist bin Laden. Now They Try To Destroy Him." *The Guardian,* November 24, 2000.
6. Khaled al-Fawwaz, interview by author in London, September 1998.
7. Peter Jouvenal, interview by author, Islamabad, Pakistan, September 1998.
8. U.S. official, interview by author, Washington, D.C., October 1998.
9. John Simpson, *A Mad World, My Masters: Tales from a Traveller's Life* (London: Macmillan, 2000), p. 83.
10. Milt Bearden, *Black Tulip* (New York: Random House, 1998), p. 59.
11. A former CIA official also confirmed the figure of six in an interview with the author, August 2001.
12. Former CIA official, interview by author, November 2000.
13. Mohammad Yousaf and Mark Adkin, *The Bear Trap: Afghanistan's Untold Story* (Lahore, Pakistan: Jang Publisher's Press, 1993), p. 81.
14. Former CIA official, interview by author, November 2000.
15. From U.S. Department of State's chronology of Rahman's visa situation.

16. Marguerite Michaels, "Martyrs for the Sheik," *Time* magazine, July 19, 1993.

17. Robert M. Gates, *From the Shadows* (New York: Touchstone, 1997), p. 146.

18. Ibid., p. 147.

19. Mark Urban, *War in Afghanistan* (London: Macmillan, 1988), p. 56.

20. Barnett R. Rubin, *The Fragmentation of Afghanistan: State Formation and Collapse in the International System* (New Haven: Yale University Press, 1995), p.197; Steve Coll, "CIA in Afghanistan: In CIA's Covert War, Where to Draw the Line Was Key," *Washington Post,* July 20, 1992.

21. Rep. William H. Gray (D–Pennsylvania), letter to Charles A. Bowser of the General Accounting Office, February 25, 1987, from U.S. National Security Archives, Microfiche #1987 02/25 (01926).

22. Henry S. Bradsher, *Afghan Communism and Soviet Intervention* (Karachi, Pakistan: Oxford University Press, 1999), p. 220.

23. I arrive at this figure by taking both Bearden's and Yousaf's estimates that 20 percent of CIA funding went to Hekmatyar and applying it to the $3 billion figure that the CIA spent on funding the Afghan resistance.Yousaf and Adkin, op. cit., p. 105, and interview by author, Karachi, Pakistan, August 6, 1993; Bearden interview by author, Washington, D.C., September 2000. Both Bearden and Yousaf have reasons for downplaying how much money the deeply anti-American Hekmatyar received, so the $600 million figure is the most conservative estimate possible. Some commentators, for instance Mary Ann Weaver, say that Hekmatyar received 50 percent of U.S. aid, in which case his share would rise to $1.5 billion.

24. Olivier Roy, *Afghanistan: From Holy War to Civil War* (Princeton, N.J.: Darwin Press, 1995), p. 86.

25. Bradsher, op. cit., p. 184.

26. Ibid., p. 185.

27. Rubin, op. cit., p. 215.

28. Lohbeck, op. cit., p. 12.

29. Ibid., p. 265.

30. Richard Mackenzie, "Afghan Games, How Pakistan Runs the War," *Insight,* April 9, 1990.

31. Asia Watch, "Human Rights Abuses by Elements of the Afghan Resistance," November 3, 1989.

32. Bradsher, op. cit., p. 330.

33. Peter Arnett, Peter Bergen, and Richard Mackenzie, "Terror Nation? U.S. Creation?" CNN documentary, aired January 14, 1994.

34. Jack Wheeler, Freedom Research Foundation Director, testimony before Congressional Task Force on Afghanistan, February 25, 1985.

35. Ibid.

36. Rubin, op. cit., p. 113; Gulbuddin Hekmatyar, speech in Pushtu defending Saddam Hussein, 1990, obtained by author.

37. Ibid.

38. Tape translated in the course of researching CNN documentary.

39. Michael Griffin, *Reaping the Whirlwind: The Taliban Movement in Afghanistan* (Sterling, Va.: Pluto Press, 2001), p. 21. Mirwais Jalil was killed on July 29, 1994.

40. Arnett et al., "Terror Nation?" CNN documentary, January 1994.

41. Rubin, op. cit., p. 220.

42. Urban, op. cit., 101–111; David Isby, *War in a Distant Country: Afghanistan, Invasion and Resistance* (London: Arms and Armour Press, 1989), p. 29.

43. Roy, op. cit., p. 63.

44. Ibid.

45. Urban, op. cit., pp. 1, 63.

46. Robert D. Kaplan, "The Afghan Who Won the Cold War," *Wall Street Journal,* May 5, 1992.

47. Arnett et al., "Terror Nation?"

48. Ibid.

49. Mohammad Yousaf interview, August 1993; Yousaf and Adkins, op. cit., p. 40.

50. Yousaf and Adkins, op. cit., p. 175.

51. Isby, op. cit., p. 114.

52. Yousaf and Adkins, op. cit., p. 187.

53. U.S. official, interview by author, August 2001.

54. Associated Press, "Opposition: U.S.-Made Stinger Missile Brings Down Taliban Jet," October 6, 1999.

55. Dilip Hiro, *Holy Wars: The Rise of Islamic Fundamentalism* (New York: Routledge, 1989), pp. 44, 55.

Chapter 4. The Koran and the Kalashnikov: Bin Laden's Years in Sudan

1. In a February 27, 1997, briefing, U.S. State Department spokesman Nicolas Burns put the number at 40,000.

2. Bernard Lewis, "License to Kill," *Foreign Affairs*, November/December 1998.

3. Saad al-Fagih, interview by author, London, September 1998.

4. Faiza Saleh Ambah, "Saudi Militant's Wish: To Die Fighting America," Associated Press, August 30, 1998.

5. Unless otherwise indicated, all information on Osama bin Laden in this chapter is from a private communication with a Middle Eastern source.

6. Osama bin Laden, interview by author and Peter Arnett for CNN, aired May 10, 1997.

7. "The Opposition," *Jane's Intelligence Review*, December 1, 1996.

8. Mamoun Fandy, *Saudi Arabia and the Politics of Dissent* (New York: St. Martin's Press, 1999) p. 61.

9. Essam Deraz, interview by author, Cairo, Egypt, December 2000.

10. Essam Deraz interview, December 2000; *U.S.A. v. Usama bin Laden*, 98 Cr. 1023 (SDNY), Testimony of L'Hossaine Kherchtou, February 26, 2001; Testimony of Jamal al-Fadl, February 6, 2001.

11. U.S. State Department White Paper, 1996.

12. Anthony Shadid, *Legacy of the Prophet: Despots, Democrats, and the New Politics of Islam* (Boulder, Colo.: Westview Press, 2001), p. 162.

13. *U.S.A. v. Usama bin Laden*, Testimony of Jamal al-Fadl, February 7 and 13, 2001.

14. Khaled al-Fawwaz, interview by author, London, February 1997.

15. Kroll Report, examined by author; *U.S.A. v. Usama bin Laden*, Cross-Examination of Jamal al-Fadl, February 20, 2001; Tom Cohen, "Affidavit Provides Rare Glimpse of Osama bin Laden as Employer," Associated Press, January 12, 2001.

16. U.S. State Department Fact Sheet on bin Laden, August 14, 1996.

17. *U.S.A. v. Usama bin Laden*, Testimony of Jamal al-Fadl, February 6, 2001.

18. U.S. State Department White Paper, 1996.

19. *U.S.A. v. Usama bin Laden*, Testimony of Jamal al-Fadl, February 7, 2001.

20. Ibid., al-Fadl cross-examination, February 20, 2001; Grand Jury Testimony of Wadih el-Hage, February 20, 2001.

21. Hamid Mir, interview by author, Islamabad, Pakistan, September 1998, and bin Laden interview by Abdel Bari Atwan of *Al-Quds Al-Arabi*, November 1996; *U.S.A. v. Usama bin Laden*, Testimony of L'Hossaine Kherchtou, February 26, 2001.

22. *U.S.A. v. Usama bin Laden*, Testimony of Essam al-Ridi, February 14, 2001.

23. Robert Fisk, "Anti-Soviet Warrior Puts His Army on the Road to Peace: Saudi Businessman Who Recruited Mujahideen Now Uses Them for Large Scale Building Projects in Sudan," *The Independent* (U.K.), December 6, 1993.

24. Scott MacLeod, interview by author, Washington, D.C., September 1998.

25. *U.S.A. v. Usama bin Laden*, Summation of Jamal al-Fadl testimony, May 1, 2001.

26. Tim Weiner, "Missile Strikes Against bin Laden Won Him Esteem in Muslim Lands, U.S. Officials Say," *New York Times*, February 8, 1999.

27. Laurence Jolidon, "Blinded by the Light, U.S. Troops Came Ashore," *USA Today*, December 9, 1992.

28. *U.S.A. v. Usama bin Laden*, Indictment, p.15.

29. Ibid. Testimony of Jamal al-Fadl, February 6, 2001.

30. Muhammad Atef also used the names Sheikh Taysir Abdullah and Abu Hafs; information from *U.S.A. v. Usama bin Laden*, Summation, May 8, 2001, and Testimony of Jamal al-Fadl, February 6, 2001.

31. Mark Bowden, "Team Members Try to Free Pilot's Body," *The Philadelphia Inquirer*, January 28, 1998.

32. Mark Bowden, *Black Hawk Down* (New York: Atlantic Monthly Press, 1999), p. 110.

33. Mark Huband, *Warriors of the Prophet: The Struggle for Islam* (Boulder, Colo.: Westview Press, 1998), p. 41.

34. *U.S.A. v. Usama bin Laden,* Testimony of FBI Agent John Anticev, February 27, 2001.

35. Ibid., Testimony of L'Hossaine Kherchtou, February 26, 2001, and Summation of Patrick Fitzgerald, May 8, 2001.

36. Ibid., May 8, 2001.

37. Hamid Mir, interview by author, Islamabad, Pakistan, September 1998.

38. Osama bin Laden, interview by Al-Jazeera television, aired June 10, 1999. Transcript at *www.terrorism.com/terrorism/BinLadinTranscript.shtml.*

39. *U.S.A. v. Usama bin Laden,* Testimony of Jamal al-Fadl, February 6, 2001.

40. Ibid., February 13, 2001; State Department White Paper, 1996.

41. *U.S.A. v. Usama bin Laden,* Testimony of L'Hossaine Kherchtou, February 26, 2001.

42. Ibid., Testimony of Essam al-Ridi, February 14, 2001.

43. Information on *Encyclopedia of the Jihad in Afghanistan* from Reuel Gerecht, who also translated the dedication.

44. Reuel Gerecht, *Talk* magazine, September 2000.

45. Rahimullah Yusufzai, interview by author, Washington, D.C., June, 2001.

46. Alan Feuer and Benjamin Weiser, "Translation: The 'How-To' Book of Terrorism," *New York Times,* April 5, 2001.

47. *U.S.A. v. Usama bin Laden,* Testimony of Jamal al-Fadl, February 6, 2001.

48. Ibid., February 7 and 20, 2001.

49. Jamal Ismail, "I Am Not Afraid of Death," *Newsweek,* January 11, 1999.

50. *U.S.A. v. Usama bin Laden,* Grand Jury Testimony of Wadih el-Hage, entered into the record February 22, 2001. According to el-Hage, Salim was the imam of al-Qaeda's mosque in Peshawar in the late 1980s and then worked as general manager of Taba investments in the early 1990s; U.S. District Court, Southern District of New York, Affidavit in Support of the Request for the Extradition of Mamdouh Mahmud Salim, October 9, 1998, pp. 11, 14.

51. *U.S.A. v. Mokhtar Haouari,* S4 00 Cr. 15 (SDNY), Testimony of Ahmed Ressam, July 5, 2001.

52. Fandy, op. cit., p. 185.

53. *U.S.A. v. Usama bin Laden,* Testimony of Jamal al Fadl, February 6–7, 2001.

54. Ali Mohamed plea agreement, reprinted as "Excerpts from Guilty Plea in Terrorism Case," *New York Times,* October 21, 2000; Hala Jaber, *Hezbollah: Born with a Vengeance* (New York: Columbia University Press, 1997), pp. 115–20.

55. Jaber, op. cit., pp. 82–83; "Truck Bomb Kills 19 U.S. Troops in Saudi Arabia; Moslem Militants Suspected; U.S. Vows to Seek Out Perpetrators," *Facts on File,* June 27, 1996, p. 441 (A1).

56. *U.S.A. v. Usama bin Laden,* Plea Agreement of Ali Mohamed, October 20, 2000.

57. Anthony H. Cordesman, *Saudi Arabia: Guarding the Desert Kingdom* (Boulder, Colo.: Westview Press, 1997), p. 77.

58. *U.S.A. v. Usama bin Laden,* Plea Agreement of Ali Mohamed, October 20, 2000.

59. Ibid., Testimony of Jamal al-Fadl, February 6–7, 2001, Testimony of L'Hossaine Kherchtou, February 26, 2001.

60. Robert Fox, "Mujahideen Move in to Fly the Militant Flag in Bosnia: Izetbegovich's New Allies Are Threatening to Split Old Alliances," *London Daily Telegraph,* February 18, 1995.

61. U.S. official, interview by author, Washington, D.C. April 1997. John Pomfret, "How Bosnia's Muslims Dodged Arms Embargo; Relief Agency Brokered Aid from Nations," *Washington Post,* September 22, 1996.

62. Steve Coll et al., "Global Network Provides Money, Haven," *Washington Post,* August 3, 1993.

63. *U.S.A. v. Usama bin Laden,* Testimony of Jamal al-Fadl, February 6, 2001.

64. Bin Laden interview by Al-Jazeera television, June 1999.

65. *U.S.A. v. Usama bin Laden,* Plea Agreement of Ali Mohamed, October 20, 2000.

66. *U.S.A. v. Usama bin Laden,* Cross-examination of Jamal al-Fadl, February 20, 2001.

67. COMPASS Newswire, May 31, 1996.

68. John Lancaster, "Saudis Shocked That Bomb Suspects Are Local," *Washington Post,* May 26, 1996.

69. Fandy, op. cit., p. 3.

70. The confessions were broadcast on Saudi TV; copy of tape obtained by author.

71. Lancaster, May 26, 1996, p. 3.

72. Fandy, op. cit., p. 3.

73. Bin Laden interview by Al-Jazeera television, June 1999.

74. Anwar Faruqi, "Opposition Claims 6 Saudis Have Confessed to Bombing U.S. Airmen," Associated Press, August 14, 1996.

75. Federal Court of Canada, Ottawa, court file # DES 1-97, *In the matter of Hani Abd Rahim al Sayegh,* March 27, 1997.

76. *Mideast Mirror,* October 25, 1996.

77. Saad al-Fagih interview, September 1998.

78. See *www.cnn.com/2001/LAW/06/21/khobar.indictments/index.html.*

79. Bin Laden CNN interview by author and Arnett, aired May 1997.

80. *U.S.A. v. Usama bin Laden,* Indictment, p. 21.

81. Saad al-Fagih, *History of Reform in Arabia,* document supplied to author.

82. *U.S.A. v. Khaled al Fawwaz,* 98 Cr. 1023 (SDNY), November 23, 1998.

83. Al-Fawwaz interview, February 1997.

84. See Fandy, op. cit.

85. *U.S.A. v. Usama bin Laden,* Testimony of Jamal al-Fadl, February 7, 2001.

86. Tina Susman, "Bin Laden's Plush Life in Sudan," *Newsday,* August 26, 1998.

87. Phase 4 from someone familiar with al-Qaeda. *U.S.A. v. Usama bin Laden,* Testimony of Jamal al-Fadl, February 7, 2001.

88. Ibid., al-Qaeda recruitment videotape, summer 2001; *U.S.A. v. Usama bin Laden,* Summation of Ken Karas, May 1, 2001.

89. *U.S.A. v. Usama bin Laden,* Testimony of L'Hossaine Kherchtou, February 21 and 27, 2001.

90. Rahimullah Yusufzai, *The News,* Pakistan, December 8, 1995.

91. U.S. official, interview by author, 1993.

92. Jamal Ismail, interview by author, Islamabad, Pakistan, September, 1998.

93. State Department White Paper, August 1996.

93. Kamran Khan, "Blast Laid to Muslim Radicals Kills 15 at Egyptian Embassy in Pakistan," *Washington Post,* November 20, 1995.

95. *U.S.A. v. Usama bin Laden,* discussion between Judge Duffy and Patrick Fitzgerald, February 26, 2001.

96. Jamal Ismail, interview by author, Islamabad, Pakistan, September, 1998.

97. Kamran Khan, "Blast Laid to Muslim Radicals Kills 15 at Egyptian Embassy in Pakistan." *The Washington Post*, November 20, 1995.

98. Jamal Ismail, interview by author, Islamabad, Pakistan, September, 1998.

99. Sandy Berger, National Security Advisor, Press Briefing, August 20, 1998. Omar Hasan Ahmed al-Bashir, interview with PBS television, transcript at: *http://www. pbs.org/wgbh/pages/frontline/shows/binladen/interviews/bashir.htm*l.

Chapter 5. From the Peaks of the Hindu Kush: The Declaration of War

1. *U.S.A. v. Usama bin Laden,* 98 Cr. 1023 (SDNY), Indictment, Testimony of Imam Siraj Wahhaj, April 19, 2001.

2. Michael Cook, *Muhammad* (Oxford: Oxford University Press, 1983), pp. 19, 22.

3. Al-Qaeda recruitment videotape, summer 2001, accessed on August 14, 2001 at *www.moonwarriors.com.*

4. Author interview of "Ali," Pakistan, March 1997.

5. Saad al-Fagih, interview by author, London, September 1998.

6. Abdel Bari Atwan, interview by author, London, September 1998.

7. Jamal Ismail and Saad al-Fagih, interviews by author, London, September 1998.

8. *Al-Hayat* newspaper, London, June 24, 1998.

9. Manifesto of the World Islamic Front, February 22, 1998.

10. Unclassified CIA document, "Fatwas or Religious Rulings by Militant Islamic Groups Against the United States," February 23, 1998, in author's possession.

11. Reuven Firestone, *Jihad: The Origin of Holy War in Islam* (New York: Oxford University Press, 1999), p. 48.

12. Max Rodenbeck, *Cairo: The City Victorious* (New York: Vintage Books, 2000), p. 79.

13. Jason Goodwin, *Lords of the Horizon* (New York: Holt, 1998), pp. 98–100.
14. Bernard Lewis, *The Political Language of Islam* (Chicago: University of Chicago Press, 1988) pp 71–90; see in general Rudolph Peters, *Jihad in Classical and Modern Islam* (Princeton, N.J.: Princeton University Press, 1996).
15. Peters, op. cit., pp. 1, 116.
16. Bernard Lewis, "License to Kill," *Foreign Affairs*, November/December 1998.
17. Ibid.
18. Akthar Raja, interview by author, London, November 1999.
19. Malise Ruthven, *Islam in the World* (New York: Oxford University Press, 2000), p. 98.
20. This document was signed by Sheikh Ahmed Azam.
21. *U.S.A. v. Usama bin Laden*, Indictment, pp. 30–31.
22. Hamid Mir, interview by author, Islamabad, Pakistan, September 1998.
23. W. Montgomery Watt, *Muhammad: Prophet and Statesman* (New York: Oxford University Press, 1974), p. 124.
24. Ismail Khan, interview by author, Islamabad, Pakistan, September 1998.
25. The author has a copy of the card. Translated from Arabic by Ferial Demy.
26. Middle Eastern source, interview by author, September 1998.
27. U.S. government official, interview by author, Washington D.C., April 1997.
28. Senior U.S. intelligence official, interview by author, November 1998; bin Laden family source, telephone interview by author, August 2001.
29. *U.S.A. v. Usama bin Laden*, Testimony of L'Hossaine Kherchtou, February 22, 2001.
30. Ibid., February 22 and 26, 2001.
31. Letter from Fazil, "The Letter From El Hage's Computer," PBS' *Frontline*, available at *www.pbs.org/wgbjpages/frontline/shows/binladen/upclose/computer.html*.
32. Rahimullah Yusufzai showed the author photos of the mosque in September 1998 during the course of an interview in Peshawar, Pakistan; Western diplomat based in Pakistan, interview by author, September 1998.
33. Hamid Mir interview, September 1998; Middle Eastern source, September 1998; U.S. official, interview by author, Washington D.C., April 1997.
34. John McWethy, ABC News, July 9, 1999.
35. U.S. government official, interview by author, Washington D.C., April 1997.
36. James Risen and Benjamin Weiser, "CIA suspects countries helped terror suspects," *The New York Times*, July 8, 1999.
37. Barry Schweid, "Senior officials quietly join probe of terrorism suspect," Associated Press, July 8, 1999.
38. Middle Eastern source, interview by author, September 1998; U.S. official specializing in Southeast Asia, interview by author, Washington, D.C., 1998. The *hawala* system is also known as the *hundi* system.
39. Ghulam Hasnain, "Money on the run: Pakistan's havala operators reap a bonanza," *Newsline* (Pakistan), August 1998.
40. U.S. government official, interview by author, Washington D.C., April 1997.

Chapter 6. Investigation and Retaliation: The Embassy Bombings

1. *U.S.A. v. Usama bin Laden,* Indictment 98 Cr. 1023 (SDNY), Summation of Patrick Fitzgerald, May 1, 2001.
2. John Miller, interview of Osama bin Laden, transcript at *abcnews.go.com/sections/world/DailyNews/miller_binladen_980609.html.*
3. *U.S.A. v. Usama bin Laden,* Indictment, pp. 16–17.
4. *U.S.A. v. Usama bin Laden,* Testimony of FBI agent John Anticev, February 27, 2001.
5. *The Nation* (Nairobi, Kenya), August 28, 1998.
6. *U.S.A. v. Usama bin Laden,* Testimony of John Anticev, February 27, 2001.
7. *U.S.A. v. Usama bin Laden,* Testimony of Jamal al-Fadl, February 6 and 7, 2001; Essam Deraz, interview by author, Cairo, December 2000.
8. Haroun used many aliases; the most common was Haroun Fazil. His real name is Abdallah Mohammed Fazul. Donald G. McNeil, Jr., "Assets of a Bombing Suspect: Keen Wit, Religious Soul, Angry Temper," *New York Times,* October 6, 1998.
9. Press release from U.S. Attorney's Office, Southern District of New York, September 17, 1998.
10. Ibid.
11. *U.S.A. v. Wadih el Hage,* 98 Cr. 1023 (SDNY), Complaint, September 17, 1998.
12. *U.S.A. v. Usama bin Laden,* Indictment, pp. 32, 33, 43.
13. *U.S.A. v. Mohamed Rashed Daoud Al-'Owhali,* 98 Cr. 1023 (SDNY), Complaint, August 25, 1998.
14. *U.S.A. v. Usama bin Laden,* Testimony of Stephen Gaudin, March 7, 2001.
15. Ibid.
16. Ibid.
17. U.S. State Department Security Warning, June 12, 1988. Travel warnings are posted and updated as circumstances dictate on the State Department's Web site at *www.state.gov.*
18. *U.S.A. v. Usama bin Laden,* Testimony of John Anticev, February 27, 2001.
19. Ibid., February 28, 2001.
20. *U.S.A. v. Usama bin Laden,* Testimony of Stephen Gaudin, March 7, 2001.
21. *U.S.A. v. Mohamed Rashed Daoud Al-'Owhali,* Daniel Coleman Affidavit, August 25, 1998.
22. David Pallister, "Fax to Newspaper Warned of Threat to 'Great Satan,' " *The Guardian* (U.K.), August 12, 1998.
23. Ibid.
24. *U.S.A. v. Usama bin Laden,* Testimony of FBI agent Stephen Gaudin, March 7, 2001.
25. Ibid.
26. Ibid.

27. *U.S.A. v. Usama bin Laden,* Summation of Patrick Fitzgerald, May 9, 2001.

28. Ibid., Testimony of Frank Pressley, March 7, 2001.

29. Ibid., Testimony of Sammy Nganga, March 7, 2001.

30. Report of the Accountability Review Board, on the Embassy Bombings in Nairobi and Dar es Salaam on August 7, 1998, known as the Crowe Report, p. 3.

31. Ibid., p. 4.

32. *U.S.A. v. Usama bin Laden,* Testimony of Ambassador Prudence Bushnell, March 1, 2001.

33. Alan Feuer, "Embassy Bombing Witnesses Recall Blood, Smoke and Chaos," *New York Times,* March 8, 2001.

34. Report of the Accountability Review Board, p. 5.

35. Louise Lief, *U.S. News and World Report,* August 17 and 24, 1998.

36. Peter Bergen, CNN, December 16, 1998. The four others indicted for the Tanzania blast are at large. See generally *U.S.A. v. Usama bin Laden* indictment.

37. Biographical information released by U.S. Attorney's Office, Southern District of New York, December 18, 1998.

38. *U.S.A. v. Usama bin Laden,* Testimony of Jerrold M. Post, M.D., June 27, 2001.

39. Ibid., Testimony of Abigail Perkins, March 19, 2001.

40. Ibid.

41. "Bombing Victims Testify in Court," Associated Press, March 14, 2001.

42. Osama bin Laden, interview by Al-Jazeera television, aired June 10, 1999. Transcript available at *www.terrorism.com/terrorism/BinLadinTranscript.shtml.*

43. Pat Milton, "Inspector Testifies in Embassy Trial," Associated Press, April 2, 2001; *U.S.A. v. Usama bin Laden,* Testimony of John Anticev, February 27, 2001!

44. Pakistani source, interview by author, Islamabad, Pakistan, December 1999.

45. See *www.state.gov/www/about_state/biography/Sheehan.html.*

46. U.S. House of Representatives, Republican Research Committee, September 13, 1993.

47. U.S. government official, interview by author, Washington, D.C., April 1997.

48. U.S. government officials, interviews by author, Washington, D.C., November 1998 and August 2001.

49. U.S. government officials, interviews by author, Washington, D.C., November 1998.

50. *U.S.A. v. Usama bin Laden,* Testimony of Daniel Coleman, February 21, 2001.

51. See *www.pbs.org/wgbh/pages/frontline/shows/binLaden/upclose/computer.html.*

52. Raymond Bonner with James Risen, "Nairobi Embassy Received Warning of Coming Attack," *New York Times,* October 23, 1998.

53. *U.S.A. v. Usama bin Laden,* Testimony of Stephen Gaudin, March 7, 2001.

54. Ibid., Affidavit of Daniel Coleman, August 25, 1998.

55. U.S. Information Agency, President's Statement, August 20, 1998. Transcript at *www.usinfo.state.gov/topical/pol/terror/98082001.htm.*

56. Statements by Secretary of Defense William Cohen and Secretary of State Madeleine Albright, August 21, 1998.

57. Sandy Berger, National Security Adviser, White House press briefing, August 21, 1998.

58. Ibid.

59. Rahimullah Yusufzai, *Newsline* magazine (Pakistan), September 1998.

60. General Henry H. Shelton, Chairman of the Joint Chiefs of Staff, press briefing, August 20, 1998.

61. *U.S.A. v. Usama bin Laden,* Testimony of L'Hossaine Kherchtou, February 22, 2001 and Jamal al-Fadl, February 6 and 7, 2001.

62. Abdel Bari Atwan, interview by author, August 21, 1998; Osama bin Laden, interview by Rahimullah Yusufzai, ABC News, aired January 1999. Transcript at *abcnews.go.com/sections/world/dailynews/transcript_binladen1_981228.html.*

63. In an interview by the author, a Pakistani official said that the government believed there would be a meeting at the camp on the twentieth. The journalist Rahimullah Yusufzai told me in September 1998 that this was probably an ISI-inspired leak.

64. French aid worker, interview by author, Peshawar, Pakistan, September 1998.

65. *U.S.A. v. Usama bin Laden,* Testimony of John Anticev, February 28, 2001.

66. Rahimullah Yusufzai, *The News* (Pakistan), September 6, 1998.

67. Robert Fisk, "Anti-Soviet Warrior Puts His Army on the Road to Peace: The Saudi Businessman Who Recruited Mujahideen Now Uses Them for Large Scale Building Projects in Sudan," *The Independent* (U.K.), December 6, 1993.

68. Khaled al-Fawwaz, interview by author, London, September 1998.

69. Laurie Mifflin, "U.S. Fury on Two Continents: What a Difference the News Makes: Clinton as Commander in Chief," *New York Times,* August 21, 2001.

70. Sandy Berger, National Security Adviser, White House press briefing, August 21, 1998; Tom Foley, deputy U.S. State Department spokesman, press briefing, August 21, 1998; Barbara Crossette, Judith Miller, Steven Lee Myers, and Tim Weiner, "U.S. Says Iraq Aided Production of Chemical Weapons in Sudan," *New York Times,* August 25, 1998.

72. Tom Tullius, interview by author, Boston, June 22, 1999.

73. Sheila MacVicar, ABC News, February 10, 1999.

74. Private Kroll Investigative Agency report for Salah Idris.

74. Michael Barletta, "Chemical Weapons in the Sudan," *Nonproliferation Review* (Monterrey Institute), Fall 1998, p. 119.

75. Andrew Marshall, "Clinton Was Angry, His White House Advisers Were Mad: They Wanted to Fight Back at the Terrorists Who'd Bombed Two American Embassies," *The Independent* (U.K.), May 6, 1999.

76. Kroll report.

77. James Risen, "New Evidence Ties Sudanese to bin Laden, U.S. Asserts," *New York Times,* October 4, 1998.

78. Kroll report.

79. Ibid.

80. Ibid.

81. Barletta, op. cit., p. 116.

82. Ibid, p. 129.

83. Vernon Loeb, "U.S. Unfreezes Assets of Saudi Who Owned Plant Bombed in Sudan," *Washington Post,* August 21, 1999.

84. My source is a U.S. lawyer familiar with the case.

85. Dexter Filkins, "World Perspective, Asia: Osama bin Laden Is Wanted Here, Too: Babies and Businesses Are Named After the Suspected Terrorist, Who Is a Hero on Pakistan's Frontier for His Battle Against the West," *Los Angeles Times,* July 24, 1999.

Chapter 7. The American Connection: From Brooklyn to Seattle

1. Norvell De Atkine, interview by author, Fort Bragg, North Carolina, November 1998.

2. Peter Bergen, Henry Schuster, and Phil Hirschkorn, "American Ties," CNN *Newsstand,* December 8, 1998.

3. Unless otherwise noted, all biographical information about Ali Mohamed is from his November 13, 1986, U.S. military record.

4. *U.S.A. v. Usama bin Laden,* 98 Cr. 1023 (SDNY), Affidavit of Daniel Coleman regarding Ali Mohamed; Colonel Robert Anderson, interview with author, North Carolina, November 1998.

5. U.S. Army Reserve Personnel Center, paper statement from Public Affairs Office, March 29, 1995.

6. Bergen et al., "American Ties."

7. Ali Mohamed plea agreement, reprinted as "Excerpts from Guilty Plea in Terrorism Case," *New York Times,* October 21, 2000.

8. *U.S.A. v. Usama bin Laden,* Affidavit of Daniel Coleman.

9. Anonymous colleague from Fort Bragg.

10. Anonymous colleagues from the Special Warfare Center.

11. U.S. Army Reserve Personnel Center, paper statement from Public Affairs Office, March 29, 1995.

12. Ibid.

13. Bergen et al., "American Ties."

14. Federal Bureau of Prisons, Inmate Locator, December 15, 1998.

15. Bergen et al., "American Ties."

16. Benjamin Weiser and James Risen, "Masking of a Militant: A Soldier's Shadowy Trail in the U.S. and Middle East," *New York Times,* December 1, 1998.

17. Anonymous colleague from Fort Bragg.

18. Bergen et al., "American Ties."
19. Bergen et al., "American Ties."
20. Colonel Robert Anderson interview, December 1998.
21. Ibid.
22. Bergen et al., "American Ties."
23. Colonel Robert Anderson interview, December 1998; Bergen et al., "American Ties."
24. Bergen et al., "American Ties."
25. Colonel Robert Anderson interview, December 1998.
26. Paul Quinn-Judge and Charles M. Sennot, "Figure Cited in Terrorism Case Said to Enter U.S. with CIA Help; Defense Says Defendants Trained by Him," *Boston Globe,* February 3, 1995.
27. Roger Stavis, interview by author, New York, October 1998; *U.S.A. v. Omar Ahmad Ali Abdel Rahman,* 93 Cr. 181 (SDNY), Testimony of Khalid Ibrahim, pp. 14280–14348.
28. Incorporation paper from the New York Secretary of State's Office.
29. Nejat Khalili, interview by author, Washington D.C., October 1993.
30. Alison Mitchell, "Missing Blast Suspect's Portrait Drawn in Shadows of Militancy," *New York Times,* March 21, 1993.
31. *U.S.A. v. Omar Ahmad Ali Abdel Rahman,* Testimony of Khalid Ibrahim.
32. Roger Stavis interview.
33. Ibid.
34. FBI inventory of contents of Nosair's apartment, November 13, 1990, pp. 2, 11; *U.S.A. v. Omar Ahmad Ali Abdel Rahman,* Indictment, p.12.
35. Peter Arnett, Peter Bergen, and Richard Mackenzie, "Terror Nation? U.S Creation?" CNN Documentary, January 1994.
36. Arnett et al., "Terror Nation? U.S. Creation?"; *U.S.A. v. Usama bin Laden,* Affidavit of Daniel Coleman.
37. Ali Mohamed Plea Agreement.
38. Ibid.
39. Phil Hirschkorn, "Passport Offers Peek Inside bin Laden's Businesses," *www.cnn.com/LAW/trials.and.cases/case.files/0012/embassy.bombing/trial.report/trial.report.02.26/,* February 26, 2001.
40. Ali Mohamed Plea Agreement.
41. Letter from Valley Media, Ali Mohamed's employer, November 6, 1998, copy in author's possession.
42. *U.S.A. v. Usama bin Laden,* Indictment, p. 41.
43. Ibid., Affidavit of Daniel Coleman regarding Ali Mohamed.
44. *U.S.A. v. Usama bin Laden,* Presentment of Ali Mohamed before Judge Andrew Peck, September 11, 1998.
45. Abdelkader Kallesh, interview by author, Brooklyn, New York, 1993; *U.S.A. v. Usama bin Laden,* Grand Jury Testimony of Wadih El-Hage entered into the

record, February 20, 2001; U.S. official, interview by author, 1997; *U.S.A. v. Usama bin Laden,* Testimony of Jamal al-Fadl, February 6, 2001.

46. Abdullah Azzam, *Jihad, News and Views,* no date; Alkhifa incorporation papers filed with New York State, September 1987; Leslie Cockburn and John Hockenberry, "Day One," ABC News, July 12, 1993.

47. Robert Friedman, "The CIA's Jihad," *New York* magazine, March 27, 1995.

48. Saad Eddin Ibrahim, interview by author, Cairo, Egypt, December 2000.

49. *U.S.A. v. Usama bin Laden,* Testimony of Jamal al-Fadl, February 6, 2001; Cross Examination of al-Fadl, February 20, 2001.

50. Saad Eddin Ibrahim interview.

51. Abdelkader Khallesh interview.

52. Ibid.

53. Author's own observations of the Seagate complex where Shalabi lived.

54. Saad Eddin Ibrahim interview; Hamed Nawaby (friend of Shalabi), interview by author, Brooklyn, New York, 1993.

55. *U.S.A. v. Wadih el Hage,* 98 Cr. 1023 (SDNY), Cause for Detention Hearing, remarks of Assistant U.S. Attorney Patrick Fitzgerald.

56. Pat Milton, "Wife of Accused Terrorist Waits Patiently for Verdict," Associated Press, May 21, 2001.

57. *U.S.A. v. Usama bin Laden,* Grand Jury Testimony of Wadih el-Hage, February 20, 2001.

58. Bergen et al., "American Ties.".

59. *U.S.A. v. Usama bin Laden,* Grand Jury Testimony of Wadih el-Hage.

60. Jamal Ismail, interview by author, Islamabad, Pakistan, September 1998.

61. *U.S.A. v. Usama bin Laden,* Grand Jury Testimony of Wadih el-Hage.

62. Marion Brown, telephone interview by author, July 29, 2001.

63. *U.S.A. v. Usama bin Laden,* Grand Jury Testimony of Wadih el-Hage.

64. Bergen et al, "American Ties."

65. Ibid.

66. Phil Hirschkorn, "Man Who Rented Kenya Bomb House Testifies," *www.cnn.com/2001/LAW/04/18/embassy.bombing.trial/index.html,* April 18, 2001.

67. *U.S.A. v. Usama bin Laden,* Testimony of L'Hossaine Khertchou, 26 February, 2001

68. U.S. official, interview by author, Washington, D.C., 1997.

69. Robert Friedman, "Trade Center Bombing: Questions the Trial Will Not Answer," *Village Voice,* March 8, 1994.

70. Craig Pyes, Judith Miller, and Stephen Engleberg, "One Man and a Global Web of Violence," *New York Times,* January 14, 2001.

71. John-Thor Dahlburg, "Pakistan Holds Suspect in Trade Center Bomb Case," *Los Angeles Times,* March 22, 1995.

72. *U.S.A. v. Usama bin Laden,* Testimony of L'Hossaine Kherchtou.

73. Phil Hirschkorn, "Trial may conclude weeks earlier than expected," *www.cnn.com/*

LAW/trials.and.cases/case.files/0012/embassy.bombing/trial.report.0323/index. html, March 23, 2001.

74. Ahmed Khan, *The Herald* (Islamabad, Pakistan), August 1993.

75. U.S. Department of State, White Paper, August 1996.

76. *U.S.A. v. Usama bin Laden,* Cross Examination of Jamal al-Fadl, February 20, 2001.

77. Rahimullah Yusufzai, interview by author, Washington D.C., June 2001.

78. Christopher S. Wren, "Terror Suspect Boasted of Bomb Plan," *New York Times,* August 13, 1996.

79. Jerry Capeci and Corky Siemaszko, "Air Terror Plotter Admitted Plan, Witnesses Say," *New York Daily News,* August 13, 1996; "Watch Links Bomb to Top Terrorist," *Toronto Star,* March 20, 2001; Western diplomat, interview with author, Islambad, Pakistan, September 1998.

80. Christine Herrera, "I don't know, Gemma; I'm upset," *Philippine Daily Inquirer,* August 11, 2000.

81. U.S. official, interview by author, Washington, D.C., 1997.

82. Osama bin Laden, interview by John Miller, ABC News, May 28, 1998.

83. Charles P. Wallace, "Weaving a Wide Web of Terror: The Plan, Officials Say, Was to Blow Up 11 U.S. Airliners in One Day," *Los Angeles Times,* May 30, 1995.

84. Former U.S. intelligence official, interview by author, Washington, D.C., 2001.

85. Terry McCarthy, "An Invasion of Paradise," *Time* magazine, May 8, 2000.

86. *U.S.A. v. Usama bin Laden,* Summation by Ken Karas, May 1, 2001.

87. See Phil Hirschkorn, "Feds allege 'unindicted co-conspirator' played key role in bin Laden's network," *www.cnn.com/LAW/trials.and.cases/case.files/0012/ embassy.bombing/trial.report/trial.report.05.04/index.html*

88. Pedro Roz Guttierez, "Case Built Against Cabbie—Ihab Ali," *Orlando Sentinel Tribune,* July 19, 1999.

89. *U.S.A. v. Usama bin Laden,* Summation by Ken Karas, May 1 and 3, 2001; Testimony of Essam al Ridi, February 14, 2001.

90. Ibid., Karas summation, May 1, 2001.

91. "Judge Cites Koran as Reason to Testify," *Orlando Sentinel Tribune,* August 8, 1999.

92. Stephen Kurkjian and Judy Rakowsky, "FBI Terrorism Probe Tracks Ex-Cabdrivers, 2 Who Left Boston, Tied to bin Laden," *Boston Globe,* February 5, 2001.

93. Ibid.; Judith Miller, "Dissecting a Terror Plot From Boston to Amman: Holy Warriors," *New York Times,* January 15, 2001.

94. Jamal Halaby, Associated Press (Amman, Jordan), December 9, 2000; Associated Press, "A Terror Conviction," Amman, Jordan, February 11, 2002.

95. Andrew Duffy, "Ressam Part of Terror 'Cell,' Expert Testifies: Montreal Ring Forged and Smuggled Passports, Says French Judge," *Ottawa Citizen,* April 3, 2001; "Bomb Plot Focused on Los Angeles International Airport," Associated Press, May 30, 2001.

96. Josh Meyer, "Border Arrest Stirs Fear of Terrorist Cells in U.S.," *Los Angeles Times,* March 11, 2001.

97. Linda Deutsch, "Prosecutor: Anti-Terrorism Arrest Was Los Angeles Tragedy Averted," Associated Press, March 13, 2001.

98. *U.S.A. v. Mokhtar Haouari,* S4 00 Cr. 15 (SDNY), Testimony of Ahmed Ressam, July 3, 2001.

99. Deutsch, op. cit.; Meyer, op. cit.

100. Alan Feuer, "Embassy Bombing Witnesses Recall Blood, Smoke, and Chaos," *New York Times,* March 10, 2001;

101. Laura Mansnerus and Judith Miller, "Bomb Plot Insider Details Training," *New York Times,* July 4, 2001; Jamal Halaby, "Jordanian, Canadian Plots Connected," Associated Press, February 29, 2000; see also chapter 9 on Yemen.

102. *U.S.A. v. Mokhtar Haouari,* Testimony of Ahmed Ressam, July 5, 2001.

103. British official, author interview, Washington DC August, 2001

104. Judith Miller, "Dissecting a Terror Plot From Boston to Amman: Holy Warriors," *New York Times,* January 15, 2001; see also p. 107 in chapter 6.

105. Christine Haughney, "Terrorist Recounts Afghanistan Training," *Washington Post,* July 7, 2001; *U.S.A. v. Mokhtar Haouari,* Testimony of Ahmed Ressam, July 5, 2001.

106. *U.S.A. v. Mokhtar Haouari,* Testimony of Ahmed Ressam, July 5, 2001.

107. Colin Nickerson, "In Canada, Terrorists Found a Haven," *Boston Globe,* April 9, 2001; *U.S.A. v. Mokhtar Haouari,* Testimony of Ahmed Ressam, July 5, 2001.

108. *U.S.A. v. Mokhtar Haouari,* Testimony of Ahmed Ressam, July 3, 2001.

109. Ibid.

110. Ibid.

111. Ibid.

112. Phil Hirschkorn, "Witness reveals details of Y2K plot," available at *www.cnn.com/2001/LAW/07/02/millennium.bomb.trial/.*

113. *U.S.A. v. Mokhtar Haouari,* Testimony of Ahmed Ressam, July 3, 2001.

114. Ibid., July 5, 2001.

115. Ibid.

Chapter 8. True Believers: The Taliban and Bin Laden

1. "Taliban Poppy-Growing Ban Will Measure Afghan's Fear," *New York Times,* November 16, 2000. In 1999 Afghanistan produced four thousand tons of opium, more than the rest of the world put together.

2. Richard Mackenzie, "America and the Taliban," in William Maley, ed., *Fundamentalism Reborn?: Afghanistan and the Taliban* (New York: New York University Press, 1998), p. 91.

3. U.S. State Department Travel Warning for Afghanistan, July 1999.

4. Steve LeVine, "Helping Hand," *Newsweek,* October 13, 1997.

5. Richard Mackenzie, "The Succession," *The New Republic,* September 14, 21, 1998.

6. Ralph H. Magnus and Eden Naby, *Afghanistan: Mullah, Marx and Mujahid* (New Delhi, India: HarperCollins, 1998), p. 182.

7. Ibid.

8. Ahmed Rashid, "Pakistan and the Taliban," in William Maley, op. cit, pp. 72–90.

9. Western diplomat, interview by author, Islamabad, Pakistan, September 1998; Peter Marsden, *The Taliban: War, Religion and the New Order in Afghanistan* (London: Zed Books, 1998), p. 90.

10. Kamran Khan, "Army Stages Coup in Pakistan; Troops Arrest Prime Minister, Seize Buildings After Firing of General," *Washington Post,* October 13, 1999.

11. Kamran Khan, "Military Coup in Pakistan; Army Chief Overthrows Government," *Chicago Sun-Times,* October 13, 1999.

12. Tim Weiner and Steve LeVine, "For Many Pakistanis, Coup Opens to Applause," *New York Times,* October 16, 1999.

13. Tim Weiner, "Pakistani Report Alleges Graft by Ex-Premier," *New York Times,* October 26, 1999.

14. Celia W. Dugger, "Coup in Pakistan: the Overview," *New York Times,* October 13, 1999.

15. Stephen P. Cohen, *The Pakistan Army* (Karachi, Pakistan: Oxford University Press, 1998), pp. 169, 128; Ahmed Rashid, *Taliban: Islam, Oil and the New Great Game in Central Asia* (London: I. B. Tauris, 2000), pp. 28–29; LeVine, op. cit.

16. Kai Friese, "Two Uneasy States of Independence," *New York Times,* August 15, 2001.

17. Malise Ruthven, *Islam in the World* (New York: Oxford University Press, 2000), p. 15.

18. Owen Bennet Jones, "Rockets Fired at Western Targets in Pakistan," *The Independent* (U.K.), November 13, 1999.

19. *Wujood,* an Urdu magazine (Islamabad, Pakistan), September 14, 1998.

20. The *fatwa* was endorsed by Madrassa Qasim al-Uloom, Shayraanwala Gate, Lahore, Pakistan, 1997, in a document obtained by author.

21. "Pakistani Islamist Party Renews Threat Against U.S. Nationals," Agence France-Presse, International News, August 5, 1999.

22. Reuters Newswire, "Scholar Accuses U.S. of War Against Muslims; Noted Pakistani Calls for Boycott of the West," *Baltimore Sun,* August 22, 1999.

23. Kathy Gannon, "Hundreds of Thousands of Religious Radicals Pay Tribute to Hardline Islam," Associated Press, April 9, 2001.

24. Kamal Matinuddin, *The Taliban Phenomenon: Afghanistan 1994–1997* (Karachi, Pakistan: Oxford Pakistan Paperbacks, 1999), p. 14.

25. Ibid., p. 18; Ahmed Rashid, "Pakistan and the Taliban," in William Maley, op. cit., p. 81: as early as January 1995 the *madrassa* had supplied "some 12,000" recruits to the Taliban.

26. Jeffrey Goldberg, "Inside Jihad U.: The Education of a Holy Warrior," *New York Times Magazine,* June 25, 2000.

27. Ahmed Rashid, *Taliban: Islam, Oil, and the New Great Game in Central Asia* (London: I. B. Tauris, 2000), p. 90.

28. Amir Zia, "Pakistani Admirers of Afghan Islamist Movement Gaining Influence," Associated Press, May 30, 2000; Ahmed Rashid, "The Taliban: Exporting Extremism," *Foreign Affairs,* November/December 1999, pp. 22+.

29. Robert Marquand, "How Islamic Extremism Can Dissolve Old Borders," *Christian Science Monitor,* August 20, 1998.

30. *Newsline* (Pakistan), February 1998.

31. Ibid.

32. Tony Clifton, "How Much Religion?" *Newsweek,* September 14, 1998.

33. Maulana ul-Haq, interview by author, Peshawar, Pakistan, September 1998.

34. U.S. State Department Travel Warning, Afghanistan, July 8, 1999.

35. Scott Anger, former Voice of America Islamabad bureau chief, interview by author, Washington, D.C., April 2001.

36. Nancy Hatch Dupree, *Afghanistan,* Afghan Tourist Organization, Publication Number 5 (Tokyo: Jagra Ltd., 1977), p. 211.

37. Edward Girardet, ed., *Afghanistan* (Geneva, Switzerland: Crosslines, 1998), p. 25. See also Mamoun Fandy, *Saudi Arabia and the Politics of Dissent* (New York: St. Martin's Press, 1999), p. 33.

38. Kathy Gannon, "Taliban Strictly Enforce Edicts," Associated Press, March 30, 1997.

39. Pathans are also called Pashtuns or Pushtuns.

40. Robert D. Kaplan, *Soldiers of God: With the Mujahidin in Afghanistan* (Boston: Houghton Mifflin, 1990), p. 49.

41. Marsden, op. cit. p. 98.

42. Louis Dupree, *Afghanistan* (New Delhi: Rama Publishers, 1994), pp. 59–64.

43. Masatoshi Konishi, *Afghanistan: Crossroads of the Ages* (Tokyo: Kodansha International Ltd., 1969), p. 9.

44. Peter D. Bell, CARE USA memo, August 1, 2001.

45. Jan Goodwin, *Price of Honor* (New York: Plume, 1995), pp. 34–35; W. Montgomery Watt, *Muhammad: Prophet and Statesman* (New York: Oxford University Press, 1974), p. 12.

46. The Koran, 24:30, translated by N. J. Dawood (London: Penguin Books, 1997.)

47. The Swedish Committee for Afghanistan, "Afghanistan, Aid and the Taliban: Challenges on the Eve of the 21st Century" (Stockholm, 1999), p. 62.

48. CNN correspondent Nic Robertson visited the school in January 2000 and was interviewed by the author in London the same month.

49. World Food Program information from spokesman Khaled Mansour. The Tal-

iban decreed in July 2000 that no Afghan women could work for Afghan NGOs, but rescinded the order within two weeks.

50. Isaac Levi, interview by author, Kabul, Afghanistan, December 1999.

51. Richard Galpin, "Taliban Executed Thousands As Troops Took Northern City," *The Guardian* (U.K.), September 4, 1998.

52. Or *pushtunwali*.

53. David M. Hart, *Guardians of the Khaibar Pass: The Social Organisation of the Afridis of Pakistan* (Lahore, Pakistan: Vanguard Books, 1985), p. 13.

54. L. Dupree, op. cit., p. 126.

55. Rahimullah Yusufzai, *The News* (Islamabad, Pakistan), August 30, 1998.

56. Ahmed Rashid, *Taliban: Islam, Oil, and the New Great Game in Central Asia* (London: I. B. Tauris, 2000), p. 20.

57. Reuters Newswire, quoting the *Al-Hayat* newspaper, October 18, 1999.

58. LeVine, op. cit.

59. Abdullah, an Afghan journalist working for the Associated Press, interview by author, Peshawar, Pakistan, September 8, 1998.

60. Ahmed Rashid, "Afghanistan: Heart of Darkness," *Far Eastern Economic Review*, August 5, 1999.

61. William C. Rempel, "Saudi Tells of Deal to Arrest Terror Suspect: Afghans Backpedaled on Hand-over of bin Laden After U.S. Embassy Blasts, Riyadh Official Says," *Los Angeles Times*, August 8, 1999.

62. Abdel Bari Atwan, telephone interview by author, February 15, 1999.

63. Tim Weiner, "Terror Suspect Said to Anger Afghan Hosts," *New York Times*, March 4, 1999.

64. Patrick Bishop, "International Mystery as Bomb Suspect bin Laden 'Disappears,'" Reuters, February 16, 1999.

65. *U.S.A. v. Mokhtar Haouari*, S4 00 Cr. 15 (SDNY).

66. *U.S.A. v. Mokhtar Haouari*, Testimony of Ahmed Ressam, July 3, 2001.

67. Further proof of the cosmopolitan makeup of the forces arriving for military training could be found among the prisoners of war captured by Massoud. Julie Sirrs, a former intelligence analyst for the Pentagon, visited the POWs in early 2000. Of the 1,200, 109 were Pakistanis, two were Yemenis, two were Chinese, and one was a British citizen of Pakistani parentage. The Chinese prisoners were Muslim Uighurs from Kashgar who attended a *madrassa* in Pakistan before going on to weapons training in Kabul. The British citizen, "Adam Rashid," had left England for Pakistan because of drug problems. Once in Pakistan he spent most of his time hanging out in mosques, after which he traveled to Afghanistan and received six months of military training, going to fight against the Northern Alliance. Significantly, about half the foreign prisoners were affiliated with the Kashmiri terrorist group Harkat ul Mujahideen.

68. Kamran Khan, "Afghan Revenge Killings Spread to Pakistan," *Washington Post*, November 28, 1998. Khan uses the figure of 500 deaths.

69. "Pak has proof of terrorist camps in Afghanistan: PM," Xinhua Newswire, Islamabad, October 7, 1999.

70. Kathy Gannon, "Pakistani Interior Minister Talks Tough with Afghanistan," Associated Press, July 7, 2000.

71. Peter Bergen, "A Dying Nation: Taliban Is Destroying More than Buddhas," *Washington Times,* March 15, 2001.

72. "Taliban to try aid workers," see *www.cnn.com/2001/WORLD/asiapcf/central/08/29/taliban.trial/index.html.*

Chapter 9. The Holy Warriors of Yemen: The Bombing of the U.S.S. *Cole*

1. U.S. official familiar with the *Cole* investigation, interview by author, December 2000.

2. John Burns, "Yemen Reports Arrests of Foreign-Born Arabs in *Cole* Attack," *New York Times,* October 26, 2000.

3. U.S. official familiar with the *Cole* investigation, interview by author, December 2000.

4. Western diplomat, interview by author, San'a, Yemen, November 2000. Militants train in remote areas of the northwest of the country.

5. Agence France-Presse, "Yemen launches arms sweep after mosque bombing," April 25, 1998.

6. Ian Henderson, British ambassador to Yemen, interview by author, San'a, Yemen, November 2000.

7. Jack Kelley, "Bombing plot stymied in Yemen: U.S. still uneasy despite 10 arrests," *USA Today,* June 20, 2001.

8. On a visit by the author to the home of the then prime minister, Dr. Abdul-Kareem Iryani, a biogeneticist in his late sixties who is an ardent fan of the British satire *Yes, Prime Minister,* he proudly showed off his state-of-the-art *mafraj,* a high-ceilinged room, lined with pillows and cushions on which to recline and with a good view of the presidential palace. The prime minister made it clear that he is not adverse to the odd chew himself.

9. Sue Lackey, "Yemen: Unlikely Key to Western Security," *Jane's Intelligence Review,* July 1, 1999. Per capita GDP in Yemen is $2,300. In the United Arab Emirates it is $24,000.

10. Western diplomat, interview by author, San'a, Yemen, November 2000.

11. Jamal Ismail, interview by author, Islamabad, Pakistan, 1998; senior Yemeni government official, interview by author, San'a, Yemen, December 2000.

12. Yemeni journalist, interview by author, December 2000.

13. Lackey, op. cit.

14. *U.S.A. v. Usama bin Laden,* 98 Cr. 1023 (SDNY), Indictment.

15. U.S. government official, interview by author, Washington D.C., 1997.

16. Western diplomat, interview by author, San'a, Yemen, December 2000; Yemeni official, interview by author, December 2000.

17. Abdul Wahab al-Anesi, Islah party official, interview by author, San'a, Yemen, December 2000.

18. Yemeni official, interview by author, San'a, Yemen, December 2000.

19. Author interview with Yemeni journalist who had previously interviewed al-Fadhli, San'a, Yemen, December 2000. My many requests for an interview with al-Fahdli were turned down.

20. Yemeni journalist, interview by author, San'a, Yemen, December 2000.

21. Ibid.

22. For a fuller account, see Brian Whitaker, *Yemen and Osama bin Laden*, at *www.al-bab.com/yemen*, August 1998.

23. Senior Yemeni official, interview by author, December 2000; *Yemen Times*, September 16, 2000.

24. Al-Anesi interview, December 2000.

25. *U.S.A. v. Usama bin Laden*, Indictment.

26. U.S. government official, interview by author, San'a, Yemen, December 2000; al-Anesi interview, December 2000; senior Yemeni official, interview by author, December 2000.

27. Salah Nasrawi, "In Yemeni Town, Muslim Militants Retain Hold," Associated Press, November 1, 2000.

28. Yemeni official, interview by author, San'a Yemen, December 2000.

29. Al-Anesi interview, December 2000.

30. Julie Sirrs, former analyst for the Defense Intelligence Agency, telephone interview by author, October 2000.

31. Ibid.

32. Interview of Osama bin Laden by Jamal Ismail, Al-Jazeera television, aired June 10, 1999.

33. Interview of Osama bin Laden by *Al-Quds Al-Arabi* newspaper, translated by *Mideast Mirror*, November 27, 1996.

34. Bin Shajea, interview by author, Yemen, December 2000.

35. Michael Becket, "Yemen Hostage Shoot-Out," *Daily Telegraph* (U.K.), December 30, 1998.

36. Ahmad al-Haj, "Four Westerners Killed in Bloody End to Yemen Kidnappings," Associated Press, December 30, 1998; "Yemen Kidnap Victims Recover After Slaughter of Four Friends," Agence France-Presse, December 30, 1998.

37. Figures from *www.al-bab.com/yemen*.

38. Abu Hassan and his lieutenant had trained with al-Qaeda; Sam Ghattas, "Freed Hostages Say Yemeni Troops Started Fatal Shootout," Associated Press, December 30, 1998.

39. Naswari, op. cit.

40. Ibid.

41. Yemeni official, interview with author, San'a, Yemen.

42. John Burns, "Little Sympathy in Yemen for Condemned Militant," *New York Times,* September 17, 1999.

43. In December 2000 interviews by the author, a Western diplomat and Abu Hamza said the Yemeni government sought Hamza's extradition, though there is no extradition treaty between Yemen and the U.K.

44. Abu Hamza, interview by author, London, November 2000.

45. Yassir al-Sirri and Muntazzir al-Zayyat, for example.

46. Abu Hamza told the *Al-Ayyam* newspaper that he worked at a nightclub at the end of the 1970s, before he was "reformed." See *www.al-ayyam-yemen.com/ freedom/ interview.html.*

47. Abu Hamza interview, November 2000.

48. See *www.supportersofshariah.org/eng/abuhamza/html.*

49. Ibid.

50. Ibid. Accounts posted for Harakat-ul-Mujahideen on the site were at the Muslim Commercial Bank, branches in Islamabad and Karachi, Pakistan.

51. *The Yemen Times,* November 13, 2000, reported that in 1998 a document was circulated by opponents of the U.S. military in Yemen saying a Marine base was being built in Aden.

52. Abu Hamza, interview with *Al-Ayyam* newspaper, August 10, 1999, at *www.al-ayyam.yemen.com/freedom/interview.html.*

53. Biographical details at *www.al-bab.com/yemen;* Western diplomat, interview by author, San'a, Yemen, December 2000.

54. See *www.al-bab.com/yemen.*

55. The best summary of this story can be found in a brilliant article by Rory Carroll, "Terrorists or Tourists," *The Guardian* (U.K.), June 26, 1999.

56. Lackey, op. cit.

57. Carroll, op. cit.

58. See *www.al-bab.com/yemen.*

59. U.S. investigator, interview by author, Yemen, December 2000; Ahmad al-Haj, Associated Press, August 9, 1999.

60. Western diplomat, interview by author, San'a, Yemen, November 2000.

61. Ibid.

62. Mary Quin, interview by author, Washington, D.C., June 2001; Stephen Farrell and Richard Duce, "Three Britons Killed in Shootout," *The Times* (London), December 30, 1998.

63. Mary Quin interview, June 2001.

64. Daniel McGrory, "My Wife Never Stood a Chance. As She Was Shot, She Said: 'Bless Me,'" *The Times* (London), December 31, 1998. One of the hostages was told by a kidnapper that they had six friends in prison and "we were to be exchanged for them."

65. Mary Quin interview, June 2001.

66. Thomas E. Ricks, "Persian Gulf, U.S. Danger Zone; Military Has Been Committed to Hot Spot Despite Risk," *Washington Post*, October 15, 2000.

67. Western diplomat, interview by author, San'a, Yemen, November 2000.

68. Steve Boggan and Andrew Buncombe, "Yemen Hostage Tragedy: When Troops Opened Fire, the Hostages Were Used As Shields," *The Independent* (U.K.), December 31, 1998; Combined News Services, "Hostages Tell of Yemen Killings: Two Survivors Say Soldiers Fired First, Triggering Gun Battle," *Newsday* (Long Island), December 31, 1998.

69. Yemeni source, interview with author, in Aden, Yemen, December 2000.

70. Ghattas, op. cit.

71. Jennifer Trueland, "I Held Edinburgh Woman's Hand As She Was Shot," *The Scotsman*, December 31, 1998.

72. Michael Smith and Tim Butcher, "Yemen Hostage Shootout," *Daily Telegraph* (U.K.), December 31, 1998; Phil Chetwynd, "Yemen Hostage Drama: A Survivor's Tale," Agence France-Presse, December 31, 1998.

73. See *www.al-bab.com/yemen*.

74. Aden newspaper editor and senior Yemeni officials, interviews with author; John Burns, "Little Sympathy in Yemen for Condemned Militant," *New York Times*, November 25, 2001.

75. See account of the trial at *www.al-bab.com/yemen*.

76. Ibid., quoting Al-Jazeera television interview with Abu Hamza, January, 14, 1999.

77. General Zinni, Testimony before Senate Armed Services Committee, October 19, 2000.

78. Reuters Newswire, "FBI Had '98 Report of Plot to Bomb Warship in Yemen, U.S. Says," reprinted in *The Washington Post*, January 31, 2001.

79. *U.S.A. v. Usama bin Laden*, Indictment, p. 32.

80. "FBI Had '98 Report of Plot to Bomb Warship in Yemen, U.S. Says" op. cit.

81. Al-Harazi also goes by the name Abdul Rahman al-Sa'afani, (Harazi is after the area in Yemen where his family is from; Sa'fan is the small village where his family actually originates). Author interview with Yemeni official, Sa'na, Yemen December, 2000

82. U.S. investigator, interview by author, Yemen, December 2000.

83. Former U.S. intelligence official, interview by author, November 2000.

84. U.S. investigator interview, December 2000; General Zinni testimony.

85. Author's visit to the house.

86. Ibid.

87. For a discussion of the significance of the "night of power" see Malise Ruthven, *Islam in the World* (New York: Oxford University Press, 2000), pp. 36–37.

88. U.S. investigator, interview by author, December, 2000.

89. John Burns, "Ship Attack Suspects Seemed Out of Place," *New York Times*, October 31, 2000.

90. Vernon Loeb, "Plot Targeted U.S., Jordan, American Warship, Official Says," *Washington Post,* December 24, 2000.

91. Agence France-Presse, Dubai, September 22, 2000; also on the tape is Asadullah Rahman, one of the sons of Sheik Omar Abdel Rahman, who urges Muslims: "Forward to shed blood."

92. Khalid Hammadi, reporter for *Al-Quds Al-Arabi* newspaper, interview by author, Yemen, November 2000.

93. U.S. investigator, interview by author, December 2000.

94. Yemeni official, interview by author, San'a, Yemen, December 2000.

95. Michael Sheehan, testimony before U.S. House Judiciary Committee, December 13, 2000.

96. John Burns, "Remote Yemen May Be Key to Terrorist's Past and Future," *New York Times,* November 5, 2000; Donna Nasr, "Wartime Loyalty Rewarded in Yemen," Associated Press, October 28, 2000.

97. David Ensor, Chris Plante, and Peter Bergen, "U.S. tightens security overseas," *www.cnn.com/2000/US/12/20/terrorism.threat/index.html,* December 20, 2000.

98. *Al-Ayyam* newspaper, Aden, Yemen, photo in the newspaper from week of December 2000

99. John Miller, "The Connection: Yemen Probe Uncovers Bin Laden Links and Missteps by *Cole* Bombers," see *abcnews.go.com/sections/world/DailyNews/yemen 001207b.html.*

100. Andrea Koppel, Elise Labott, Susan Bassals, and Rym Brahimi, "Remains of 1 *Cole* bomber found, U.S.officials say," *www.cnn.com/2000/US/11/17/usscole.02/index.html,* November 17, 2000

101. Ibid.

102. See *www.cnn.com/2000/US/10/13/shipattack.thumbnails.02.ap/.*

103. ABC News, *Primetime Live,* January 18, 2001.

104. Abdul Aziz Hakim, interview by author, Aden, Yemen, December 2000.

105. U.S. counterterrorism official, interview by author, Washington, D.C., October 15, 2000.

106. Official at FBI's New York office, interview by author, October 2000.

107. Ibid.

108. John Burns, "Yemenis Seem to Hinder Inquiry," *New York Times,* November 1, 2000.

109. Neil MacFarquhar, "Saudis Say They, Not U.S., Will Try 11 in '96 Bombing," *New York Times,* July 2, 2001.

110. John Burns, interview by author, Yemen, December, 2000.

111. In December 2000 a Yemeni journalist told me that 1,800 people were interviewed; John Burns, "Yemen Links to bin Laden Grow at FBI in *Cole* Inquiry," *New York Times,* November 25, 2000.

112. Massimo Calabresi, "How Feuds and Culture Clashes Have Stymied the U.S.S. *Cole* Investigation," *Time,* July 16, 2001.

113. U.S. State Department, "Patterns of Global Terrorism," Middle East Overview, 1998.

114. Howard Schneider and Roberto Suro, "In Yemen, A Search for Clues," *Washington Post*, October 15, 2000: the *Cole* is an "Arleigh-Burke class-guided missile destroyer."

115. Western diplomat in Yemen, interview with author, December 2000; Abdul Walid, at Salafi bookstore in Birmingham; Sheikh al-Wadi'i, interview by the *Yemen Times*, July 17, 2000.

116. Margie Mason, "An American Taliban in Yemen: John Walker Lindh Bumbled His Way Through the Mideast," Associated Press, January 15, 2002.

117. Ibid.; "At Least Two Killed in Bomb Explosion at Islamist Mosque in Yemen," Agence France-Presse, April 24, 1998; *Yemen Times*, September 18, 2000.

118. *Yemen Times*, July 17, 2000.

119. Ibid.

120. Agence France-Presse, "At least two killed in bomb explosion at Islamist mosque in Yemen," San'a, April 24, 1998.

121. See *www.qoqaz.com.my/qoqaz/fatwa/muqbil.htm.*

122. *Yemen Times*, July 17, 2000.

123. John Burns, "FBI's Inquiry in *Cole* Attack is Nearing Halt," *New York Times*, August 21, 2001.

124. "Bin Laden verses honor *Cole* attack," Reuters Newswire, reprinted in *The Seattle Times*, March 2, 2001.

Chapter 10. The Global Network: Around the World in Eighty Jihads

1. Giles Tremlett, "Spanish Police Arrest bin Laden Suspect," *The Guardian* (U.K.), June 23, 2001; Sarah Lyall and Judith Miller, "Hunting bin Laden's Allies, U.S. Extends Net to Europe," *New York Times*, February 21, 2001; Alessandra Stanley, "Italy Arrests 5 Islamists in Failed Bomb Plot," *New York Times*, April 6, 2001; the arrests appear to have been connected to a planned bombing in Strasbourg, France.

2. John Micklethwait and Adrian Wooldridge, *A Future Perfect: The Challenge and Hidden Promise of Globalization* (New York: Times Books, 2000), p. 225.

3. *U.S.A. v. Usama bin Laden*, S (6) 98 Cr. 1023 (SDNY), Indictment, p. 6.

4. Stephen Kinzer, "Jordan Links Terrorist Plot to bin Laden," *New York Times*, February 4, 2000; "Bin Laden Supporter Detained in France," Agence France-Presse, March 3, 1999; Katherine Ellison, "Terrorism May Wear Normal Face," *Houston Chronicle*, February 19, 1999; "Australians Being Recruited for bin Laden Jihad, Court Told," Associated Press, April 29, 1999.

5. Arlinda Causholli, "Member of Jihad Dies in Shootout with Police," Associated Press, October 23, 1998; Patrick Kennedy, State Department Briefing, December 1998; Peter Bergen, "Official: Bin Laden group major threat to U.S. embassies," see *www.cnn.com/US/9902/25/bin.laden/*, February 25, 1999 and author interview of U.S. counterterrorism official, February 1999.

6. David Carpenter, Testimony before the U.S. House of Representatives Committee on International Relations, March 12, 1999.

7. Sayantan Chakrarty, "The discovery of a plan to bomb the U.S. embassy in Delhi," *India Today*, July 2, 2001.

8. Ibid.; *Yemen Times*, February 19, 2001; see chapter 9, note 81.

9. Rajesh Mahpatra, "Indian Police Charge Osama bin Laden with Plotting to Bomb U.S. Embassy in New Delhi," Associated Press, August 24, 2001.

10. Mamdouh Mahmud Salim, handwritten statement to FBI, copy in author's possession.

11. Ibid.; Tribune News Services, "Suspect in Bombing of U.S. Embassies Awaits Extradition," *Chicago Tribune*, September 23, 1998.

12. *U.S.A. v. Usama bin Laden*, Summation by Ken Karas, May 1, 2001.

13. Phil Hirschkorn, "Trial reveals a conspiracy of calls, but only tidbits about bin Laden," April 16, 2001, see *www.cnh.com/LAW/trials.and.cases/case.files/0012/embassy.bombing/trial.report/trial.report.04.16/index.html*.

14. Ian Black and Nicolas Pelham, "Egypt's Quiet Militant Protests His Innocence," *The Guardian* (U.K.), January 19, 1996.

15. See *www.cairotimes.com/content/issues/Islamist/london21.html*.

16. Yasser al-Sirri, interview by author, London, September 1998.

17. Abu el-Ela Mady, interview by author, Cairo, December 2000.

18. See generally Max Rodenbeck, *Cairo: The City Victorious* (New York: Vintage, 2000).

19. Gilles Kepel, *Muslim Extremism in Egypt* (Berkeley, Calif.: University of California Press, 1993), p. 39.

20. Malise Ruthven, *Islam in the World* (New York: Oxford University Press, 2000), pp. 312–13; Dilip Hiro, *Holy Wars, The Rise of Islamic Fundamentalism* (New York: Routledge, 1989), p. 66.

21. Kepel, op. cit., pp. 24, 37, 41, 51, 54–55, 155.

22. Saad al-Fagih, interview by author, London, October 2000.

23. John Burton, *An Introduction to the Hadith* (Edinburgh: Edinburgh University Press, 1994), p. 39.

24. Abu el-Ela Mady, "Violent Groups Connected to Islam: The Historical Roots, Theological Foundations and Future," International Center for Country Studies, Cairo, March 1998, Arabic monograph.

25. Ibid.

26. Abu el-Ela Mady interview, Cairo, Egypt, December 2000.

27. Abu el-Ela Mady interview.

28. Hiro, op. cit., p. 78.

29. Ibid.

30. Anthony Shadid, *Legacy of the Prophet: Despots, Democrats and the New Politics of Islam* (Boulder, Colo.: Westview Press, 2001), pp. 77–78.

31. Kepel, op. cit., p. 192.

32. Abu el-Ela Mady interview, December 2000.

33. U.S. State Department background paper, 1993, copy in author's possession.

34. Montasser al-Zayyat, interview by author, Cairo, Egypt, December 2000.

35. Robin Wright, *Sacred Rage* (New York: Simon & Schuster, 1985), p. 186.

36. Abu el-Ela Mady interview, December 2000.

37. Abu el-Ela Mady interview.

38. Mike Boettcher, "Authorities target bin Laden's second-in-command," September 28, 2001, see *www.cnn.com/2001/US/09/28/inv.second.command/index.html.* I am indebted to CNN's Phil Hirschkorn for this important observation.

39. "The Retreat from Fundamentalism," *The Economist,* May 1, 1999.

40. Shadid, op. cit., p. 1.

41. Ibid.

42. Saad al-Fagih, interview by author, London, September 1998; Jamal Ismail, interview by author, Islamabad, Pakistan, September 1998; Rahimullah Yusufzai, interview by author, Peshawar, September 1998; Montasser al-Zayyat, interview by author, Cairo, December 2000; U.S. intelligence officials, interview by author, Washington, D.C., October 1999. All told me that Ayman al-Zawahiri has had a profound influence on bin Laden.

43. Biographical information from the U.S. Department of the Treasury, Office of Foreign Assets Control; Jamal Ismail interview, September 1998.

44. Montasser al-Zayyat interview, December 2000.

45. Montasser al-Zayyat interview.

46. Al-Qaeda recruitment videotape, accessed on August 14, 2001, at *www.moon-warriors.com.*

47. Osama bin Laden biography in Urdu, pp. 46–47; Rahimullah Yusufzai, *Newsline* (Karachi, Pakistan), September 1998.

48. *U.S.A. v. Usama bin Laden,* Testimony of Stephen Gaudin, March 10, 2001.

49. Nancy Peckenham, Phil Hirschkorn, Peter Bergen, and Douglas Wood, "Bin Laden, millionaire with a dangerous grudge," September 27, 2001, see *www.cnn.com/2001/US/09/12/binladen.profile/index.html.*

50. David S. Cloud, "Around World, al-Qaeda arrests top 350," *Wall Street Journal,* November 30, 2001.

51. "Suspected Militants on Trial in Egypt; 107 Face Charges Tied to Alleged Roles in Outlawed Group," Associated Press, February 2, 1999.

52. Montasser al-Zayyat interview, December 2000.

53. Hassan Mekki, "Egypt Sentences to Death 9 bin Laden Followers," Agence France-Presse, April 18, 1999.

54. Montasser al-Zayyat interview, December 2000.

55. BBC World Service Summary of *Al-Hayat* newspaper, February 12, 1997.

56. Larry Neumeister, "Fresh Links Made to U.S. Terrorism by Latest Arrests in Europe," Associated Press, July 13, 1999.

57. *U.S.A. v. Usama bin Laden,* Summation by Patrick Fitzgerald, May 3, 2001.

58. *U.S.A. v. Usama bin Laden,* Summation by Ken Karas, May 1, 2001.

59. Abdel Bari Atwan, interview by author, London, November 1998.

60. *U.S.A. v. Usama bin Laden,* Testimony of L'Hossaine Khertchou, February 10–11, 2001.

61. Ali Mohamed plea agreement, October 21, 2000.

62. *U.S.A. v. Usama bin Laden,* Summation by Ken Karas, May 1, 2001.

63. Ibid., Testimony of Jamal al-Fadl, February 6, 2001.

64. Ibid., Testimony of L'Hossaine Kherchtou, February 10–11, 2001; Summation by Ken Karas, May 1, 2001.

65. Jason Burke, "Britons Hold Key to Master Terrorist Trial: A 'Holy War' Manual Found in Manchester is Claimed to Link 4 Men Accused of Bombing Embassies in East Africa," *The Observer* (U.K.), May 20, 2001.

66. Ibid.

67. Daniel McGrory, "UK Muslims Volunteer for Kashmir War," *The Times* (London), December 28, 2000.

68. *The Nation* (Islamabad, Pakistan), January 5, 2000.

69. Pamela Constable, "Kashmir Tension Knows No Season: Multiple Factors Trigger New Strife in Disputed Region," *Washington Post,* July 10, 2000.

70. Barry Bearak and Celia W. Dugger, "Kashmir Impasse: India and Pakistan Are Stuck on Semantics," *New York Times,* July 22, 2001.

71. Rahimullah Yusufzai, "Over a dozen Harakat members missing since US attack," *The News* (Pakistan), August 26, 1998.

72. Western diplomat, interview by author, Islamabad, Pakistan, September 1998.

73. Douglas Jehl, "Prominent Muslim Is Named a Suspect in Pearl Case," *The New York Times,* February 7, 2002.

74. Kathy Gannon, "Taliban's Image Getting a Shine with Their Handling of Hijacking Drama with Indian Airlines," Associated Press, December 28, 1999.

75. U.S. counterterrorism official, interview by author, Washington, D.C., January 2000.

76. Uli Schmetzer, "Hijacked Passengers Faced Fear, Threats; American Schoolteacher Survives 'In Good Health,'" *San Diego Union-Tribune,* January 2, 2000.

77. Ibid.

78. David Graves, "Militants Set Free in Deal Can Return to Britain," *Daily Telegraph* (London), January 4, 2000.

79. Patrick French, "Dangerous Neighbours: India and Pakistan Have Long Fought Over Kashmir. Now, as Nuclear States, They Have Never Needed Peace So Badly," *The Independent* (U.K.) May 30, 1999.

80. Salim Wani, interview by author, Muzaffarabad, Pakistan, January 2000; Sumit Ganguly, *The Crisis in Kashmir* (Cambridge: Cambridge University Press, 1997), p. 41.

81. Salim Wani interview.

82. Western diplomat, interview by author, Islamabad, Pakistan, December 1999.

83. Abdullah Muntazir, interview by author, Islamabad, Pakistan, December 1999. Muntazir said 500,000; a U.S. government official in Pakistan said 200,000.

84. U. S. Department of State, *Patterns of Global Terrorism,* Appendix B, p.16.

85. Thomas B. Hunter, "Terror in the Philippines," *Journal of Counterterrorism & Security,* vol. 9, no. 3, June 2001, p. 1; Carl H. Yeager, *Journal of Counterterrorism & Security,* vol. 6, no. 4, May 2000.

86. Thomas B. Hunter, op. cit.

87. Rahimullah Yusufzai, interview by author, Washington, D.C., June 2001.

88. U.S. State Department, *Patterns of Global Terrorism* (2000), Appendix B, section on Abu Sayyaf; Thomas B. Hunter, op. cit.

89. Charles P. Wallace, "Weaving a Wide Web of Terror: The Plan, Officials Say, Was to Blow Up 11 U.S. Airliners in One Day," *Los Angeles Times,* May 30, 1995.

90. Yaeger, op. cit; Rajiv Chandrasekaran, "Gunmen Take Foreigners Hostage in Malaysia," *Washington Post,* April 25, 2000.

91. Christine Herrera, "Khalifa: I don't know Gemma; I'm upset," *Philippine Daily Inquirer,* August 12, 2000.

92. "Suspect in Terror Gang Being Held in East Bay," *San Francisco Chronicle,* April 17, 1995; Marc Van der Hout, telephone interview by author, April 1992.

93. Louise Lief and Ian James, *U.S. News & World Report,* May 15, 1995.

94. Van der Hout interview.

95. Ibid.

96. Christine Herrera, op. cit.

97. *U.S.A. v. Usama bin Laden,* Testimony of Jamal al-Fadl, February 6 and 7, 2001.

98. Leo Tolstoy, *The Cossacks* (London: Penguin Books, 1975).

99. See generally Carlotta Gall and Thomas de Waal, *Chechnya: Calamity in the Caucasus* (New York: New York University Press, 1998).

100. W. Montgomery Watt, *Muhammad: Prophet and Statesman* (New York: Oxford University Press, 1974), p. 78.

101. Yo'av Karny, author of *Highlanders: A Journey to the Caucasus in Quest of Memory,* telephone interview by author, January 2000.

102. U.S. officials, interview by author, Washington, D.C., January 2000.

103. All information about Khattab is from Middle Eastern sources or U.S. government officials unless otherwise noted.

Afterword: The Endgame

1. Laurie Goodstein, "After the Attacks: Finding Fault; Falwell's Finger-Pointing Inappropriate, Bush Says," *The New York Times,* September 15, 2001.

2. Samuel P. Huntington, *The Clash of Civilizations and the Remaking of World Order* (New York: Simon & Schuster, 1998), p. 125.

3. Ibid., p. 258.

4. Ibid., p. 209.

5. Ibid., p. 34.

6. However, Israeli defense minister Binyamin Ben-Eliezer told Reuters in June 2001 that bin Laden was trying very hard to penetrate the country. See also Roger Crabb, "Israel Fears bin Laden is Plotting to Attack," *The Washington Times,* June 26, 2001.

7. Jodi Wilgoren, "On Campus and On Knees, Facing Mecca," *The New York Times,* February 13, 2001; see Robin Wright, *The Last Great Revolution: Turmoil and Transformation in Iran* (New York: Vintage, 2001), chapters 4 and 5; Camelia Entekhabi-Fard, "Behind the Veil, A New Symbol for the Women of Iran," *Mother Jones,* August 2001; Gilles Kepel, "Islamism Reconsidered," *Harvard International Review,* Summer 2000; and Malise Ruthven, Islam in the World (New York: Oxford University Press, 2000), p. 400.

8. Jonah Blank, "Kashmir: Fundamentalism Takes Root," *Foreign Affairs,* Nov./Dec. 1999. Blank writes: "Both Pakistanis and Indians are clouded by self-delusion. In the valley of Kashmir (the main area under contention) the population remains profoundly alienated from the Indian government and the radical Islamist guerrillas alike."

9. Kosovar nationalist, interview by author, New York, February 1999; former senior U.S. official, interview by author, London, November 2000.

10. Michael Ignatieff, *The Warrior's Honor: Ethnic War and the Modern Conscience* (New York: Holt, 1998), pp. 34–71.

11. Final Report to Congress: Conduct of the Persian Gulf War (Washington, D.C.: U.S. Department of Defense, April 1992), pp. 498–500.

12. Peter Partner, *God of Battles: Holy Wars of Christianity and Islam* (Princeton, N.J.: Princeton University Press, 1998), p. 260.

13. Huntington, *The Clash of Civilizations,* p. 247.

14. Barnett R. Rubin, *The Search for Peace in Afghanistan: From Buffer State to Failed State* (New Haven: Yale University Press, 1996), p. 135. Between April 1992 and December 1994 alone, 20,000 died in Kabul—a figure based on conservative estimates of victims at Kabul hospitals.

15. Samuel R. Berger and Mona Sutphen, "Commandeering the Palestinian Cause, Bin Laden's Belated Concern," an essay in James H. Hoge Jr. and Gideon Rose, eds.: *How Did This Happen? Terrorism and the New War* (New York: Public Affairs, 2001).

16. Tim Witcher, "Schroeder Joins West's Bid to Bolster Pakistan Leader," Agence France Presse, October 28, 2001.

17. United Press International, "Poll: Muslims Have Low Opinion of US," February, 27, 2002.

18. Agence France Presse, "Al-Qaeda Threatens More Suicide Plane Attacks against U.S., Britain," October 13, 2001.

19. Wolf Blitzer, "Unreleased Interview with Osama bin Laden Goes Public," *www.cnn.com/TRANSCRIPTS/0201/31/wbr.02.html,* January 31, 2002.

20. Elisabeth Bumiller, "Bin Laden, on Tape, Boasts of Trade Center Attacks," *The New York Times,* December 14, 2001.

21. David Ensor, Kelly Wallace, Brad Wright, CNN, "Bin Laden named 9 hijackers on tape," www.cnn.com/2001/US/12/21/ret.bin.laden.translation/index.html, December 21, 2001.

22. *The Washington Post,* "These young men have done a great deed," December 29, 2001.

23. Neil MacFarquhar, "Father Denies 'Gentle Son' Could Hijack Any Jetliner," *The New York Times,* September 19, 2001.

24. Strobe Talbott and Nayan Chanda, eds.; Charles Hill, "A Herculean Task: The Myth and Reality of Arab Terrorism," an essay in *The Age of Terror: America and the World After September 11,* p. 103.

25. Ibid, pp. 101–103.

26. See *www.worldbank.com/data/countrydata/countrydata.html* and Energy Information Administration, *International Energy Outlook* (Washington, D.C.: United States Department of Energy, Office of Integrated Analysis and Forecasting, 2001).

27. Nedra Pickler, "Levin says U.S. military should consider quitting Saudi Arabia," Associated Press, January 15, 2002.

28. Wolf Blitzer, "Late Edition: Interviews with Andrew Card, Joe Lieberman, and Mitch McConnell," *www.cnn.com/TRANSCRIPTS/0201/27/le.00.html,* January 27, 2002.

29. Agence France Presse, "US military presence in Saudi will be adjusted over time: Rumsfeld," February 20, 2002.

30. Charles J. Hanley, "America and Saudi Arabia: They've made it work, but for how much longer?" Associated Press, January 28, 2002.

31. Edward L. Morse and James Richard, "The Battle for Energy Dominance," *Foreign Affairs,* volume 81, number 2, March/April 2002.

32. See generally Genevieve Abdo, *No God but God: Egypt and the Triumph of Islam* (New York: Oxford University Press, 2000).

33. See generally Anthony Shadid, *Legacy of the Prophet: Despots, Democrats, and the New Politics of Islam* (Boulder, Colo.: Westview, 2001).

34. Abdul Wahab al-Anesi, interview by author, San'a, Yemen, November 2000.

35. Karen Armstrong, *The Battle for God* (New York: Knopf, 2000), p. 163.

36. Joseph Coleman, "Islam Grows Deep and Wide in Asia," *The Washington Times,* August 19, 2000.

37. See generally Bernard Lewis, *The Assassins, A Radical Sect in Islam* (New York: Oxford University Press, 1987).

38. Zalmay Khalilzad in a speech delivered at Johns Hopkins School of Advanced International Studies, February 18, 2002.

39. Andrea Kannapell, "Frontlines: February 25–March 2," *The New York Times*, March 3, 2002.

40. Michael Gordon, "New Plan: Join the Fray," *The New York Times*, March 4, 2002.

41. President George W. Bush's address to a joint session of Congress, September 20, 2001.

42. Paul Richter, "US Efforts in Caucasus Underscore Global Fight," *Los Angeles Times*, February 28, 2002; Bruce Wilson, "Hunt for bin Laden moves to Kashmir," *The Advertiser* (UK), February 25, 2002; Martin Abbugao, "US personnel, naval vessels targeted by militant group in Singapore," Agence France Presse, January 11, 2002; Walter Pincus, "Al-Qaeda Leader Talked of Plot Against US Embassy," *The Washington Post*, January 23, 2002; Agence France Presse, "Philippines, Malaysia to beef up cooperation to fight terrorism," March 20, 2002; Agence France Presse, "Four Dead, 40 Injured in Pakistan Church Blasts," March 17, 2002.

43. Agence France Presse, "One of Masood's assassins was al-Qaeda member in Belgium," December 7, 2001; John Tagliabue, "Claim of Plot Against Embassy in Paris," *The New York Times*, October 3, 2001; John Lumpkin, "So far, al-Qaida cells have failed in attempts to follow Sept. 11," Associated Press, March 1, 2002.

44. Robert Novak, et al., "Novak, Hunt and Shields: Interview with Bob Graham," *www.cnn.com/TRANSCRIPTS/0202/23/en.00.html*, February 23, 2002.

45. Agence France Presse, "One of Masood's assassins was al-Qaeda member in Belgium," December 7, 2001; John Tagliabue, "Claim of Plot Against Embassy in Paris," *The New York Times*, October 3, 2001; John Lumpkin, "So far, al-Qaida cells have failed in attempts to follow Sept. 11," Associated Press, March 1, 2002; Omar Samad, Afghan Foreign Ministry spokesman, interview by author, Washington, D.C., March 2002.

46. D. Ian Hopper, "Computers used by al-Qaida could be treasure trove of intelligence data," Associated Press, December 31, 2001.

47. "I Am Not Afraid of Death," interview of Osama bin Laden by Jamal Ismail, *Newsweek*, January 11, 1999; Hamid Mir, "Osama claims he has nukes: If U.S. uses N-arms it will get same response," *The Dawn* (Pakistan), November 10, 2001.

48. *The New York Times*, "Countless Questions, a Few Answers," October 7, 2001; *The New York Times*, "Arrests suggest water plot," February 21, 2002; *The Guardian*, "In Brief: Anthrax Balloon," November 29, 2001; Edward Alden, "CIA chief warns of 'clear and present' dangers," *Financial Times*, February 7, 2002.

49. Zahid Hussain, "Two Pakistani nuclear scientists acknowledge meeting Osama bin Laden," AP Worldstream, November 11, 2001.

50. Bill Gertz, "Nuclear plants targeted for terror attacks," *The Washington Times*, January 31, 2002.

51. Agence France Presse, "Iranians stage anti-US protests on anniversary of revolution," February 11, 2002.

52. Pentagon official, interview by author, Washington, D.C., February, 2002.

53. Pentagon official, interview by author.

INDEX

American Protective Services, Sunnyvale, California, 131
Amin, Hafizullah, 71
Amin Shah, Wali Khan, 141, 222
Amnesty International, 162
al-Amoudi family, 45
Anderson, Robert, 133
al-Anesi, Abdul Wahab, 101, 178, 192
al-Ansar training camp, Afghanistan, 59
al-Aqsa mosque, Jerusalem, 47–48
Arabian Sea, 124, 172
Aramco, 79
Arbusto, 49
ARIANA, 16
Arnett, Peter, 6, 18, 23
Assassins, the, 238–39
Associated Press, 23, 165
Atef, Muhammad, 102, 107, 208, 242
Atomic bomb, 21–22
Atta, Mohamed, 37–39, 234, 238, 242
Atwan, Abdel Bari, 96, 207–8
al-Auda, Salman, 81
Azerbaijan, 20, 89
Azhar, Maulana Masood, 212, 215, 221
al-Azhar University, Cairo, 55, 203
al-Aziz bin Baz, Abd, 58
Azzam, 111
Azzam, Abdullah, 30, 50, 54–57, 59, 64–65, 87, 136, 138, 140, 182, 206
Azzam, Ibrahim, 65
Azzam, Muhammad, 65
Azzam.com, 40

Baaboud family, 127
Babar, Naseerullah, 148
al-Badawai, Jamal, 190
al-Badr training camps, Afghanistan, 29, 103, 123
Ba'eshn, Said Mohamed, 197
Bahrain, 230
Bakri Muhammad, Sheikh Omar, 211–12
Baku, Azerbaijan, 89
Bangladesh, 32
al-Banshiri, Abu Ubaidah, 109, 208, 209
al-Barakati, Mansoor, 61–62
Baroum family, 45
Basayev, Sail, 223
al-Bashir, Omar Hassan Ahmad, 82
Bath, James, 48–49
Bayat (oath of allegiance), 29, 63
BBC (British Broadcasting Corporation), 6, 74, 114
Bearden, Milt, 58, 68, 76
Begin, Menachem, 205, 235

Beirut, Marine barracks bombing (1983), 88, 144
Beit al-Ansar (House of the Supporters), 54, 62, 93
Beit al-Salaam guest house, 93
Beit al-Shuhadaa (House of the Martyrs), 140
Belle Glade, Florida, 38
Berger, Sandy, 231
Bhutto, Benazir, 36, 63–64
Bhutto, Zulfikar Ali, 63
Bin Laden: Behind the Mask of a Terrorist (Robinson), 34–35
bin Laden, Osama. *See* listing under L
Bin Laden: The Man Who Declared War on America (Bodansky), 34
Bismarck, Otto von, 229
Black Hawk Down (Bowden), 85
Black Stone, 150
Black Tulip (Bearden), 68
Blessed Fruits Company, 83
Blowback, 70–71
Bodansky, Yossef, 34
Bodine, Barbara K., 193
Bojinka plot, 37
Bosnia, 36, 42, 89, 114, 183, 228
Bowden, Mark, 85
Bradsher, Henry, 72
Brown, Marion, 138
Brunei, Sultan of, 45
Brydon, Dr., 53
Brzezinski, Zbigniew, 66
Bureau of Alcohol, Tobacco, and Firearms, 119
Burns, John, 26, 28, 182
Burqa (garment), 13, 16, 158
Bush, George, 22, 80, 84
Bush, George W., 33, 48–49, 106, 165, 236, 241, 244
Bushnell, Prudence, 112–13
Buzkashi (sport), 14–15

Cambodia, 159
Cannistraro, Vince, 68, 77, 140
Card, Andrew H., Jr., 237
Carey, Caroline, 48
Carpenter, David, 200
Carter, Jimmy, 51, 66, 71, 205
Catholic Church, 3, 227
CBS News, 6, 73
Central Intelligence Agency (CIA), 33, 34, 212
  Afghan war and, 1, 66–72, 74–78
  Counterterrorist Center (CTC), 119

Gardez, Afghanistan, 240
Gates, Robert, 71, 76
Georgia, 244
Ghaith, Suleiman Abu, 232
Gondal, Saifullah, 123
Gore, Al, 5
Graham, Bob, 242
Grand Mosque, Mecca, 51
Grand Trunk Road, 7
Guardian, The, 67
Guevera, Che, 75
Gul, Hamid, 64
Gulf War, 6, 73, 92, 130, 230, 237

al-Habshi, Nabil, 45–47
Hadda, Afghanistan, 12, 168
Hadramawt, Yemen, 44–46, 190, 197
Hafeezullah, Maulvi, 146, 164
Hafs, Abu, 85, 103
el-Hage, Wadi, 109, 120, 137–40, 142,
    201
Hajj (pilgrimage), 46, 48
Hakim, Abdul Aziz, 191
Hamas, 88, 222
Hamza, Abdul Baset, 127
Hamza, Abu, 42, 181–84, 187
Hamza, Mohammad, 182, 184
Hanif, Qari Din Mohammad, 163–64
ul-Haq, Maulana Sami, 129, 152–54
Haqqani, Jalaluddin, 57
Harakat ul-Mujahideen (HUM), 125,
    183, 212–16, 218, 219
al-Harazi, Mohammed Omar, 188, 190,
    201
Harvard University, 49
Hassan, Abu, 183–85, 186–88
Havala system, 106
al-Hawali, Safar, 81
Al-Hayat newspaper, 111
Hazaras, 156, 159
Hekmatyar, Gulbuddin, 6, 56–57, 71–76,
    168
Help Africa People, 139
Hemingway, Ernest, 51
Henderson, Victor, 48
Herat, Afghanistan, 159, 161, 169
Hezbollah, 21, 88, 91, 222
Hijazi, Raed, 142, 143
Al-Hijra Construction Company, 83
Hill, Charles, 234–35
Hindu Kush mountains, 7, 30
Hindus, in Afghanistan, 160, 169
Hitler, Adolf, 228
Hizb party, 71–74

Holy Kaaba operation, 108
Holy Roman Empire, 21
Hotaki, Abdul Khabir, 154–55
al-Hudaifi, Ali, 103
Huffman Aviation, Venice, Florida, 38
Huntington, Samuel, 227–30
Hussain, Mushahid, 116, 156
Hussein, Saddam, 3, 73, 80, 122, 230,
    237, 244
Hutus, 229

Ibn Taymiyyah, 102
Ibrahim, Saad Eddin, 137, 206
Idris, Salah, 127, 128
Ignatieff, Michael, 229
Al-Ikhlas Company, 83
Ilyas (driver), 217–18
Independent, 84
India, 241
    airline hijacking (1999), 212–16, 219,
        221
    Kashmir and, 36, 212, 216, 218–21,
        229
Indonesia, 27, 238
Indus River, 7
Intercontinental Hotel, Kabul,
    Afghanistan, 155, 158
Internet, 28–29, 40, 42
Inter-Services Intelligence agency (ISI),
    67, 69, 71, 76, 148, 220
Iran, 34, 51, 71, 77, 89, 91, 119, 155, 158,
    236, 237, 244
Iraq, 3, 19, 21, 22, 23, 27, 34, 37, 40, 80,
    101, 102, 127, 128, 130, 227, 229,
    230, 236, 244–45
Irish Republican Army (IRA), 21
Irvine, Walter, 8
Isby, David, 74
Islah party, 177, 192, 196, 237–38
Islamabad, Pakistan, 6–7, 69, 93, 150–51,
    242
Islambouli, Khalid, 205, 208
Islambouli, Mohammed Shawki, 208
Islamic Army of Aden (IAA), 41, 180–81,
    183, 184, 193
Islamic Coordination Council, 140
Islamic Group (Egypt), 69–70, 89, 98,
    193, 199, 204, 206
Islamic Observation Centre, 202–3
Islamic People's Congress (1995), 88
Islamic University, Islamabad, 55
Ismail, Jamal, 54, 58, 59, 62, 138
Israel, 5, 21, 27, 39, 51, 55, 132–33, 150,
    204–5, 227, 234, 237

Jaamiah Darul Uloom Haqqania,
    Pakistan, 7, 152–53
Jahiliyyah (state of ignorance), 51, 204
Jais-e-Mohammed (JEM), 221
Jaji, battle of, 59–60
Jaji, Pakistan, 63
Jalalabad, Afghanistan, 6, 12–14, 16, 61,
    68, 96, 157, 167
  siege of (1989), 73
Jamaat e-Jihal al-Suri organization, 89
Jambiya (Yemeni dagger), 189
Jamiat-e-Ulema Islam (JUI), 152–53
Jan, Mullah Khan, 162
Jane's Intelligence Review, 33
Janjalani, Abdurajik, 221
Al-Jazeera television station, 39, 86, 90,
    116, 232–34
Jeddah, Yemen, 46, 47, 194
Jesus, 99–100
Jews, 161–62, 206–7, 228, 234
Jihad Group "Vanguards of Conquest"
    (Egypt), 62, 89, 98, 111, 131, 186,
    203–5, 209
Jihadist movement, 50–51, 55–56
Jihad magazine, 94
Jihad Media, 189
Jihad Wal training camp, Afghanistan,
    92
Jobe, Henry, 127
John F. Kennedy Special Warfare Center,
    130–34
John Paul II, Pope, 37, 141, 222
Jones, Jim, 241
Jordan, 89, 142, 143, 189, 199, 222, 237
Jouvenal, Peter, 6, 18, 57, 63, 68

Kaaba, 150
Kabul, Afghanistan, 6, 14, 73, 75, 106–7,
    124, 147, 157–59, 159, 161, 168, 169
Kabul Museum, Afghanistan, 14
Kahane, Rabbi Meir, 134, 209
Kamal, Mustafa. See Hamza, Abu
Kandahar, Afghanistan, 15, 61, 98, 148,
    161, 165, 169, 189, 213–16
Kaplan, Robert D., 52
Kargil operation, 219
Karzai, Hamid, 239
Kashmir, 27, 32, 36, 212, 216–21, 229
Kenya. See African embassy bombings
    (1998)
Kepel, Gilles, 59
Khadijah, 160
Khaldan training camp, Afghanistan, 92,
    110, 143

Khalid bin Walid training camp,
    Afghanistan, 92, 123, 125
Khalidi, Tarif, 28
Khalifa (caliphate), restoration of, 20, 21,
    55–56
Khalifa, Mohammad Jamal, 222
Khalifa, Muhammad Abdurrahman, 57,
    141
Khalili, Nejat, 134
Khalilzad, Zalmay, 239
al-Khamri, Hassan Saeed Awad, 190
Khan, Ismail, 103, 104
Khartoum, Sudan, 81, 123
Khartoum Tannery, 83
Khashoggi, Adnan, 47
Khattab, 42, 223–24
Kherchtou, L'Hossaine, 87, 92–93, 142
Khmer Rouge, 159
Khobar Towers bombing (1996), 91
Khomeini, Ayatollah, 51
Khost, Afghanistan, 67, 123, 124, 168
Khumram Agency, 140
Khyber Agency, 9, 10
Khyber Pass, 7, 9–11
Khyber Rifles regiment, 9
King Abdul-Aziz University, Jeddah, 50
Knights Templar, 149
Koran, 20, 51, 66, 73–74, 76, 101–99,
    106, 152, 160, 171, 189, 230
Koresh, David, 241
Kosovo, 36, 229
Kroll Associates, 127
Kuchis, 18
Kurds, 229, 230, 244
Kuwait, 3, 23, 80, 230
Kyrgyzstan, 166

Labevière, Richard, 34
bin Laden, Abdullah (son), 61
bin Laden, Abdullah (uncle), 45–47
bin Laden, Bakr, 92
bin Laden, Mohammed bin Awad
    (father), 31, 45–48, 55, 104, 197
bin Laden, Mohammed (son), 208
bin Laden, Osama. See also al-Qaeda
  ABC News interview (1998), 27, 32,
    124
  Aden hotel bombings (1992) and, 176
  Afghan war and, 3, 7, 12, 13, 33, 43,
    44, 53–55, 57–61, 67, 68, 74, 125–26
  aliases of, 31
  ancestral village of, 45, 46, 197
  assassination attempts against, 4, 92,
    135

bin Laden, Osama (*cont.*)

ABOUT THE AUTHOR

Born in Minneapolis but raised in London, Peter Bergen received his B.A. in Modern History from Oxford and moved to New York in 1984. He worked first for ABC News and later for CNN, for which he produced a variety of news stories and documentaries, including one on the 1993 bombing of the World Trade Center. In 1997, he produced the first televised interview with Osama bin Laden.

Currently CNN's terrorism analyst, he has written about Islamist militants and related subjects for *The Washington Post, Foreign Affairs, The Times* of London, and *Vanity Fair;* in 2001, he served as a Pew Journalist-in-Residence at the School for Advanced International Studies at Johns Hopkins University. He is now a fellow of the New America Foundation.

Peter Bergen has received many awards and honors, among them The Leonard Silk Journalism Fellowship and a 1994 Edward R. Murrow Award, for best foreign affairs documentary, from the Overseas Press Club.

For more information, please visit www.peterbergen.com.